The Most
Dangerous Cinema

ALSO BY BRYAN SENN

A Year of Fear: A Day-by-Day Guide to 366 Horror Films (2007)

*Golden Horrors: An Illustrated Critical Filmography
of Terror Cinema, 1931–1939* (2006; paperback 1996)

BY BRYAN SENN AND JOHN JOHNSON

*Fantastic Cinema Subject Guide: A Topical Index
to 2,500 Horror, Science Fiction, and Fantasy Films* (2008; paperback 1992)

BY MARK CLARK AND BRYAN SENN

Sixties Shockers: A Critical Filmography of Horror Cinema, 1960–1969 (2011)

ALL FROM MCFARLAND

The Most Dangerous Cinema

People Hunting People on Film

BRYAN SENN

*To John—
With many thanks for all your help. This hunt would not have gone near as well without you!*

McFarland & Company, Inc., Publishers
Jefferson, North Carolina, and London

ISBN 978-0-7864-3562-3
softcover : acid free paper ∞

LIBRARY OF CONGRESS CATALOGUING DATA ARE AVAILABLE

BRITISH LIBRARY CATALOGUING DATA ARE AVAILABLE

© 2014 Bryan Senn. All rights reserved

No part of this book may be reproduced or transmitted in any form or by any means, electronic or mechanical, including photocopying or recording, or by any information storage and retrieval system, without permission in writing from the publisher.

Front cover: poster art for *The Most Dangerous Game*, 1932 (RKO Radio Pictures)

Manufactured in the United States of America

McFarland & Company, Inc., Publishers
Box 611, Jefferson, North Carolina 28640
www.mcfarlandpub.com

For Gina
You make it all worthwhile

Table of Contents

Acknowledgments   ix
Introduction   1

1. Pride of Place: *The Most Dangerous Game* (1932)   13
2. Carbon-Copy Game: *A Game of Death* (1945)   23
3. Teenage Game: *Bloodlust!* (1960)   33
4. Dangerous Roughie: *Confessions of a Psycho Cat* (1968)   42
5. Sexploitation Game: *The Suckers* (1972)   50
6. Filipino Danger: *The Woman Hunt* (1973)   60
7. Post-War Game: *Open Season* (1974)   70
8. Dangerous Ozploitation: *Escape 2000* (1982)   78
9. Dangerous Action: *Avenging Force* (1986)   87
10. Sci-Fi Game: *Slave Girls from Beyond Infinity* (1987)   96
11. Rambo Game: *War Cat* (1987)   105
12. Dangerous Style: *Hard Target* (1993)   113
13. Wilderness Hunt: *Surviving the Game* (1994)   125
14. Comedy Game: *The Pest* (1997)   138
15. DTV Danger   146
16. *Almost* Dangerous Games   179
17. Dangerous Game Shows and Deadly Diversions   215
18. Dangerous Alien Games   231
19. Television Games   242

A Most Dangerous Conclusion   270
Chapter Notes   273
Bibliography   276
Index   279

Acknowledgments

Thanks to Anthony Ambrogio, Mark Clark, Cindy Collins-Smith, Bruce Dettman, Holger Haase (for his assessment of *Copeland Saves His Skin*), David Hogan, Bruce Holecheck, Lenny Kohl, Arthur Lundquist, Jonathan Malcolm Lampley, Dave Maska, independent moviemaker Ted V. Mikels, Mark Miller, Ted Okuda, Bob Sargent (founder of the *Eurotrashparadise*), director/producer Stu Segall, Brian Smith (who planted the idea for this book in my head in the first place), Midnight Marquee's Gary Svehla, Dan Taylor (the *Hungover Gourmet* himself), Steve Thornton, comic book artist extraordinaire Neil Vokes, Laura Wagner, Tom Weaver, the late Oscar-winning filmmaker Robert Wise, and David Zuzelo for their suggestions, insights, anecdotes, and amazing knowledge of film.

A special note of thanks to John Gibbon, whose extraordinary detective and procurement skills made the impossible possible; I quickly came to learn that if John can't find it, it simply can't be found.

And, most of all, special thank yous are owed to Dr. Gina Beretta, my oh-so-patient wife (and unofficial editor), and my son Dominic Beretta-Senn, for re-teaching me all about perseverance.

Introduction

"There is a passion for hunting something deeply implanted in the human breast."—Charles Dickens

"It is very strange, and very melancholy, that the paucity of human pleasures should persuade us ever to call hunting one of them."—Samuel Johnson

Hunting: the solid reassurance of the weapon in your hands, the thrill of spotting your prey, the adrenalin rush when you know you've hit your mark — it all culminates in a feeling of power, specifically of power over nature, staking your claim as *the* top predator in the food chain. It's a primal impulse and an archetypal one — the wielding of power over life and death. Carry that to the *n*th degree — to, some might say, its logical conclusion — and you apply that power to fellow human beings.

People hunting people for sport — it's an idea both shocking and fascinating. In 1924 prolific novelist, playwright and screenwriter Richard Connell[1] published a short story that introduced this concept into the public zeitgeist, where it has remained embedded ever since. Since its publication, Connell's O. Henry Memorial Award–winning "The Most Dangerous Game" has been continuously anthologized and studied in classrooms throughout America and abroad. Raising questions about the nature of violence and cruelty, the needs of society vs. those of the individual, and, of course, the ethics of hunting purely for pleasure, the thrilling story spawned a new cinematic subgenre, beginning with RKO's 1932 production of *The Most Dangerous Game*.

The storyline of Connell's "The Most Dangerous Game" is one of those timeless classics, like Robert Louis Stevenson's *The Strange Case of Dr. Jekyll and Mr. Hyde* or Mary Shelley's *Frankenstein*, which continue to fascinate as the years go by. It is the tale of a man who takes an obsession to the extreme. The clever title is a double-edged sword, as it can denote either the hunt itself (which Connell's hunting-obsessed antagonist, General Zaroff, sees as sport of "the most dangerous" type) or the quarry of man, who, given his intelligence and ingenuity, certainly is the "most dangerous game" to hunt (as Zaroff himself enthuses).

Why has such a brutal and violent concept remained so popular through the years, as evidenced by the immense staying power of the story via not only the printed page, but the sheer numbers of cinematic and television adaptations and variations (well over 100) over the last eighty-odd years? It's almost as if Connell's concept touched a genetic nerve, or at least awakened some collective cultural memory. Perhaps it is modernized society's repression of, and subsequent longing for, the "joyful exercising of natural predatory instincts and indulgence in electrifying thrills associated with threatening and being threatened," as described by cultural analyst and author Gregory Desilet.[2] Or perhaps it's as simple as the explanation put forth by thriller novelist Andrew Klavan, who unapologetically defends

Title lobby card for the first cinematic adaptation of Richard Connell's "The Most Dangerous Game."

violent fiction by pointing out that "it's fun. Like sex: it's lots of fun.... This business of violent fiction as therapy—the modern-jargon version of Aristotle—it's a defense, isn't it, as if these stories needed a reason for being. In order to celebrate violent fiction—I mean, *celebrate* it—it's the joy you've got to talk about. The joy of cruelty, the thrill of terror, the adrenaline of the hunter, the heartbeat of the deer—all reproduced in the safe playground of art."[3]

Hunting is a polarizing issue. In today's more P.C.-minded world (at least in America), fewer and fewer modern hunters will admit to hunting simply for the "love of the game," insisting instead that they seek fresh and unsullied meat as an answer to the food industry's use of chemicals and hormonal growth-enhancements, and that hunting is necessary to control the animal populations that have been knocked out of balance by the encroachment of Man. Even more telling, African safaris nowadays are almost universally geared towards cameras rather than firearms.

Hunting for food is one thing; hunting for sheer pleasure is something else entirely. Back in the 1920s, when Connell penned his classic tale, hunting was still considered legitimate "sport," and many a Hollywood adventure tale from the Golden Age of cinema involved a protagonist of the Great White Hunter variety—as did real life. For instance, President Theodore Roosevelt, who founded the U.S. National Parks System, was an avid hunter who, both before and after his presidency, traveled the globe to hunt on safari. In

Africa, Roosevelt and his son killed a reported 512 animals, including 29 zebras, 20 rhinoceroses, 17 lions, 11 elephants, 9 giraffes and 8 hippopotamuses. In his 1910 book *African Game Trails*, Roosevelt describes the thrill of the blood sport when he bagged one particular rhino:

> The big beast stood like an uncouth statue, his hide black in the sunlight; he seemed what he was, a monster surviving over from the world's past, from the days when the beasts of the prime ran riot in their strength, before man grew so cunning of brain and hand as to master them. So little did he dream of our presence that when we were a hundred yards off he actually lay down.
>
> Walking lightly, and with every sense keyed up, we at last reached the bush, and I pushed forward the safety of the double-barreled Holland rifle which I was now to use for the first time on big game. As I stepped to one side of the bush so as to get a clear aim, with [fellow hunter Captain Arthur] Slatter following, the rhino saw me and jumped to his feet with the agility of a polo pony. As he rose I put in the right barrel, the bullet going through both lungs. At the same moment he wheeled, the blood spouting from his nostrils, and galloped full on.
>
> Before he could get quite all the way round in his headlong rush to reach us, I struck him with my left-hand barrel, the bullet entering between the neck and shoulder and piercing his heart. At the same instant Captain Slatter fired, his bullet entering the neck vertebrae. Plowing up the ground with horn and feet, the great bull rhino, still headed toward us, dropped just thirteen paces from where we stood.[4]

In the second big-screen adaptation of Connell's tale, *A Game of Death* (1945), Connell's famous big-game hunter protagonist is asked why he keeps hunting all around the world year after year. "It isn't the money, really," answers Rainsford. "Love of the game, I guess. Adventure. Color. Excitement. Never knowing what you'll meet around the next corner. To me it's the greatest sport in the world." One can easily envision Teddy Roosevelt espousing these very same sentiments.

Hunting is Man proclaiming his superiority at its most basic level — by killing anything and everything that moves. Though big game hunters don't eat their prey, they generally stuff their heads and mount them on the wall in a sort of symbolic savoring — drinking in their victory, their superiority, with a glance above their mantle whenever they feel the need. The psychology of hunting for sport, then, may stem from Man's basic need to dominate, to stay top of the food chain — a very natural urge.

Man is predatory by nature — hence the classic characterization of a successful modern man as being "a good provider" (with food being the most basic of provisions, naturally). And what makes Man such a great provider, allowing his relatively frail physique to stand atop nature's pyramid, looming over such better physically-equipped species as lions and tigers and bears (oh my)? His intellect and ability to reason. According to the laws of nature, the aim of each individual is to master those qualities that set its species apart in order to dominate other members of the species — Darwin's "survival of the fittest" — allowing said individual to procreate and so enhance the species' collective gene pool.

In Man's case, one could argue that the ultimate extrapolation of that quality — human intellect — is to employ it to dominate others. And, at the most basic level, what could be more dominating than hunting down and killing one's rivals? In the animal kingdom, however, most battles for dominance (over food, territory, and mating rights) don't generally end in *lethal* confrontations. That is what makes Connell's concept so fascinating — what happens when individuals perversely abandon societal dictates and take it upon themselves to carry their competitive natures to the ultimate by hunting other humans for sport?

Nevertheless, philosophers, religious leaders, and people of conscience (in fact, some of the most intellectually advanced members of our species, such as Albert Einstein) will tell you that what truly separates man from beast is humankind's emotional (or spiritual, if one leans in that direction) component — man's capacity for compassion, empathy and, at its highest level, altruism. (Of course, this last concept opens up a whole can of philosophical worms; for instance, how can one call an act altruistic if there is indeed something to be gained from it? At the very least, an altruistic action — even something done or donated anonymously — will instill a positive feeling in the person committing it, even if he or she is the only one to know of it; hence, how can it truly be called "altruistic"? But this particular worm is too wriggly for the scope of this book.)

In any case, Man is a social animal. Alone and naked in the wilderness, a human being is nigh on defenseless; but surrounded by others, or even equipped with the collective power of society (everything from the rudimentary mastery of fire to the technological advantage of firearms), he becomes the true king of the jungle. So Man must use his intellect to forge societal bonds, allowing the human race to reign supreme. (The many apocalyptic stories and films that deal with the breakdown of society and the resultant chaos illustrate our fascination with — and fear of — this concept.) But this can come into conflict with the individual, and even the logical.

It is our intellect that allows us to construct society, and our emotions (compassion, empathy) that allow us to live within it. That makes man an animal of dichotomies (if one chooses to see reason and emotion as opposites). When a member swings too far one way or the other, he or she becomes either a beast relying solely on instinct, or a heartless, cold, calculating "machine." Neither can survive long nor succeed within the society Man has created. So which is the hunter-of-men of Connell's story and so many cinematic updates? On the surface it appears that Zaroff and his successors are of the latter type — those who've taken their reasoning, their logic, to an absurd level. But looking deeper, it becomes apparent that these societal misfits, who consider themselves above moral dictates (which, after all, are simply society's *rules*), have allowed their emotions — their obsessions — to cloud their reason to the point that they fly in the face of what they ultimately need: society. Consequently, their outward intellect and obvious intelligence are simply a mask for what we would consider mental illness and emotional instability — something seen as both mysterious and frightening to most "normal" people. And what to do with mysterious and frightening concepts? Why, explore them via stories — on the page and on the screen.[5] So it's little wonder that Connell's concept grabbed the public as it did and has remained so vibrant over the years.

The Story

"The Most Dangerous Game" tells the tale of Sangor Rainsford, a famous big-game hunter and author on a yacht sailing through the Caribbean for "some good hunting up the Amazon." As the ship passes a desolate spot known as "Ship-Trap Island" in the night, the sound of distant gunshots startles Rainsford, on deck alone smoking his pipe, resulting in his falling overboard. Helplessly watching the receding yacht, Rainsford swims to the island where he finds an incongruous chateau on a high bluff overlooking the sea. Answering his knock "was the largest man he had ever seen — a gigantic creature, solidly made and black-bearded to the waist." But this mute monster is not the castle's owner, who approaches to extend his hand and announce, "It is a very great pleasure and honor to welcome Mr. Sanger Rainsford, the celebrated hunter, to my home.... I've read your book about hunting snow

This 1957 paperback short story collection centered on Richard Connell's famous tale "The Most Dangerous Game."

leopards in Tibet, you see." This is General Zaroff, a Cossack with an imposing visage. Ivan, Zaroff's deaf and dumb servant, shows Rainsford to his room to rest.

Later, in a dining hall festooned with the mounted heads of many animals, Rainsford finds the general to be "a most thoughtful and affable host, a true cosmopolite." However, whenever he looked up from his plate, Zaroff seemed to be staring at him. Zaroff tells him, "I have but one passion in my life, Mr. Rainsford, and it is the hunt." Rainsford compliments Zaroff on his collection of trophy heads, observing, "That Cape buffalo is the largest I've ever seen.... I've always thought the Cape buffalo is the most dangerous of all big game." At this Zaroff smiles and counters, "No, the Cape buffalo is not the most dangerous big game. Here in my preserve on this island I hunt more dangerous game." Zaroff continues, "I think I may say, in all modesty, that I have done a rare thing. I have invented a new sensation." He goes on:

> God makes some men poets. Some He makes kings, some beggars. Me He made a hunter.... My whole life has been one prolonged hunt. I went into the army — it was expected of noblemen's sons — and for a time commanded a division of Cossack cavalry, but my real interest was always the hunt. I have hunted every kind of game in every land. It would be impossible for me to tell you how many animals I have killed.

But all was not right in Zaroff's hunter's world. As the general explains:

> I was lying in my tent with a splitting headache one night when a terrible thought pushed its way into my mind. Hunting was beginning to bore me. And hunting, remember, had been my life.... Now mine is an analytical mind, Mr. Rainsford. Doubtless that is why I enjoy the problems of the chase. So I asked myself why the hunt no longer fascinated me.... Hunting had ceased to be what you call "a sporting proposition." It had become too easy. I always got my quarry.

What was he to do? "I had to invent a new animal to hunt," explained Zaroff. "So I bought this island, built this house, and here I do my hunting." At Rainsford's bewilderment, Zaroff continues, "I wanted the ideal animal to hunt. So I said: 'What are the attributes of an ideal quarry?' And the answer was, of course: 'It must have courage, cunning, and, above all, it must be able to reason.'" When Rainsford reacts with undisguised horror at the obvious implication, the General only laughs off what he calls Rainsford's "naive, mid–Victorian point of view."

The General explains how he acquires his prey. "This island is called Ship-Trap," he says. "Sometimes an angry god of the high seas sends them to me. Sometimes, when Providence is not so kind, I help Providence a bit" — by activating channel lights where there is no channel. He then shelters the survivors, getting them into "splendid physical condition" in what Zaroff terms his "training school." When it's time for the hunt, says Zaroff, "I suggest to one of them that we go hunting. I give him a supply of food and an excellent hunting knife. I give him three hours' start. I am to follow, armed only with a pistol of the smallest caliber and range. If my quarry eludes me for three whole days he wins the game. If I find him — he loses." And if someone refuses to be hunted? "I turn him over to Ivan," answers the general. "Ivan once had the honor of serving as official knouter for the Great White Czar, and he has his own ideas of sport. Invariably they choose the hunt."

The next day, after Rainsford categorically rejects Zaroff's invitation to hunt with him ("I'm a hunter, not a murderer"), the general has an "inspiration." Raising his glass to Rainsford, he enthuses, "I drink to a foeman worthy of my steel — at last." The General continues, "You'll find this game worth playing. Your brain against mine. Your woodcraft against mine. Outdoor chess!"

Introduction

When Zaroff retires for his afternoon nap, Ivan sends Rainsford out into the jungle armed only with a hunting knife. After his initial panicked flight, Rainsford "got a grip on himself.... He saw that straight flight was futile; inevitably it would bring him face to face with the sea." Rainsford then "executed a series of intricate loops; he doubled on his trail again and again, recalling all the lore of the fox hunt, and all the dodges of the fox." Taking refuge in a tree as night falls, Rainsford waits. He tells himself that no one, not even Zaroff, could trace his tracks in the dark. But towards morning, Zaroff is there, having miraculously followed Rainsford's convolutions. But rather than taking down his quarry then and there, the general simply smiles and walks away. "The general was playing with him! The general was saving him for another day's sport! ... Then it was that Rainsford knew the full meaning of terror."

Rainsford now decides to set a trap for his pursuer. Finishing his work, he takes up position a hundred feet away. "He did not have to wait long. The cat was coming again to play with the mouse." Intently following Rainsford's trail, the general's "foot touched the protruding bough that was the trigger. Even as he touched it, the general sensed his danger and leaped back with the agility of an ape. But he was not quite quick enough; the dead tree, delicately adjusted to rest on the cut living one, crashed down and struck the general a glancing blow on the shoulder as it fell." With his mocking laughter ringing through the jungle, Zaroff calls out, "Let me congratulate you. Not many men know how to make a Malay man-catcher. Luckily for me, I too have hunted in Malacca.... I am going to have my wound dressed; it's only a slight one. But I shall be back. I shall be back."

After the general departs, Rainsford takes flight again. Narrowly avoiding some quicksand at the swampy end of the island, Rainsford has an idea. He digs a pit and lines it with sharpened stakes made from nearby saplings, then again he waits. But the trap catches not Zaroff but the general's hunting dog, which he'd brought with him for this stage of the hunt. "'You've done well, Rainsford,' the voice of the general called. 'Your Burmese tiger pit has claimed one of my best dogs.'"

At daybreak Rainsford awakens to the sound of baying hounds. With Ivan reining in the dogs before him, Zaroff once again pursues Rainsford. "They would be on him any minute now," Rainsford realizes. "He thought of a native trick he had learned in Uganda." Using his knife to set his final trap, Rainsford then flees for his life. Hearing the noise of the hounds abruptly stop, he shinnies up a tree to look back. Unfortunately, the knife, driven by the recoil of a springing tree, had felled Ivan rather than Zaroff.

Rainsford turns again to flee, this time towards a blue gap between the trees ahead. "It was the shore of the sea. Across a cove he could see the gloomy gray stone of the chateau. Twenty feet below him the sea rumbled and hissed. Rainsford hesitated. He heard the hounds. Then he leaped far out into the sea..." Reaching the spot from which Rainsford jumped, the general stands for a few moments regarding the blue-green water, then simply shrugs his shoulders.

Once back at the chateau, General Zaroff enjoys "an exceedingly good dinner" in his dining hall. Retiring for the night to his bedroom, the general is startled by a shadowy figure waiting there—Rainsford. Sucking in his breath and smiling, the General says, "I congratulate you. You have won the game."

> Rainsford did not smile. "I am still a beast at bay," he said in a low, hoarse voice. "Get ready, General Zaroff."
>
> The general made one of his deepest bows. "I see," he said. "Splendid! One of us is to furnish a repast for the hounds. The other will sleep in this very excellent bed. On guard, Rainsford...."
>
> He had never slept in a better bed, Rainsford decided.

Life Imitates Art: A Real-Life Zaroff?

> *"To big game hunter Robert Hansen, Alaska was a paradise. But for his victims, it was a terrifying wilderness where no one could hear their screams."*

Amazingly, the above is not a tagline for another Most Dangerous Game film but a jacket blurb from the nonfiction account of a real-life serial rapist/killer. Bernard DuClus' book *Fair Game* relates the story of Robert Hansen, a mild-mannered baker and family man — and an avid big-game hunter and world record holder (including the number one spot for a Dall Sheep taken by a bow) — who abducted women, many of them topless dancers or prostitutes from Anchorage's seedy Tenderloin district, drove them or flew them in his private plane into the Alaskan wilderness, raped them, and sometimes killed them and buried their bodies in shallow graves. Finally caught in a web of mounting evidence in 1983, Hansen admitted to killing 17 women in the 1970s and early '80s (though the evidence points to many more). Convicted on numerous counts, he is currently serving a 461-year prison sentence at the maximum security Spring Creek Correctional Center in Seward, Alaska.

Media conjecture, and even some scholarly writings, indicate that Hansen may have let some of his victims run in order to experience the thrill of hunting them before killing them. For instance, the authors of the book *The Serial Killers: A Study in the Psychology of Violence* write of Hansen, "He had not killed all the women he had taken out to the wilderness. What he wanted was oral sex. If the woman satisfied him, he took her back home. If not, he pointed a gun at her, ordered her to strip naked, and then run. He gave the girl a start, then would stalk her as if hunting a game animal."[6] While the first part of this description was verified by testimony and evidence, the second is pure conjecture, speculation springing mainly from an impassioned speech given before the court by Assistant District Attorney Frank Rothschild during Hansen's sentencing:

> This hunter who kept trophies on the wall, now has trophies scattered throughout south-central Alaska [the wilderness grave sites of his victims, which Hansen had marked on an aviation map]. And while he doesn't talk about or admit to it, it's obvious from looking at where things started and where women ended up, he hunted them down. He'd let them run a little bit, then he enjoyed a hunt, just like with his big-game animals. He toyed with them, he got a charge out of it. We don't think for a moment that he's told us the whole story...[7]

Hansen never admitted to hunting his victims for sport, and such a notion may be merely an imaginative leap on the part of attorney Rothschild, so the line between fact and Most Dangerous fiction remains blurred. Even so, Hansen, a champion hunter, with his world records and his lust for the kill, certainly had the capabilities and the twisted psyche to put this heinous notion into practice. Whether he did so or not, only Hansen and his victims know. (Note: As of this writing, a cinematic adaptation of the Robert Hansen story, *Frozen Ground*, starring Nicholas Cage as detective Jack Halcombe and John Cusack as Hansen, is in production but has yet to be released.)

On a much lighter note, the case of out-of-work Utah laborer Mork Encino garnered some bemused media attention in 2011 when he created a tongue-in-cheek website to advertise his services as human prey. On his site *Hunt Me 4 Sport*, Mr. Encino claimed, "I'm faster than a wild turkey, smart as any GODDAMN wild boar and willing to make the ultimate sacrifice for the monetary health of my family.... If I am trapped and killed you stand to earn the RESPECT of your fellow hunters, a PRIZE HUMAN MOUNT for your wall and

Connell's concept has permeated nearly every form of popular culture—including comic books. In issue 4 of the 1970s Marvel comic *Werewolf by Night*, a big-game hunter sets out to hunt the lycanthropic protagonist for sport.

ALL INCOME from any organ harvest. For this I ask the reasonable sum of $10,000 US DOLLARS per hunter/per round."[8] He even offered to run *naked* for an extra two grand...

About This Book

The Most Dangerous Cinema: People Hunting People on Film is the first book to examine all the cinematic, video and television permutations of Connell's iconic short story (whether officially credited as such or not). In order to qualify for full-chapter treatment, the film in question had to have been released theatrically in English (prior to May 2013) and must focus on hunting humans for *sport*— rather than for revenge (e.g., *Deadly Game*), for pay (*Human Target*), to keep a secret (*Run for the Sun*), or simply for survival (*The Eliminator*). Each of the fourteen theatrically-released cinematic adaptations of the tale are explored in individual chapters, with each chapter containing the following sections: "Synopsis," "How '*Dangerous*' Is It?" (comparing and contrasting the film's story with Connell's original), "Critique" (analyzing the picture for both cinematic and thematic merits — or lack thereof), "Production" (detailing the movie's production history and the principals involved), and "Credits."

In addition, the book offers five further chapters. "DTV Danger" covers all those humans-hunting-humans-for-sport films that went direct to video or were made specifically for television. "*Almost* Dangerous Games" covers those movies that include the basic concept of hunting humans but which show little or no fidelity to Connell's story by having its antagonist(s) motivated by something other than the "sport" of hunting. Also, here you will find a few films that, like *My Son, the Hero*, utilize Connell's concept as a secondary subplot, with the hunting-humans theme merely a brief interlude. The "Dangerous Game Shows and Deadly Diversions" chapter details those movies in the (surprisingly large) cinematic subset featuring hunting-humans-as-entertainment-for-the-masses (exemplified by *The Running Man* and the more recent *The Hunger Games*). Films in which people are paid to hunt others for the vicarious thrill it provides third-party observers, such as a television audience, are included here. These pictures, though definitely inspired by Connell's story and concept, are distinct in that the hunt becomes voyeuristic rather than participatory. Yes, there are people hunting people, but they do so for motives other than pleasure (though there may be some of that, too) — generally money. The "Dangerous Alien Games" chapter explores those movies in which *aliens* hunt humans for sport (highlighted by the *Predator* films). And finally, "Television Games" features the numerous TV shows that have utilized the people-hunting-people-for-sport concept for one or more episodes (everything from *Get Smart* and *Gilligan's Island* to *Star Trek* and *Buffy the Vampire Slayer*).

Just a glance at the myriad titles detailed within this book shows that there's no denying the basic power of, and outright fascination with, the disturbing notion of hunting humans for sport. And it remains a germane and controversial subject today, as evidenced by a story picked up by the press in late 2012 bearing the headline: "Sarah Timme, Colorado Mom, Wants School to Ban 'The Most Dangerous Game.'" Reported the article, "[U]pset that her 8th-grade son was assigned to read a short story about a man who hunts humans for sport ... Timme says that 'The Most Dangerous Game' only serves to encourage school violence, adding that she was 'outraged and appalled' by the story and assignment, which were disturbing to both her and her son."[9] Even after nearly ninety years Connell's powerful tale can still provoke serious thought and strong emotions (not to mention "outrage and appall"

French movie card highlighting scenes from the 1932 *The Most Dangerous Game*, the first and most faithful cinematic adaptation of Connell's tale to date.

certain readers). And even *humor*, with immensely popular shows like *30 Rock* name-checking the notion for laughs (Jack: "*I've hunted the world's most dangerous game: man—[coughs]—excuse me, manatee*"). So for those among us with stronger literary stomachs and braver cinematic sensibilities (Colorado moms apparently need not apply), it's time to sharpen our cinematic "woodcraft," hone our skills at "outdoor chess," and delve into the Most Dangerous Cinema.

1

Pride of Place
The Most Dangerous Game (1932)

"Only after the kill does man know the true ecstasy of love."— Count Zaroff

Synopsis

A yacht bearing Robert Rainsford (Joel McCrea), a famous big-game hunter, and four companions returning from a hunting expedition makes its way through the treacherous Malay archipelago. While Rainsford and the men discuss the contradictions inherent in "civilized" hunting, the boat suddenly lurches as it hits a hidden reef. All is chaos when the sea water rushes in below deck and hits the hot boilers, ripping the ship apart in a spectacular explosion. Rainsford is the only one to make it safely through the shark-infested waters and reach the shore of the nearby island.

After wandering through the jungle, he looks across a steamy clearing and spies a castle-like structure in the distance. It is the home of Count Zaroff (Leslie Banks), a Russian aristocrat who fled the revolution with most of his fortune intact. "Welcome to my poor fortress," says the cordial Count, "built by the Portuguese centuries ago. I have had the ruins restored to make my home here." Rainsford soon meets two more of Zaroff's impromptu "guests," Eve (Fay Wray) and Martin Trowbridge (Robert Armstrong), survivors of a previous shipwreck. There had been four survivors, but neither Eve nor Martin has seen their two sailor companions for three days. Zaroff claims they are out hunting, but Eve doesn't think so and relays her suspicions to Rainsford.

The Count is impressed by Rainsford, whom he considers to be a "kindred spirit" in his passion for hunting. Zaroff tells him, "God made some men poets, some he made kings, some beggars; *me* he made a hunter! ... Hunting is my one passion." That evening the conversation turns mysterious as Zaroff talks of his growing ennui, and how he rekindled his passion for hunting. "I have done a rare thing," he boasts. "I have invented a new sensation." But he prefers not to elaborate, saying only, "It is my one great secret."

Eve's suspicions are soon proven to be justified when she and Rainsford sneak into a secret trophy room. There they find a horror to shock the senses — a room filled with *human* trophies. The pair are discovered when Zaroff returns with his latest "trophy"— the body of Eve's brother, whom Zaroff had just "hunted." With fire in his eyes, Zaroff tries to enlist Rainsford in his sadistic sport of hunting "the most dangerous game." Rainsford will have none of this and so becomes the Count's next "prey." While Zaroff's henchmen restrain Rainsford and Eve, the Count sets the ground rules for his game of "outdoor chess," as he terms it. Rainsford and Eve (who insists on going along) will be given a knife and a head start, and if they survive until 12:30 the following day they will be set free. (Of course, to date no one has met the challenge and won.) There then ensues a deadly game of wits as Rainsford uses his hunter's knowledge to set various traps for the pursuing Zaroff, but ultimately fails to kill his adversary. Finally there is nowhere left to run and the pair are cornered above a waterfall. Zaroff lets his hound loose, and as Rainsford struggles with the vicious brute, the Count fires his rifle. Man and dog topple over the cliff into the raging torrent. Stroking the scar on his forehead, Zaroff leers at Eve — his "prize."

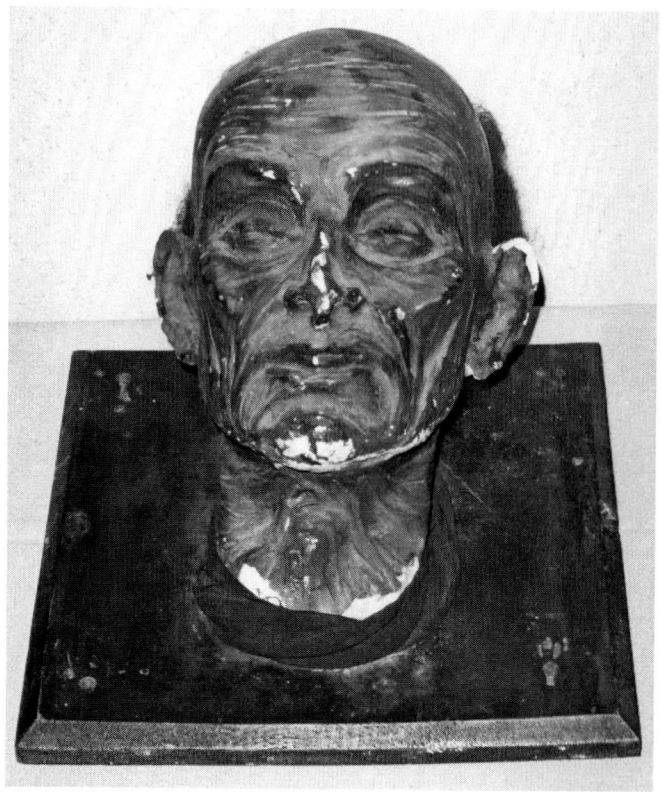

Original head prop seen on the wall of Zaroff's grisly trophy room in *The Most Dangerous Game* (photograph: Lynn Naron, 1993).

Returning to his fortress, Zaroff plays the piano after ordering that Eve be brought to him. The door opens and Rainsford enters — torn, tattered, but alive. "You hit the dog, not me," he relates to the surprised Count. "You have beaten me," replies an admiring Zaroff, but the treacherous Count is not yet finished. When Zaroff reaches for a hidden pistol, Rainsford leaps at him. In the ensuing melee Zaroff grasps his bow, but Rainsford wins out and stabs the Count in the back with his own arrow. Rainsford grabs Eve and they rush to the launch. The Count is not yet dead, however, and he staggers to the window to raise his bow as the escaping boat moves into view. His strength is gone, though, and Zaroff collapses onto the window ledge, only to roll over and fall into the jaws of his own vicious hunting dogs waiting below. The boat, carrying our hero and heroine, speeds safely away.

How "Dangerous" Is It?

This first, and best (as it turns out), adaptation of Richard Connell's 1924 classic short story is astoundingly faithful to the spirit — and even the letter, at times (lifting dialogue and even complete conversations from the story) — of Connell's original. Of course, having learned the hard way from their previous action-adventure pictures the importance of "romance" to a film's success, the producing/directing team of Merian C. Cooper and Ernest

B. Schoedsack made certain their film adaptation featured a love interest in the form of the ethereally beautiful Fay Wray (the classic screamer from *King Kong*) as Eve Trowbridge, a fellow castaway and prisoner on Zaroff's island. And along with Eve came her blustery, besotted brother, played by Robert Armstrong (*Kong*'s Carl Denham), who not only provides some amusing comic relief, but also a grim portent of things to come when he becomes the first victim (that we see) of Zaroff's "most dangerous game."

The inclusion of a female constitutes the movie's major departure from Connell's story, though the filmmakers made numerous changes in the details. For instance, the film transfers Connell's Caribbean setting to the even more exotic-sounding (and more forbidding) "Malay archipelago." It's a shipwreck rather than the story's clumsy accident (in which the hero rather stupidly falls overboard while trying to grab his dropped pipe) that places Rainsford on the benighted isle. The odd first name of "Sanger" Rainsford is changed to the more generic moniker of "Robert" (or "Bob") in the film; and Connell's "General" Zaroff becomes "Count" Zaroff—undoubtedly to reinforce the character's "decadent" aristocratic background, while not giving too great a weight to the antagonist's authority (by making him a general). The film compresses the original story's three-day "contest" into a single day and night. And, of course, the deliberate (though "unseen") killing of Zaroff at the end of the short story is softened to the simple wounding of the Count in the film, thus allowing Rainsford to preserve his innate humanity while he and Eve take flight (with the Count ultimately falling to his death of his own accord).

Zaroff's unwholesome, Sadean view of sexuality displayed in the film through both imagery (in the form of the satyr-themed doorknocker and wall tapestry) and the Count's pointed, almost salacious dialogue was created out of whole cloth by scripter James Ashmore Creelman. Such a suggestive and disturbing portrayal would have been impossible to film only two years later, when the revamped Production Code became an all-powerful censorial entity under William H. Hayes in 1934.

While the Connell story hints at the results of Zaroff's gruesome game ("'And now,' said the general, 'I want to show you my new collection of heads. Will you come with me to the library?'" to which Rainsford icily replies, "'I hope ... that you will excuse me tonight, General Zaroff. I'm really not feeling well.'"), the movie takes the more cinematic approach and places the protagonists (and viewer) inside the horrific sanctuary, thereby creating one of the great visual shocks of the film (and decade), as Rainsford's flashlight shines upwards into the darkness and illuminates a hideous sight—a human head preserved and mounted on the wall like some perverted deer trophy. As Eve backs away, she bumps into another human head, this one bobbing in a tank as the dim light silhouettes its grotesque twisting and turning. This was strong stuff for 1932, and a scene possessing enough gruesome style to unsettle a viewer even eight decades later.

Critique

The Most Dangerous Game is a film in two parts. The first half carefully builds the mood, creating a feeling of unease and dread, a feeling validated by the sheer fast-paced terror of the second half. From the moment we meet Count Zaroff, with his passion for hunting, his cultured yet cold manner, his cryptic talk of the "most dangerous game," and his sadistic views of love and sex ("What is woman, even a woman such as this, until the blood is quickened by the kill?"), we sense the sinister undertones to the seemingly innocuous events unfolding. The bizarre setting, Eve's vague fear, and Zaroff himself all set the stage for the symphony of terror and violence soon to commence, as the two protagonists are forced to flee for their lives, hunted as "the most dangerous game."

James Ashmore Creelman's screenplay adapts Connell's story into a taut, intelligent, literary work of cinematic art. The characters are well drawn, the dialogue is excellent, and the screenplay's structure draws the viewer into this nightmare situation and holds him or her fast until the final reel. Of course, credit must be given to co-directors Ernest B. Schoedsack and Irving Pichel for their masterful pacing and camerawork, which find a base in the literate screenplay and leap forward to create a rollercoaster ride of excitement. Schoedsack deliberately set out to achieve this effect, saying:

> When I read the script I felt that nobody would believe it. I decided the main thing was to keep it moving so they wouldn't have time to think it over. I didn't know a damned thing about stage direction, but I tried one thing that worked: I brought a stopwatch to the stage and sometimes I'd say, "That scene took 30 seconds; I think we could do it just as well in 20," and we'd speed it up that way.[1]

Scriptwriter Creelman wisely avoided falling into the age-old love-interest trap. Though Hollywood wisdom demanded that the filmmakers add a feminine element to Connell's all-masculine tale, the film's romance, what there is of it, is only implied (simply by the fact that the two protagonists are man and woman, and that Rainsford is dedicated to protecting her). Rainsford and Eve never kiss or exchange any romantic banter; they are merely two people thrown together who must fight for their lives. The only talk of love comes from Zaroff himself, and it is a twisted, savage form of love. "First kill, then love," is Zaroff's credo. Other than this Sadean view of sex, there is no romantic interlude to intrude upon the terror and dark mood of the film, no moments of romantic respite to lessen the horror of the situation. This absence of romance strengthens the impact of *The Most Dangerous Game*, allowing the audience to identify with the two people caught in this horrible competition without being distracted by their sudden romantic interest in each other (which so often comes across as implausible and unconvincing).

One of the most striking aspects of *The Most Dangerous Game* is the literate and insightful dialogue. Surprisingly, though screenwriter Creelman wisely incorporated a number of phrases and even whole conversations from the original story, much of the memorable dialogue came directly from Creelman's pen rather than Connell's. For instance, when Rainsford expresses how "incredible" the deaths of his companions seem, Zaroff counters with this sagacious observation: "Such things are always incredible. Death is for others, not for ourselves." The script is filled with juicy lines, particularly when Zaroff verbally spars with Rainsford or elucidates his sadistic theories of life, love, and the hunt. Creelman provides Zaroff with a diverse array of illuminating phrases, utilizing lines both blatant and subtle to reveal this man's warped and twisted character. Towards the beginning, as we first get to know Zaroff, he makes a revealing statement. "One night as I lay in my tent with this, this head of mine," he relates while unconsciously reaching up to stroke the scar on his forehead, "a terrible thought crept like a snake into my brain — hunting was beginning to bore me." "Is that such a terrible thought, Count?" asks Eve, her voice full of sarcastic reproach. "It is, my dear lady," Zaroff continues, "when hunting has been the whip for all other passions. When I lost my love of hunting I lost my love of life —" he says and, after a significant pause, adds "— of love." Compare this to Connell's handling of the same moment: "I was lying in my tent with a splitting headache one night when a terrible thought pushed its way

1. Pride of Place

into my mind. Hunting was beginning to bore me! And hunting, remember, had been my life. I have heard that in America businessmen often go to pieces when they give up the business that has been their life." Creelman often cleverly adapts — and improves upon — Connell's scenes and dialogue, upping the dramatic ante.

Later, when Rainsford and Eve discover the horror of the "trophy room" (a sequence devised solely for the film), the true nature of Zaroff's cruelty and sadism is revealed with a few understated and euphemistic lines. "You see," Zaroff explains to his two horrified captives, "when I first began stocking my island, many of my guests thought I was joking, so I established this trophy room. An hour with my trophies and they usually do their best to keep away from me." Then, just before the hunt is to begin, a bit more of Zaroff's twisted perspective is revealed in this exchange: "I'm going to be hunted," an angry Rainsford tells the frightened Eve, but Zaroff interrupts to reassure her. "Oh no, no Miss Trowbridge — outdoor chess, his brain against mine, his woodcraft against mine, and the prize — " he trails off, with a pointed look at Eve. She insists upon going with Rainsford, but our hero protests that "he'll kill you too"; to which Zaroff counters, "Not at all — one does not kill the female animal."

The film is far more blatant in its anti-hunting theme than the more subtle underpinnings found in Connell's short story. From the opening, in which Rainsford and his com-

Zaroff (Leslie Banks) explaining his mania for *The Most Dangerous Game* to Eve (Fay Wray) and Rainsford (Joel McCrea).

panions discuss the morality of hunting, to the inexorable climax of human beings stalked for the thrill of the hunt (which, after all, is just the concept taken to its ultimate extreme), the picture focuses on the cruelty of this blood sport. At the film's beginning, one of Rainsford's companions makes a wry observation: "I was thinking of the inconsistency of civilization. The beast of the jungle, killing just for his existence, is called 'savage'; the man, killing just for sport, is called 'civilized.' It's a bit contradictory, isn't it." (No such dialogue is found in Connell's story.) Rainsford responds with this poor argument: "What makes you think it isn't just as much sport for the animal as for the man?" His companion presses the issue by asking this Great White Hunter if "there'd be as much sport in the game if you were the tiger instead of the hunter?" "Well, that's something I'll never have to decide," is Rainsford's evasive reply. "This world is divided into two kinds of people, the hunter and the hunted. Luckily, I'm a hunter. Nothing can ever change that," he continues confidently—just as the ship lurches under him and his "hunter's world" is turned upside-down. (This latter "hunter and hunted" diatribe is the one sentiment adapted directly from Connell's dialogue.) In the end, even Rainsford, whose life is dedicated to the deadly pastime of hunting for pleasure, comes to realize the wasteful brutality of the sport. When treed like a wild beast by Zaroff, he learns what it's like to be on the other side of the gun barrel. "Those animals I cornered, now I know how they felt," he empathizes. (Connell offers a similar observation towards the end of his story with the simple "Rainsford knew how an animal at bay feels.")

Co-directors Ernest B. Schoedsack and Irving Pichel utilize the satyr motif, with all its bestial and sexual implications, throughout the film to underscore the dark themes of the Hunt and its brutal relationship to sex. Beginning with the opening credits, it is the first thing the viewer sees. Focusing on a heavy wooden door, the camera moves in to rest on the unusual and forbidding door knocker — a satyr-like figure holding a swooning girl in its arms. Suddenly a hand rises up into the frame, raps with the knocker, and the first credits appear.

This imagery also plays an important role in Zaroff's introduction. Rainsford, his head full of suspicions about his unusual host, walks up the massive staircase towards his room. On the wall he notices a gigantic mural. Again it is the satyr with the captured woman in his arms, but in much more revealing detail. Shocked, Rainsford stops his ascent and the camera closes in on the tapestry, revealing the swooning woman to be half nude, with one breast exposed. The camera then cuts to Zaroff gazing up at it, an unhealthy gleam in his eye and a cruel half-smile on his lips. The man obviously identifies with the brutal, amorous satyr. Schoedsack makes good use of this nice symbolic touch provided by art director Carroll Clark.

In his American film debut, Leslie Banks gives a wonderfully sinister performance as the sadistic yet cordial Count Zaroff. With his glaring eyes, his small but significant gestures and mannerisms (such as lovingly stroking the scar on his forehead when his bloodlust is aroused), and his exquisite dialogue delivery, he makes a perfect villain. Banks receives all the best lines, and he takes full advantage. "One passion builds upon the other," he says, "Kill, then *love*." Banks rolls the word "love" on his tongue, stretching it out, changing its meaning into something dark and degenerate.

Henry Gerrard's photography makes excellent use of the wonderfully medieval interiors of Zaroff's castle, with its huge stone fireplace, massive steps, and spectacular masonry, as well as the lush jungle sets, all towering plants, decayed logs, and hanging creepers (the same jungle seen in the original *King Kong*). In one of the most exciting sequences, Gerrard's

Zaroff (Leslie Banks) gloats over his latest kill in *The Most Dangerous Game.*

mobile camera takes the viewer on a wild ride through this hellish setting. As Rainsford and Eve flee through the jungle, the camera moves in front of them, keeping pace with their panic-stricken flight. We are shown their faces in close up, each in turn. First comes Rainsford — grim, determined; then Eve — frightened, almost in a panic; and finally Zaroff — eyes bulging in a bloodlust frenzy. The camera then turns to the point of view of the fleeing protagonists as they rush through the jungle; leaves and plants slap our face as now we, the viewers, join the panicky flight. This use of the subjective camera brilliantly draws us into the characters' plight and inspires an exciting urgency and involvement not found in many films of the day (or of *any* day, for that matter).

One of the few faults that can be leveled at *The Most Dangerous Game* is the sometimes dated dialogue mouthed by Rainsford. (Paradoxically, the rich dialogue written for Zaroff is one of the picture's strongest assets.) For instance, when Zaroff suggests that Rainsford join him in his deadly hobby, an incensed Rainsford answers with, "You murderous rat, I'm a hunter, not an assassin." While this line gets the point across, it conjures up images of an Edward G. Robinson gangster picture. Earlier, when Rainsford tells Zaroff of his shipwreck and the friends he'd lost, he describes them as "the swellest crowd on Earth"—a rather quaint thirties-ism. Thankfully, only Rainsford utters these little slices of dated slang, which remind us that the film is indeed set firmly in the 1930s. However, this does set up a nice contrast between the two rival characters: Zaroff, sophisticated and proud in his mad obsession — and Rainsford, simple yet honest in his convictions, an Everyman for the times (who thus must speak like the Everyman of his time).

As the first-ever adaptation of Connell's short story, *The Most Dangerous Game* stands as an exciting, intelligent, involving film — a genuine classic from the Golden Age of Hollywood. The mobile camerawork, fast-paced direction, strong themes (not least of which is Connell's take on man's ultimate inhumanity to man), and generally effective dialogue make it a thrilling and timeless piece of cinema history that continues to delight after repeated viewings.

Production

The Most Dangerous Game was made by the team of Merian C. Cooper and Ernest B. Schoedsack, the men responsible for *King Kong* (1933). Another *Kong* alumnus was screenwriter James Creelman. (Cooper had promised the job of writing *The Most Dangerous Game* to Edgar Wallace after receiving the prolific English writer's original treatment for *King Kong*, but Wallace's premature death in 1932 cut short his involvement in both projects.) Tragically, the talented Creelman took his own life in 1941 by leaping from a New York high-rise. He was 40 years old.

Though released before *King Kong*, *The Most Dangerous Game* was actually filmed *after* the start of that classic ape movie (which took close to a year to complete, mostly due to the time-consuming animation work). Recalled Cooper:

> We needed a project while the [*King Kong*] script was rewritten and while the animation for *Kong* was being done, so I picked up this short story and got Jimmy Creelman to write the script. The title means when man hunts man, instead of animals, and I thought Monty [Schoedsack] and I could introduce all those things that we used in *Chang* [1927] — the traps and the dead falls, and all those things. None of them are in the original story, neither was the love story. [Actually, the deadfall and traps *did* feature in Connell's original short story.] ... *The Most Dangerous Game* was a cheap picture to make — it only cost about $150,000. [Once again, Cooper's memory is *slightly* faulty, as the production was budgeted at a more substantial $202,662 for a three-week shoot; Cooper and Schoedsack brought the picture in about $16,000 over budget and a week over-schedule.] We saved money by using Fay Wray and Robert Armstrong in between sessions on *Kong*. Since both films were laid in the jungle, we were able to use the same sets for both, switching back and forth; I'd be shooting *Kong*, then Monty would move in and do *The Most Dangerous Game*. There's a shot in *The Most Dangerous Game* where you see Leslie Banks, the villain, running through the fog; as soon as Schoedsack did that shot, I moved in and took the same set and did the shot in *Kong* where the sailor is being chased by the dinosaur. The same thing where Kong shakes the men off the log; when I was through doing the live action, Monty came in and shot a scene for *Dangerous Game* showing Fay and Joel McCrea, playing the hero, crossing the log trying to escape from the madman. We had a lot of fun, and the picture was a hit, and it's been remade several times, but each time the people who did it used our concept, the traps and the love story and all.[2]

As reported by film editor Archie Marshek, director Schoedsack didn't always see eye-to-eye with his producer and partner Merian C. Cooper while making *The Most Dangerous Game*. According to Marshek, Schoedsack would sometimes hide in the editing room when Cooper was on the set because the two each had their own ideas of how the chase scenes should be shot. By avoiding Cooper, Schoedsack could do things his own way. Even so, Schoedsack was not at all convinced that they had a "classic" on their hands. The director later admitted that he "didn't think it would be very good so I just decided to keep it moving so fast that nobody would notice.... We didn't know what a good picture we had until it was finished."[3]

Cooper and Schoedsack originally envisioned *The Most Dangerous Game* as a big-budget spectacular, but the RKO head office set strict limitations for the production. This demanded significant revisions in the script, including the elimination of *nine* actors (set to play Rainsford's fellow passengers) from the proposed cast. Among those lost before the yacht ever went down were Leon Waycoff (fresh from Universal's *Murders in the Rue Morgue*), Creighton Chaney (later Lon Chaney, Jr.), and a young Ray Milland. Cooper and Schoedsack's reworking of the shipwreck sequence (which would have been much more expensive had it been shot as originally planned) is illustrative of their cost-cutting process. In a note to production supervisor Val Paul, dated May 4, 1932, Schoedsack outlined the proposed alterations:

> Mr. Cooper and I have discussed and approved a change in the yacht sequence which should result in considerable economy, while improving and adding realism to the wreck with a more modern and convincing method...
>
> At the instant that the ship scrapes bottom, we leave the interior of the dining salon as the sets rocks over, but before the water enters. We cut to the flash on the bridge as the officer discovers the water has reached the boilers. We cut to a miniature explosion of flash powder on our miniature hull and instantly dissolve to a series of overlapping and rapidly dissolving flashes such as falling wreckage (all in close-ups), a man being washed along a deck, falling spars and gear, drowning sailors, hissing steam, etc., accompanied by screams, crashes and the roaring of water. Over all will be exposed flashes of foaming and churning water, and the last flash might be the last of the masthead disappearing under the water. Inasmuch as these scenes are fast and impressionistic, I think they could be very cheaply made, or perhaps a great many found in stock. At the end of the series, we dissolve to the scene of the boy in the water, as in the present version. As you will see, this lineup eliminates the following items:
>
> 1. Building a salon set in tank, with water dumps.
> 2. Possibly eliminate rockers on both bridge and salon.
> 3. Eliminates deck set in tank entirely.
> 4. Simplifies miniature yacht work to some extent.
> 5. Eliminates costume changes for extras in cabin.

Irving Pichel, co-director of *The Most Dangerous Game*, worked in front of as well as behind the camera. As an actor he appeared in such genre films as *Murder by the Clock* (1931), *Dracula's Daughter* (1936; in which he was unforgettable as Sandor, the slimy, evil, scheming servant of the title character), and *Torture Ship* (1939). Behind the camera he co-directed *She* (1935) with Lansing C. Holden and later helmed George Pal's milestone science fiction film *Destination Moon* (1950). "The front office was afraid I couldn't handle dialogue," stated Ernest B. Schoedsack, "so they sent Irving Pichel over and he just stood behind me and watched." Co-star Fay Wray, however, remembered Pichel as doing more than just "standing and watching." She remembered that, while Schoedsack directed the action scenes in *The Most Dangerous Game*, it was Pichel who actively supervised the dialogue portions.[4]

Along with Ms. Wray, three other actors from *Kong* featured in *The Most Dangerous Game*. Robert Armstrong, who here plays Martin Trowbridge (Eve's besotted brother), had the pivotal role of Carl Denham in *King Kong*. Steve Clemento (a Yaqui Indian named Esteban Clemente who was known in vaudeville as the world's greatest knife thrower) appears as Zaroff's "Tartar" servant in *The Most Dangerous Game* and later as the "Witch King" in *Kong*. Noble Johnson, here playing Ivan, Zaroff's strong, silent henchman, was the imposing village chief on Kong's island. Johnson, a well-known local dog breeder, was originally contracted to provide several of Zaroff's hounds for the picture, but his stature and imposing presence earned him a spot in the film alongside his animals. *Most Dangerous Game* star Joel McCrea was *almost* in *Kong* as well. McCrea told John Kobal (for his book, *People Will Talk*) that Merian C. Cooper wanted McCrea for the role of Jack Driscoll in *Kong*, but he turned the director down and instead recommended Jacques de Bujac (who became Bruce Cabot) for the role.

While working on *King Kong*, Bruce Cabot made a bid for the role of Count Zaroff in *The Most Dangerous Game*. Though he submitted portraits of himself made up as Zaroff, RKO passed him over in favor of English stage star Leslie Banks, then appearing on Broadway. Banks subsequently returned to England, where he continued his film career, though he never made another picture in America.

Whether Leslie Banks' subsequent avoidance of American productions had anything to do with his experiences on *The Most Dangerous Game* is purely a matter of conjecture, though the English actor did suffer at least one embarrassing (and painful) mishap during filming. Remembered Schoedsack:

> Once, when we were working on the Fog Hollow set, Leslie came bounding out of the fog, clutching his rear end, and told us, "I say, one of those dogs bit me!" The lady from the training school [five of the twenty Great Danes used were provided by the Hollywood Dog Training School] said, "Oh, no, it's impossible! None of those dogs would do that!" Leslie said, "Well, perhaps it was a cameraman, but *something* bit me in the ass." He was bleeding and had to have first aid and stitches.[5]

According to Joel McCrea, producer Merian C. Cooper had more than a professional interest in his star, Fay Wray, though he never acted on it. "He got me and Fay Wray," stated the actor, "because he loved Fay Wray ... he loved Fay Wray, but he married Dorothy Jordan, and she [Wray] was married to John Monk Saunders, who wrote *Wings*."

Clarence Linden ("Buster") Crabbe earned $5 a day as Joel McCrea's stunt double on *The Most Dangerous Game*. An Olympic athlete-turned-stuntman-turned-actor, Crabbe is best remembered for his portrayal of *Flash Gordon* in the 1936 serial and its subsequent sequels. It's interesting to note that McCrea himself began his life in motion pictures as a stuntman in the 1920s. By 1932, however, he was much too valuable a star for the studio to risk his neck performing dangerous stunts, and so RKO hired Crabbe to take the *Most Dangerous* risks.

CREDITS: Alternate Titles: *The Hounds of Zaroff* (British release title); *Skull Island* (1938 reissue title); Directors: Ernest B. Schoedsack and Irving Pichel; Associate Producer: Merian C. Cooper; Executive Producer: David O. Selznick; Screenplay: James Ashmore Creelman ("From the *O. Henry Prize Winning Collection* story by Richard Connell"); Cinemaography: Henry Gerrard; Art Director: Carroll Clark; Editor: Archie F. Marshek; Music: Max Steiner; Makeup: Wally Westmore*; Recorded by: Clem Portman; Production/Distribution Company: RKO Radio Pictures; Release Date: September 9, 1932; Running Time: 63 minutes.

CAST: Joel McCrea (Bob), Fay Wray (Eve), Leslie Banks (Zaroff), Robert Armstrong (Martin), Noble Johnson (Ivan), Steve Clemento (Tartar), William Davidson (Captain), Dutch Hendrian (Scar-face), Hale Hamilton* (Bill Woodman), Landers Stevens* (Doc), James Flavin* (First Mate).

*Uncredited on film print.

2

Carbon-Copy Game
A Game of Death (1945)

> "Let me tell you Rainsford, there is no game in the world that can compare with it for a moment." — Erich Kreiger

Synopsis

Famous big game hunter and author Don Rainsford (John Loder) is sailing back to New York when his yacht captain (Jason Robards, Sr.) notices some safety buoy lights don't match the reefs on his charts. They decide to turn back, but it's too late — the ship hits a reef and the cold seawater streaming through the breach in the hull quickly explodes the ship's boilers.

His companions are taken by sharks, but Rainsford makes it to the nearby island. There, Rainsford finds a castle, built by pirates but now owned and occupied by Erich Kreiger (Edgar Barrier), a man with an all-consuming passion for hunting, and who is more than pleased that his latest "guest" is a world-renowned hunter. At Kreiger's castle, Rainsford also meets Robert and Ellen Trowbridge (Russell Wade and Audrey Long), survivors of a previous shipwreck. While Bob overindulges in Kreiger's fine brandy, their host tantalizes Rainsford with his boast of having stocked his private island with "the most dangerous game." Mysteriously, he is unwilling to disclose the nature of said game (nor open up his locked "trophy room"). Meanwhile, Ellen surreptitiously relates her concern to Rainsford. "Don't trust him," she warns, "Don't believe anything he tells you ... there's something evil going on in this place — we're all prisoners."

That night Ellen comes to Rainsford's room, worried because her brother Bob has disappeared. Hearing a scream from outside, they creep downstairs, only to find the trophy room unlocked. Inside they discover Kreiger's "trophies" — human heads mounted on the wall and bobbing in tanks. They also find Bob, who only pretended to be drunk to keep Kreiger off-guard, and who has been nosing around on his own. Rainsford slips out of the castle and sets traps in Kreiger's private jungle, intending to "beat him at his own game."

The next day Rainsford confronts Kreiger. "You hunt human beings," Rainsford states, before adding, "Kreiger, you're a genius — I congratulate you." Kreiger is surprised. "Really, Rainsford? I was afraid you might have some romantic notion about the value of human life." After gaining his confidence and accepting Kreiger's invitation to join him that night in hunting Ellen's brother, Rainsford reveals his plan to Ellen: "Don't worry, when I get Kreiger out in that jungle the hunt will be short and the victim won't be your brother."

Evocative one-sheet poster for *A Game of Death*, RKO's 1945 remake of their own *The Most Dangerous Game* (1932).

Unfortunately, Kreiger discovers Rainsford's ruse and traps him in his room, guarded by Kreiger's "man-killing" monster of a dog. Kreiger then hunts Bob, using a bow (Kreiger's favored weapon after having become too proficient with a gun)—with the expected result. When Kreiger and his men return with his newest "trophy," Rainsford goads Kreiger into hunting *him* that same night, and Ellen insists on going with Rainsford.

After Kreiger spots Rainsford's previously-set deadfall trap, the madman trades his bow for a high-powered rifle. When Rainsford and Ellen seek cover in the island's foggy swamp, the hunter calls for his dogs to track them. Finally cornered on a seaside cliff, Rainsford is set upon by one of the dogs. As Rainsford struggles with the brute, Kreiger shoots, and man and dog tumble over the cliff to their doom.

With Ellen locked safely away back at the castle, Kreiger smugly plays his piano, reveling in his triumph. Suddenly, the castle's door opens and in walks Rainsford, disheveled but very much alive. "Rainsford, I congratulate you, you beat me," stammers the astonished Kreiger. "Not yet," growls Rainsford, "You hit the dog, not me. I took a chance and went over with him." Kreiger grabs for a Luger in a drawer and the two men struggle. Kreiger's henchman joins the fray, but Rainsford overpowers him and continues grappling with Kreiger. They fall over the back of a couch, with Kreiger clutching the pistol. A shot rings out ... but it is Rainsford who stands up from behind the sofa, Luger in hand. As Rainsford and Ellen flee through the horrid trophy room to the hidden boat launch and speed away, the wounded Kreiger grabs his rifle and staggers to the window—only to topple onto the terrace below, into the slavering jaws of his own vicious hounds.

How "Dangerous" Is It?

A direct remake of the 1932 *The Most Dangerous Game*, *A Game of Death* follows the same pattern as its predecessor, hewing closely to Connell's classic storyline and deviating only in a few details. Apart from the various name changes (Connell's exotic-sounding "Sanger" Rainsford becomes the more mundane—and approachable—"Don"; while "General Zaroff" transforms into the topically Teutonic "Erich Kreiger," no doubt to take advantage of the then-current anti–German sentiment), *A Game of Death* deviates from Connell's story along the same lines as its 1932 template: adding a female character (and her brother); telescoping the three-day hunt into one night; staging a more dramatic shipwreck rather than having Rainsford simply fall overboard; and keeping the hero's hands relatively clean at the end of the tale by avoiding Connell's deliberate-killing-of-the-antagonist closer.

As a result of such fidelity, *A Game of Death*, like its predecessor, retains much of the power of Connell's original story, with the various changes made either to (1) increase the drama (the added characters and tightened time frame), (2) play to the camera by making events more "cinematic" (adding the exciting shipwreck sequence), or (3) appease the censors (modifying the ending). Apart from the last, each of these alterations actually strengthens the story's power to help create yet another cinematic triumph—though one that, as we shall see, ultimately becomes redundant.

Critique

A Game of Death is the country cousin—or, more appropriately, given the studio's insistence on slavishly aping their own original, the slightly-less-attractive younger sister—

of RKO's 1932 hit *The Most Dangerous Game*. Almost a carbon copy of the 1932 film, *A Game of Death*, just like a literal facsimile from the old mimeograph days, is a little bit fainter and features a few more smudges when compared to the original.

When it comes to visual symbolism, for instance, this *Game* is far less dangerous than its predecessor, no doubt due to the more stringent demands of the Production Code, which was updated in 1934. The satyr doorknocker of the 1932 version has given way to a generic gargoyle face here, while the woman held in the arms of the satyr in the huge tapestry prominently displayed in the madman's castle is no longer topless. *Game* makes a half-hearted attempt to put the sexual subtext over via a line of dialogue when Kreiger pronounces, "First the hunt, then the kill, then the woman. Only when you have experienced all that can you know complete ecstasy." But it seems only a token effort to recapture the significant subtext running through James Ashmore Creelman's more adult *Most Dangerous Game* screenplay.

Speaking of Creelman, had he not died by his own hand in 1941, that scribe could very well have brought a plagiarism suit against RKO, since so much of *A Game of Death* is simply Creelman's 1932 script with a few words and incidents changed by "new" screenwriter

Hunting enthusiast Erich Kreiger (Edgar Barrier, center) introduces hunter/author Don Rainsford (John Loder, right) to his imposing mute servant Caribe (Noble Johnson, more-or-less reprising his role from 1932's *The Most Dangerous Game*) before forcing Rainsford to play *A Game of Death* (lobby card).

Norman Houston, a veteran scribbler of mostly B-oaters whose credits stretched back to the Silents. When Rainsford marvels that all his companions are now dead, labeling such a thing "incredible," Kreiger counters with "Death is always incredible, always for others, never for ourselves." It's nearly a word-for-word steal from the original ("Such things are always incredible; death is for others, not for ourselves").

Unfortunately, few of those dialogue changes that Norman *did* make turned out to be improvements. A case in point:

> Zaroff in *The Most Dangerous Game*: "One night as I lay in my tent with this, this head of mine, a terrible thought crept like a snake into my brain — hunting was beginning to bore me.... When I lost my love of hunting, I lost my love of life — of love."
>
> Kreiger in *A Game of Death*: "Then one night, lying in my tent, unable to sleep, my head throbbing, a terrible thought began pushing its way into my mind. The idea gave me actual, very real physical pain. Hunting had begun to bore me. It had ceased to be a sporting proposition."

Case in point number two:

> Zaroff: "An hour with my trophies and [my guests] usually do their best to keep away from me."
>
> Kreiger: "After seeing my trophy room, my guests invariably accept my invitation [to hunt]."

Not content with stealing much of the original's script, *A Game of Death* re-uses actual footage from *The Most Dangerous Game*, including all of the shipwreck sequence and various shots of the pursuing hounds. The original Zaroff, Leslie Banks, even stands in for Edgar Barrier's Kreiger at one point, when, in silhouette, he urges on his hounds. There's also one instance in which John Loder and Audrey Long magically transform into Joel McCrae and Fay Wray as they flee through the fog!

Sometimes, however, Norman makes a few minor improvements. The first is having the heroine's brother only feign inebriation. Not only is Russell Wade's character far less obnoxious than the original's Robert Armstrong, his alertness to danger and cleverness at pulling off the ruse makes his fate that much more chilling — particularly since we actually see him run for his life, something we don't in the original.

The concept of Rainsford having discovered Kreiger's secret and making plans to pre-emptively respond by building traps and working a deception (pretending to go along with the madman's obsession) adds a further layer of suspense to the already taut story. Quickly recovering from the initial horror of Kreiger's trophy room, Rainsford indeed lives up to "the most dangerous game" appellation by applying logic and cunning, formulating a plan to string Kreiger along and then kill him at the first opportunity. Of course, circumstances are against him and he's found out, but this little twist on the original offers moments of additional suspense and character revelation.

To his credit, Norman cleverly tapped into the World War II zeitgeist by transforming a Russian Count (or General in Creelman's story) into a German (his henchmen answer with "Javol" and deferentially refer to him as "Herr Kreiger"). Norman even makes Kreiger something of a Nazi spokesman, as he spouts such sentiments as "The weaklings of this world were put here to give us pleasure, to die for us if need be."

Further reflecting the war-torn times, particularly the World War II–America gung-ho/can-do attitude, in which Rosie the Riveter and war hero Audie Murphy were the role models of choice, *A Game of Death* makes a few further subtle alterations. Rainsford taunts

Kreiger into hunting him immediately (rather than after resting) by accusing, "You stack the deck. No, Kreiger, tonight or not at all.... The trouble with you is you want all the odds. You wouldn't dare match your brain against my brain, your skill against mine." This puts the challenge into the mouth of the hero rather than the villain, like in the 1932 version, casting *A Game of Death*'s Rainsford in a more proactive light than the hero of the original, who simply *re*-acted. Additionally, Rainsford sets his traps well before he becomes the prey, showing a far-thinking preparedness not exhibited by the 1932 protagonist.

Like the original, *A Game of Death* touches on the morality of hunting for sport. At the film's beginning, Rainsford discusses this issue with his photographer friend, Collings, aboard the ship.

> Rainsford: "To me it's the greatest sport in the world."
> Collings: "Sport for the hunter, I imagine, not for the hunted. Take this jaguar, for instance [holds up photo of Rainsford about to shoot the big cat]. Look at the expression on that face. What do you suppose his feelings are?"
> Rainsford: "Look Collings, there are two kinds of creatures in the world, the hunter and the hunted. I happen to be a hunter. Frankly, I'm not concerned with that fellow's feelings. As a matter of fact, he's probably enjoying himself just as much as I am. After all, he has a sporting chance of getting me."

Of course, such a nonchalant dismissal of the morality of hunting comes back to bite this Great White Hunter when he himself becomes the prey. Though nothing explicit arises in the subsequent dialogue, the film suggests that Rainsford's outlook may indeed have changed over the course of his ordeal. Near the climax, after Rainsford has turned the tables on Kreiger, Rainsford pointedly asks, "Kreiger, you're the hunted now, and I'm the hunter; how does it feel?" Rainsford, in asking the very same question that Collings posed about the jaguar, appears now to side with the animals. It's a subtle shift that suggests that the issue is far more complex and worthy of consideration than Rainsford's earlier "two kinds of creatures" dismissal.

Art directors Albert D'Agostino (*The Invisible Ray, Dracula's Daughter*, various Val Lewton films) and Lucius Croxton, along with set decorators Darrell Silvera and Jame Altweis, create a studio jungle setting that, while not up to the impressive (and oppressive) vine-strewn, overgrown jungle hell of the original (itself constructed for the bigger-budgeted *King Kong*), prove perfectly serviceable. So too do the smaller-scaled but well-dressed castle interiors, with massive wooden and iron door, stone flagstones, solid-looking walls festooned with animal heads, and heavy furniture.

Likewise, Kreiger's trophies are equally effective and a truly ghastly sight. In a particularly grisly moment, director Robert Wise offers us a horrified reaction shot, as Rainsford's eyes widen and Ellen sucks in her breath, then a close-up of their object of horror — a head suspended in a glass tank. The low-key lighting makes it seem to glow in all its hideousness, the warped features, sunken eye sockets and exposed teeth bared in decay seeming to push forward out of the surrounding darkness. It's a startling and gruesome tableau, and one that hammers home the horror of Connell's concept.

Given that *The Most Dangerous Game* boasts such thespian heavyweights as Joel McCrae, Fay Wray, Leslie Banks, and Robert Armstrong, the cast of lesser lights in *A Game of Death* come off remarkably well by comparison. At least partial credit should go to director Robert Wise, as confirmed by actor Russell Wade (who played Bob Trowbridge): "Bob Wise was helpful to me, always giving me little tidbits. Bob deserves the great success he has attained."[1]

Affecting a slight accent, precise speech patterns and an aristocratic bearing very much in the vein of Leslie Banks' original Count Zaroff, Edgar Barrier offers up an involving portrayal of Connell's archetypal hunter. When Kreiger asks Rainsford if he slept well, and receives the response "Like the dead," Barrier pauses ever so slightly before giving a slight, knowing smile as he answers, "My guests always do." Barrier's subtle expression adds a whole other meaning — and a welcome touch of black humor — to the innocuous idiom. Later, Barrier's eyes shine with a mad excitement as Kreiger, his bloodlust aroused, calls for his dogs and urges his quarry to "Run, run, run, give them a good chase!"

Though often painted with a "bland" brush by critics, John Loder puts forth an impression of level-headedness and dependability, so that one can easily posit him turning the tables on his blood-maddened host. Loder's calm, confident and authoritative (but not overbearing) demeanor, coupled with a natural likability and lack of arrogance, makes him an ideal choice for the story's hero. When Kreiger excitedly proclaims upon learning the identity of his new guest, "Rainsford — not the famous author and hunter?!" Loder gives a self-deprecating laugh and answers, "I don't know about the 'famous' part," immediately endearing him to the viewer.

As already mentioned, Russell Wade's doomed character in *A Game of Death* is far more engaging than Robert Armstrong's counterpart in the original film. In contrast to the blustery Armstrong's obnoxious drunk, Wade's quietly inebriated, even apologetic Trowbridge becomes a far more likable and identifiable character — particularly when we learn of his clever deception and masked alertness. Wade, never the most dynamic of actors, is well cast as the quiet, unassuming, gentle Trowbridge, making his plight and eventual demise that much more affecting.

Not all the *Game of Death* principals measure up to their predecessors, however. While attractive enough in her own right, Audrey Long lacks that ethereal beauty and innate vulnerability possessed by *Most Dangerous Game* heroine Fay Wray. As the de facto heroine-in-peril, Long fails to recreate the desperation and sheer terror so convincingly put across by Wray in the 1932 film. And the people at RKO seemed to agree, since her screams in *A Game of Death* were dubbed from an old soundtrack recording of Ms. Wray!

As Kreiger's stony-faced right-hand man Preshke, Gene Stutenroth makes a poor substitute for Noble Johnson's scowling, imposing and forbidding "Ivan." Sleepy-eyed Stutenroth comes off as a bland Raymond Burr-type heavy, too soft-spoken and polite to generate much menace. (Ironically, Noble Johnson appears as Kreiger's secondary henchman, Carib, but makes little impression.) Stutenroth, renamed Gene Roth, found a home in low-budget Bs and on television, playing support in such fare as *She Demons* (1958) and *Attack of the Giant Leeches* (1959).

Though constrained by a nearly word-for-word and incident-for-incident script that offers too-few innovations, director Robert Wise, working with cinematographer J. Roy Hunt, was still able to invest a few flourishes in this remake.

The mobile camerawork of Hunt (whose career stretched all the way back to 1916, and whose credits include *I Walked with a Zombie* [1943] and 1949's *Mighty Joe Young*) keeps things visually active, even during the early dialogue scenes, while his low-key lighting enhances the ambiance and helps set the mood. When Rainsford and Ellen sneak into the trophy room at night, the lighting casts ominous shadows as they make their way through the castle's main room. The shadows from some ornate iron grill work fall across them, subtly suggesting prison bars and reflecting the duo's trapped condition.

Though early in his career (*Game* was only his fourth picture), director Robert Wise's camera placement and choice of angles displays the superb craftsmanship and good cinematic judgment that would lead him to the Oscar podium two decades later. For instance, when Kreiger gives his self-revelatory "hunting was beginning to bore me" monologue, which segues into his hint-dropping about his having "found a new animal to hunt," Wise positions his camera and actors so that Rainsford and Ellen are seated in the foreground, their backs to us, while Kreiger stands in the background, looming larger than the two seated listeners. The placement, coupled with Kreiger's vaguely threatening dialogue and Edgar Barrier's mannered yet intense delivery, creates an ominous, brooding mood and offers a foretaste of the terrors to come.

When said terrors materialize in the form of the chase—the centerpiece of the film's second half—Wise utilizes some quick editing (a former editor himself, Wise cut such classics as 1939's *The Hunchback of Notre Dame*, *Citizen Kane* and *The Magnificent Ambersons*) and clever camerawork (with the camera alternately pursuing and running alongside the frantic, fleeing Ellen and Rainsford) to make the scene as exciting as it is disturbing. Though not quite capturing the raw energy and large-scale grandiosity of the original, it still remains a thrilling pursuit; and there would be no cause for complaint had not the brilliant original *Most Dangerous Game* sequence preceded it.

When Kreiger returns from another successful hunt, his servant places the body, wrapped in burlap, on a table in the trophy room. As Kreiger steps up to gloat over his latest kill, Wise's camera moves forward, *over* the body on the table, forcing the viewer to come into horrifically close proximity to the covered corpse, stopping only in close-up on Kreiger, whose distant gaze and trance-like expression, as he unconsciously strokes the scar on his forehead, hammers home the subtle madness of the man and the situation.

Near film's end, Kreiger sits triumphantly playing his piano. The shadow of the huge castle door slowly opening appears on the wall in front of him, followed by Rainsford's silhouette, which towers over the sitting—and startled—Kreiger. The tables have been turned and the balance of power shifted, and Wise's clever presentation and use of angles underscores this.

A worthy, well-acted and well-crafted thriller in its own right, with a few token changes and even the occasional improvement, *A Game of Death* remains too slavish a remake for its own good. Back in 1945, with *The Most Dangerous Game* only a hazy 13-year-old memory for most moviegoers, the project was a viable one, reintroducing the classic tale to a new generation of cinemagoers. And had the 1932 *Most Dangerous Game* disappeared into the limbo of the lost film, this remake would enjoy pride of place among fans today. But with the advent of video and home entertainment, *A Game of Death* has become superfluous.

Production

Though not the most prestigious of the Dangerous Game adaptations, and nowhere near the best-known or most popular (having received no legitimate video or DVD release to date, and only sporadic television airplay), *A Game of Death* boasts the most prestigious *director* ever to tackle Connell's story—Robert Wise, who went on to helm such classics as *Curse of the Cat People* (1944), *The Body Snatcher* (1945), *The Day the Earth Stood Still* (1951), *I Want to Live!* (1958), *West Side Story* (1961), *The Haunting* (1963), *The Sound of Music* (1965), and *The Sand Pebbles* (1966). Consequently, *A Game of Death* holds the distinction of being the only adaptation of Connell's story to have been helmed by an Oscar-winning director (Wise won *two*—for *West Side Story* and *The Sound of Music*).

Given his immense stature among both critics and moviegoers, Robert Wise has given many, many interviews over the years. Rarely, however, has anyone ever asked about *A Game of Death*, which seems to be his own personal "forgotten film." And, truth be told, the director himself wishes it *were* forgotten. In a 1996 interview with this author, Wise, when asked if he screened the original prior to shooting his remake, answered, "Yes," before adding, "unfortunately." The director continued:

> I was not too keen about doing it but I was under stock contract at RKO. I don't like the idea of remakes and wasn't keen to do this, but yes, I had to look at the original picture because there were shots of these Great Danes going through the jungle or whatever in the hell it was, lots of shots of those. They wanted me to use those out of the original picture in order to save money and not have to re-shoot them. So I had to run the whole picture just to see those eight or ten or twelve shots of the Great Danes going through the forest or jungle just to see how I could use them. And what was bad about it for me was that every time — because it was a remake, there were similar scenes between the new one and the old one — and every time I'd get into a sequence not to do with the dogs but the story part of it, I kept getting flashes back to the original scene I'd seen. It was just terrible; it kept haunting me. Every time I got into it I couldn't get the original out of my mind, and that's no way to make a picture. I did it but it was not a favorite experience.[2]

New York–born stage and screen actor Edgar Barrier was a member of Orson Welles' prestigious Mercury Theatre group, and lent his voice to a number of Welles' radio productions before making a minor name for himself in Hollywood in various B pictures in the early 1940s, including several Jon Hall–Maria Montez fantasy costumers. Barrier played Banquo to Orson Welles' *Macbeth* in that director's 1948 film adaptation of the famous Shakespearean play. Among his more "interesting" credits are Universal's 1943 remake of *The Phantom of the Opera*, *The War of the Worlds* (1953; uncredited as a scientist), and *The Giant Claw* (1957, as another scientist, this time credited — though no doubt wishing he hadn't been). Beginning in the early 1950s Barrier made frequent appearances on television until his premature death in 1964 of a heart attack at age 57.

The son of a British general, John Loder served as a lieutenant at Gallipoli in World War One, where he was captured and became a prisoner of war. After appearing in a number of German silents, Loder came to Hollywood in the late 1920s, where he played in early talkies. Returning to his native England in 1931, he became a star of the British screen, even appearing opposite Boris Karloff in 1936's *The Man Who Changed His Mind* (aka *The Man Who Lived Again*). Loder went back to Hollywood during World War Two and appeared in a score of pictures over the next seven years (including the intriguing 1945 poverty-row witchcraft entry *The Woman Who Came Back*). Failing to attain the level of screen stardom he had achieved in Britain, Loder turned to Broadway and then finally returned to England, where he made several more pictures before retiring to his fifth wife's ranch in Argentina. Hedy Lamarr was among his previous wives.

Russell Wade is best remembered for a trio of Val Lewton horrors: *The Ghost Ship* (1943), *The Leopard Man* (1943), and *The Body Snatcher* (1945). After earning his first studio contract at age 18, Wade worked primarily in B films for the next decade before forging a new career in real estate in Palm Springs. "I still haven't seen the original [1932 *Most Dangerous Game*]," he said in the 1990s, "so I don't know if [*A Game of Death*] was a worthy remake. I would assume that our version was better than the earlier one, but then, some of that antique footage was put into our film and it looked it. You could easily see that the footage didn't match."[3] (Wade's observation notwithstanding, said footage is integrated fairly well into *A Game of Death*.)

Audrey Long had a relatively brief decade-long career in B movies, with her starring turn in *A Game of Death* being a highlight (though she did appear this same year in the Ray Milland classic *The Lost Weekend*— uncredited, as a cloak room attendant). In 1952 she became the fourth wife of novelist and screenwriter Leslie Charteris (creator of "The Saint") and retired from the screen. The union lasted until his death in 1993.

CREDITS: Director: Robert Wise; Executive Producer: Sid Rogell; Producer: Herman Schlom; Screenplay: Norman Houston (From an Original Short Story "The Most Dangerous Game" by Richard Connell); Music: Paul Sawtell; Musical Director: C. Bakaleinikoff; Director of Photography: J. Roy Hunt; Special Effects: Vernon L. Walker; Art Directors: Albert D'Agostino, Lucius Croxton; Set Decorators: Darrell Silvera, Jame Altweis; Recorded by: Phillip Mitchell; Edited by: J.R. Whittredge; Gowns: Renie; Assistant Director: Doran Cox; Rerecording by: James G. Stewart. Production/Distribution Company: RKO Radio Pictures; Release Date: November 23, 1945; Running Time: 72 minutes.

CAST: John Loder (Don Rainsford), Audrey Long (Ellen Trowbridge), Edgar Barrier (Erich Kreiger), Russell Wade (Robert Trowbridge), Russell Hicks (Mr. Whitney), Jason Robards (Captain), Gene Stutenroth (Pleshke), Noble Johnson (Caribe), Robert Clarke (Helmsman).

3

Teenage Game
Bloodlust! (1960)

"HE HUNTED HUMANS for the sheer sport of killing ... and made his island paradise into a Hell on Earth!"—poster

Synopsis

Two young couples, Johnny and Betty, and Pete and Jeanne (Robert Reed, June Kenny, Gene Persson, Joan Lora), charter a small boat for some fishing and skeet shooting. When their drunken captain, Tony (Troy Patterson), passes out, they decide to go explore a nearby island. Walking through the jungle, Johnny falls into a pit trap—just as Mr. Balleau (Wilton Graff) and two servants arrive. Back at Balleau's house, their host explains, "I came here shortly after the war. I wanted to live in a world of my own—a world completely free from any kind of outside pressure." He also ominously adds, "I've developed a kind of passion for hunting." Though the four are uneasy, their host politely but forcefully insists that they stay the night

The foursome surreptitiously learns that Balleau's wife, Sandra (Lilyan Chauvin), and another man stranded on the island, Dean (Walter Brooke)—who pretends to be "a useless drunk"—are being held against their will. "He can never allow anyone to leave this place alive," Sandra laments. "And he's made sure no one ever will."

Meanwhile, Pete and Jeannie have found stairs leading to an underground tunnel and cave. There they find a room that appears to be some kind of butcher's workshop—except that there's a woman's corpse floating suspended in a glass tank set into the wall! When one of Balleau's henchmen enters, the two terrified teens hide, only to observe him removing a severed human foot and what looks like treated skin (including a human face mask!) from a vat of liquid.

With the four youngsters now certain of the danger of their situation, Dean convinces them to cover for he and Sandra while the two make a run for a hidden cove and the boat that's moored there, promising to return with help. But Balleau is on to them, and he follows the pair into the jungle...

Two days pass and, with no word of Dean and Sandra, the quartet stumble across a secret door leading to a cave that serves as Balleau's "private trophy room." They find Balleau there, reclining in his throne-like chair, and the urbane madman proudly displays his trophies—human bodies posed in their death throes. Balleau explains, "I merely preserved my trophies as they were at the moment of my triumph"—just as he illuminates another alcove to reveal the preserved bodies of Dean and Sandra.

U.S. one-sheet poster.

Back upstairs, the madman explains that he intends to hunt Johnny and Pete, leaving the two girls to supply him with "feminine company." Just then a henchman enters with a reluctant (and now sober) Tony. "I've paid you well to provide me with subjects in the past," an angry Balleau tells the cowering captain. "But since you've been so foolish as to allow these young people to find their way here without my knowledge, I think it only right that you should share their fate." Balleau further explains that Tony "was my source of supply for my subjects. In the past they were always convicts escaped from the penal islands."

Balleau plans to hunt the three men with a crossbow, armed with only three arrows. He gives Tony an unloaded gun and tells the trio that they'll find ammunition at the starting point of the hunt (a place "the natives call the 'Tree of Death'"). "When that gun is loaded, my life will also be subject to how the hunt goes," says the sporting Balleau. But when they find only one bullet at the designated tree, Tony takes the gun and abandons the two boys. Balleau tracks Tony, but the desperate man gets the drop on his pursuer, only to learn that the gun won't fire! "You've known me long enough to realize that I wouldn't give you a gun without first taking the precaution of removing the firing pin," deadpans the duplicitous Balleau — before sending an arrow through Tony's chest.

During the hunt the two girls escape from their room and make it to the sinister workroom, searching for weapons. One of Balleau's henchmen accosts the girls and tries to rape Betty, but she uses her judo skills (her father is an instructor) to flip her assailant into the standing acid vat!

The girls meet up with Johnny and Pete in the jungle, and elude Balleau (whose tracker, Jondor, has fallen into quicksand — with a displeased Balleau merely smiling as the man sinks) before doubling back to the house. When Balleau returns, the quartet hides in his trophy room. But Balleau, now armed with a pistol, finds them. As he contemplates how he'll "arrange" his soon-to-be-victims, Jondor staggers in — he has escaped the quicksand and leeches!

Balleau frantically fires his pistol at the steadily advancing Jondor, but the brute impales Balleau on the display stand meant for the teens before dying from his wounds. Contemplating their lucky escape, Johnny concludes, "I guess Balleau never thought he'd be the prize exhibit in his own museum."

How "Dangerous" Is It?

Though snubbing Connell completely (making no mention of the author's classic story), *Bloodlust!* remains more faithful than most to its source — which is just as much the 1932 RKO film *The Most Dangerous Game* as Connell's short story. As *Bloodlust*'s "unit manager" Bri Murphy (who later married *Bloodlust* writer-producer-director Ralph Brooke) related, "[*Bloodlust!*] was a remake of *The Most Dangerous Game* — Ralph figured that was one of the best horror pictures he'd ever seen, so why not do it again?"[1] Why not indeed? To that end, Brooke adapted the story to his decreased budget, keeping the premise but changing the details. For instance, he dispensed with the rather costly use of trained dogs from the original, replacing them with a few extra actors (that could be had on the cheap), one even serving as the antagonist's lapdog, so to speak, who tracks the quarry through the jungle. Brooke also changed "Zaroff" to "Balleau" (dropping Connell's military leader status and RKO's aristocratic origin) and transformed RKO's two main adult protagonists (or the solo protagonist of Connell's story) into a quartet of attractive young people, no doubt in a savvy effort to ride the coattails of the teen-targeted horror films then ruling the drive-ins (as led by AIP and their teenage monster movies like *I Was a Teenage Werewolf*, *I Was a Teenage Frankenstein*, and *Blood of Dracula* [all 1957]). In fact, it's rather surprising that *Bloodlust!* wasn't titled something like "I Was Teenage Prey." Unfortunately, these teens apparently aren't resourceful enough to set any of the traditional jungle traps, so *that* thrilling portion of Connell's (and RKO's) story fell by the wayside.

Brooke did keep the tale's (and film's) private-tropical-island hunting ground setting, as well as the grotesque "trophy room" concept. He even expanded upon the latter by including some gruesome "trophy prep" imagery when the protagonists stumble across various body parts in Balleau's secret workroom.

Additionally, *Bloodlust!* offers a rather intriguing variation on the hunt, as Balleau, ever the sportsman, reduces his own odds by choosing to hunt his trio of victims with a crossbow and only *three* arrows — one for each. He also gives his quarry a gun and one bullet, though this turns out to be a ruse, as he's removed the weapon's firing pin (Balleau is not quite the "sportsman" he makes himself out to be).

Providing a somewhat different (and topical) take on the mad hunter's motivation, *Bloodlust!* posits that Balleau was *made* into a hunter of men by sanctioned killing — war. Upon displaying his "trophies" to the horrified teens, Balleau explains:

> I hunted them. And shall I tell you why? I'd been a scholar all my life. I was curator of a large museum when the war began. I, who had never killed anything in my life, found myself assigned to duty as a sniper, a "sharpshooter," because of my steady hand and keen eyesight [chuckles]. It amuses me now that I found it distasteful — at first. Then as time went by I adjusted to my new activity, and what had been an unpleasant duty became a pleasure. Then it developed into a passion, and then into a *lust*— a lust for blood — a lust that has grown with the years, and one that I spend my entire life trying to satisfy.

It's a rather clever — and unsettling — extrapolation on the motivation of Connell's antagonist, made all the more chilling because it smacks more of logic than madness (particularly since there's no talk of an old head wound, as in Connell's story, or debilitating headaches, as in the RKO film, as a kind of motivational malady).

Critique

Here's your chance to see the father of *The Brady Bunch* hunted down like a wild animal (and who among us that grew up in the 1970s could resist such a satisfying concept?). Long before Robert Reed became a household name and face on television via "the story of a man named Brady," he was chased through a forest of potted plants by a crossbow-wielding madman thirsting for his blood.

This third "Most Dangerous Game" adaptation is the first truly low-rent version (though it wouldn't be the last). Budgeted at a mere $80,000, and starring a bunch of then-no-name actors, *Bloodlust!* turned out far better than its straitened circumstances should have allowed.

First-time director Ralph Brooke, aided by cinematographer Richard E. Cunha (a director in his own right, whose credits include *She Demons, Giant from the Unknown, Missile to the Moon*, and *Frankenstein's Daughter*— all from 1958!), seems remarkably self-assured in the visuals department, utilizing varied camera angles and evocative lighting to augment what little resources he has. For instance, the first shot of the goatee-sporting,

Connell's General Zaroff figure morphs into Mr. Balleau (Wilton Graff) for this early '60s updating.

rifle-bearing Balleau (appearing at the lip of the pit into which Johnny has fallen) is an up-angle perspective (accompanied by a dramatic chord sounding on the music track) that emphasizes the man's power and menace. The next scene fades in on a roaring lion's head, with the camera pulling pack to reveal it to be a stuffed and mounted trophy in Balleau's study, where Balleau serves as host to the quartet of "rescued" teens. The sudden juxtaposition of Balleau and the predatory beast furthers the unsettling feeling surrounding their mysterious "host."

Shortly thereafter, Balleau has a private word with Dean, warning, "I've worked out a very satisfactory design for living here. I think you realize that." The shot, focusing on Balleau, displays two lion heads mounted on the wall behind him, framing him on either side — three predators, with the deadliest of the trio firmly in the foreground. The camera then begins to slowly dolly forward as Balleau continues: "I hope you also realize that the presence of those four young people here changes nothing as far as we're concerned." As he concludes with "I've taken care of *everything*," the advancing camera is now tight enough to reveal the slight upturn of Balleau's lip and the faraway look in his eyes as he imagines that certain "everything." The subtle camerawork — and even subtler playing by Wilton Graff (augmented by his self-satisfied and calm-yet-menacing tone) — generates an ominous sense of unease that propels the story forward and *almost* overcomes the vapid characterizations and dull playing of the "four young people."

Unfortunately, Ralph Brooke the Screenwriter fares worse than Ralph Brooke the

Director. The four clean-cut "kids" (i.e., 20-something adults) are far too *Leave It to Beaver*-ish, with their bland politeness and gee-wiz demeanor, to take seriously. The banal dialogue they spout further scuttles their already-sinking credibility. For example, when told by Balleau of their impending doom, Johnny blandly retorts: "Listen, Mr. Balleau, fun's fun, but if you think we're going to be the day's pigeons in your shooting gallery, you're just a little far out."

Or how about this dreary exchange in which Pete relates his and Jean's horrific experience in discovering Balleau's gruesome "workshop":

Pete: "You'll never believe what we saw; I don't believe it myself."
Johnny: "We just heard about it [from Dean and Sandra]. I guess it's true then."
Pete: "If they told you about an unbelievable nightmare, it's true all right."
Johnny: "Well that settles it. We've got to try and get out of here tonight."

Adding dull insult to desultory injury is Brooke's (non)direction of his actors in this pivotal scene. As Johnny, Robert Reed's reaction offers nothing more than a furrowed brow and mild concern in his voice; while, as Pete, Gene Persson's bland delivery makes him appear no more excited or shocked than had he been talking of his high school football team's recent loss to their cross-town rivals. While Brooke could get away with leaving his veteran actors to their own devices, the younger thespians—including Reed—obviously needed far more coaching than Brooke would, or could, give. Consequently, amateurish and passionless exchanges such as these tend to undermine the horror of the story. (To be fair to Brooke, time constraints may have been the *real* villain here, with eliciting nuanced performances rather far down on the day's to-do list.) "He had us alone in here with an unloaded gun," seethes Johnny after Balleau reveals his horrific plan—and the fact he's really unarmed. But the irony is that Johnny doesn't seem to realize that he *still* has them in the same room and Balleau is *still* unarmed. Plus, they outnumber him three to two (Johnny, Paul and Tony vs. Balleau and a solitary henchman). Why the two strong youths and sea captain don't grab and overpower Balleau and his toady instead of lamenting a lost opportunity that *is still there* becomes an obvious, and unaddressed, question—and smacks of rather disingenuous (or perhaps simply careless) scripting.

Fortunately, the subtly menacing playing of Wilton Graff as Balleau helps offset such banalities and gaffs, and injects some real style into the scenario. Graff receives the script's best lines—and delivers them with aplomb. During Balleau's explanatory soliloquy (quoted earlier), Graff begins by speaking calmly, levelly; but when he talks of his pleasure becoming a passion, Graff's voice quickens, becoming louder as he mentions his "lust for blood." Finally, his voice softens and slows again—almost in resignation—as he tells of trying to satisfy that lust, as if such a thing could never truly be satisfied. It's a well-modulated and subtly revelatory delivery on the character's own madness.

Later, when Balleau reveals his latest trophies—Sandra and Dean locked in a death embrace—in his underground lair, Betty screams. At this, Graff gives a wry smile and observes, "I see that my latest trophy has *really* impressed you. I'm glad, because I think it's the best thing I've done—" here Graff pauses ever so slightly, and the smile fades to a malevolent coldness as he pointedly adds, "—so far."

Bloodlust! suffers from those seemingly unavoidable shortcomings arising from having more ambition than cash. Some of the most blatant evidence of the production's poverty lies in the faux cave, whose walls look like what they are—crumpled construction paper, and its *single* clichéd human skeleton and *two* accompanying rats (any more would have required a professional handler — far too expensive). The above-ground settings suffer just as badly. As the teen foursome creep around Balleau's house trying to figure out what's going on, the obvious redressing of the same sparse sets (including using the same two candelabras in room after room after room in a vain attempt to add some elegance to the meager set dressings) all but scream the word "cheapjack."

Additionally, the lengthy early sequences in which Archie and Betty and Jughead and Veronica ... er, Johnny and Betty and Pete and Jeanne, creep about the house trying to Find Out What's Going On engenders an unwelcome feeling of juvenalia. It gets to the point where one almost expects Deborah Wally or Erich Von Zipper to pop up on their way to some AIP beach party movie. (And the fact that Balleau's nondescript henchmen all sport striped shirts like some landlocked Disney pirate gang doesn't up the maturity level any.)

But just when you tire of the Hardy Boys/Nancy Drew-like shenanigans, Brooke and company toss out some genuine shocks. When two of the teens stumble across Balleau's underground workroom, they hide when one of his henchmen arrives. The servant promptly rolls up a window shade, revealing a glass tank inset into the wall with a woman's body floating in it (nightgowned, of course). Brooke then treats us to the gruesomely macabre sight of the henchman retrieving human body parts from another tank — first a foot, then what looks like a batch of human skin, then a head (but with the skull removed, so that he promptly starts filling the skull-less skin with cloth packing material before carefully setting the gruesome relic on the table). The human taxidermy show concludes with the man dumping a load of offal into a second tank, the bubbling mist rising from it indicating its acidic nature. This is strong stuff for the time, and a rude awakening from the earlier '50s-style pleasantries. "It's a pretty gory film for the time," remembered co-star Joan Lora. "I remember they had actual animal body parts on the set. In the scene where June [Kenny] and I are in the room and encounter the guy putting things into the boiling tub of water, on that table were sheep hearts and eyeballs. And the large mass that the man throws into the boiling water was actually a huge hunk of stomach lining."[2] Combine such unexpected grue with some evocative camerawork and a well-played villain worthy of the title, and *Bloodlust!* often manages to escape from the many traps set by its budgetary and scripting deficits. Often ... but not always.

"I saw it again recently and I enjoyed it," recounted unit manager Bri Murphy thirty-five years after working on *Bloodlust!*, "but maybe that was partly because of the sense of déjà vu. The paper caves — I wondered, how did we ever dare to try to get away with that? ... [Nevertheless,] I think it was very good for what it was."[3] Indeed, one could do much worse than this moderately entertaining Most Dangerous Game-on-a-shoestring outing

Production

Though *Bloodlust!*'s beach scenes were shot at Paradise Cove in Southern California, all the interiors *and* jungle sequences were filmed on a Hollywood soundstage, near the CFI Lab. "The jungle was all done on the stage," reported Bri Murphy, "every set-up, [director-producer-screenwriter] Ralph [Brooke] changed things around so it looked like a different part of the jungle. Ralph was production-managing that, too, so he had all the plants brought in from a plant supplier, but they didn't have any banana trees. Ralph got very upset — 'How am I gonna do a jungle without banana trees?' Robert Reed said, 'Ralph, trust me, I'll fix it for you. Watch this take.' So they go to shoot the take and the kids are finding their way through the jungle, and Robert Reed says, 'Who ever saw a jungle without banana trees??' And the line stayed in!"[4]

Robert Reed (born John Robert Rietz) is by far the best-known (*only* known) actor in *Bloodlust!* A drama major at Northwestern University, he journeyed abroad to further his studies at the Royal Academy of Dramatic Arts in London. Returning to the States, he joined an off–Broadway company called "The Shakespearewrights," playing leads in *Romeo and Juliet* and *A Midsummer Nights Dream*. Reed appeared in a number of television shows before landing the role that would make him famous, Mike Brady in *The Brady Bunch* (1969–1974), a role the method-trained, serious-minded actor reportedly hated. Post-*Brady* he appeared in dozens of television shows, TV movies and miniseries, earning three Emmy nominations along the way. Though he was HIV positive when he died in 1992, it was colon cancer that ended his life at age 59. Reed had a daughter from a brief 2-year marriage in the late 1950s, but it was Reed's *TV* offspring, Barry Williams (who played eldest son Greg Brady on the series), who helped make the arrangements for Reed's memorial service.

"[*Bloodlust!*] was Robert Reed's first picture," commented Bri Murphy, "and he was delightful. We called him 'the Boy Scout,' and the only problem we had with him was that his armpits sweated so much that it drove the wardrobe lady, Marge Corso, crazy — she was constantly changing sponges in his armpits. Unfortunately, she didn't realize that this was going to be a problem until after it was established that he was in a T-shirt, because it's hard to have sponges in your armpits and have them not show when you're wearing a T-shirt." In fact, there are several scenes in which Reed's sweat-stains show quite prominently, sponges or no sponges. According to co-star June Kenny, Reed was none-too-enamored of his first movie job. "In between scenes," recounted Kenny, "he would make it known that he would rather not have been in this kind of picture."[5] Laughed Murphy, "I was going to 'blackmail' Robert Reed with that picture. I had a 35mm print for a long time — but then he went and died, so I gave the print to Lilyan Chauvin, who was also in it [as Balleau's doomed wife, Sandra]. She teaches acting now, and still acts whenever she can."[6]

Born Wilton Calvert Ratcliffe, Wilton Graff got his start on the stage, appearing in over a dozen Broadway productions before moving to Hollywood in the early 1940s. There he appeared in supporting roles in scores of (mostly B) movies up until the early Fifties, usually playing judges, doctors, DAs and the like. Apart from *Bloodlust!* (his only starring role), Graff appeared in two other horror films, the Lon Chaney, Jr.–starrer *Pillow of Death* (1945), and the Poverty Row entry *Valley of the Zombies* (1946). For the last decade of his career, until his death in 1964 (at age 65), Graff mostly worked in television, appearing on such shows as *The Virginian*, *The Alfred Hitchcock Hour* and *Dr. Kildare*. *Bloodlust!* co-star June Kenny remembered Graff as "very pleasant and professional," while Joan Lora labeled him "a real gentleman. He was a seasoned radio and New York stage actor."[7]

Walter Brooke, brother to *Bloodlust!* director Ralph Brooke, made a handful of mostly uncredited appearances in the movies in the 1940s before turning to television as early as 1949 to make his living. For almost fifty years, until his death in 1986 at age 71, he appeared on the small screen, guesting on such series as *The Wild Wild West* and *Dragnet* in the 1960s, *M*A*S*H* and *Charlie's Angels* in the '70s, and *St. Elsewhere* and *The A-Team* in the 1980s. Among his sparse film credits were supporting roles in *Conquest of Space* (1955) and 1967's *The Graduate* (Brooke once confided to his nephew that had he known his famous line about "plastics" would take off like it did, he would have invested in it himself!). Brooke's other genre credits include *The Andromeda Strain* (1971) and *The Return of Count Yorga* (1971).

3. Teenage Game

Actress June Kenny (ne: Kenney) was something of a drive-in stalwart in the late 1950s, having played female leads in such teen-targeted terrors as *Attack of the Puppet People*, *Earth vs. the Spider*, and Roger Corman's *The Saga of the Viking Women and Their Voyage to the Waters of the Great Sea Serpent* (replacing Abby Dalton's sister, who injured herself in a fall from her horse during production), all in 1958. She left the industry in 1962 after a handful of TV appearances (including the "Waxworks" episode of Boris Karloff's *Thriller*).

Director-producer-screenwriter Ralph Brooke, the younger brother of actor Walter Brooke, began as a bit player in the late 1940s/early 1950s before moving behind the camera (first working as art and second unit director for the infamous Jerry Warren on 1956's *Man Beast*) when he hooked up with low-budget director Richard Cunha as production manager on four of Cunha's sci-fi/horror features, all in 1958: *Frankenstein's Daughter*, *She Demons*, *Missile to the Moon*, and *Giant from the Unknown* (which Brooke also co-wrote). Brooke returned the favor by hiring Cunha as cinematographer on *Bloodlust!* Reported Murphy:

> Ralph was marvelous with the crews, he loved working with them; it was always light and fun and happy. We had one very complicated dolly shot through the jungle which took a lot of setting up. We rehearsed it several times and then we went to shoot it, and just at the end the sound man sneezed. Everybody gasped, "Oh, my God!" expecting a big blow-up. But Ralph said, "*O-k-a-y*, somebody plug up the sound man and we'll do it again." That got a big laugh, which was very nice, and that was typical of the way he directed.[8]

Bloodlust! was Brooke's first feature as director, and he helmed only two other short films before his untimely death in 1963 at age 43 from a heart attack.

CREDITS: Director/Producer/Screenwriter: Ralph Brooke; Executive Producer: Robert H. Bagley; Cinematographer: Richard E. Cunha; Film Editor: Harold V. McKenzie; Unit Manager: Bri Murphy; Camera Operator: Wilbur Bradley; Visual Effects: Harold Banks; Makeup: Jack Dusick; Music: Manuel Francisco; Sound Mixer: Phil Mitchell; Assistant Director: Leonard J. Shapiro; Script Supervisor: Diana Loomis; Chief Electrician: Charles Becket; Key Grip: Grant Tucker; Costumes: Marge Corso; Properties: Richard M. Rubin; Sound: Ryder Sound Services. Production Company: Cinegraf; Distribution Company: Westhampton Film Corportation. Running Time: 70 minutes.

CAST: Wilton Graff (Dr. Albert Balleau), June Kenny (Betty Scott), Walter Brooke (Dean Gerrard), Robert Reed (Johnny Randall), Gene Persson (Pete Garwood), Joan Lora (Jeanne Perry), Troy Patterson (Captain Tony), Lilyan Chauvin (Sandra Balleau), Bobby Hall (Jondor), Bill Coontz (insane man).

4

Dangerous Roughie
Confessions of a Psycho Cat (1968)

"What secrets are harbored deep within the sinister highways of the mind — what are the 'Confessions of a Psycho Cat'?!" — trailer

Synopsis

After a brief prologue in which a woman sees her brother off at the airport, bound for a hunting safari in Africa, *Confessions of a Psycho Cat* opens at a cheap apartment where an in-progress swingers' party shows various people talking or having (simulated) sex. They also seem to be waiting for their friend the dope dealer to arrive. "I'd like to do something stronger here than just pot," complains one dissatisfied partygoer, "— like real narcotics."

The scene abruptly switches to a man walking through the city streets suddenly attacked by a woman and another man, who chases the victim into some nearby woods. The woman shoots a crossbow bolt at him, grazing his leg and dropping him into a river, whereby he makes his escape.

Suddenly the film cuts back to the grope-and-fondle gathering. The victim from the previous scene walks — or limps — in. It turns out he is the drug pusher everyone's been waiting for, but he has no "stuff." Instead, he offers a story. "It all started when I got this note to go to this apartment, this fancy apartment..." — and it's flashback time.

At said fancy apartment, three men — a washed-up actor named Charles Freeman, an ex-wrestling champ named Rocco (played by ex-boxing champ Jake LaMotta), and our storyteller Buddy — have been summoned by Virginia Marcus (Eileen Lord) for a little proposition: "I'll give either, any, or all of you 100,000 dollars — *if* you can stay alive in Manhattan for 24 hours." When asked, "What's the catch?" Virginia coolly responds, "Simple — I'm going to hunt you down, then I shall kill you." The men ask her why she picked them, and she answers, "You three men are all bona fide killers. Each of you has killed. Oh, I know you were *all* acquitted, you *all* went free. But each of you has killed." She then relates how each will receive a certified check, post-dated to the next day, which will signal that the hunt is on.

Back at the party, his listeners ask Buddy about the "killers." Cue three more flashbacks. First, Charles the actor, "shacking up with some guy's wife," is interrupted by her husband, who receives the sharp side of a straight-razor for his troubles. Second, the wrestler gets "carried away in the ring ... *stomp*!" And Buddy himself (as related by one of his "friends" at the party) accidentally overdoses a young girl on heroine.

4. *Dangerous Roughie* 43

Sex sells—or so thought Chancellor Films, the distributor of *Confessions of a Psycho Cat*, whose advertising played up the sex angle (one-sheet poster).

After scenes of more party "fun" (consisting of topless girls and hairy guys trying to overcome either their natural ennui or nervousness), Buddy continues by relating the fates of the other two human targets. First, Virginia moves behind the scenes to secure a last-minute theatrical job for Charles, who, vain and desperate enough, accepts — despite having received the fateful check that morning. After Charles' performance that evening, Virginia traps him in the deserted theater and sends an arrow into his chest.

Next we see "the Champ" sitting in a cheap hotel room with a young prostitute on the bed opposite him. Virginia keeps phoning him to taunt the once-proud pugilist into facing her. Finally he's had enough and tears out after his tormentor, who meets him at her apartment dressed as a matador(!). Virginia's manservant (named "Bi") sneaks up behind the raging wrestler and sticks two toreador spears into his back. Virginia then steps forward and twirls her matador's cape, dodging and weaving before finishing off the wounded man with a sword.

Back at the party, Buddy can no longer go without a fix. So, despite the protestations of his friends, he leaves the safety of the crowded apartment for the mean streets of Manhattan to score some dope. After he makes his score, he walks around a corner only to receive an arrow through the throat.

Meanwhile, Virginia's psychiatrist has become concerned about her increasingly erratic behavior, and has summoned her brother, Anderson, back from Africa. When Anderson and the doc arrive at Virginia's apartment, they discover the three bodies in her walk-in freezer. The picture ends with a close-up of Virginia shrieking in a straitjacket.

How "Dangerous" Is It?

Not very, actually. Besides the central concept of hunting humans for pleasure, *Confessions of a Psycho Cat* takes little else from "The Most Dangerous Game" (unless one considers the crowded island of Manhattan to be analogous to the deserted Caribbean isle of Connell's story).

Connell's characters are largely unrecognizable here. Instead of the world-traveling big-game hunter Sanger Rainsford, *Confessions* offers a trio of New York lowlifes: a womanizing over-the-hill actor, a barely-articulate ex-wrestler, and a cocky junkie. Zaroff's servant — the mute "gigantic creature" Ivan the Cossack — has transformed into a drink-making, average-sized houseboy whose ambiguous sexuality is reflected in his name, "Bi." Then, of course, the imperious and calculating Zaroff himself ("mine is an analytical mind, Mr. Rainsford") has morphed into a neurotic, ultimately psychotic, Manhattan socialite! And apart from a throwaway line at the beginning about her not being able to accompany her brother on his African safari (due to her recent "nervous breakdown"), and the fact that her "fancy" apartment is furnished like a taxidermy shop, nothing in the film addresses her obsession with hunting, nor why she's taken the "sport" to its ultimate amoral level. There's no revelatory monologue, no shocked reaction from the protagonist, and no human trophy room.

Even the hunts are only a pale reflection of Connell's gripping scenario. In fact, two of the three hunts are little more than simple murders, as Virginia lures her prey out of hiding and then strikes them down. The only real "hunt," in the purest sense of the word, comes at the very beginning, before we even know who's who or what's what, as Virginia and her toady chase a man through the woods. The prey initially escapes, only to be perfunctorily shot down at film's end when his need for a "fix" forces him to leave his sanctuary. There are no uncanny tracking abilities, no terror inspired by pursuing hounds, and no cleverly-laid traps. Gone is the sick and deadly concept of "outdoor chess ... your brain against mine, your woodcraft against mine, your strength and stamina against mine." And gone is the pulse-pounding excitement of the terrifying hunt itself, the very core of Connell's engrossing story.

Critique

"ADULTS ONLY" warns the ads for *Confessions of a Psycho Cat*. Indeed, this New York–shot "roughie" (a more violent counterpart to the "nudie cuties" that proliferated in low-rent grindhouses during the 1960s) is one of the sleaziest adaptations of Connell's tale to date — as well as cheapest. (Authors Eddie Muller and Daniel Faris explain the origin of the "roughie" in their book *Grindhouse*: "As the titillation of nudity wore off, filmmakers sought new ways to maintain the audience's interest [and their own]. With any depiction of physical intimacy below the waist outlawed by every state censor board, violence became a substitute adrenaline rush.")

"Dangerous Game" adaptations live or die by their antagonist, and *Confessions* at least offers a fresh twist: for the first time, the human hunter of Connell's story is a *woman*. "See the female cat as she really is!" dares the trailer, playing up this novel angle. This "female cat" is a wealthy, mentally unbalanced socialite denied a hunting trip to Africa with her brother (due to a recent nervous breakdown), and making up for it with her own special "safari."

"EXCITING. EXOTIC.. EVIL...!" screams the poster in reference to the female antagonist. When it comes to Eileen Lord's performance, however, a more accurate tagline would be "REACTIONARY. RIDICULOUS.. RISIBLE...!" Lord is more petulant schoolgirl than clever master of the hunt, as evidenced by her sudden angry outbursts and gleeful cackling.

For instance, when Charles protests, "You must be joking," Virginia nearly screams, "I'm not joking!" Her over-shrill, over-the-top reaction, meant to suggest her unstable psyche, is about as necessary — and subtle — as a 10-pound sledge pounding on a one-inch nail. Even in more mundane conversation, Lord's voice sounds forced, her lips held taut, her eyebrows dancing in wild abandon.

When Virginia calls Rocco to taunt him into facing her, she mocks, "I challenge you, *Champ*. Come outside and fight." While she talks on the phone, Lord's free hand can't seem to stay still, as it tugs her hair and rubs her face like an agitated snake while she veritably spits out her mocking lines, her eyes and brows involved in some insane ocular calisthenics. At the end of the call she laughs maniacally, her mouth going impossibly wide. On the one hand, it's a shrill, painful, overplayed performance. On the other, however, it's never dull (unlike so many of the other amateur players in this half-baked movie), and makes up in sheer outrageous gusto what it lacks in verisimilitude.

With ad lines like "SHE WAS THE MISTRESS OF PLEASURE—AND THE SLAVE OF HER DESIRES!" and "HER BED WAS HER LAIR!" it's rather surprising that Virginia never engages in any of the erotic activity that comprises fully half the picture, remaining completely asexual and focused on the hunt. Of course, given that said undraped activity appears to have been added as an afterthought, it's little wonder Lord took no part in the frisky festivities.

Speaking of which, though the picture offers up nudity in quantity, it definitely skimps on the quality. Very little of the lethargic, half-hearted couplings could be considered even mildly erotic, as the amateurish (and uncredited) participants look alternately uncomfortable and bored, with some being only marginally attractive at best. Consequently, despite all the casual nudity and unenthusiastic simulated sex, the film only comes (half) alive during the three stalking sequences, and when Lord indulges in her wild histrionics.

The only other performer of note is Jake "Raging Bull" LaMotta as Rocco. The ex-boxing champ looks lost. Granted, his punch-drunk performance occasionally suits the role, but he's unable to vary his delivery enough to make this "kill-hungry grunt-and-groaner" (as the trailer labels him) into anything more than a one-note caricature. Of course, the fractured script does little to aid this Raging Thespian, with perhaps the worst moments coming when Rocco alternately responds to Virginia's taunting on the phone and the (creepily underage-looking) topless prostitute's jibes from the bed (it's obvious said femme fatale is *not* in the same room with the ex-champ). LaMotta, bare-chested (and barely coherent) sits in a chair and "delivers" lines like "I'm not afraid of nothin'" and "Okay lady, now you get yours" with all the conviction of a, well, *Sleeping* Bull.

The film's very structure works against it. By opening on a dull "party" exchange and various sex scenes, then abruptly switching to a man fleeing through the woods before we've had any hint of introduction or explanation (it's as if a completely different movie had suddenly popped up), the viewer has no investment — nor any real interest — in what *should* be a thrilling, suspenseful centerpiece, making it all seem both disjointed and ridiculous. Rather than the multiple flashbacks, the story would have made far more impact had it run in a straight timeline, with the "hunts" escalating in action and intensity (the actor, the wrestler, and finally Buddy's frantic run) *after* the set-up had been established. Of course, this would have made it more difficult to shoehorn in the "titillation" scenes, so...

Besides structural problems, the script offers some dialogue humdingers as well. Not surprisingly, most of them come from the movie's sexed-up portion. How about this exchange between two partygoers idly waiting for the "stuff" to arrive:

Man: You wanna ball?
Woman: Groovy.

Later, one of the somnambulant chippees responds to Buddy's shocking tale with a vapid "That woman sounds real goofy." Indeed.

"All these people running around naked — look at them!" disdainfully sniffs one demure attendee (who nonetheless soon doffs her top as well). This line becomes comical when the viewer realizes that none of the sex scenes feature more than three people in the same shot! Rather than a group gathering, this "party" is merely a disconnected series of two- and three-person vignettes.

But it's not just the tacked-on distaff portion of the script that contains head-scratching moments. During Buddy's flight through the woods, he ends up climbing a tree. The next shot shows him literally out on a limb, hanging above the river. Now *why* would he place himself in such an open and perilous position when running for his life? (So he could conveniently be shot in the leg with an arrow and drop into the water, that's why.) Later, in talking about Charles' demise, Buddy comments that it was "a spear right through the heart" when we clearly see said spear (an arrow, actually) sticking out of the victim's right *side*, nowhere *near* his heart. And how does Buddy know all this anyway, since he wasn't there?

In among its many fleapit flaws, *Confessions* does manage to pull off two effectively disturbing sequences. The first comes when Virginia tells her psychiatrist about a childhood trauma. With a distorted camera lens reflecting her fractured psyche, Virginia narrates an incident in which as a little girl she happily plays with her new puppy on the roof of a New York high-rise. "It was the cutest little thing," she says, before her voice abruptly changes, hardens: "I was glad when it died." Suddenly, a slightly older boy — her brother — rips the dog from her arms and shockingly hurls it over the roof edge! We watch as the (obviously *stuffed*) puppy spirals downward, even hitting the side of the building as it drops to its death. Here Virginia devolves into shrill shouting: "Killing is bad. I've never killed anything. I couldn't — I hate killing. I hate guns. Killing is bad!" Both shocking and disturbing, the sequence simultaneously answers and asks questions.

The second memorable moment is remarkable more for its jaw-dropping bizarreness than its shock effect. It begins as Rocco, lured out of hiding by Virginia's mocking phone calls, enters her darkened apartment and creeps through a set of patio doors, only to have Bi sneak up behind him and jab two toreador spears into the big man's back. The bleeding and enraged Rocco then staggers and lunges towards the cape-swirling Virginia, all decked out in a matador costume! The sequence's sense of disturbing surrealism is heightened by the fact that at the center of this bizarre human bullfight is Jake LaMotta, the former "Raging Bull" himself. The icing on this outré cake arrives when Virginia offers this epitaph: "He died like a brave bull."

While the huntress' lair exposes the production's poverty (all we see of Virginia's "fancy apartment" is an entryway and one cramped and cluttered room), it also reflects the chaotic mind frame of its owner. Nearly every inch of the two walls we see are covered with all manner of animal trophies — everything from a huge swordfish head to wolf pelts — while the floor is covered with animal-skin rugs, and every available surface displays stuffed ducks, weasels, badgers and god-knows-what. (Perhaps the picture's main investor was a taxidermist?) Disappointingly, however, there's no human trophy room. Undoubtedly, such was beyond the film's meager budget.

Behind the camera, producer-director Herb Stanley, aided by cinematographer Paul Guffee, makes a few valiant attempts to create a mood, enhance a scene, or at least generate some visual interest — and even succeeds on occasion. During Buddy's panicked flight, the handheld camerawork, shooting from various angles, and moving both behind and in front of the frantic "prey," adds some much-needed motion and urgency. (Too bad we have so little investment in the moment, since at this point we've no idea what's going on.) Fast edits and some frenetic music (no doubt taken from a stock library, but well-chosen nonetheless) further enhance the feeling of immediacy.

Later, as Virginia visits her psychiatrist, the camera shoots solely from Virginia's point of view as she enters the waiting room, talks with the nurse, picks up a magazine, and flips to an ad with a dog (triggering the pivotal soon-to-be-related memory of her doomed puppy), effectively forcing the viewer to identify — and sympathize — with the unbalanced Virginia. Stanley uses a wide-angle lens that slightly distorts what Virginia (and we) see to an almost fish-eye perspective, and occasionally goes in and out of focus (particularly when Virginia — and we — stare at the dog in the magazine), reflecting the instability of Virginia's state of mind.

Such occasional flashes of competence and creativity makes it doubly disappointing that Stanley's efforts are effectively undone by the static, poorly-filmed, tinny-sounding party and sex inserts; the jumbled and poorly-edited story structure; and the alternately toneless and wildly inappropriate playing of his non-actors. "See this shocking and bizarre motion picture," ordered the trailer. Well, they got it half-right, as it certainly lives up to the "bizarre" adjective in that claim. But apart from a few memorable moments, some unintentionally amusing dialogue, and the outrageously outré thespian shenanigans pulled by Eileen Lord as Virginia, the seedy *Confessions of a Psycho Cat* prove hardly worth hearing — or watching.

Production

Besides the fact that *Confessions of a Psycho Cat* was filmed on location in and around New York City, very little is known, or has been recorded, about the making of this (rightfully) obscure movie. Given the film's two different titles (the other being *3 Loves of a Psycho Cat*), and the different footage contained in each of the two respective trailers that exist, it appears that the movie was originally shot as a straight horror/suspense film but then morphed into a sex-laden "roughie" when the various nude/sex scenes were added later. The *3 Loves of a Psycho Cat* trailer contains none of the characters from the party sequences besides Buddy, and features plenty of footage not included in the *Confessions of a Psycho Cat* print (the only one available as of this writing). In the *3 Loves* trailer, Jake LaMotta interacts *directly* with an underwear-wearing prostitute during his big phone scene, as opposed to his tangential verbal jousting with the obvious cut-ins of a topless prostitute (a different actress) seen in the *Confessions* print. The only character featured in both the hunt and party scenes is Buddy, and his variable appearance indicates some passage of time between the two sets of footage.

The only "name" attached to the production, either in front of or behind the camera, is former middleweight boxing champion Jake LaMotta, known as "the Bronx Bull" and "the Raging Bull." Beginning in 1941 at age 19, Lamotta enjoyed a highly successful boxing career over the next decade and a half, recording 83 wins (30 by knockout), 19 losses and 4 draws. Most famously, he was the first man to beat the great Sugar Ray Robinson. Most infamously, LaMotta later testified during an FBI investigation into the workings of organized crime that he'd thrown a 1947 fight with Billy Fox in order to curry favor from the Mafia and secure a World Title bout with French boxing champion Marcel Cerdan (which LaMotta won by technical knockout in 1949). Of the fixed fight with Fox, LaMotta wrote in his autobiography *Raging Bull: My Story*:

> The first round, a couple of belts to his head, and I see a glassy look coming over his eyes. Jesus Christ, a couple of jabs and he's going to fall down? I began to panic a little. I was supposed to be throwing a fight to this guy, and it looked like I was going to end up holding him on his feet.... By [the fourth round], if there was anybody in the Garden who didn't know what was happening, he must have been dead drunk.

After retiring from boxing, LaMotta bought a couple of bars and began a spotty career as an actor (winning mostly bit parts in 15 different films, the most famous being 1961's *The Hustler*, in which he played the bartender) and occasional stand-up comedian. He also wrote his tell-all biography detailing his often-violent life (at one point even confessing to rape!), upon which the Martin Scorsese-directed, Robert DeNiro-starring film *Raging Bull* (1980) was based.

CREDITS: Alternate Title: *3 Loves of a Psycho Cat*; Director/Producer: Herb Stanley [as "Eve"]; Screenplay: Bill Boyd; Camera: Paul Guffee; Sound: Tom Dougher; Lab: Arta;

4. Dangerous Roughie

Sound Transfer: Magno Sound; Props: L. Little; Location: Peter Falk; Script Girl: Mary Marlin; Production Company: World Wide Pix; Distribution Company: Chancellor Films Inc.; Release Date: February 1, 1968; Running Time: 69 minutes.

CAST: Eileen Lord (Virginia Marcus), Ed Garrabrandt [as Ed Brandt], Frank Geraci [as Frank Grace], Dick Lord, Arlene Lorrance, Jake LaMotta (Rocco), Rita Bennett.

5

Sexploitation Game
The Suckers (1972)

Sheer suspense that will leave you RIGID in your seat!! — tagline

Synopsis

Photo agency owner George Stone (Norman Fields), his photographer wife Cindy (Barbara Mills), and two "fifty-dollar-an-hour fashion models," Barbara (Sandy Dempsy) and Joanne (Lori Rose), travel down a dusty dirt road in the wilderness towards a photo-shoot assignment only to have their jeep stopped by two armed men. These rifle-toting "guards" work for Steve Vandemeer (Vincent Stevens), "at one time one of the top five big-game hunters in the world." Vandemeer has contracted with Stone's agency to do a photo-layout on his planned hunt this weekend. As George tells his worried wife, "It's a little weird, but the money's good." After wining and dining them on his estate, the retired big-game hunter tells his curious guests, "Let's call this a touch of nostalgia. Only instead of African Blacks we have very lovely ladies. Instead of African rhinos we have a very special game to hunt." But Vandemeer remains cagey about just what said game might be — even to professional hunter Jeff Baxter (Richard Smedley), whom Vandemeer hired just a few days earlier to help with the hunt, scheduled to begin in the morning.

That night Barbara seeks out Baxter and tells him how spooked she is by Vandemeer and his mysterious hunt. Baxter consoles her by making passionate love to her. Soon after, Barbara retires to the waiting arms of Joanne, her lesbian lover.

The next morning Vandemeer leads his hunting party, along with his two well-armed guards, out into the surrounding wilderness, promising to finally "tell you about the animals we're going to hunt today." When they stop to rest, Vandemeer announces, "Ladies and gentlemen, you are here today because *you* are the hunt." The group of prey apparently disperse (the sole existing print of the film appears to suffer from some missing footage at this point), as the next scene shows Barbara and Joanne alone, with Barbara imploring, "He is our only chance." Joanne disagrees and runs off in a different direction. (One assumes that the "he" Barbara refers to is Baxter, whose hunting experience might help them survive.)

Joanne makes it back to the jeep alone, but Vandemeer is waiting with one of his guards (Lynn Vann). "Predictable," sneers the hunter. "One thing you learn in hunting is that prey always returns to safe quarters — a stream, a hidden cave, or a jeep one drove in on." Turning to his henchman, Vandemeer observes, "You know, it's hard to tell what she's more afraid of — being raped or what's going to happen afterwards." Vandemeer orders his

Poster for the "EXPLICITY ADULT!" Dangerous Sex Game oddity *The Suckers*.

toady to take Joanne back to the house, where the henchman viciously rapes her and then stabs her to death.

Back in the wilderness, Vandemeer's second guard (Jim Dannin) spots the fleeing Barbara and takes a shot but misses. Then Vandemeer himself spies the panicked Barbara and takes aim. But he, too, misses the mark. (Some hunter.)

After another abrupt splice (suggesting more missing footage), guard number two suddenly whacks George on the head with his gun butt. "You killed him," shrieks Cindy (she and her husband George had obviously stuck together) and flees. The guard catches her, but she bargains for her life with both her body and a promised "safety deposit box full of cash that the government knows nothing about." After the guard finishes having his way with Cindy, out from the bushes steps Vandemeer. The henchman panics, claiming, "I was just stringing her along.... I'll kill her now for you, just say the word." But Vandemeer isn't buying and tells the duplicitous guard to "Start running"—before coldly shooting him in the back. He then turns his sights toward the cowering Cindy.

Meanwhile, the first guard has rejoined the hunt and is now after Barbara, firing his shotgun at her (and, once again, missing). Hearing a yell off in the brush, he runs toward the sound, only to be surprised by Baxter, who jumps down from a tree and dispatches the rapist by jamming a pointed stick into his neck.

As Vandemeer continues the hunt, Baxter, now armed with the dead guard's shotgun, finds Barbara first. They also come across George, who's not dead after all but seriously concussed. Baxter formulates a plan to use Barbara as bait in order to lure Vandemeer within shotgun range. Leaving the wounded George to rest, Baxter and Barbara come across Cindy's naked corpse, but they step into a snare Vandemeer has laid next to the body. Vandemeer drags them to him and ties his captives to two trees. While Vandemeer menaces Barbara with a knife and talk of "skinning his prey," Baxter works on his bonds with a blade he'd hidden down the back of his pants. Baxter spies George staggering towards them and distracts Vandemeer with taunts of "You're an impotent freak!" When Vandemeer turns his angry attention to Baxter, George manages to sneak up and hit the hunter from behind. While George, hopelessly outmatched, wrestles vainly with Vandemeer (who finally simply tosses him aside), Baxter finally frees himself. But in the ensuing struggle, Vandemeer stuns Baxter and advances upon the still-tied Barbara. George staggers to his feet once more and recovers Vandemeer's pistol, which had been knocked aside earlier. George fires at Vandemeer, then collapses (presumably dead from his wounds).

Baxter recovers, cuts Barbara loose, and approaches the mortally wounded Vandemeer. "Didn't you forget something—" the prone Vandemeer asks of Baxter, who stands over him, before pointedly adding, "—as one hunter to another." Baxter answers, "No, I didn't forget. I'd do the same for any sick animal." He takes aim with the pistol and shoots, killing Vandemeer. Baxter and Barbara then set off through the brush.

How "Dangerous" Is It?

Most obviously, *The Suckers* deviates from "The Most Dangerous Game" in terms of sex (both noun *and* verb) and numbers. Connell's story includes a lone protagonist and *no* women, much less any hanky-panky. *The Suckers* not only offers a trio of females among its *five* protagonist prey (rather than the solitary Rainsford), it shows (in great detail) them all "getting busy," some multiple times. Similarly, whereas Connell provides General Zaroff a sole servant/henchman in the form of the hulking mute Ivan, *The Suckers* offers Vandemeer *two* rape-happy guards — and makes them just as much hunters-of-men as Vandemeer himself, with each lackey at one time or another chasing and shooting at the quarry (in Connell's story, Ivan merely handled the dogs, leaving the actual hunting to Zaroff alone). Consequently, this takes some of the power and mystique *away* from Vandemeer, leaving the impression that this Zaroff figure either needs direct help hunting his prey or simply can't properly rein in his human hunting dogs.

While *The Suckers* offers an experienced, Rainsford-like big-game hunter among its quintet of protagonists, it gives Baxter very little to do, focusing more on the female prey and their actions/fates than on the "woodcraft" or "outdoor chess" of the big-game hunter, who disappears for long stretches of the hunt. Baxter's only seeming proactive move is to lure one of the guards under the tree in which he hides so he can drop down and take him by surprise. Unlike Rainsford, Baxter sets no traps; in fact, he (along with Barbara) falls into one himself— the noose snare laid out by Vandemeer near Cindy's body. "Well, Mr. Baxter," gloats Vandemeer, "it seems my *dead* bait was more effective than your live, very attractive one [indicating Barbara]." Indeed.

Other significant departures include the scrub-land wilderness setting of Vandemeer's private hunting preserve (actually the familiar Bronson Canyon area in the Hollywood hills) replacing Zaroff's Caribbean island; the absence of Zaroff's all-important hunting hounds (no doubt such an expense was beyond the budget of this three-day wonder); and a disappointing disregard for the grisly "trophy room" implied in Connell's story (again no doubt due to cash constraints, naked girls being far more economical than costly make-up effects and props).

Talk being cheap, there's plenty of it in *The Suckers*. And screenwriter Ted Paramore (as "Edward Everett") fills Vandemeer's mouth with much of it, capturing the gist (if not the near-poetic verbiage) of Connell's Zaroff, including the jaded predator's soliloquy on his growing ennui with ordinary hunting, and his inventive solution. After leading the party into the wilderness, Vandemeer finally reveals his "game":

> You know I've tracked down and hunted just about every living species of mammal there is on earth today. And in my years of doing so I've discovered one horrible fact. There's no more joy in hunting and killing ordinary game. But, being that hunting is a way of life for me, it's made my existence meaningless. Now, if I could hunt a creature as inherently clever and resourceful as I, that would be a challenge. Contemplating that, my life has become meaningful again. Mr. Baxter, I would have thought that you would have guessed the nature of our hunt by now. It's a logical conclusion. Come now, I'll say it for you. Ladies, gentlemen, you are here today because *you* are the hunt.

Vandemeer has intentionally stocked his human hunt with the most challenging game of all — a fellow hunter like himself. "Mr. Baxter," he tells his disbelieving prey, "you're a trained hunter, an ex–Green Beret. You're a formidable opponent even without contemporary weapons." But Vandemeer goes beyond Zaroff's brutal bloodlust in at least one respect. "As for the lovely ladies," he leeringly continues, "with what I have in mind for them…" This being an "adults-only" sexploitation picture, Vandemeer isn't satisfied with just hunting and killing his human prey (at least of the female variety). When Joanne demands, "Why us?!" Vandemeer bluntly answers, "Because rape and slaughter go hand in hand when one is hunting human beings. And that ancestral pleasure is part of our little game." At this, Cindy spits, "You sick bastard." Vandemeer's response: "Hardly sick, Cindy, just bored. Bored with the ordinary games of life."

Critique

A (soft-core) sex film aimed at the adults-only specialty market of the early 1970s (before XXX porn took over a few years later and made such relatively tame skin flicks seem quaint and obsolete), *The Suckers* remains a rather curious hybrid of titillation and brutality. For its first two-thirds *The Suckers* appears to be a more-or-less straightforward "T&A" flick, as director Stu Segall (employing the pseudonym "Arthur Byrd") labels it. After the character introductions and a bit of banal blather, the film awkwardly takes us into a flashback involving George and his wife Cindy discussing their latest lucrative assignment. Though Cindy remains nonplussed, observing, "He wants to kill animals ... and wants *me* to photograph the kill?" it's a living. So the two soon retire to bed. There ensues a seriously off-putting six-minute sex scene in which the scrawny, comb-over-creepy George laboriously noshes on his wife's nipples, engages in simulated cunnilingus, then climbs aboard for the full monty, hairy backside and all.

Back in the present (thankfully) at Vandemeer's estate, Barbara seeks out Baxter, and the two share their concerns about their respective assignments (Barbara worries about being photographed with dead animals, while Baxter wonders about what type of big game they'll hunt and why Vandemeer remains mum on the subject). Soon they're sharing a bed as well, and we're into the film's *second* sex scene, which pretty much follows the same pattern as the first. Though repetitive, at least it's an improvement on the preceding romp, as Richard Smedley makes a far less repulsive lothario than Norman Fields, and Sandy Dempsy, as Barbara, even manages to act like she's enjoying it (rather than just enduring it, like Barbara Mills in the previous scene). And for a bit of novelty, Barbara even climbs on top to close out the 10-minute sequence.

But wait, *The Suckers*' extended voyeurism hasn't finished with us yet. Barbara soon returns to the room she shares with fellow model Joanne, only to take a sunken-tub bubble bath with *her*, revealing the two to be longtime lovers! After sensuously slathering each other with soapy water, this five-minute lesbian exercise ends just as they start to get down and, er ... dirty.

After 50-plus minutes of sexual shenanigans, however, *The Suckers* abruptly takes a 90-degree turn towards savage violence when Vandemeer begins his human hunt. It starts with the big-game hunter's brutal talk of rape and killing, extends into the physical hunt itself (including the cold-blooded shooting in the back of one of the guards; the discovery of Cindy's bloody corpse; and Vandemeer's intention of *skinning* Barbara), and climaxes (so to speak) with the film's two explicit *rape* scenes. Titillation turns to torment (both for the participants *and* the viewer) when the first guard takes Joanne to the house, throws her on the bed, and proceeds to brutally violate her. Actress Lori Rose contributes the film's most effective performance here, crying, pleading and screaming with disturbing verisimilitude. Shots of her face contorting in pain and disgust as her attacker roughly kneads her breasts and forces himself on her (for a full five minutes) makes this the most unpleasant and hard-to-watch segment of the whole movie. Even the stock musical score agrees, as what sounds like a discordant theremin adds to the distressing effect. The scene concludes with the rapist maniacally stabbing Joanne to death in a harrowing point-of-view shot. "That disturbed the shit out of me, if you want to know the truth," admitted director Stu Segall. "That was pretty grisly."[1] About Lori Rose, Segall noted "she was a real trouper [who] did a good job. The actor [Lynn Vann] was kind of a brute, and he helped her get into it." (Note: Lori Rose ended up on the wrong end of a human hunt again the very next year in the Filipino-shot

5. Sexploitation Game

Woman Hunt [as Lauri Rose]. But she fared much better in that feature, for instead of ending up on the point of a rapist's knife, she ended up in the arms of co-star John Ashley by film's end.)

The film's fifth and final sex scene arrives when Cindy, caught by guard number two, offers herself to him (along with some promised cash) if he'll let her go. He takes her up on it then and there, crudely pawing her, slobbering over every inch of her torso with his tongue, then mounting her while she lies on the dried grass and tries hard not to look disgusted. The degrading scene is anything but erotic, and one wonders what audience the filmmakers were aiming at here. The brutality and overwhelming unpleasantness of these final two sex scenes surely couldn't have pleased the raincoat brigade. Said Segall, "That was still for the same crowd; that crowd was presumed to be the same group. That's how they wrote it, and that's what I did with it." Continued Segall, "We were all really into making the movie. The T&A part was no big deal to us — we were all 24, 25-year-old kids doin' this (except for the guys like Dave Friedman, Ted [Paramore] and the cameraman [Hal Guthu]). We were a bunch of young ne'er-do-wells just makin' movies however we could make 'em."

The script takes a few halfhearted stabs at exploring the moral issues of hunting. Early on, Baxter reflectively reveals to Barbara, "Big-game hunting is a dying profession, what with all the emphasis on ecology and rapidly expanding game preserves. Sometimes I think it's men like Vandemeer and myself that are becoming extinct." Later, Barbara asks Baxter, "Why do you like to hunt?" He answers, "Because I enjoy the excitement of the chase." She then asks, reasonably, "But do you always have to kill?" At this, he responds, "No, not always"— and makes his move on her, launching us into another extended sex scene (apropos, perhaps, given that the onscreen boinking is the film's true *raison d'etre*).

The picture's production values are better than one might expect from a cheap "adults only" flick from 1972 (and certainly superior to that other Most Dangerous sexploitationer *Confessions of a Psycho Cat*). The photography is competent and far more expansive than most of its contemporaries, helped by the final third being shot out-of-doors (a rarity in the generally cheap-set, studio-bound world of soft-core sex flicks). And the actors don't embarrass themselves too badly (at least regarding their *acting*). One exception being the bland, toneless playing of Richard Smedley as Baxter, whose supposed self-assuredness comes off as a general blankness. "He was a little too morose in that movie for me," admitted Segall, "but that was his acting ability — that's why he never really made it as an actor."

Segall related a funny story about Smedley:

His claim to fame was that he married Natalie Wood's sister [Lana Wood, of *Diamonds Are Forever* fame].... When Natalie Wood married Robert Wagner, Richard Smedley shot the stills of their wedding because they didn't want to trust anybody to shoot their marriage. So he shot their wedding, and they had paparazzi trying to get photos and all. So he shoots this wedding, and Natalie Wood and her husband go off to Europe on their honeymoon. So Richard says, I can make some money with these, and they'll never know because they're out of the country. So he gets $10,000 from a tabloid, and they ran the stills of the wedding in that magazine. And he thought they'd never find out. But, of course, they did. And they went crazy on him.... Oh boy were they pissed. But Richard was a good guy, we had a lot of laughs.

As the pivotal figure of Vandemeer, Steve Vincent (as "Vincent Stevens"— the most poorly-considered pseudonym since Count Dracula's "Alucard" gambit!) gives a haughty, theatrical performance that, while not particularly convincing in its own right, serves the character well in his portrayal of a man who sees himself apart from and above his fellow human beings. His studied superiority (he even deigns to shake George's proffered hand) and once-removed demeanor makes his climactic downfall — in which he literally dies in the dirt — all the more satisfying. "Steve Vincent," recalled Segall, "he was a stage actor, very broad; booming voice. He was a really good guy."

Directing only his third feature (and his first in 35-millimeter, the previous two having been shot in 16mm), Segall manages to add a few inventive and involving touches on a miraculously short *three-day*(!) shooting schedule. At the close of the first rape scene, for instance, the attacker terrorizes Joanne further by running the blade of a huge bowie knife over her naked body. ("That was a real knife he dragged across her body, too," said Segall, "it wasn't like a plastic studio knife, it was a real knife, so we obviously had to be very careful and take our time.") Segall then switches to Joanne's point of view, with the camera looking up at the menacing rapist as he frenziedly stabs downward over and over again. The victim's p.o.v., coupled with Joanne's dying shrieks, powerfully brings home the sheer terror and horror of the killing.

Later, when Vandemeer dispatches his second guard, Carl, for conspiring with Cindy, Segall switches to slow-motion to show a fleeing Carl shot in the back — twice — with the bullet squibs exploding in painfully realistic fashion. ("We did have a couple of squibs," recounted Segall, "that was a big deal in those days.") Then, at film's end, Segall again switches to a p.o.v. shot when Baxter aims a pistol at the wounded Vandemeer, forcing the viewer to stare directly into the muzzle of the gun, the forced perspective making the weapon appear huge and inescapable, and hammering home the disturbing finality of the act.

Up until the final scene in which Vandemeer taunts and terrorizes his two trussed-up captives, this Zaroff stand-in has been hidden beneath an obfuscating pith helmet and reflective aviator sunglasses. Segall cleverly utilizes these twin mirrors almost like a metaphor, at one point capturing the image of Vandemeer's terrified victim in the two reflective lenses. If the eyes truly are the "window to the soul," Vandemeer's sees people only as prey. Additionally (whether by conscious choice on Segall's part or merely expediency due to time constraints), Vandemeer receives only one brief close-up of note during the hunt itself (and this merely to reveal his cowering victim reflected in his sunglasses). Consequently, this hunter-of-men becomes more distant visual symbol than approachable character. For the finale, however, in which Vandemeer finally becomes violently intimate with his prey (having let his henchmen do all the "dirty" work up to then), he finally discards his protective headgear and glasses to reveal himself fully. No longer the dispassionate big-game hunter-of-humans he claims to be, Vandemeer now displays the sadistic madman that is his true nature by terrorizing his prey with a knife and talk of skinning them alive — all visually realized by the physical exposure of Vandemeer himself. (Segall laughingly admitted that, rather than any intentional symbolism here, "we might of just lost his glasses, or he might have left his hat at home. [laughs] We weren't that smart to do symbolism — unless it was so over-the-top. There was nothing in those days that was real subtle. Now that doesn't mean that somebody on the set didn't say something, and then, 'Oh, let's do that,' but there wasn't a lot of pre-thought. It was really, 'Let's get to the set and we'll figure it out.'") Segall's overall approach "was more intuitive," he said. "You don't really get a chance to storyboard a show like that.... It was just kind of a visceral thought—'This would be fairly interesting'—and that's what I'd do."

Directorial decisions (and/or intuitive happy accidents) like these makes one wish that Segall had slipped his sexploitation bonds and received more opportunities to make "straight" films, a wish reinforced by his lone foray into "legit" territory with the quirky, moderately entertaining 1976 no-budgeter *Drive-In Massacre*— a movie he completed in an amazingly brief four days (Segall was nothing if not speedy).

Production

Long thought lost to the "sinematic" ages, *The Suckers* was resurrected in 2013 via an unexpected DVD release. The resuscitation wasn't *completely* successful, however, as the lone surviving print (from a 1976 re-release by an obscure outfit called Lee Ming Film Company) appears to feature at least two significant instances of missing footage. And, most unfortunately, it's footage of the Most Dangerous type — the hunt — rather than the already-too-long simulated sex scenes (much of *that* would not have been missed). But it is what it is, and *The Suckers* lives once again.

The Suckers was shot in the Bronson Canyon area of the Hollywood hills over a Friday, Saturday and Sunday with a minimal crew ("less than ten," recalled Stuart Segall). Segall utilized a huge, heavy 35mm Mitchell BNCR camera, "which is basically a studio camera ... so nothing was very portable, you had to really schlep a camera and then set up tripods. We used gyros and things like that to get smoother shots." This makes it all the more remarkable that he and his crew were able to get the footage they did in so short a time span.

Despite its obvious hardships and limitations, Segall found working quickly and cheaply to be "a lot of fun. You ran like you were on fire because you didn't have any time, and you certainly had no money to get more time, so wound up doing very creative and innovative things in those days to make those movies." Recounted the filmmaker:

> I made movies for different folks as producer/director, because I was fast and cheap, and they knew I could do it. It was like, "I got a movie for you to do," and, "Great, I'm on my way." "It doesn't pay much," which was the standard line in those days. But I didn't care. When you pay only 100 bucks in rent [in those days], believe me, when they tell you you're going to make $50 or $75 a day, you were a rich man for workin' three or four days.

"*The Suckers* was very cheaply made," continued Segall, who estimates the budget being about $30,000. "We had no money for anything other than the actors and the equipment. None of us got paid a lot of money." Segall himself made "probably a couple of hundred bucks a day, no money for prep; I can't remember exactly, but it wasn't much.... Some of the crew would make $50 a day, and a day was as long as it took. The actors probably got $150."

Speaking of the actors, they were all sexploitation veterans who went on to ... well, more sexploitation (with a few minor exceptions, such as Richard Smedley's appearance in a couple of Al Adamson schlockfests). Said Segall of his a actors:

> It was a group of people that [executive producer] Dave [Friedman] knew, that he liked. Dave probably had his pick of women at the time. I don't even know if we read many people. It was like we'd have two or three people in, "I like the blonde. She's got great tits." So I think Dave had his finger on the casting probably more than I did.... It was fairly loosey-goosey. You'd pick up the phone and say, "Hey, we're doing a movie this week; you wanna work for three days?"

Barbara Mills (Cindy in *The Suckers*) looked back with bemusement on her work in these more "innocent" early adult films:

> I wasn't crazy — I was completely nude in my film appearances but no penetration, no genitalia and no oral sex. That would have been stupid. If you're going to sell it, you might as well keep your anonymity. They never tried to get me to do more. When I remember my former work in

films, I believe we left behind a really free spirit. We weren't condemned for what we did. We were sometimes greatly appreciated for our work. It was interesting. It was an innocent time, it wasn't considered real.[2]

The Suckers was written and produced by Ted Paramore, son of Edward E. Paramore, Jr., an old-time Hollywood screenwriter with credits like *The Santa Fe Trail* (1930), *Three Godfathers* (1936) and *The Oklahoma Kid* (1939). Trying to follow in his fathers footsteps led Ted down the primrose path of sexploitation, where he wrote and produced (often employing the *nom du cinema* Harold Lime) such soft and hard-core titles as *Sensual Encounters of Every Kind* (1978), *The Ecstasy Girls* (1979), and *Summer Camp Girls* (1983). "Ted always prided himself on being a writer," remembered Segall, "but he didn't write very many *big* things. It was all those kinds of things [sex films]. But he was a writer and went to work in a suit and tie. He was of that generation. We were in Levis and bell-bottoms and long hair; we were products of the '60s, and he was a product of the '40s."

Despite its rushed schedule, *The Suckers* shoot went relatively smoothly — with one exception. Recounted Segall about the mishap:

> The fellow who played the agent [Norman Fields], on the set he swallowed a bee. And his throat started to enlarge. And we've got three pages left of dialogue with this guy, and he's got to go to the hospital. I'm thinking, "When can I get him back," because I'm fucked if this guy doesn't get back in time. So I wasn't quite caring about his health [laughs], I just needed him to finish.... Fortunately we got him back a couple of hours later, and it didn't kill us completely. But I just remember thinking, "The movie's going to go in the shitter because we have an actor that died." [laughs] That's how your mind goes sometimes.

Stuart Segall got into the moviemaking biz in a rather, er, unusual way — "by making up tits and ass and crotches." Explained Segall:

> I used to be a private investigator. And I ran into a guy through a mutual female friend who was a make-up artist in titty movies, the T&A business. He was fascinated by me being an investigator, and I was fascinated by what he did, so he said to me, "Why don't you come on up to the set, and you'll help me on the movie." So I said, "Yeah sure, but I don't know what I'm doin.'" He says, "Aw, come up." So I hit it off with him, the guy's name was Ray Sebastian. And Ray Sebastian was a very well known make-up artist in the early days of—we'll call it the T&A business. And we got to be very very good friends. So I worked for Ray as an assistant make-up artist on my first time on the set. My first job was to take make-up and put it on naked women. This was a movie that was made by — it might have been Russ Myer, I don't remember the name of it. But they were all large-busted women; they were all 44D and above. So my job that day was to put body make-up on all these girls that were naked.... You know, you have them lined up on tables, and you just went down this line and put make-up on these girls. That was my first [movie] job that I got paid for.

After a few more assistant make-up jobs, some grip work, and generally doing whatever needed doing on a low-budget movie set, "one thing led to another and I said, 'I think I can do this.'" So Segall borrowed some money to produce and direct his own "T&A" movies (1969's *Harvey* and its sequel, *Harvey Swings*, 1970). "I had no clue about anything," he admitted. "We were all a bunch of newcomers. But we were young, it was great."

The way Segall came up with his "Arthur Byrd" pseudonym for *The Suckers* was: "I took the 'R' out of Stuart [for 'Arthur'] and the 'Segall' I made into a 'Byrd.' I never put my name on any of the low-budget movies I made because they were T&A." After a few more early-seventies soft-core entries, like *Teen-Age Jail Bait* (1973), Segall eventually joined the early wave of hard-core porn that formed in the middle of the decade, directing and

5. Sexploitation Game

producing under a variety of pseudonyms (with Godfrey Daniels being a favorite) such XXX fare as *The Spirit of Seventy Sex* (1976, with Annette Haven) and the "classic" *Insatiable* (1980), with Marilyn Chambers and John Holmes. Under his real name, Segall also produced and directed the slightly more "legit" early slasher pic *Drive-In Massacre* (1976). Abandoning porn (and directing altogether) in the mid–1980s, Segall (sans pseudonym) became a television producer/executive producer, overseeing series like *Hunter* (1984–87), *Renegade* (1992–97), and *Silk Stalkings* (1991–99, something of a return to his sexploitation roots), as well as a whole slew of low-budget made-for-TV movies like *Beastmaster: The Eye of Braxus* (1996), *I Married a Monster* (1998), and *Alien Fury: Countdown to Invasion* (2000). Since 1991 he has owned and operated a 70,000-square-foot studio facility, Stu Segall Productions, in San Diego. Among others, the popular cult TV series *Veronica Mars* was shot there. After 9/11, Segall transformed his production studio into a military training facility called Strategic Operations, Inc., and garnered contracts with the Navy, the Marines, and Special Forces. Explained Segall:

> We use all the movie and TV effects in actual training. We brought that to military training. We've supported the training of about 700,000 soldiers, sailors, marines and coast guard.... We've got an "Afghan village" in the back that's now full of sailors and corpsmen, explosions going off. We've run 130,000 marines through this space before they went into combat in Iraq and Afghanistan.... It's kind of similar to traditional movies in a way — battlefield special effects, movie special effects, make-up special effects. We do a tremendous amount of medical training. We'll take amputees and we'll put gore on them, put eviscerations and huge wounds on them so the corpsmen can train on something that looks very realistic.

About his adults-only film career, Segall concluded:

> It was low-budget, down and dirty stuff. I never really wanted to be big or anything. I loved doing what I did because I was in control. On anything of any size or consequence, you've pretty much lost that control, and you're just another person doin' the job.... I always like working for myself, and if I wanted to move on and move up — I might not have had the talent to do it, either; it's not just about what I wanted. It just didn't happen to me, and I'm fine with that. Some people aspire to that, but I just never had that aspiration.
>
> I was very proud of what I did. It got me to where I'm doing whatever I've done in my life. Producer of a thousand hours of television. Probably every studio in Hollywood, from Disney on down, we've made shows for — not as a director but as a production company.

When asked if he was pleased with how *The Suckers* turned out, Segall responded, "I was never happy with anything I made. Because I could see through all the problems. 'Oh shit, oh god, why did we do that?!' Well, I know why we did that — because we had to. I never sat back and went, 'Wow, look what we did.' It was a movie, it was fun making." And while not always "fun" watching, *The Suckers* offers just enough, both sexploitation- and Most Dangerous Game–wise, to keep viewers from feeling like one.

CREDITS: Director: Stu Segall (as Arthur Byrd); Producer/Screenplay: Ted Paramore (as Edward Everett); Executive Producer: David F. Friedman; Cinematographer: Hal Guthu; Sound Recording: George Manly; Key Grip: Jerry Jade; Script Supervisor: Kelly Green; Editor: Lawrence Avery. Production Company: Cromwell Pictures; Distribution Company: Entertainment Ventures; Release Date: 1972. Running Time: 79 minutes (approximate).

CAST: Richard Smedley (Baxter), Lori Rose (Joanne), Steve Vincent (as Vincent Stevens) (Vandemeer), Sandy Dempsy (Barbara), Barbara Mills (Cindy), Norman Fields (George), Lyle Vann (First Guard), Jim Dannin (Second Guard).

6

Filipino Danger
The Woman Hunt (1973)

Set your sights on the Tastiest Game of all.—ad line

Synopsis

A woman, Magda (Lisa Todd), enters a shanty complex where she's shown a group of young girls in cages. Dissatisfied, she berates their long-haired, headband-sporting captor, Karp (Ken Metcalfe), until one girl catches her eye. The girl is stripped for inspection but takes her guards by surprise and dashes out the open door. Running onto a jetty (they're at a harbor), she plunges into the water, but two guards swim after her and drag her back. The mysterious woman pays the man $2500 for the girl. "You see, we don't haggle over price when the merchandise is right. You have the specs on the other four. Don't waste your time trying to get us to take *substitutes*."

The next day, Karp and seedy boat captain Silas (Sid Haig) take two women out on their boat—resulting in one woman being taken prisoner and the other killed when she tries to escape. The remaining girl is caged and transported, along with three others, to a house in the jungle by Karp, Silas and a third man, Tony (John Ashley), who treats the girls kindly and looks uncomfortable about this "business."

Once they reach their destination—a luxury mansion in the jungle—the girls are shown to their rooms by Magda, while Tony goes to the boss, Spiros (Eddie Garcia), to warn him of the danger of his present course of action—and basically tender his resignation. This doesn't sit well with Spiros, who, despite considering Tony the son he never had, sends Silas to Tony's room to kill him. But Silas, dismayed by his boss' coldness, has second thoughts during the subsequent confrontation, and lets Tony live—for the moment. "I'm going to try and make a break for it and take the women with me," announces Tony.

A pair of helicopters deposits a quartet of "distinguished gentlemen" at the compound. The kidnapped girls are dressed for dinner and instructed to act as companions to the men. After dinner, Spiros sends the girls to their rooms and addresses his four guests, informing them that their evening's "entertainment" will be a "woman hunt." When one of the men balks at "hunting them down and murdering them in cold blood," and rises to leave, Spiros shoots him dead with a crossbow. At this point, the women, who've been plotting an escape, break out, aided by Tony. Tony and the girls kill several guards and raid the armory, heading off into the jungle with rifles and machine guns. One girl is killed during the escape, but Tony and the other three manage to get away into the jungle. Upon hearing

Pressbook cover.

the first gunshots, Spiros announces, "I believe we're ready to begin," and his "hunting party" sets out after them (sans Silas, who has been killed by Karp because of Silas' duplicity).

During their flight, one of the girls, McGee (Pat Woodell), slips and falls down a slope, breaking her leg. Asking to be left behind with a gun, she stoically lies in wait for their pursuers. When the hunting party reaches this point, she kills several guards and one of the "guests" (while another is dispatched by Spiros' own man when the would-be-hunter flees in panic) before being gunned down herself.

Meanwhile, Tony and the two remaining girls, Lori (Laurie Rose) and Billie (Charlene Jones), spend a restless night, particularly after Billie is bitten by a cobra! Tony builds a spring trap lined with bamboo spikes in anticipation of the final showdown. Billie dies of the snake bite during the night.

Spiros awakens in the morning to find his camp deserted by all but Magda. "Where would I go?" she sadly responds when asked why she didn't flee with the others.

In a final shoot-out, Tony wounds Spiros, while the trap impales Magda. Spiros crawls to the mortally-wounded Magda and puts her out of her misery by shooting her in the head. As Tony and Lori reach the river (and presumed safety) and frolic in a cool mountain pool, the bloodied Spiros takes aim from a nearby rock. But as he raises his weapon, images of Magda flash through his mind and he hesitates to pull the trigger, finally turning the gun on himself.

The hunted McGee (Pat Woodell) gets set to turn the tables on her hunters, courtesy of a loaded carbine.

How "Dangerous" Is It?

Connell's central premise receives a Filipino facelift here that's about as appealing as the overstretched countenance of a past-her-prime Beverly Hills dowager. Gone is the excitement and vibrancy of the solitary hunt, not to mention the mano-a-mano idea of "your brain against mine, your woodcraft against mine, outdoor chess," replaced instead by a quartet of girls (and one man) facing off against a troupe of nondescript guards, with everybody sporting automatic weapons. Missing is the focused purity-of-evil when one man takes his obsession to the ultimate, replaced by the tawdry sleaziness of a white slaver looking for a new sensation. The intelligent, terrifying prowess of Connell's Zaroff here gives way to the bullying sadism of Spiros, a man more interested in a quick "thrill" (and buck) than pursuing his obsessive passion, whether that comes from beating and raping women for himself, or shooting them down in the jungle for his guests. This lack of thematic focus and underdeveloped characterization leaves a gaping hole at the center of *Woman Hunt* that director Eddie Romero tries to fill with women-in-prison exploitation tropes (the lesbian captor, the victim who retreats into a bottle, the leering guards). As a result, this *Woman Hunt* strays far from Connell's tale — and far from good filmmaking.

They say the devil is in the details, and *Woman Hunt* features so few effective elements that it couldn't even conjure up a mischievous leprechaun, much less Ol' Scratch himself. As mentioned, Connell's imposing, hunting-obsessed Zaroff is here replaced by the run-of-the-mill pimping villainy of Spiros, who espouses no particular interest in hunting per se, just in finding a new "thrill" sensation for himself and his guests. Instead of the terrifying giant mute Cossack Ivan, here we have the low-rent henchman Karp, who, with his long hair and blank expression, looks

Ad for *The Woman Hunt*.

more like a zoned-out hippy than a murderous minion. And the substitution of a platoon of nameless guards for Zaroff's vicious and relentless pack of hounds not only replaces the terror of being tracked by tireless canines with the more mundane notion of pursuit by low-rent underlings, but deleteriously overpopulates the jungle with people, transforming the tense stalk-and-flee scenario into an automatic weapons firefight.

The horrifying notion of the hideous trophy room remains conspicuous solely by its absence, as this appears to be Spiros' *first* hunt (again, making the antagonist no more than some thrill-hungry sadist ready to try anything for kicks, rather than the intelligent yet amoral madman pursuing his obsession to its extreme). Our nominal hero does follow Connell's lead when he manages to set one solitary trap (a spring-loaded set of bamboo spikes) that takes out Spiros' female follower Magda, clearing the deck for a final shootout between the hero and villain. However, the quieter, intimate terror represented by the weaponry — bows, knives and one's own wits — of Connell's original tale here gives way to the noisy, distancing anonymity of machine guns. So in the end, Connell's hero experiencing for the first time the feel of a hunted animal, the hopeless sense of being cornered and trapped (resulting in his desperate final gambit to leap from the seaside cliff to his uncertain fate), is lost in a perfunctory exchange of gunfire.

This *Woman Hunt* does, however, offer up a unique (if inexplicable) epilogue not found in Connell's story — in which the antagonist, with his unknowing prey literally in

Spiros (Eddie Garcia, center) and his faithful, beautiful assistant Magda (Lisa Todd) lead their bloodthirsty guests on *The Woman Hunt*.

his sights (as the two surviving protagonists embrace in a mountain stream), decides to commit suicide! Has the sadistic Spiros been transformed by Magda's loyalty (love)? Or has the sight of the two lovers frolicking in the cleansing waters somehow triggered his conscience? It's a novel notion worthy of exploration, but one so clumsily presented as an ad hoc development that it becomes little more than a final, confusing afterthought.

Critique

"Women are made for men ... TO HUNT!" With a tagline like this, it's a sure bet that *The Woman Hunt* is no feminist treatise. But it's not exactly a misogynist's dream either, as the female characters are not only attractive, but tough and resourceful as well. Still, it's difficult to get past the exploitative nature of the story (not to mention the presentation, as most of the women end up topless at one point or another). But, to paraphrase Shakespeare, when in the Philippines making low-budget exploitation movies, do as the low-budget Filipino moviemakers do...

It doesn't help that the titular concept fails to raise its intriguing head until nearly two-thirds into the movie. Consequently, the majority of the film becomes little more than a rattier-than-usual white slavery/women-in-prison exploitationer, with the story focusing on the four females being captured, transported, "instructed," bemoaning their fate, and planning their escape. This was a result of New World Pictures' head Roger Corman draining his women-in-prison Filipino franchise dry. After having produced such financially successful Philippines-shot drive-in winners as *The Big Doll House* (1971) and *The Big Bird Cage* (1972), Corman was looking for yet another W.I.P. (women in prison) angle to exploit. As former New World trailer editor-turned-filmmaker Steve Carver explained, "Roger liked that there, where they were the game, the naked prey—literally—having to flee for their lives and having to fight the hunter, was a new way in which to present the women-in-jeopardy theme." As a result, only the final 20 minutes comprise the hunt, and it's a disappointingly desultory affair, spiced only with a few moments of gunfire and some orange stage blood.

When the film finally gets around to the subject at hand, things (as well as the viewer's interest) do admittedly perk up, beginning with the "dinner party" scene in which Spiros introduces the topic of hunting their female companions for sport to his four guests. He begins by stating, "Every man in this room has at one time or another unmistakably proved his contempt for the law and for morality.... All I want to do now is to make it clear, not just by word but by actual deed, that we will not be held back in our efforts by any kind of law or moral principle."

"And we're supposed to do this," shoots back one of his doubting guests, "by treating ourselves to a fancy woman hunt? By turning them loose, hunting them down, and murdering them in cold blood?"

It's an intriguing twist on Connell's theme, with Spiros basically throwing down the gauntlet on society's restrictions by positing hunting humans for sport as a slap in society's—and morality's—face. But just as the script seems poised to boldly step into a field of thematic richness, it does an about-face and retreats back down the path of mundane exploitation from whence it came. To Spiros, it seems, the woman hunt is simply "learning to follow our desires to their ultimate consequences." In this light, it becomes an act of pure hedonism, as Spiros adds, "Naturally, there would be no point in doing this if we did not believe we would enjoy it." After all, he continues, "There is no one here who does not tremble with delight at the thought of inflicting pain." So what we have here is not a man obsessed, nor even a man intentionally flying in the face of society's mores, but a man simply offering the latest thrill to a group of sadists. What had begun so promising as an exploration of moral issues devolves once again into mere exploitation.

On the technical front, *The Woman Hunt* looks about like what one expects from a Filipino-American co-production on a budget of $150,000 to $200,000 (the figure quoted by co-producer/star John Ashley). It offers the dull, almost washed-out color photography (not to mention the unconvincing day-for-night shooting) so common to low-budget '70s fare. Cinematographer Justo Paulino's flat lighting and mundane camerawork makes even the exotic Filipino jungle look drab and uninviting (which, admittedly, given the subject matter, may actually work *for* the picture to some extent).

The poorly-modulated, atonal dubbing, however, definitely works against the movie. (Though filmed in English, sound was added later to save on production costs during the shoot.) The voices often sound exactly like what they are — substandard voice actors in a cheap dubbing studio. Also, minimal foley (sound) effects give everything a disjointed, almost disconnected feel.

Eddie Romero's perfunctory direction does little to alleviate the technical tedium. For instance, when one of Spiro's guests panics and bolts after McGee shoots a guard during the hunt, Spiros orders Karp to chase down and kill the fleeing man. The subsequent "action" is not only half-hearted but *half-speed*, as an ambling Karp quickly catches the "panicked" man and draws a blade across his throat, producing little more than a slight grimace on the victim's face — and not a drop of blood. Nor is there any shock, excitement, or anything else of note. Philippine native Romero made a number of horror and exploitation pictures, including several with John Ashley (such as *Beast of Blood*, 1971; *Beast of the Yellow Night*, 1971; and *The Twilight People*, 1973). While none of them would qualify as award-winners, most evince more energy than the desultory *Woman Hunt*.

The acting in *The Woman Hunt*, with one notable exception, remains as substandard as the rest of the production. The four female protagonists (played by Pat Woodell, Laurie Rose, Charlene Jones, and Alona Alegre) display some welcome enthusiasm (not to mention bare torsos), but offer little else in terms of convincing dramatics. As the hero Tony (the Rainsford figure), John Ashley turns in his usual flat performance, his bland expressions and toneless delivery sucking the life from whatever urgency the dialogue and situation might demand. For instance, when Tony, confronted by a pistol-pointing Silas, admits, "Ok, so I've had it; I'm going to try and make a break for it and take the women with me," he does so with all the emotion of a man deciding where to go for dinner. "Maybe the key to my success with exploitation films is that I always liked those movies," postulated the actor. "I just enjoyed doing them."[1] From Ashley's demeanor in *The Woman Hunt*, one could never tell.

Most disappointingly, Eddie Garcia's Spiros mouths the words but lacks the conviction to make this primary antagonist anything more than a cardboard cutout, marking him as one of the poorest Zaroff stand-ins ever to raise a rifle. Lisa Todd, as Spiros' female counterpart (the heartless lesbian procurer Magda), conveys more of a passive blankness than a calculating coldness. Ken Metcalfe's Karp (the Ivan substitute) is little more than a (ahem) cold fish, offering nothing to delineate his character other than long hair and a silly headband. And Spiros' four (unnamed) "guests" receive so little screen time or characterization that they're simply a quartet of warm bodies.

6. Filipino Danger

The sole thespian exception to this disappointing rule comes in the form of veteran exploitation stalwart Sid Haig, who cut his acting teeth on low-budget horror (*Spider Baby*, 1968), blaxploitation (*Coffy*, 1973) and women-in-prison films (*The Big Bird Cage*, 1972). Haig imbues his underwritten part of Silas with some natural likability that breathes life into the stock proceedings, and manages to deliver his lines with a smarmy, sleazy charm.

> Captive Girl: Where are we going?
> Tony (John Ashley): To a house.
> Captive Girl: What kind of a house?
> Silas (Sid Haig): Oh, kind of a *funhouse*. You gonna like it. You'll be able to spread your wings — and other things. Hey, wanna sit up here? You can play with my gearshift, ha ha ha ha."

While unsubtle (and more than a little crass), such dialogue comes to life in Haig's capable hands, as his grin and the twinkle in his eye overlays the sleaze with a layer of self-aware good humor. Though Silas enjoys the sordid banter, he's fully aware of just how corny it is, and doesn't appear to take it too seriously. At other moments, however, Haig reveals that there's more to his character than just a goofball with questionable morals. When Silas relates to Tony how Spiros has coldly instructed him to shoot Tony, Silas notes how Spiros asked him to perform the murder "as soon as convenient." Incredulous, Silas observes, "He might as well been asking me to go out for a *box of cigars*." Haig's wonder, tinged with disgust, at this turn of events, shows that even this white-slaver has limits, and that there might be more going on beneath his amoral veneer than meets the eye. Couple this with his apparent sense of humor, and Haig's ambivalent henchman becomes the film's one bright spot. Consequently, it's a real pity that he's dispatched before the hunt even begins, robbing the movie of its one intriguing character (and actor). The filmmakers really shot themselves in the foot when they shot Haig's Silas in the chest.

Production

Roger Corman's then-nascent New World Pictures distributed *The Woman Hunt*. The company encouraged theater owners to target the youth audience. "Hit the underground youth-oriented [radio] stations," they advised in their *Woman Hunt* pressbook. "Turn the youth on to a film with a new bizarre twist." Obviously, the New World PR department hadn't seen the five previous Dangerous Game take-offs, or "new" would not have been one of their chosen adjectives (particularly since said cinematic "twist" was actually 40 years old!). Among New World's other promotional suggestions were bumper stickers that read, "COME JOIN THE WOMAN HUNT." Undoubtedly these were very popular among the feminist crowd of the 1970s...

Of course, New World apparently adhered to the old adage that "there's no such thing as bad publicity," since they recommended theaters "cash in on 'Women's Lib' by staging a mock picket line in front of the theatre on opening night," resulting in "great local news coverage." Or how about: "Stage a mock 'woman hunt' in imitation of the 1-sheet [poster], with three local lovelies and enthusiasts at a local shopping center. Watch the public join the fun and flock to your theatre when the film opens." Indeed.

The Woman Hunt came about through John Ashley's (and his production company, Four Associates, Ltd.) association with Roger Corman and his New World Pictures (Ashley starred in *The Beast of the Yellow Night*, one of New World's first releases). "[Roger Corman] called me and told me about this picture [*The Big Doll House*, 1971, also with Sid Haig] that they were going to do in Puerto Rico," recounted Ashley. "I told him, 'You ought to come down and take a look at the Philippines. I mean, it's all right here.'"[2] According to Ashley, Corman flew to the Philippines, "took one look and asked me, 'Would you stay around and exec-produce the show [*The Big Doll House*]?'" Ashley continued this successful partnership with *The Woman Hunt*, with Ashley's company putting up the above-the-line costs, while Corman's New World covered the below-the-line costs. About his partnership with Corman, Ashley recounted:

> The thing that's fun about Corman is, Roger's a tough deal-maker — a very fair deal-maker, but he's tough — but once you make your deal, he leaves you alone and doesn't bother you. He lets you go off and make your movie. And I think that's why so many people have started with him, because he does let you go off and do it your way.[3]

Oklahoma-raised John Ashley fell into acting while on vacation in California. Work as an extra on John Wayne's *The Conqueror* (1956) led to an appearance (with Wayne's helpful promotion) on William Castle's television series *Men of Annapolis*. From there he was chosen to play the male lead in AIP's *Dragstrip Girl* (1957), leading to further roles in teen-targeted JD films (*Motorcycle Gang*, 1957; *Hot Rod Gang*, 1958; *High School Caesar*, 1960) and horror movies (*How to Make a Monster*, *Frankenstein's Daughter* [both 1958]). Ashley also dabbled in singing, releasing several singles on the Dot label in the late '50s. Then came a string of beach party movies — five between 1963 and 1965, including *Beach Blanket Bingo* (co-starring Ashley's then-wife Deborah Walley) — before Ashley journeyed to the Philippines to star in a pair of low-budget but inventive 1968 Filipino-American horrors, *The Mad Doctor of Blood Island* and *Brides of Blood*. As well as acting in front of the camera, Ashley stepped behind the lens to become a producer, founding his own Philippines-based company, resulting in over a dozen productions over the next decade (many of them starring Ashley himself). In between making movies in the Philippines, Ashley also owned and ran a string of theaters in Oklahoma. Ashley continued producing (and sometimes starring in) Filipino films up until 1979, with his final project involving behind-the-scenes location support on Francis Ford Coppola's *Apocalypse Now* ("Coppola and his people used my Philippine company as a kind of base of operations, so that they could deal through me," explained Ashley[4]). He returned to the States permanently in the 1980s, and turned his hand to producing television shows, including *The A-Team*, *Werewolf*, and *Walker, Texas Ranger*. John Ashley died of a heart attack in 1997 at the age of 62.

CREDITS: Alternate Titles: *Womanhunt*, *Escape* (UK video); Director: Eddie Romero; Producers: Eddie Romero, John Ashley; Executive Producer: David J. Cohen; Screenplay: David Hoover, based on a story by Jack Hill and David Hoover; Cinematographer: Justo Paulino, A.S.C.; Music: Jerry Dadap; Editors: Ben Barcelon, Joe Zucchero; Production Design: Roberto Formosa; Set Construction Supervisor: Francisco Balangue; Make-up Supervisor: Toni Artieda; Hair Dresser: Remy Amazan; Propmaster: David Delina; Wardrobe: Lolita Parafina, Tony Abeto; Unit Manager: Cenon Gonzalez; Production Manager: Mario David; Assistant Director: Maria S. Abelardo; Script Supervisor: Boots Fernandez; Recording Director: Angel Avellan; Sound Mixer: Gabriel Castellano; Second Unit Cameraman: Johnny Aracijo; Special Effects Supervisor: Teofil O. Hilario; Ordinance: Lopezino Juban, Maj., AFP, Ret.; Sound Effects Editor: Tony Gosalvez. Production Company: Four Associates, Ltd.; Distribution Company: New World Pictures, Inc.; Release Date: September 30, 1973; Running Time: 75 minutes.

CAST: John Ashley (Tony), Pat Woodell (McGee), Sid Haig (Silas), Laurie Rose (Lori), Charlene Jones (Billie), Lisa Todd (Magda), Alona Alegre, Eddie Garcia (Spiros), Ken Metcalfe (Karp), Liza Belmonte, Lotis Key, Alfonso Carvajal, Ruben Rustia, Don Lipman, Tony Gosalvez, Paquiteo Salcedo.

7

Post-War Game
Open Season (1974)

Their license to kill has expired!—ad line

Synopsis

Open Season begins with a district attorney (William Layton) telling the mother of rape victim Alicia that there's no point in prosecuting "these three boys [that] typify the very best of American youth. Football, rowing teams, debating societies, fraternity officials.... No, no judge and no jury is going to believe they're rapists." Flashbacks show moments, indistinct and disturbing, from the rape, seen through the rain-distorted window of the car in which Alicia is being assaulted.

Cut to a suburban Michigan backyard, where the families of college chums Ken (Peter Fonda), Gregg (John Phillip Law) and Artie (Richard Lynch) have a typical Saturday afternoon get-together, complete with impromptu football game, activities for the kids, and a friendly picnic. An older man (William Holden) arrives to drop off a young autistic boy, who'll be staying with one of the families while he's away. Ken, Gregg and Artie then leave for their annual two-week hunting trip in the northern part of the state. After a sordid tryst with some waitresses at their motel stop, the trio kidnaps a couple on the road, Martin and Nancy (Albert Mendoza and Cornelia Sharpe), dump Martin's car in a lake, and takes the pair to their isolated cabin situated on an island in a remote lake.

When Martin, thinking they're being kidnapped for ransom because he works at a bank, offers to raise $50,000 for their release, an affronted Ken protests. "You are guests," he reassures them. "This cabin—we provide everything; you cook and clean. We hunt. In the evenings maybe we have a little fun. Everybody's happy. *Guests*, Martin, *polite guests*."

After hunting the local wildlife all day, Ken, Gregg and Artie get drunk, play monopoly, then coerce Nancy into having sex with them. The next day, while Martin, chained in the kitchen, cleans the dishes, the three and Nancy all skinny-dip in the lake.

Come the end of the week, the trio hands Martin a compass and rucksack with "everything that you and Nancy could possibly need" and sets them free. But Nancy sees through their ruse. "You're going to hunt us, aren't you—like animals," she proclaims. Indeed they are, and the terrified couple, given half an hour head start, begin to run for their lives. Martin and Nancy find the inflatable boat that was planted, but when Nancy falls out, Martin, embittered by her liaison with the three men, just keeps going, leaving Nancy on the island. Martin makes it to shore, with the three in hot pursuit in another boat. Martin

7. Post-War Game 71

One-sheet poster.

manages to jump Ken and take his rifle, but Artie corners him with the sun in Martin's eyes and guns Martin down.

Meanwhile, Nancy has doubled-back to the cabin and taken a shotgun. Artie and Gregg return in one of the boats, and Artie flushes Nancy from the nearby abandoned sawmill in which she's taken refuge. Terrifying her to the point of dropping her shotgun, Gregg closes in for the kill. Suddenly, a shot rings out, and Gregg goes down, mortally wounded. Artie scrambles to his aide but is shot in the arm himself. Artie struggles to his feet and flees.

Now Ken arrives back at the cabin, finds the wounded Artie, and shoots Nancy. Ken then goes searching for the unknown perpetrator. Artie cracks and swims across to the shore — only to be cut down by a bullet. Suddenly, a recording rings out over the island:

> Good morning, Ken. This is the end of the line. Remember Alicia? I'm her father. Your child was born but Alicia died. She committed suicide. It's taken me a long time to find you, to get to know you, become a friend. I had to change my name. Time was beginning to make my memory of Alicia fade. Until last year, when I followed you up here. I saw what an army education had done to improve your game, and the game had to be stopped. But how, Ken, how? Appeal to the law? No. You and I and Alicia know that. So *I* am the law.

As Ken takes refuge in the old mill, he hears the same calm voice again: "Good morning, Ken. This is *not* a recording. You have less than a minute to live. And in that time I'm going

Artie (Richard Lynch, with rifle) bags the first kill (Albert Mendoza) of this *Open Season*.

to kill you." Ken turns to see Wolkowski, the older man who dropped off the boy at the film's beginning, pointing a rifle at him. Wolkowski fires, and Ken's hunt is over. Wolkowski then takes a boat and heads for shore.

How "Dangerous" Is It?

Open Season takes little from Connell's "The Most Dangerous Game" except the all-important theme of hunting humans for sport. While it shares the story's isolated island setting (though replacing its exotic Caribbean isle with the rather more prosaic island in the middle of a Northern Michigan lake), the film veers sharply away from Connell's tale by offering three antagonists to fill Zaroff's shoes, and presenting a pair of human targets in place of the story's solitary Rainsford. Straying further afield, these two are simply panicked "civilians," not hunting experts, so there's no supreme test of the characters' "woodcraft," nor are there any traps laid and sprung. Not unsurprisingly, these changes more accurately reflect the more cynical sensibilities of the times (the mid–1970s, when America had been rocked not only by the divisive Vietnam War, but the Watergate scandal and subsequent resignation of President Richard Nixon). So the admittedly misguided and Sadean-tinged "nobility" of Connell's Zaroff here makes way for the hedonistic amorality of Ken, Gregg and Artie, who are more interested in the "thrills" gleaned from partying and killing than truly challenging their skills as hunters of men (hence their choice of an ordinary couple with no particular skill-set as their prey). "Ferchrissakes," exclaims Martin when faced with the truth, "we can't beat you out here, and you know it!" At this, Gregg protests, "I disagree with you. That's a big forest out there. And you're a man — with a brain potentially more lethal than any rifle." This is as close to Connell's "your brain against mine; your woodcraft against mine; outdoor chess!" notion as *Open Season* comes. But Martin is right — the untrained, unprepared couple has no chance. As a result, the climactic hunt is short and not-so-sweet — at least until the third, heretofore unknown, party makes his presence known.

Said party, the calmly vengeful Wolkowski, adds a welcome wrinkle to the Most Dangerous Game scenario by cleverly turning the tables on the hunters and making *them* the prey for the final few minutes. After an hour of watching the two protagonists be humiliated and terrorized at the hands of Ken, Gregg and Artie, seeing the trio placed in a similar position offers some much-needed relief via its tables-turned catharsis. To the filmmakers' credit, however, this deadly development ultimately carries a very disturbing element in its own right, as the audience comes to realize that, while Wolkowski ostensibly carries "right" on his side, in the final analysis there's little to separate him from the sadistic trio he dispatches. Wolkowski's vengeance-at-any-price attitude is little different, really, than the antagonists' kicks-at-any-price approach.

Critique

Ken, Gregg and Artie revel in their power over the couple, and their secret knowledge. What makes the scenario even more disturbing is the fact that the trio appear to enjoy the build-up just as much as — if not more than — the actual hunt itself, which seems almost perfunctory after all their subtle humiliation of their "prey."

In particular, Peter Fonda's Ken comes off as truly villainous, but not through any mustache-twirling or ham-handed outbursts — just the opposite. He speaks calmly, charmingly, to his "guests," and performs such shocking deeds as attaching a chain to Nancy's leg with the utmost casualness, as if such a thing was an everyday occurrence.

In fact, the three are a personable, fun-loving bunch, fond of impersonations (Ken does John Wayne and Artie does Bogart when they first confront Martin and Nancy on the road). But their good humor and surface politeness occasionally gives way to little cruelties (such as Artie offering Martin a piece of gum, then, after Martin says nothing, taking some from his own mouth and forcing Martin to chew it), which causes their mask of civility to slip and reveal the sadism lurking underneath. They delight in their captives' discomfiture, responding with mock-sincere reassurances (such as Ken insisting on calling Martin and Nancy "guests").

When Nancy seems distraught about her complicit sexual activities the night before, for instance, Ken attempts to reassure her by saying, "C'mon Nancy, listen. So you got drunk last night and had a good time. So what? That's what life's all about, baby, no matter what your mother told you." And when the cuckolded Martin loses his temper and slaps Nancy for what she did, shouting, "Whore!" Gregg restrains him and sneers, "Make love, not war, Martin."

Augmenting the naturalistic acting, screenwriters David Osborn and Liz Charles-Williams' dialogue sounds like real conversation, as the trio argue about some triviality, make mundane bets, and try to make the others laugh with lame jokes or half-funny remarks. Director Peter Collinson sometimes allows the dialogue to overlap, with characters talking over one another. These slices of realistic interactions, in which characters speak out of turn, begin a sentence without finishing, or even mumble at times (in short, converse like people in real life) not only enhances the scenario's realism, it underscores the banality of evil.

These men are not world-weary big game hunters, nor aristocratic Counts or foreign generals; they are regular guys whose middle-class privilege has allowed them to basically do what they want for most of their adult lives, and whose recent training and experience in war has whetted their hedonistic and amoral appetites for the sadistic. These suburban-dwelling monsters even drive a station wagon! Consequently, like much of what '70s cinema appeared to strive for (though frequently falling short), it all feels oh-so-real. And as such, Connell's central concept becomes that much more disturbing.

Equally disturbing is this notion of the utter banality of evil. These three going-on-middle-aged men are virtual scions of suburbia, as evidenced by the opening scene. The film offers no comforting *Psycho*-like explanations, no sensibility-warping abuse from the past as a reason for their behavior. They're just looking for "kicks," and their pursuit of thrills has merely evolved from college football to raping girls in the backseat of cars to hunting humans for fun — the implied result of their experiences in the Army. In other words, this brand of evil is simply the ultimate hedonism turned to sadism via some military training/experiences.

The film makes no effort to detail what happened to the three in Vietnam to turn them into heartless killers. They experience no flashbacks, no moments of shell-shocked terror. This, coupled with their reprehensible behavior even before the war (personified by their gang-rape of Alicia), makes it clear that it wasn't the war that turned them into monsters, it simply made them more *efficient* monsters by training them to kill. It's a subtle distinction that indirectly reflects a more modern and progressive view of the Vietnam conflict than what was generally held by anti-war factions in the mid–1970s. At the time of the war (which didn't officially end until the fall of Saigon in 1975, eight months after *Open Season*'s

7. Post-War Game

release), protesters in America blamed—and reviled—the soldiers. With hindsight, American attitudes have changed, so that most now blame the impossible situation itself rather than the unlucky participants.

Director Peter Collinson, aided by some evocative photography by cinematographer Fernando Arribas and impactful splicing by editor Alan Pattila, uses visuals to both illuminate his story's characters and provoke unease in his viewers. For instance, during the hunting montage of the three men shooting birds, rabbits, even squirrels, the edits (and gunshots) come faster and faster until the sequence finishes with Ken pointing his rifle directly at the camera (and viewer) and pulling the trigger. This cleverly builds the mounting unease in an effectively disturbing manner as we watch the three engage in their bloodsport (particularly given the quick shots of fowl falling from the sky and various animal carcasses delineating the results of their "sport").

Though it offers an added twist to the expected Dangerous Game scenario with the appearance of the avenging Wolkowski at the end, the script raises several disturbing questions without providing any pat answers. For instance, why did Wolkowski, who had planned everything out so carefully, wait until his trio of targets had already killed one of their victims and was on the verge of dispatching the second before stepping in to exact his vengeance? And even after he does intervene to kill one of the three hunters and wound another, he still leaves the terrified Nancy alone to her own devices, resulting in the third hunter ultimately shooting her down like a dog. Apparently, Wolkowski, in seeking vengeance, has as little regard for human life as the hunters themselves. While it may have been the intent of scripters David Osborn and Liz Charles-Williams to show how the thirst for vengeance, no matter how justified, taints even the most noble among us, the characterization of Wolkowski, as portrayed by the soft-spoken William Holden, displays nothing but sympathetic tendencies (as seen in his interaction with his autistic grandson). On the other hand, while the viewer derives satisfaction from seeing the three hunters shot down at their own game, the audience is left with a feeling of unease at the seemingly needless demise of Martin and Nancy, and the callous disregard for anything but his own brand of "justice" by the hitherto sympathetic Wolkowski. Rather than a heroic rescuer, Wolkowski is simply another killer. In *Open Season*, seemingly no one is innocent (even Martin and Nancy are painted with the distasteful brush of adultery)—and all must pay the price for their lack of morality. Except Wolkowski, who seemingly gets off Scott-free after his killing spree and blatant disregard for human life. This final development leaves the viewer with the rather disturbing message that the winner of this "game" will always be the one who's most clever and most single-minded of purpose.

The acting in *Open Season* is first rate from all concerned, but especially noteworthy are Cornelia Sharpe as Nancy and Richard Lynch as Artie. When Artie and Gregg corner Nancy, they shoot all around her until, terrified, she holds up her shotgun and drops it, sobbing. "Please..." she pleads forlornly, then collapses to her knees in supplication and terrified exhaustion. Sobbing to herself, she mumbles, "God, get me out of this. Don't shoot—I'll do anything." Then, as Gregg approaches for the kill, she almost mindlessly paws at the sand, as if subconsciously trying to dig her way out of her terror, while mumbling, "Please no, please no." As Nancy, Cornelia Sharpe presents a harrowing picture of abject terror and despair, powerfully hammering home the horror of her situation. Likewise, the wide smile on John Phillip Law's countenance as he happily glances over at Lynch, only to be met by Lynch's look of delight and anticipatory satisfaction, speak volumes about *their* characters.

Collinson aims his camera upwards at Law and Lynch for this sequence, so that the camera angle makes them loom over the scene — and viewer — in a show of raw power. As Gregg strides closer, aping the manner of a Western gunfighter, rapid edits between him and the supplicating Nancy, with nothing but her pathetic, almost incoherent pleadings on the soundtrack, ratchets the tension to a near-unbearable degree. Then, when the unexpected shot rings out and Gregg collapses, a brief freeze-frame of the bewildered Nancy makes literal the notion of time standing still for that fatal few seconds.

Though Peter Fonda's Ken is obviously the focal point of the antagonistic trio, it's Lynch's Artie that remains the most intriguing character. Wearing a goofy hat and even goofier thick-rimmed glasses, he's the jokester/clown of the group (though more in line with Gacy than Bozo). He also appears to be the low man on this triangular totem pole, for he generally observes rather than partakes in the debauchery, whether it be with the floozy waitresses or Nancy, leaving his two cohorts to carry on. And it's the wounded Artie who seems to have some inner reckoning that makes him cut and run, talking to himself as he strips to swim across the lake: "You just gotta understand, I can't do it. Sorry Kenny, I'm sorry. I don't know how the whole goddamned thing began but I want outta this. I want out of it. *Sick. Sick!*"

Lynch's death scene may be the most powerful sequence of the film. After Artie swims across the lake to the shore, he laughs and even capers like he's gone a little mad. "Up you!" he shouts. But a shot rings out, a red hole appears in his chest, and Artie collapses right in front of the camera. With his face in close-up, blood oozing from his mouth, he whispers, "Oh God, oh my God, help me." With Lynch's countenance filling half the foreground, we see a figure approach from behind, walking steadily towards him (and us) until all we can see are the intruder's legs, then only his boots, as he steps near Artie. Artie utters one last, "Oh God," and dies. The lack of music, the purposeful but unhurried approach by the mysterious avenging figure, and Artie's plaintive prostrate pleadings make this a harrowing—and cathartic—death sequence.

Though Collinson and company make very few missteps with *Open Season*, one glaring eyesore (or "ear-sore," as it turns out) comes in the form of the awful ballad "Casting Shadows" at the film's beginning—in which reedy-voice singer John Howard plaintively whines, "Now shadows block the sun, the houses freeze / The cars go nowhere past the silent trees / The faceless clouds above..." etc. Fortunately, after this appalling audio assault, the musical choices become more judicious, frequently adding to the tension or setting the mood of a scene, whether by its presence or, at times, complete absence (such as at Artie's death).

Production

The film's credits state that *Open Season* is based on David Osborn's novel *The All-Americans*. Osborn's book, however, which came out in tandem with the film, was actually called *Open Season*, like the film. Obviously, *The All-Americans* was the novel's working title when the picture's producers bought the rights to the work before publication. Osborn had been writing for the screen since the late 1950s, when he penned episodes of *Armchair Theatre* before graduating to feature film screenplays like the excellent Eurospy thrillers *Deadlier Than the Male* (1967) and *Some Girls Do* (1969) (both also co-written with his *Open Season* writing partner Liz Charles-Williams), and the "horror hag" offshoot *Whoever Slew Auntie Roo?* (story only) in 1971.

British-born director Peter Collinson also got his start in television, before moving on to make numerous features in Europe and the UK. Among his credits are *The Italian Job* (1969, starring Michael Caine) and *The Spiral Staircase* (1975, again with John Phillip Law). Collinson's final film before his death from cancer that same year was *The Earthling* (1980), starring another *Open Season* alumnus, William Holden.

"Oh man, I had a good time on that one," enthused Peter Fonda when asked about *Open Season*. "That was my first chance to play a really evil guy. I liked working with Richard Lynch and John Phillip Law.... I wish that film was available on video. I really like that film."[1] (Unfortunately, as of this writing, *Open Season* can only be seen via out-of-print videocassette.)

Richard Lynch labeled *Open Season* "a very strange movie." Lynch did enjoy the shoot, however, particularly while filming in Spain. "The European lifestyle is more laid back and cavalier and easier than working in the industry over here." Of his director, Lynch recalled, "I got along with Peter [Collinson], but he was pretty tough. He was a bit of a cantankerous guy.... He was a very competent director, but he had a lot of difficulties. He had a lot of personality conflicts with a lot of people, but I seemed to have gotten around that."[2] One such "conflict" involved Peter Fonda's then-girlfriend. As Fonda himself wrote in his autobiography, "My girlfriend was barred from the [Madrid] set because of her jealousy. I agreed."[3]

Lynch was in awe of his co-star William Holden. "I grew up on his movies, and I still had the naivete of a kid from Brooklyn who's suddenly sitting on a movie set with William Holden." A "quiet and gentle man," Holden gave Lynch some very useful advice: "'*Kid, you're lucky to get one hit out of every ten movies.*' He was very realistic and pragmatic."[4]

The hunting lodge interiors of this international production were filmed on a set in Pinewood Studios in England, while most of the exteriors were shot on location in Spain (with additional footage lensed in Michigan). Apparently, U.S. distributors Columbia altered the picture's original ending before its release. The somewhat longer Scandinavian release of the picture, titled *Jaktoffer*, reportedly concludes with William Holden's character of Wolkowski surrendering to the police outside of Ken's house. Excising this denouement significantly altered the ending's tone by allowing Wolkowski to seemingly walk free.

Open Season shared a similar critical fate with the same year's *Texas Chainsaw Massacre*, as both were lambasted at the time of release for excessive violence — when, in fact, very little bloodshed occurs onscreen (in either movie). It's the *tone* of each of these two films that makes them so disturbing.

CREDITS: Alternate Title: *The Recon Game* (UK); Director: Peter Collinson; Producer: Jose S. Vicuna; Executive Producer: George H. Brown; Screenplay: David Osborn and Liz Charles-Williams (based on Osborn's novel *The All-Americans*); Cinematography: Fernando Arribas; Art Director: Gil Parrondo; Editor: Alan Pattila; Make-up: Cristobal Criado; Special Effects: Antonio Balandini; Music: Rugger Cini; Song "Casting Shadows" written and sung by John Howard; Production Supervisor: Fancisco Malero; Production Manager: Manola Amigo; Assistant Director: Adiafa Aristarain; Countries of Origin: Spain/Switzerland/U.K./U.S.A./Argentina. Production Company: Impala/Arpa. Distribution: Columbia Pictures. Filmed in Panavision. Release Date: August 1974. Running Time: 104 minutes.

CAST: Peter Fonda (Ken), Cornelia Sharpe (Nancy), John Phillip Law (Gregg), Richard Lynch (Artie), Albert Mendoza (Martin), William Holden (Wolkowski), Helga Line (Sue), Didi Sherman (Helen), Conchita Cuetos (Joyce), Norma Castel (Annie), May Heatherly (Pat), Gudrun McCleary (Mrs. Rennick), and guest artists Blanca Estrada (Alicia Rennick), Simon Andreu (Barman), William Layton (District Attorney).

8

Dangerous Ozploitation
Escape 2000 (1982)

"It is 1995. Hunting is the national sport. And people are the prey." — trailer

Synopsis

In the dystopian future of 1995 (at least according to the film's trailer — the "2000" of the movie's title notwithstanding), a trio of prisoners arrive at Camp 97. Welcoming them is the camp sign:

> CAMP 97
> Re-Education and Behaviour Modification
> WELCOME
> Your Stay Here Will Make You an Asset to Society

Equally welcoming are the brutal, lascivious guards and the cooly sadistic Camp Master, Charles Thatcher (Michael Craig), who orders his head guard, Ritter (Roger Ward), to provide a demonstration for the new "deviates" (as the prisoners are labeled) — by arbitrarily beating a hapless young woman nearly to death. Thatcher's motto: "Freedom is obedience. Obedience is work. Work is life." The three arrivals are Paul Anders (Steve Railsback), a *Radio Freedom* revolutionary who's escaped from several camps in the past; Chris (Olivia Hussey), a naive young shop girl who was taken in for questioning when police chased a man into her shop ("guilt by proximity"); and Rita Daniels (Lynda Stoner), who's there because "some asshole turned me in for being a whore — which I am not."

At this prison camp, in between pointless work details, the prisoners — the "undesirables of society" — are beaten and tortured. But that's not the worst of it. Also at the camp are the powerful Secretary Mallory (Noel Ferrier), there for an official inspection, and two wealthy, influential guests, Tito (Michael Petrovitch) and weapons designer Jennifer (Carmen Duncan). They are all there for a very special reason, as we learn when Thatcher gathers four hand-picked prisoners in his office — Paul, Chris, Rita, and the wormy Dodge (John Ley) — to make them a proposition. "All you have to do is lead my guests on a chase for one day," he tells them. "A little sport.... If you survive, you'll be free." The quartet accept the offer (refusing means permanent confinement ... or worse) and prepare for tomorrow's "hunt." Chris will be Mallory's prey, Rita will be Jennifer's, Dodge will be Tito's, and Paul will be Thatcher's himself. At the last minute, Thatcher adds a fifth target, the resourceful prisoner Griff (Bill Young), who has been causing trouble in the camp.

The next morning Thatcher sets the five loose at half-hour intervals, isolating them

8. Dangerous Ozploitation

Head guard Ritter (Roger Ward) beats a female prisoner (Orianna Panozzo) as an example — and warning — to the other "deviates" in *Escape 2000*.

from their fellows and allowing their hunters to focus on each specific prey. First Tito, whose weapons of choice are a dune buggy/bulldozer contraption armed with a machine gun, and a hairy half-man/half-animal "circus freak" with cats' eyes and fangs named Alph (Steven Rackman). Using Alph as his hunting hound, he runs Dodge to ground. But Tito orders Alph only to wound Dodge and let him go, therefore prolonging the hunt.

Next, Thatcher finds Paul crossing a rocky cliff by a waterfall. Though Thatcher has him in his rifle sights, he intentionally misses ("No, too easy," he mutters), spurring Paul to dive into the water to make his escape.

Meanwhile, the resourceful Griff enters the jungle and plants a false trail, then waits for Red (Gus Murcurio), the guard Thatcher has sent to track him. Griff jumps Red, overpowers him, and takes his gun. Griff leaves Red trussed up as bait for a trap that Ritter later inadvertently springs, leaving Red dead. Elsewhere, Tito finally corners Dodge for the kill and sets Alph on him. After delivering a sound beating, Alph breaks Dodge's spine.

Griff seeks out Thatcher, but just as Griff engages the Camp Master in a gun battle, the crossbow-wielding Jennifer rides up on her horse and pins Griff down in a grassy field with her exploding arrows. After Jennifer wounds Griff, Thatcher finishes him off by running him over with his land rover. Thatcher then takes Griff's body back to the camp to put on display as a "lesson" for the other inmates.

Jennifer rides off in search of *her* prey, Rita. Finding her bathing in the river, Jennifer makes short work of Rita after terrifying her with her exploding arrows.

Fleeing along a stream, Paul literally runs into Alph. As Alph holds Paul against a tree, Tito drives forward, with the blade of his scoop raised to "cut him down to size." But at the last second Paul shoves a broken branch into Alph's eye and slips out of his grasp, leaving Alph to be literally cut in half in his place.

Ritter leads Mallory in pursuit of *his* target, Chris, tracking her to a cane field. Ritter circles around and sets fire to the foliage to drive her out. Mallory finds Chris and starts to force himself upon her, but Paul arrives, wrestles Mallory's gun from him and shoots him in the crotch. As the spreading fire consumes the screaming Mallory, Paul and Chris flee. Ritter tracks the two to the sea. "Goddamn, it's an island!" exclaims Paul. "There never was a way out." With nowhere left to run, Paul and Ritter fight. After Paul makes a dash for it, Ritter pulls his gun and takes aim. Chris runs up behind the guard and chops off Ritter's hands with his own machete. She runs, panicked at what she's done, but Paul catches her and pleads, "We can't quit now. Because if we quit now, everything we believe in dies."

Paul and Chris head back towards the camp, only to run into Tito, enraged over Paul having killed his "pet," Alph. As a diversion, Chris makes a break for it, and Paul sneaks up and buries a machete in Tito's head. Paul and Chris take Tito's rig and head for the camp, taking out guards with the machine gun and freeing the prisoners.

Meanwhile, Jennifer has gone back to camp and called the "Department," triggering a "wipe-out" order. As the jets scramble, Thatcher and his men make it back to camp and engage the now-armed prisoners in a gun and grenade battle. While Chris struggles with Jennifer, turning her own exploding arrow on her, Paul literally blows Thatcher's head off with machine-gun fire. As Paul and Chris lead the remaining escapees into the nearby mountains, the jets bomb the camp into oblivion. The film ends on a quote from H.G. Wells: "Revolution begins with the misfits."

How "Dangerous" Is It?

The makers of *Escape 2000* obviously never took the expression "Less is more" to heart, as this Australian film features more protagonists, more antagonists (if one Zaroff is good, how about *four*?), and more outlandish action than ever found in Connell's already action-packed tale. Ironically, while it offers more ostensible bang for its (Australian) buck (at least in terms of gunfire, explosions, and gory set-pieces), *Escape 2000* makes far less of an impact than Connell's more intimate, thoughtful and powerful story.

The film offers no real characterization of the hunters, not even of Thatcher himself, with their motivation left unexplained and unexplored. About the best screenwriters Jon George and Neill Hicks can come up with is having one antagonist state, "Excess is what makes life worth living—for people like us"; while another comments to Thatcher, "I think your little ... turkey shoot will be well appreciated in the right quarters. I commend your imagination." In other words, they are merely decadent sadists; and as such, these Zaroff stand-ins are far less intriguing than Connell's obsessed hunter-of-men.

Thatcher's very name belies the ham-fisted political nature of the entire enterprise (in fact, it's rather surprising someone didn't slip and refer to him as "Maggie" at one time or another). The Fascism comes so thick and fast that it becomes almost cartoonish at times, as Ritter states at one point that if he were in charge he'd just "kill them all," earning an approving "Ah, the final solution" from Mallory. And, of course, there's Thatcher's camp "motto," which is a veritable paean to the Nazi's "Arbeit Macht Frei." Admittedly, it's a novel twist on Connell's concept to set the hunt at an island prison camp for a dystopian society, but so little is made of the background (and breakdown) of society that ultimately led to this, that the set-up seems more simple contrivance than motivational guide. (Actually, as originally planned, there would have been far more made of said societal situation, but budget cuts at the last minute cost the filmmakers their opening salvo; see the "Production" section below for more details.)

The pivotal hunt itself actually consists of *five* different hunts conducted simultaneously, since the quartet of antagonists each have their own hand-picked "prey." As Thatcher tells the other three hunters, "Now remember, you only have your own targets, so no poaching." With so many possibilities on offer (Thatcher even adds a fifth "target" at the last minute when another prisoner, Griff, causes trouble at the camp — "not for sport," explains Thatcher, "but for execution"), it becomes truly disappointing that only one of the five has the wherewithal to engage in any proactive activity besides running blindly. Said protagonist (Griff) lays a false trail and sets a trap after ambushing one of the camp's sleazy guards, Red. When Thatcher's right-hand man, Ritter, finds Red, trussed up and hanging by his heels from a tree, Ritter cuts the rope holding the man, which in turn releases a log tipped with wooden spikes that swings down and disembowels the hapless Red. Though it's gratifying to see at least one of the film's protagonists take a page from Connell's original story by using his "brain" and "woodcraft" to set a trap, the "brain" part comes into question by the fact that the logic of constructing such a trap is nearly unfathomable. First off, where did Griff find the time, with Ritter so close on his heels, to build this complicated contraption? (In Connell's original, Rainsford quickly rigged *his* trap, a "Malay man-catcher," by modifying an existing deadfall.) Second, Griff could have simply killed the guard in the first place and then put more distance between him and his other pursuers — why the elaborate set-up just to dispatch Red in front of someone else? Obviously, Griff put a lot of thought into the trap's construction — far more than scripters Jon George and Neill Hicks put into their screenplay on this point.

Critique

"I thought that I would make a high-camp splatter movie with a lot of dark humor," declared director Brian Trenchard-Smith some twenty-odd years after the fact.[1] It's a somewhat disingenuous comment, as, despite its plentiful gore, there's nothing tongue-in-cheek nor even mildly satirical about *Escape 2000*. A montage of real-life riot scenes and mob violence opens the film. As the credits roll, we see makeshift barriers smashed, and protestors brutally clubbed and beaten by police. Opening with such disturbing scenes of real-life violence sets a definite tone, one that's miles away from "high camp." Said tone continues with the frequent make-believe violence on offer during the film's first half (before the hunt begins), starting with a brutal, bloody beating of a petite woman prisoner by the hulking guard Ritter, and continuing through the deliberate and tortuous immolation of another inmate who tried to escape.

Once the hunt begins, however, realism appears to take a back seat to shock value, as things head further over the top (and often slide down the other side). For instance, when Tito first captures Dodge, he orders Alph to hobble his prey by ripping off Dodge's little toe. After accomplishing this near-impossible feat with his bare hands, Alph then *eats* the tiny member! At this, Tito asks, "All right, Alph? Good. Tea break's over." Though it is indeed a darkly humorous line, this bizarre, sadistic, and ridiculous moment adds nothing but a minor outré shock. Later, Tito chases the now-limping Dodge around for a bit—almost comically so, as at one point the wounded Dodge desperately hops on one foot—before letting Alph beat him to death.

Later, when Tito accidentally drives his bulldozer blade into Alph rather than the intended Paul, we see the lower half of Alph's body separate and fall away in a grisly mess. Tito proclaims, "Oh shit!" and picks up a miniature bazooka(!) from the floor of his vehicle to fire at the fleeing Paul. Again, such uber-gore and violence may be somewhat shocking in the moment, but (much like the unfortunate Alph's internal organs) it slides into the realm of the ridiculous.

None of the characters are well-developed (nor, in some cases, well-acted) enough to inspire much more than idle curiosity about how and when they will meet their demise. Steve Railsback's Paul comes off as a walking political slogan machine (and a none-too-eloquent one at that). His smarmy stubbornness and haughty defiance backfire, lessening viewer sympathy, as he appears more cocky and arrogant than heroic and noble. And the strident delivery of Method-trained Railsback, only a few short years after his triumph in *The Stunt Man* (1980), fails to breathe life into clichéd dialogue like "I'm the one you can't break; I'm what you've been afraid of all your life." Though Paul Anders may be a tough-minded prison camp escape artist á la Hilts in *The Great Escape* (1963), Railsback is miles away from Steve McQueen. Remembered co-star Michael Craig, "Steve Railsback, he was a bit difficult ... everything was Method, had to be *felt*."[2]

The movie's other name "star," Olivia Hussey, does no better with her role of Chris. Projecting an air of doe-eyed innocence, Hussey's Chris is nothing but a shrinking violet whose transformation at the end into a machine gun–toting action heroine is about as convincing as most of the film's gore (including the moment when Chris chops off both of Ritter's hands, resulting in a pair of bloody stumps on the level of a backyard 8mm production — with the actor's hands obviously tucked inside his sleeves). According to co-star Michael Craig, such a timid characterization on Hussey's part may not have been simple acting, as she was deathly afraid of the local flora and fauna: "[She] was absolutely terrified of being in Australia, in Queensland.... She was very difficult about doing anything outside the set."[3]

The remaining three protagonists, Rita, Dodge and Griff, are so underdeveloped and one-dimensional that their characters could each be easily defined with a solitary word: "weary" for Rita, "slimy" for Dodge, and "tough" for Griff. As a result, the film generates little suspense during the pivotal hunt, since suspense requires empathy and identification with a character, which these cyphers fail to inspire to any significant degree.

Fortunately, the villains here prove far more intriguing than the heroes (as is often the case). Though given little more to work with character-wise than Railsback, Hussey and company, the quartet of character actors who flesh out these elegantly-dressed antagonists are good enough to make them interesting. As the corpulent Mallory, Noel Ferrier's haughty demeanor and mild-yet-assured dialogue delivery immediately paints a portrait of a man used to wielding power and getting what he wants. Carmen Duncan's Jennifer, with her elegant gowns and riding gear, her self-assured air and sarcastic double entendres, is obviously a woman who needs no man to achieve her decadent goals. Michael Petrovitch's Tito, with his black garb, satanic widow's peak and goatee, receives the best lines, fully illustrating his sadistic sense of humor. For instance, after calmly watching on closed-circuit TV the spectacle of Thatcher's guards burning a prisoner alive, Tito takes a drink from his brandy snifter and quips, "Beats the hell out of network television." And Thatcher, as played by Michael Craig, is the coolest customer of all. He need never raise his cultured voice to be heard or obeyed, and nothing so banal as conscience can trouble a man of his position. When Jennifer complains about Thatcher adding Griffith to the hunt ("I thought you said only one apiece"), Thatcher coolly responds, "Griffin is not for sport, he's for execution." Then, without missing a beat, he civilly inquires, "Would you like some breakfast?"

While having *twelve* principals — seven antagonists (the four hunters, the two guards Ritter and Red, and Alph) and five protagonists — involved in the hunt provides plenty of opportunity for gory set-pieces, it makes for some disjointed continuity, as the constant cutting between the various parties further dilutes the tension. Consequently, the filmmakers must rely on excess to hold the viewer's interest. But to be fair, they do a pretty good job at doing just that.

Director Brian Trechard-Smith keeps things moving at a brisk pace, and the hunt itself, which lasts well over half an hour, culminates in a blood-and-thunder full-scale battle back at the camp that, while not particularly realistic, remains lively nonetheless. This climactic battle offers gunfire and pyrotechnics galore, with plenty of impressive stunt work and explosions. It reaches a level of near-comical absurdity, however, when wave after wave of guards keep coming, making one wonder if there were more guards at this prison camp than prisoners (or if some futuristic clown car had pulled up to the camp). But the hated Thatcher's demise, though perhaps no more realistic than the rest, is definitely memorable, as Paul aims a rapid burst of machine-gun fire at the commandant and literally blows his head off. Though unimpressed with most everything about the film, Railsback did admit he was pleased by this one special effects gag: "But I tell you what did work — when I blew that [Thatcher] head off. *That* one worked."[4] Indeed it did.

Trenchard-Smith offers plenty of flourishes that indicate what this film *might* have been had things worked out according to plan. For instance, the introductions of pivotal characters are carefully staged for maximum impact. For Thatcher's first appearance, the camera, holding on the Camp 97 sign, suddenly changes focus as Thatcher's profile enters the frame so that everything but his stony countenance becomes a blur. Thatcher is the man in charge, and to which everything in the camp is subservient and (literally) fades into the background. Such carefully planned visual foreshadowing effectively represents Thatcher's all-encompassing power.

The introduction for Ritter, Thatcher's sadistic right-hand man, is equally potent. It comes when Paul is struck from behind by an unseen blow, and the camera shifts to his point of view from on the ground. Looking up, he (and we) see the bald-pated, hulking Ritter towering over him (and the viewer), with nothing but blue sky behind, his malevolent presence filling the screen.

Trenchard-Smith works with cinematographer John McLean to employ unusual camera angles (up-angle shots of Thatcher's imposing death vehicle passing overhead, for instance) and mobile camerawork to generate immediacy. At times the camera moves in front of a fleeing protagonist, gazing up at Dodge's panicked face, for instance, then switching to glide alongside his fleeing feet.

Trenchard-Smith makes good use of the local Australian landscape, offering everything from rocky outcroppings and cascading waterfalls to jungle ravines (complete with decomposing skeletons), mysterious cane fields, and even a mangrove swamp. Unfortunately, the sets come off poorly in contrast to the realism of the Aussie outdoors. The camp, with its flimsy corrugated plastic walls and squeaky-clean fixtures (not to mention the two-dollar

Turkey Shoot (renamed *Escape 2000* for its U.S. release two years later) fared poorly in both Australia and America but cleaned up at the box office in the U.K. (thanks in large part, according to director Brian Trenchard-Smith, to posters like this British quad).

blow-up plastic air mattresses the inmates sleep on), never looks truly lived-in, appearing just like what it really is—a hastily constructed movie set.

In the end, though sporadically engaging and occasionally amusing, *Escape 2000* remains too unevenly acted and poorly fleshed-out to make it more than a sometimes effective but more often risible, gory exploitation take on Connell's classic theme.

Production

Two weeks before shooting began, director Brian Trenchard-Smith lost nearly a quarter of his $3.2 million budget, with the schedule cut from 44 to 30 days. "We had a huge prison camp built for 500 extras," recalled the director. "We could afford 70 on one day and 20 on other days."[5] Due to this last-minute cost-cutting, the production lost a "huge *1984* scene to sort of set up the repressive society that requires these re-education and behavior modification camps," according to Trenchard-Smith. "The first 15 pages [of the script] were torn out because they were too expensive. A helicopter chase torn out, four pages of it, because that was too expensive. It was a mess."[6] Lynda Stoner felt that because of the cuts, "it went from having some kind of social message ... to being an absolutely putrid, puerile bunch of crap."[7]

Shot as *Turkey Shoot* (and titled as such for its native Australian release), *Escape 2000* failed to make back even half its cost during its North American release, making it something of a box-office ... er, turkey. Some of the principal participants apparently shared the general audience's disdain. Michael Craig, for instance, labeled it "85 minutes of kind of *schlock*, really"[8]; while Roger Ward observed, "Everybody knew it wasn't a piece of art."[9] Lynda Stoner went even further:

> Look, we knew we weren't making *War and Peace*. But I think that each and every actor that took this project onboard believed that we at least had the potential to make something that was watchable and interesting. And it just became a caricature; it became the most *grotesque* thing. I saw it once and don't ever want to see it again.[10]

According to the director himself, the film nearly ruined his career. "It certainly was not a good career move for me.... That one certainly put about as many nails in the coffin as possible."[11] Consequently, after toiling for another decade in the low-budget Australian arena, making films like *BMX Bandits* (1983) and the Wings Hauser vehicle *The Siege at Firebase Gloria* (1989), Trenchard-Smith turned to American television in the 1990s, working on series such as *Silk Stalkings* and the revived *Flipper* in between low-budget assignments like *Night of the Demons 2* (1994) and several entries in the lowly *Leprechaun* franchise.

In the documentary *Not Quite Hollywood* (2008), Steve Railsback recalled, "This thing was turning into a piece of crap, and I hated to see it.... When you have no beginning [due to the missing pages], you're screwed." To this, producer Antony Ginnane responded, "With all due respect to Steve, I'm not sure the state of *his* mind during that film was such that he'd remember *any* of the pages."[12]

Escape 2000 was "Dangerous Ozploitation" in more ways than one, as it was not the safest of film shoots. As related by special makeup effects man Bob McCarron:

> David Hemmings was the second unit director. [Note: Actor-turned-filmmaker Hemmings (*Blow-Up, Barbarella, Deep Red*) also served as an executive producer on the project.] And I remember the scene where one of our actors [Roger Ward] gets his hands chopped off. Olivia had that bloody machete in her hands, and David says, "And cut," meaning cut, stop the film. She thinks he means "cut," so she goes for it — missing his real hands by inches.[13]

McCarron continues:

> We actually had live ammunition fired at actors to hit rocks nearby. We had a stuntman, Glen Boswell, he was crossing the river. When the scene was finished he got up and found he was still bleeding. On examination we found there was a *bullet* embedded in him.[14]

Summing it up, director Brian Trenchard-Smith wryly admitted, "It has professional shortcomings as well as moral shortcomings." Actor Michael Craig's final assessment: "I think if you watch it in the right way, it will probably give you a good laugh, actually."[15]

Note: *Escape 2000* was the film seen playing on the screen in Trenchard-Smith's later *Dead End Drive-In* (another dystopian exploitation flick, in which disaffected youth are lured to — and interred in — a camp disguised as a drive-in theater).

CREDITS: Alternate Titles: *Turkey Shoot* (Australia), *Blood Camp Thatcher* (UK video); Director: Brian Trenchard-Smith; Producers: Antony I. Ginnane, William Fayman; Screenplay: Jon George and Neill Hicks (based on a story by George Schenck, Robert Williams and David Lawrence); Director of Photography: John McLean, A.S.C.; Production Designer: Bernard Hides; Editor: Alan Lake; Costume Designer: Aphrodite Kondos; Music Composed and Conducted by: Brian May; Associate Producer: Brian W. Clark; Executive Producers: John Daly, David Hemmings; Production Companies: Hemdale / FGH Ltd. / Filmco; Distribution Company: New World Pictures. Release Date: November 18, 1982 (Australia),

October 1983 (USA); Running Time: 93 minutes / 80 minutes (USA); Panavision and Eastmancolor.

CAST: Steve Railsback (Paul Anders), Olivia Hussey (Chris), Carmen Duncan (Jennifer), Noel Ferrier (Mallory), Micheal Craig (Thatcher), Lynda Stoner (Rita), Roger Ward (Ritter), Michael Petrovitch (Tito), Gus Mercurio (Red), John Ley (Dodge), Bill Young (Griff), Steve Rackman (Alph), John Godden (Andy), Oriana Panozzo (Melinda).

9

Dangerous Action
Avenging Force (1986)

> Now, in the ultimate form of savage combat, *they* are the hunters, and *he* is the target. — trailer

Synopsis

Two men frantically flee through the Louisiana swamps, pursued first by what appears to be a white-masked Ninja (complete with samurai sword), then a camouflage-sporting commando, next by an S&M-masked gladiator(!) carrying a deadly trident, and finally by a fourth man wearing a Japanese ceremonial mask whose weapon of choice is the garote. After the pair are dispatched we learn they were two C.I.A. agents (note: though one of the killers mentions that the victim was from the "Secret Service," every subsequent reference indicates C.I.A.). Standing over a corpse, the jubilant victor tells the other three, "You boys owe me $50,000.... My, my, my, my, this is a great game, boys. Gentlemen, to the Pentangle Hunting Fraternity!"

Next we see Matt Hunter (Michael Dudikoff), his little sister Sarah (Allison Gereighty), and their grandfather (Richard Boyle) traveling from their horse ranch to New Orleans to spend Mardi Gras with their good friend Larry Richards (Steve James), a black man running for senator. Says Larry, "Here's to the future — the future of living together and working together, and a future of peace for our young people, so they won't make the same mistakes we did." Here here; but for some it is not to be...

With Larry, his family and Matt all riding a float in the Mardi Gras parade, a team of assassins open fire with Uzis, killing a number of innocent bystanders before Matt and Larry (both former agents) put them down. One of the killers gets away, however, and one of Larry's two young sons is killed.

Meanwhile, the four hunters-of-men — Professor Elliot Glastonberry (John P. Ryan), head of "the giant Hadly Corporation"; young senator Wade Delaney (Bill Wallace); Commander Jeb Wallace (Karl Johnson), holder of the World Iron Man Championship title; and Charlie Lavell (Marc Alaimo), millionaire businessman — enjoy a kendo martial arts exhibition presented by the "American Survival Association." Afterward, Glastonbury delivers a speech to the influential gathering:

> We're living in dangerous times. They call us paranoid because we love our country, because we want to survive the economic collapse of our land. You know it's comin,' dontcha — riotin' in the streets of our cities, civil disorder everywhere. Dope-crazed savages, gangs of nigger rapists! Snivelling politicians tryin' to enforce gun control. Commie guerilas in Central America pointin' their

A Mardi Gras parade turns tragic for Larry Richards (Steve James, standing at top) and his family, despite the protective efforts of friend and former C.I.A. partner Matt Hunter (Michael Dudikoff, lower left).

guns north, just waitin' to cross the Rio Grande. Just waitin' to terrorize *your* mama and *your* children, and *your* neighborhood and *your* churches.... Oh no, gentlemen, it is our constitutional right to bear arms. It is our sacred duty to do so as efficiently as we know how. Become soldiers in the cause of freedom and the American way of life.

The escaped assassin gets word to Glastonbury that they failed to kill senatorial candidate Larry Richards, and they learn that it was Matt Hunter, one of the Agency's youngest and best agents (and former partner of Larry) who thwarted their plot. Glastonbury decides that Pentangle (whose inner circle consists of the four wealthy and influential man-hunters, and a fifth as-yet-unseen silent partner) must now eliminate *both* of these threats to their neo–fascist organization.

Briefed at the Agency's headquarters after the attack, Matt learns from his former commander, Admiral Brown (James Booth), that the Agency has been unsuccessfully trying to infiltrate Pentangle — "some sort of secret society with extreme right-wing views.... They have a weakness — they have a hunting club. Except they don't hunt animals, they hunt men." The authorities have "found literally dozens of mangled bodies in the bayou, all of them branded with the sign of the pentangle [a five-pointed star]." Brown asks Matt to rejoin the Agency and "beat them at their own game," but Matt declines, focused instead on protecting Larry and what's left of his family.

To this end, after he and Larry have battled their way out of another Pentangle assassination attempt, he has the beleaguered Richards family brought to Matt's own ranch, along with a contingent of agents for protection. But Pentangle has somehow found out about this impromptu "safe house," and the four Pentangle elite, intent on doing it them-

9. Dangerous Action

The four neo-fascist hunters-of-men that make up the Pentangle elite (L-R): Lavall (Marc Alaimo), Delany (Bill Wallace), Glastonbury (John P. Ryan), and Wallace (Karl Johnson).

selves this time, launch a surprise attack on the ranch house, burning it to the ground and cold-bloodedly murdering everyone there (including Larry and his family, and Matt's grandfather), leaving only Matt and his 12-year-old sister Sarah alive. After disabling Matt with an arrow in the leg, they "invite" him to participate in "the great game." Adding, "your sister is insurance that you'll turn up," they take her away and order Matt to come alone to a certain Cajun bayou village in two weeks time.

Matt arrives on the appointed evening, finds his sister, and then flees with her into the swamps. Giving Matt a 30-minute head start, the four Pentangle leaders begin their hunt. One by one they track Matt and his sister, and one by one Matt overcomes the odds to kill his pursuers — until only Glastonbury remains. Matt manages to wound him and escape with Sarah to freedom. After delivering her to safety, he heads to Glastonbury's palatial mansion, where, among Glastonbury's collection of medieval weaponry in his great hall, the two battle to the death.

Victorious, Matt goes to see Admiral Brown at the Agency one last time. Pointedly asking about the identity of the mysterious fifth Pentangle leader, and how they seemed to know Matt's every move, he ominously tells his former boss, "If what Glastonbury said is true, and Pentangle is not finished but just starting, I want you to know something — so am I." Brown narrows his eyes, and the implication is clear, as is the promise of a sequel (a promise that remained unfulfilled).

How "Dangerous" Is It?

Following the Most Dangerous Trend of "more is more" began in the 1970s with *The Woman Hunt* and *Open Season* (and carried forward with 1982's *Escape 2000*), *Avenging*

Force offers not one, not two, not even three, but *four* Zaroff figures. While in some cases (such as with *Woman Hunt* and *Escape 2000*) this can lead to sketchy characterizations or choppy storytelling, *Avenging Force* does it right, painting some intriguing variations on the hunter-of-men concept by giving each of the four villains their own distinct personality and favored weapons. The film also points up the extreme (to the point of sickness) competitive nature of these antagonists, as they bet against each other making the "kill," and revel in their triumph not only over their prey but in besting their fellow hunters (or "warriors" as they like to label themselves).

The well-constructed script (by actor-writer James Booth, who plays Matt's former boss, Admiral Brown) adds a none-too-subtle subplot about racism, with the antagonists bandying about the "N" word on several occasions, and Glastonbury even positing that Hitler was "a visionary." So rather than Connell's intellectual uber-predator who's grown bored with hunting mere animals, these Zaroff stand-ins are cast as despicable bigots who bask in their own skills and power, show off for their fellow fascists, and attain status in the organization by hunting men.

With its emphasis on action, the two hunts the film presents (the opening sequence with the two agents, and the climactic bayou showdown with Matt as the prey) are more chase-and-fight scenarios than big-game stalking sequences. Matt lays no traps (he's not a hunter himself, and so knows little of the "woodcraft" Connell writes about), relying instead on his fighting skills and turning his pursuers' own weapons against them. Also, for much of the chase, Matt is not alone but must contend with (and even carry) his 12-year-old sister. Though a departure from Connell, little Sarah's presence during the terrifying ordeal emphasizes Matt's dire situation and underscores his grim, desperate determination, as it's not only *his* life he must fight for but that of the person he loves most in the world.

Avenging Force's ending parallel's Connell's in one very important aspect. Just like Rainsford in Connell's story, Matt heads back to his pursuer's palatial mansion for a final mano-a-mano confrontation (on equal terms this time) after the hunt has ostensibly concluded — bearding the lion in his den, so to speak. In this case, however, Glastonbury, unlike Zaroff, knows Matt escaped alive and so is expecting, even anticipating, Matt's arrival. Connell's tale ends with a few deft suggestive closing lines:

> "I see," [Zaroff] said. "Splendid! One of us is to furnish a repast for the hounds. The other will sleep in this very excellent bed. On guard, Rainsford...." He had never slept in a better bed, Rainsford decided.

Avenging Force, however, finishes with a visually-realized violent battle involving a plethora of medieval weapons scattered about Glastonbury's great hall. But it's refreshing to see Connell's dramatic coda retained and brought to action-filled life.

Critique

"The action film of the year," boasted the *Avenging Force* posters. Back in 1986, such hyperbole might not be too far wrong. Filled with exciting set-pieces; disturbing gun violence; more brutal fight scenes than you can shake a kendo stick at; and dangerous, jaw-dropping stunts, the movie lives up to its hype as "A pulse-quickening, bare-knuckled, boot-in-the-face action film." According to an enthusiastic production piece, "We're talking fist fights, sword fights, crossbows, nasty Cajuns, lots of gunfire and a black-and-white

9. Dangerous Action

moral universe. We're talking Michael Dudikoff and Steve James, the heroes of Cannon's highly successful *American Ninja*, out to kick some serious butt."[1] Indeed.

"Everyone enjoys a good, rip-snortin' action film," stated another publicity article. "It heats the blood, perks up the spirit and, according to most sociologists, provides an outlet for our aggressions."[2] Therapeutic claims aside, *Avenging Force* delivers its action in spades, right from the outset when the two agents must flee and then fight for their lives in the swamp. Follow this with a brutal Mardi Gras parade massacre and subsequent pursuit across the rooftops of New Orleans; a multiple-vehicle high-speed car chase over a partly raised drawbridge down to the docks which ends in savage fistfights and shoot-outs; a vicious assault on a ranch home resulting in nearly a dozen bloody deaths, a hellish conflagration, and a spectacularly collapsing burning staircase (with Matt hanging on for dear life); four exceedingly ferocious fights to the death in the filthy mud and water of the rain-drenched swamplands; and a final violent battle between the two principals in an elegant hall filled with medieval weaponry, and *Avenging Force* should satisfy even the most demanding action fan.

Recounted *Avenging Force* director Sam Firstenberg:

> My talent was to be able to take a written page and turn it into a visual story. The Action genre is pure cinema magic; in my films I enjoy 6–7 minute action sequences. Usually in a script these scenes are very vaguely described. Now on-set you must collaborate with your crew to come up with a choreographed sequence that will later cut together in the editing room. Something is created from nothing. All action sequences should have a beginning, middle and end, some type of conclusion. It should tell a mini story.[3]

And tell a story he does, as Firstenberg stages these set-pieces with a firm grasp of pacing and editing to generate maximum suspense and impact. Given that the two principal actors, Dudikoff and James, performed "90 percent of their own stunts" (with *100 percent*

Prey Matt Hunter (Michael Dudikoff) faces off with one of his masked hunters.

of the action being actual physical stunts in this pre–CGI era), realism stands paramount. And this realism often extended to brutal extremes. One of the most impressive—and appalling—stunts comes during the Pentangle attack on Matt's ranch house. When Matt rescues Larry's young son from the burning structure, he climbs atop the gabled roof with the child in his arms. One of the killers takes careful aim with his crossbow and shoots Matt in the leg, causing him to tumble off the upper gable, striking it end over end, with the child flying from his arms to hit the roof and then plummet to the ground below. Adding brutal insult to devastating injury, one of the Pentangle killers walks up to the two prone protagonists and casually shoots the 5-year-old child gazing up at him with frightened eyes. This stunt (and scene) leaves a mark.

But *Avenging Force* is more than just a series of falls, rolls, chases, and crashes, for James Booth's screenplay offers enough character development and interaction to go beyond the stereotypical cardboard characterizations found in so many other action flicks of this time. Several scenes concisely reveal the genuine affection Larry and Matt share, as well as the love they both have for their families. Contrasted with this are scenes displaying the bigotry and monomania of the four antagonists, portrayed through their interactions with their underlings, peers and one another, their vaunted social positions and affected manners masking an arrogance and sadism that explodes in their sick, competitive game of hunting humans.

"*Avenging Force*'s villains," posited a publicity article, "represent the American individualist dream gone off the paranoid deep end, and are a reflection of certain disturbing political currents—i.e., the emergence of a New Right radical fringe—observed in the U.S. recently." (Take *that*, Ronald Reagan!) Scripter James Booth even took some dialogue inspiration from a then-recent court case involving a White Supremacist group who claimed responsibility for the assassination of a liberal radio talk-show host in Oregon. "A couple of them were led out of the courthouse, and someone yelled, 'You guys are finished!'" recounted Booth. "And one of them answered back, 'We're just beginning.' That isn't just idle talk."[4] This made it into Booth's script in the form of Glastonbury's response to Matt Hunter's observation that Pentangle was finished: "No, we're only just beginning."

Such obvious moral politicizing, with Glastonbury even touting the merits of Adolf Hitler at one point as "a man ahead of his time"(!), though about as subtle as the movie's *raison d'etre* (its action scenes), still remains a secondary (though colorful) subtext. It bleeds into but doesn't preach at nor detract from the movie's real point—good guys taking out bad guys in spectacular fashion. "The political material," explained director Firstenberg, "is beneath the action, which gives it a certain resonance. But it's not the main order of business. *Avenging Force* is about thrills, suspense, excitement."[5]

Avenging Force packs a punch—and then some. Killing off one of the two heroic protagonists half-way through the movie *and* his entire family (not to mention the survivor's kindly grandfather to boot!) offers a real shock to the viewer's system. But it's far from gratuitous—and not simply there for a cheap "thrill"—as this disturbing twist drives the story forward, providing motivation not only for the protagonist but for the viewer as well, who's invested plenty of time in these likable and engaging characters, only to see them die senselessly and horribly.

Firstenberg makes excellent use of authentic New Orleans and bayou locales in which to stage his action. "There had been discussions about possibly filming in Los Angeles," he said, "but the film is so closely linked to New Orleans and surrounding areas, there was really no choice but to film there."[6] From the gilt and glitter of a Mardi Gras parade down an historic New Orleans street to the otherworldly cypress trees and rain-drenched oppression of the Louisiana bayous, Firstenberg makes the most of the exotic environment. During the brutal battles in the swamp, one can almost smell the decaying foliage and feel the muddy slime as the principals grapple in the clinging muck and snake-infested waters. This location shooting posed more than logistical challenges to the filmmakers. "You can be walking in mud up to your knees, you take another step and suddenly you're in up to your chest," recounted Firstenberg, who had his crew lay sections of chain-link fence and plywood sheets down under the mud to prevent such calamities.[7] As for snakes, the production employed what they dubbed "Snake Wranglers" to form a protective perimeter around the filming area to keep the potentially dangerous animals away from cast and crew. "They killed maybe 40, 50 snakes during the three weeks we were there," reported stunt coordinator B. J. Davis. "I was bitten by a water moccasin but his teeth didn't penetrate my boots."[8]

Several things keep *Avenging Force* from being the perfect action movie, however. While Michael Dudikoff injects plenty of enthusiastic athleticism into his role, his baby face and youthful demeanor fail to convince as a hardened former C.I.A. operative whose barked commands are instantly obeyed by other, more mature agents. And while he tries valiantly to let emotions play across his generally stoic countenance, he rarely succeeds. But this immaturity is almost made up for by Dudikoff's physical efforts, as he flees, fights and falls through scene after scene of violent confrontation, often while covered with, or even immersed in, muddy swamp slime. "The methodology of breaking down a character," declares Dudikoff on his official website, "is similar to the regimen of martial arts training. I rehearse and prepare for a scene with the repetition and focus I learned in doing my katas (karate forms), to the point that the scene flows with dance-like fluidity."[9] And at least in its physical aspect, he succeeds admirably.

Fortunately, Dudikoff's co-star, Steve James, brings a natural charm and likability to his supporting role (despite having to ridiculously rip off his shirt to expose his muscular chest at nearly every opportunity). James had a rocky relationship with Dudikoff, however, dating back to their first co-starring encounter on *American Ninja* the previous year. On that film, said James, "Michael knew boxing but didn't know martial arts, so he had to learn it on the set. I'm sure having this big muscular guy around who studied martial arts [James was a black belt] didn't help his insecurities. There was a little jealousy on his part that I was going to show him up.... There was a lot of tension between us at times."[10] Said tension certainly didn't show on *Avenging Force*, as the two have an easy chemistry together, and (perhaps on the more mature James' part, who was a better actor than Dudikoff) display what appears to be genuine affection. This last was vitally important to the film's story, since it's Matt's loyalty toward his friend and former partner that drives the plot and even creates the eponymous *Avenging Force* partnership itself.

The script, though generally well-constructed and fast paced, also contains the occasional inconsistency and even a few "huh-what?" moments. For instance, when Larry and Matt realize Pentangle has set up a second assassination attempt, they decide to take the bait and walk into the trap anyway—though neither one has a gun! So they face down a horde of armed killers at an abandoned shipyard with nothing but Matt's pickup truck, using their fists and feet to overpower the machine-gun and shotgun toting assassins. And they often neglect to even pick up the dropped weapons of the numerous killers they beat into submission one by one. Though a well-staged and exciting sequence, it makes no logical sense.

The climactic confrontation between Matt and Glastonbury, while excitingly choreographed, incorporating various spears, maces and swords, contains a near-fatal flaw: The stunt double for John P. Ryan looks nothing like the rather long-in-the-tooth actor. And while Ryan does an excellent job of bringing out this arrogant hunter-of-men's egomaniacal menace during his various dialogue scenes, the 50-year-old actor can't bring the same conviction to his physical confrontations, so that those shots of Ryan himself in action look slow and over-choreographed when intercut with his much more agile (and obvious) stunt double. After all the fantastic fight and chase scenes and spectacular stunt work that came before, it's a pity the ultimate combat remains so unconvincing.

The film's somewhat open-ended finish also disappoints. The obvious implication that Admiral Brown is the secret fifth leader of Pentangle and will continue its nefarious activities sacrifices a satisfying closure for a moment that all but becomes a giant neon sign flashing "Sequels Welcome."

Even with these flaws, however, *Avenging Force* succeeds where it matters most. "I did not intend the Cannon movies to be serious, they are fun movies," recounted Firstenberg on his stint for the company (*Avenging Force* was the fifth of seven action-oriented movies he helmed for Cannon). "So the stereotyping and the over the top action is intentional so action fans can just watch and enjoy and have good time."[11] Flesh out its MDG skeleton with some political food for thought, and this actionful entry becomes a cinematic *Force* to be reckoned with in the Most Dangerous Action arena.

Production

Avenging Force was originally intended as a vehicle for Chuck Norris, with some suspecting that it was written as a sequel to Norris' hit 1985 film *Invasion USA*. According to director Sam Firstenberg, however, this was not quite the case:

> It's not a sequel but there is a story behind that rumor. Cannon was producing *Invasion USA* with Chuck Norris starring. They immediately wanted to come up with a sequel in order to use Chuck again, to continue squeezing the lemon if you will. The script that was written for the proposed sequel eventually was turned into *Avenging Force*. From a story point it's not a sequel; however, it does have the same characters. When Chuck Norris finished shooting *Invasion USA* he read the script and he didn't like it at all. The original draft was about a father and daughter, and he didn't want to do the film. By this time *American Ninja* had come out and Cannon recognized that Michael Dudikoff was also going to be a mini-star. So the producers gave Michael the script and he responded well to it. The only change that we made to the final draft was the story was now about a brother and sister, because Michael was too young to have a daughter.... Otherwise it's the same script that was presented to Chuck Norris, that's why the main character is named Matt Hunter in both *Invasion USA* and *Avenging Force*.[12]

California-born Michael Dudikoff got his showbusiness start as a professional model, appearing in print ads for such publications as *Seventeen*, *GQ*, and *Esquire* before starting to act in commercials. Television soon followed, with his first appearance coming as Joni's boyfriend on the popular sitcom *Happy Days*. After a number of other appearances on shows like *Dallas* and *Gimme a Break!*, he moved into features, becoming a minor action star with *American Ninja* (1985) and a decade of mostly low-budget sequels and action clones that followed.

Dubbed "the black Rambo" by *Variety*, Steve James had no pretensions about his movies or his roles in them. "Who ever said action films were art?" asked the actor. "These films are about bigger-than-life fantasies that allow audiences to escape the real world for a couple of hours. And I would say that I'm perfectly suited for these films. My agent would like me to be the new Sidney Poitier, but I keep saying that I *really* want to be the new Jim Brown."[13] About *Avenging Force*, James said:

I *hated* that movie. I didn't like the idea that I was playing just another black sacrificial lamb who gets killed along with his family. I told the writer, "You should let my family die and me live so that I could take revenge." I didn't think Michael would go for that, so then I suggested, "Kill me but let my family live." Ultimately, I managed to get them to give the character some substance, but I was still killed off. The only worthwhile thing about doing that movie was being in New Orleans, eating some great food and being around some fine-looking women.[14]

Stuntman/martial artist/actor Steve James began his career in the theater and television commercials, then moved into stuntwork on films like *The Warriors* (1979) and *Dressed to Kill* (1980). He had his first major acting role in the cult favorite exploitationer *The Exterminator* (1980). James went on to play sidekicks to the likes of David Carradine (*P.O.W.: The Escape*), Chuck Norris (*The Delta Force*), and, of course, Michael Dudikoff. According to his wife Christine, James "had a photographic memory, and his happiness came from films.... He was a true actor because even though he was so muscular and forbodeing [sic] on screen, he was caring and protective in life." As a youth, James often served as his smaller classmates' "protector," and went on to become an Eagle Scout, "which gave him excellent values in life."[15] James died in 1993 of pancreatic cancer, age 41. Sidney Poitier delivered his eulogy.

Something of an in-house talent at Cannon Films in the 1980s, Poland-born and Israeli-raised filmmaker Sam Firstenberg came to the U.S. in 1971, attending film school at Columbia College. After meeting producer Menahem Golan (co-founder, along with Yoram Globus, of the prolific 1980s action-movie-making company Cannon Films) while still in school, Firstenberg went to work for the company as an assistant director, graduating to full director in the early '80s when offered *Revenge of the Ninja*. Among his over 20 films are *American Ninja*, *American Ninja 2*, and the inexplicable *Breakin' 2: Electric Boogaloo*(!). When asked what he considers to be his best, Firstenberg responded:

The most interesting from a cinematic standpoint is *Avenging Force*. Unfortunately it wasn't as successful as *American Ninja* financially, but it has deeper complexity in the story. We had a large budget for that film and we were able to shoot in and around the bayous of New Orleans; we even re-created Mardi Gras. That sequence itself involved over 4000 extras and took two days to shoot. All of this helped give the film a certain "look," and I feel the action is very compelling. We tried to capture the dark side of New Orleans, and after all these years the story still holds together.[16]

Though it didn't completely fail financially, *Avenging Force* was not the *American Ninja*–sized hit that Cannon's executives sought, as it grossed just under $5 million domestically upon its initial theatrical release. Consequently, any sequel plans were scuttled in favor of other franchise pursuits (like *American Ninja 2, 3, 4,* and *5*, two of these with Dudikoff).

CREDITS: Director: Sam Firstenberg; Producers: Manahem Golan, Yoram Globus; Screenplay: James Booth; Cinematographer: Gideon Porath; Music: George S. Clinton; Production Designer: Marcia Hinds; Editor: Michael J. Duthie; Production Company: Golan-Globus; Distribution Company: Cannon; Release Date: September 13, 1986; Running Time: 104 minutes; MPAA Rating: R.

CAST: Michael Dudikoff (Matt Hunter); Steve James (Larry Richards); James Booth (Admiral Brown); Bill Wallace (Wade Delaney); John P. Ryan (Professor Elliott Glastenbury); Karl Johnson (Commander Jeb Wallace); Marc Alaimo (Charlie Lavall).

10

Sci-Fi Game
Slave Girls from Beyond Infinity (1987)

Big Movie. Big Production. Big Girls.—ad line

Synopsis

A scantily-clad woman races through a jungle, pursued by a strange, mutant monster with a laser gun. As the creature closes in on its prey, a man steps out of the shadows and dispatches the beast, then advances on the girl.

Cut to a spaceship moving through space. Inside is a dank dungeon with two more scantily-clad beauties chained to the floor (apparently captives of space slavers). One of them, Darla (Elizabeth Cayton), breaks her chains(!), then helps free the other, Tisa (Cindy Beal). Stealing a space shuttle, they pick up a "beacon" from a "small planetoid." The beacon turns out to be a tractor beam that forces them to crash into the planetoid's ocean.

Darla emerges from the surf alone, and walks through the alien jungle to find a castle-like structure whose portal slides open to admit her into a large hall festooned with animal skins and trophy heads. Inside, she's confronted by an imposing robot, which remains silent until its owner, Zed (Don Scribner), makes his presence known on the staircase. Zed tells her that he and his two "androids" live alone in this "old fortress built by space pirates" on this, his private island. Tisa makes her appearance; she survived the crash as well, and preceded Darla to the castle.

At dinner, Zed introduces the two girls to his other "guests," brother and sister Rik (Carl Horner) and Shela (Brinke Stevens), survivors of an earlier wreck. The conversation turns to the sport of hunting, of which Zed is an avid devotee. He goes out to hunt every night, relates a tipsy Rik. But Rik only feigns drunkenness, and as Zed plays a weird musical instrument as entertainment for his guests, Rik relates his suspicions to Darla. "One night, after dinner, he took our pilot into the trophy room. Last night he took our navigator. We haven't seen them since.... He says they've gone hunting."

That night Rik goes to Darla's room, telling her that now his own sister has gone missing. The two sneak downstairs and enter Zed's mysterious trophy room, where they find Tisa already there ("Somebody had to find out what's in this place," she explains). When Zed suddenly returns from his most recent nocturnal hunt, the trio scurries from the trophy room. Zed opens the sack his two robots had been carrying for him and lifts out a human head! Zed then produces the captive Shela and rapes her.

Darla determines that they've got to prepare for what's to come, and she and Rik sneak

Tisa (Cindy Beal, left) and Darla (Elizabeth Cayton) as the *Slave Girls from Beyond Infinity*.

out to rig several deadly traps in the jungle, while Tisa covers for her two friends by distracting a robot sent to check on them, insisting it accompany her to the beach for a topless swim! After setting their traps, Darla and Rik sneak back into Darla's room just after dawn and feign having sex when they hear Zed come to check on them. The phony embrace develops into a real one, and the two become lovers.

As Rik leaves Darla's room, one of Zed's robots knocks him unconscious. That night, Zed sets Rik loose with a laser gun (but it "won't activate for 10 minutes"), and hunts him down. Out in the jungle, Rik backs into a huge spider web, and Zed coldly shoots two (laser) bolts into him with his crossbow.

Back at the castle, Darla, Tisa and Shela awaken to find themselves decked out in the doeskin bikinis they wore when they arrived (where Shela's came from is anybody's guess, as she was *not* one of the "slave girls") and chained to a post in the trophy room. "I intend to hunt you," Zed tells them. He gives them each a knife and an hour's head start, and informs them of "a temple on the far side of my island containing high-powered laser weapons. If you can make it that far, those weapons will give you more than a fighting chance."

During the subsequent hunt, Zed avoids the traps previously set by Darla and Rik, shoots Shela, but then falls prey to a sharpened spike left by Darla on the path. As Zed's robots tend to his wound, the girls find a huge stone wall (presumably the temple Zed mentioned). Fortunately, Darla can read the hieroglyphics etched into the stone, and so can open the portal. Inside the mysterious fog-shrouded structure the girls find not only the laser weapons, but the humpbacked mutant monster seen at the film's beginning *and*

SLAVE GIRLS FROM BEYOND INFINITY

BIG MOVIE. BIG PRODUCTION. BIG GIRLS.

TITAN PRODUCTIONS Presents "SLAVE GIRLS FROM BEYOND INFINITY" Starring ELIZABETH CAYTON, CINDY BEAL, BRINKE STEVENS, DON SCRIBNER and introducing CARL HORNER as the Director of Photography KEN WIATRAK Edited by TOM CALLAWAY Music Composed and Conducted by CARL DANTE Screenplay by KEN DIXON Co-Producers JON ENG and MARK WOLF Produced and Directed by KEN DIXON

R — RESTRICTED UNDER 17 REQUIRES ACCOMPANYING PARENT OR ADULT GUARDIAN

two alien zombies! Escaping the monsters, Darla and Tisa race back into the jungle, where they run into Zed and exchange laser fire. Darla is knocked off a log into a chasm, and Zed takes Tisa prisoner. Back at the castle, Zed is about to rape Tisa when the door opens and in strides Darla, armed with a gladiator's sword and shield. (Darla didn't fall to her death after all, having hung onto a branch.) Zed grabs an axe from the wall, and the two fight. Tisa, meanwhile, takes out one of the robots by deflecting its laser blast with a piece of armor. As the remaining robot advances on her, the humpbacked monster from the temple bursts in and shoots the robot with its own laser gun. It also delivers a debilitating blow to Zed before advancing towards Tisa. Darla lays into the beast with a mace-like weapon, and the creature inexplicably disappears in a flash of lavender light! Darla and Tisa escape in Zed's hidden spaceship, while the wounded Zed crawls to his trophy room and activates a self-destruct mechanism. As Zed's fortress blows up, Darla and Tisa speed away into space.

How "Dangerous" Is It?

Amazingly, the science fiction entry *Slave Girls from Beyond Infinity* is a fairly faithful adaptation of Connell's classic story (with sci-fi trappings, of course). In fact, it so slavishly apes the two previous most faithful cinematic versions (1932's *The Most Dangerous Game* and 1945's *A Game of Death*) that a visit from the plagiarism police would not be out of order. Entire dialogue passages are taken, often nearly word-for-word, from James Ashmore Creelman's *The Most Dangerous Game* screenplay, with a few steals from Norman Houston's *A Game of Death* script for good measure (not to mention the direct borrowings from Connell).

Sample dialogue swipes:

Zed: "The barbarians know that it is only after the chase that man indulges. You know the saying of the Altair chieftains? 'Hunt first the enemy, then the woman.'"
Zed: "One passion builds on another. Kill, then love. When you know that, then you know ecstasy."
Sheila: "Every night he [Zed] packs us off to bed like bad little children."
Zed: "No my dear, *charming* children."
Zed [giving knives to the protagonists]: "Here are your claws and fangs."
Zed: "Death is always incredible — always for others, never for ourselves!"

And on and on. The audacity of not only leaving Connell unacknowledged in the credits, but Creelman and Huston as well, borders on the criminal.

From Connell the film takes the intriguing discourse on hunting itself.

Shela: "This obsession with hunting you call 'sport'— isn't it just a little inconsistent? The beast in the jungle killing for merely his existence is called 'savage'; the man killing just for sport is called 'civilized.' Isn't that a bit contradictory?"
Zed: "What makes you think it isn't just as much sport for the animal as it is for the man? Take that fellow right there, for instance [motioning to a saber-toothed, cat-like beast mounted on the wall]. There was never a time when he couldn't have gotten away, but he didn't want to. He got interested in hunting *me*. He didn't hate me for stalking him any

---

Opposite: "Big Movie. Big Production. Big Girls." Had they added "Big Guns" to this tag-line, they at least would have been part-right.

> more than I hated him for trying to charge me. As a matter of fact, we admired each other."
> Shela: "Perhaps. But would you change places with him?"
> Zed: "Not now."
> Tisa: "Don't evade the issue. Would there be as much sport in the game if *you* were the prey instead of the hunter?"
> Zed: "That is something I will never have to decide. This universe is divided into two types of people—the hunter and the hunted."

These sentiments, uttered by the protagonist Rainsford in both Connell's original story and the first two cinematic adaptations, are here espoused by the antagonist Zed, the Zaroff character. While they retain their thought-provoking qualities, the comments carry far less resonance here, as they lack the irony generated when postulated by a hunter who is soon to become the prey. Additionally, this reversal denies the power found in Connell's story when the protagonist, Rainsford, is forced to re-examine his whole philosophy of hunter and hunted—of life itself.

Strangely, given the sheer volume of his thefts, *Slave Girls from Beyond Infinity* producer-director-screenwriter Ken Dixon chose not to include the all-important reasoning for Zed's decision to hunt humans. There's no talk of Zed losing his passion for hunting—for life—because he had become too proficient a killer of animals. There's no mention of ennui or how he suffered at the thought of having no new challenges. There's no prideful boasting of "having done a rare thing" in creating a new type of "game" to hunt. As a result, Zed becomes little more than a madman and rapist who just happens to enjoy hunting. Rather than having taken an obsession to the extreme out of a crazed necessity (according to his own warped viewpoint, anyway), he's just a thug who enjoys killing whatever and whoever he can.

Shamelessly, Dixon doesn't stop at pilfering dialogue snippets—he apes incidents, set-ups, and entire *scenes* from both Connell's tale and the earlier films. For instance, when heroine Darla (nee Rainsford) first enters the castle, she's confronted by an imposing-looking robot (né Ivan), who remains menacingly silent in response to her inquiries until its master, Zed (né Zaroff), makes his presence known on the staircase.

Then, upon their first meeting after dinner that evening, a survivor of a previous wreck, Rik, steers Darla towards a window as Zaroff ... er, Zed, plays the piano ... er, "holographic audiosibeoscope," for his guests' enjoyment. There Rik surreptitiously relays his suspicions to the newcomer. It's an exact replica of a sequence from the 1932 *Most Dangerous Game*, except the genders have been reversed — Darla takes the Rainsford role, while Rik plays the "Eve" part.

Other steals from the previous films include Zed spying the deadfall trip vine at the last second and firing a bolt into it to bring it down — just like Zaroff in the '32 and '45 versions (in Connell's tale, Zaroff merely jumps back to avoid the falling log, receiving a slight injury to his shoulder); Zed warning his prey not to venture into "the Phantom Zone" (a futuristic stand-in for "Fog Hollow" in the films and "Death Swamp" in the story); and the surviving pair speeding away in Zed's boat ... er, spaceship, at the end.

To Dixon's credit(?), he was astute enough to steal the best from *both* worlds (the '32 *Most Dangerous Game* and the '45 *Game of Death*) when he borrows from the 1945 version the improved notion of having the brother (Rik) only *pretend* to be an obnoxious drunk in order to mislead their sinister host, thus making the throwaway character from the first film far more intriguing and sympathetic. Dixon steals another major enhancement found in *A*

Game of Death by having his protagonist, Darla, rig her traps *before* the climactic hunt, anticipating Zed's intentions and demonstrating the heroine's intelligence and resourcefulness. And, just like in *A Game of Death*, Dixon includes a preliminary hunt in which Zed tracks and kills Rik, making this character's demise far more poignant (particularly since — in a rare *original* twist — he and the heroine had become lovers).

Critique

From the opening shot, in which a blank-faced, big-breasted blonde in a doeskin bikini runs out of the fog between some potted plants towards the camera — and then hugs herself to accentuate her considerable cleavage — you know that this is not your father's "Most Dangerous Game." (Of course, the title *might* be something of a giveaway as well.) You also know, after watching said blonde's careful, half-speed "flight" through the cramped soundstage "jungle," pursued by a goofy-looking humpbacked mutant creature with an impossibly large laser-gun, that this sci-fi exploitation take on Connell's tale is, well, just not very good.

The next sequence, however, raises one's hopes a bit higher via some decent-looking spaceship model work and convincingly dingy sets for the prison ship's *Alien*esque interior. Of course, said rising hopes immediately plummet to the depths of cinematic despair when we're introduced to our two heroines and realize they're far more plastic than the aforementioned models. Additionally, the special effects — so important to a science fiction movie such as this — become less and less special as the film unspools. Though the budget (reportedly only $120,000 at final tally) imposed obvious restrictions, producer-director Dixon showed little inventiveness in surmounting his fiscal difficulties. The heroines' crash into the ocean, for instance, consists of a primitive computer monitor showing (in blue monochrome) an approaching aerial shot of what looks like a lake (*not* an "ocean"). Then the screen simply goes black, while the next thing we see is Darla walking out of the surf onto a rocky beach and collapsing (with *dry*, perfectly-coiffed hair, no less). Sad. But it only gets worse when Darla strolls into a rocky cave by the shoreline and steps out the other side moments later right into a thick, steamy jungle (complete with swirling fog, hanging creepers, and exotic bird sounds)! Both of these ridiculously abrupt transitions only point up the fact that the filmmakers have bitten off far more than they can chew.

Further events do little to aid one's celluloid mastication. When Rik backs into a ratty, ropey giant spider web during his "hunt," it conjures up images from *Queen of Outer Space* or *Missile to the Moon*. Except even those risible '50s cheapies offered a giant spider to go with it (goofy as it may have looked), which Dixon and co. fail to provide! Zed's two robots, dubbed Vak and Krel (the latter a nod, perhaps, to *Forbidden Planet*?), sport vaguely skull-like faces (more than a little reminiscent of *The Terminator*) atop bulky, awkward and impractical armored bodies obviously assembled at the back of a combination Army Surplus/Hoover repair shop.

During the final hunt, Darla and Tisa cross a chasm-spanning log (à la *King Kong*) that actually spans a matte painting whose realism fails to match even that of a Frazetta fantasy painting. Adding improbable insult to unrealistic injury, Dixon returns to this same spot (and painting) not once but *twice* more! And the picture concludes with the girls in Zed's stolen (model) spaceship making their escape by zigging and zagging (for no particular reason) through a *Land of the Lost*-level, Saturday morning kids show-style papier mache rock canyon.

Unfortunately, Ken Dixon's direction is right in line with the shoddy effects and plagiarized script. As Darla advances warily (i.e. slowly) through his cut-rate "jungle," Dixon's camera moves in front of her in a slo-mo replication of the mobile cinematography from *The Most Dangerous Game* and *A Game of Death*. Here, however, it's not so much to create any sense of motion or excitement (things move too slowly for that), but to give viewers a good, long look at her bikini-clad body. Dixon utilizes this technique again during Zed's hunting of Rik, with the camera chasing Rik through the jungle in close-up. While no doubt the intent was to ape the exciting camera movement found in the chase scenes from the first two films, here the camera is so tight on Rik that it generates more claustrophobia than excitement. And the scene moves into the realm of the ridiculous when Rik literally turns on his heels and heads straight back *at* the camera, with the lens now retreating in front of him down the path he'd just come!

Dixon completely botches the pivotal trophy room sequence, which serves as a shocking highlight in the previous film versions. When Darla asks, "Did you *see* what's on those walls?" Tisa responds, "Yeah, that's what he's planning for all of us." This dialogue is chock full of unintentional irony for the viewer, as Dixon neglects to reveal *anything* on said walls. The lighting in the chamber is so dim as to render whatever "trophies" might be lurking there all but invisible. Dixon offers no startling shots of human heads mounted on the wall or bobbing grotesquely in tanks, no chilling tableaus of victims in their death-throes, and no shocked reactions from the principles. Had the audience no prior knowledge of the plot, the viewer would have no idea what the two girls are talking about.

Only in the next scene, when Zed returns from his hunt and the protagonists retreat from the room, does Dixon finally reveal any gruesome trophies (with these exposed so casually and only in the background that they make little impact). For the big shock, Zed opens the sack his two robots had been carrying and lifts out a human head. Dixon's poor timing—waiting until now to produce his trophy-room surprise, when the protagonists are not only missing from the scene but safely back in their rooms—greatly diminishes not only the terror of the revelation (by removing the protagonists' horrified reactions) but any suspense the sequence might hold. And the phony-looking Styrofoam Halloween head (totally exposed for what it is by the harsh spot-lighting) completely negates whatever impact might have been left.

As a screenwriter, Dixon fares no better than as producer-director. It speaks volumes about Dixon's scribbling abilities that the film's best dialogue is all stolen. When he's forced to come up with his own lines, the hackneyed result falls well short of Dixon's prototypes. For example:

> Tisa: "You're brilliant."
> Darla: "Dazzling—people have to wear sunglasses."
> Darla: "Did we have to steal such an expensive ship? Do you know how much time these things spend in the shop?"
> Darla: "He's ventilated with laser holes; he's history now."
> Tisa: "History has a way of repeating itself."

Then there is Dixon's attempt at comedy relief when he has the two thrift-store *Robocop* clones bicker among themselves:

> Vak: "The Master will not be pleased with your absence."
> Krel: "*You* displease *me*."
> Vak: "And *I* ignore *you*."
> Krel: "I'm going to inform the master."
> Vak: "Tattletale!"

It's not only the clichéd and/or childish dialogue that bedevils Dixon's screenplay; there are the various "sci-fi" details. When Darla and Tisa escape from their prison-ship cell, for instance, they do so by "reversing the polarity on these cuffs," thus somehow shorting out the electronic lock. They accomplish this by simply holding up their manacles to the keypad! With security (and polarized manacles) such as this, it's no wonder these two seem to be the only slave girls aboard, as all the rest obviously escaped long ago.

Then come the frequent continuity errors, demonstrating how haphazardly the script (and film) was put together. When Darla asks Rik where they can find some laser guns, Rik replies, "You *heard* what he said about hunting with bow and arrow; if he has any laser rifles he must keep them locked up here somewhere." Zed has mentioned *nothing* about hunting with "bow and arrow." Later, the three girls find a body hanging in their previously-set snare trap. But the camera never reveals quite who—or what—it is, and the girls don't elaborate, nor even act surprised; they simply move on. Having seen only nine characters (with three of those being either monsters or robots), it's a major head-scratching moment.

Further scripting problems force the fleeing girls to behave downright stupidly. When Tisa loses the map Zed had given them, she suggests she go back alone to find it, and the other two agree—just moments after Darla had insisted they all stick together for safety!

Then there are such unexplained—and ridiculous—anomalies as Darla bursting into Zed's castle decked out like a Roman gladiator (where did she get the anachronistic weaponry after falling off that log?); a pair of zombies lurking in "the Phantom Zone" (why zombies—apart from a desperate attempt to inject a few kitchen-sink monsters into the proceedings?); the humpbacked mutant from scene one arriving suddenly to strike down Zed at the end (what *is* it and *why* is it there?); and said monster literally disappearing in a flash of lavender light when struck in the back with a mace (???). Such a game of plug-the-plot-holes quickly grows wearisome. Though only 74 minutes long (with four of those comprising the end credits), *Slave Girls from Beyond Infinity* feels *muuuch* longer.

Acting-wise, the cast of unknowns (with '80s low-rent "scream queen" Brinke Stevens being the only thespian who could pass as any kind of "name") offers up what one might expect from a movie called *Slave Girls from Beyond Infinity*. As the pivotal Zaroff character Zed, newcomer Don Scribner is at least fairly animated, his facial muscles twitching and his speech quickening as he talks of the "ecstasy" of the hunt. But his dull, lifeless eyes cause his theatrical expressions to ring false, and ultimately he fails to convince. Of course, juxtaposed with the passive plasticity of Elizabeth Cayton and Cindy Beal as the two main heroines (to whom the word "inflection" is utterly foreign), Scribner—whose subsequent career consisted of appearances in straight-to-video actioners like *Rapid Assault* (1997) and soft-core thrillers like *The Escort III* (1999)—nearly becomes Sir Lawrence Olivier, proving Einstein's theory that indeed it *is* all relative.

Production

While *Slave Girls from Beyond Infinity* looks, sounds and acts like a low-budget straight-to-video exploitationer, it, amazingly, received a (limited) theatrical distribution. But that's not due to its quality or the faith of Charles Band's Empire Pictures in same, but rather to a marketing tool. As low-budget filmmaker/distributor Fred Olen Ray (*Hollywood Chainsaw Hookers*, *Deep Space* [both 1988]) explained, "They need[ed] these small theatrical releases to help boost up their video sales. That was the only reason that guys like Charlie Band would put out movies like *Slave Girls from Beyond Infinity*, because of the home video sales."[1]

Of the haphazard shoot, production assistant (and "Mutant" player) Fred Tate remembers:

> I was the alien mutant thing in the film *Slave Girls from Beyond Infinity*, and it was officially supposed to be an "alien zombie," but the production could only afford to get an old coat and a set of "alien hands" and an "alien facemask," so if you look really hard at the feet when I surprise the two in the "jungle," you will see a set of New Balance running shoes! [I] also worked as set painter, set builder, production assistant, sometimes boom man. [I was] the only person the studio [Empire] would trust to go down to the bank every week and pick up the cash to pay everyone and actually bring it back to the set (ex-military). [I was also] the person who told them to set that really stupid booby trap that nails Zed's leg (and it was really stupid!), the person who told them *not* to load the real crossbows on the set (walls like paper, 150 pound pull crossbows — see the problem), and the all around set slave (as most of us crew members/extras were on the set!), because we did everything![2]

According to Tate, "The production only had $90,000 to make the film, and when it didn't get made for that (only about 45 minutes of film ready for edit), we got $30,000 to do two weeks of re-shoot to complete the film. Yes, $30,000 for *everything*, and we not only did it, we came in under budget!"[3]

Well, at least they accomplished *something*.

CREDITS: Director/Producer/Screenplay: Ken Dixon; Directors of Photography: Ken Wiatrak, Tom Callaway; Special Effects Supervisor: Mark Wolf; Androids and Phantazoid Warrior Created by: John Buechler, Mechanical & Makeup Imageries, Inc.; Zombie and Mutant Created by: Joe Reader; Special Visual Effects: John Eng; Music Supervisor: Jonatahn Scott Bogner; Music Composed and Conducted by: Carl Dante; Editors: Bruce Stubblefield, James A. Stewart; Production Company: Titan Productions; Distribution Company: Urban Classics; Release Date: September 18, 1987; Running Time: 74 minutes.

CAST: Elizabeth Cayton (Darla), Cindy Beal (Tisa), Brinke Stevens (Shela), Don Scribner (Zed), Carl Horner (Rik), Kirk Graves (Vak), Randolph Roehbling (Krel), Bud Graves (Phantazoid Warrior), Jeffrey Blanchard (Phantazoid Warrior), Mike Cooper (Guard), Greg Cooper (Guard), Sheila White (Girl), Fred Tate (Mutant), Jacques Schardo (Zombie).

11

Rambo Game
War Cat (1987)

"She was hunted like an animal, until they became the prey..." — ad line

Synopsis

Tina (Jannina Poynter), a pretty, young writer, returns to her father's small home town to research a book on her dad, a military expert. In between typewriter sessions, she jogs and fishes in a stream—with a pointy stick, cooking the speared fish over an open fire! Local creep and convicted sex offender Manny (Macka Foley) breaks into her cabin, resulting in Manny's arrest after being felled by an elbow to the face (Tina is well-versed in military combat and self-defense).

Meanwhile, a group of survivalists, run by Major Hargrove (David O'Hara), sets up their paramilitary camp in the nearby desert to gird themselves against the coming "war." As the Major explains, "When the shit hits the fan, every asshole out there is gonna be killin' and eatin' each other in a week's time. There's gonna be no law. Well, we got the organization and the firepower to establish a *new* law in this area—*our* law."

The Major goes into town to bail Manny, one of his underlings, out of jail. On the way back to the compound, the Major and Manny run across a biker gang called "the Thrill Killers" (an obvious nod to original director Ray Dennis Steckler; see the Production section). But the Major scares off the bikers with his handy AK-47.

Undeterred, the gang decides to "have some fun" by following the Major and storming the compound, brandishing pistols. The survivalists hit them with everything from machine guns to bazookas in the biggest show of military overkill since the invasion of the Falklands, leaving all but three of the bikers dead. After coldly executing two of the survivors (including a woman!) with a bullet to the head, the Major gives the third (another woman) to Manny as a plaything.

Back at town, Manny and a compatriot run across Tina out jogging (yet again) and force her at gunpoint to return to their compound. There they lock her up with the other girl, then systematically rape her.

Meanwhile, two killers (Jason Holt and Ed Walters) rob a gun store, shoot the clerk, then head for the mountains, stopping to kill a couple at their home—for no discernible reason.

Back at the camp, the Major decides it's time to dispose of Tina and the other girl "because we can't afford to feed the extra mouths"(!). In a bid to stave off her execution,

War Cat, with Jannina Poynter, was retitled *Angel of Vengeance* for its U.K. video release.

Tina taunts the Major. "I now know why you didn't take me last night; that gun is the only prick you've got!" Bartering for her life, she continues: "I want a chance — give me one chance, you bastard! ... Let me go, and you and your men hunt me. You think you're tough? Hunt a woman, an unarmed woman." The idea appeals to the Major, and he posits, "I think we can use the exercise. What do you guys think? Want to have a little fun?" So the "fun" hunt is on, with Tina given a two-hour head start.

Meanwhile, the two killers strike again, murdering a picnicking couple and taking their sportscar.

In the woods, Tina kills one of her pursuers with two pointy sticks (jabbing them in his eyes), then lures another into a snare trap and blows him up with his own grenade. A third she kicks off a cliff, while she shoots a fourth with a crossbow (taken from an earlier victim), leaving only Manny and the Major still on the hunt. Tina lures Manny with a tape recorder (apparently considered standard issue military gear by at least one of the survivalists) and slits his throat. Then she heads back to the compound and blows everything up (along with the few remaining men), before tossing the Major into a rattlesnake pit.

Making her way to the highway, Tina is spotted by the two killers in their stolen sportscar. When the duo offer her a ride, she answers, "Sure, why not?" — while hiding a hand grenade behind her back.

How "Dangerous" Is It?

Connell's name is conspicuous in *War Cat*'s credits only by its absence — which may not be unreasonable given that the film takes nothing but the general concept from the author's story. (When asked if he was familiar with Connell's famous short story, director Ted V. Mikels responded, "Never heard of it."[1]) The tropical island setting has been replaced by a desert/mountain tableau, while the lone madman obsessed with hunting has transformed into half a dozen yahoo survivalists obsessed with, well, survivalism. Likewise, the male protagonist/prey well versed in woodcraft has become a female protagonist/prey well versed in military survival skills. Consequently, the intimate, almost sadistically noble (at least in the eyes of Connell's antagonist) mano-a-mano struggle from the original story, in which two worthy opponents participate in a crafty dance of death ("Your brain against mine; your woodcraft against mine," as Zaroff describes it), devolves into a human-hounds-in-pursuit free-for-all as a whole group of yabbos chase after their ostensibly helpless prey with everything from automatic rifles to hand grenades and bazookas! Gone is the air of intelligence from Connell's story (no "outdoor chess" here), leaving only a cut-rate *Rambo* action-movie in its place. "You have two hours ... and I'm sending my animals after you," the Major tells Tina, literalizing the level of thought and sophistication this "hunt" offers.

The film does put a novel spin on the concept, however, by having the protagonist *volunteer* to become the prey, as she challenges the man who's about to execute her to play the Most Dangerous Game in a frantic gambit to give herself "a chance." It's an intriguing twist — one that shows her sheer desperation and dire mindset — that unfortunately remains largely unexplored. The survivalists immediately jump at the idea, wanting simply to "have a little fun" and "hunt a lady," with nary a comment or moment of thought; while she goes about her business of dispatching her hunters, again with nary a thought or moment of introspection. (Note: This hunting a human for sport or "fun" — rather than training — is what separates *War Cat* from such "*Almost* Dangerous Game" examples as 1988's *Deadly Prey* and 1995's *Pure Race*.)

War Cat borrows one other notion from Connell — that of the prey setting traps for the hunter(s). At one point Tina sets a rope snare, which results in a pursuer hanging upside down by one leg from a tree, leading to the film's one truly inspired (and blackly comedic) moment: Tina drops one of the man's own live hand grenades on the ground beneath him, just out of reach of the frantic hunter; when the subsequent fireball clears, we see only the man's foot dangling from the rope — all that's left of the sadistic survivalist. Unfortunately, such a brutal moment of cold, calculating and poetic justice becomes a risible spectacle of low-budget fringe filmmaking when the transparent phoniness of the superimposed explosion explodes all sense of reality. And the lighting is so dim that the scene ultimately looks as dark as its intended comedy, inspiring more eye strain than morbid chuckles.

Critique

One of the biggest (of many) problems with *War Cat* is its simplistic screenplay and ill-defined characters and motivations. Original scripters Gary Thompson and Jeffrey C. Hogue obviously drew much of their "inspiration" from the 1978 exploitation classic *I Spit on Your Grave*, which was about a woman writer come to a small town who's raped by a gang of creeps and then exacts brutal revenge. Unfortunately, Thompson and Hogue took the basic scenario but forgot to pilfer the characterization, emotion, moral dilemmas and visceral qualities of that earlier film. "There was very little to the script of *War Cat*," admitted director Ted V. Mikels.[2] He was right.

First off, we know nothing about the protagonist's background, apart from the fact she likes to go jogging and her dad was a military man. Second, we know even less about the Major and his group, and the dynamics involved. They're just a bunch of interchangeable losers dressed in green and carrying automatic weapons who hang out at their desert compound waiting for some vague societal collapse. The one exception is Manny, whose infantile psychosis and history of incarceration for sexual assault single him out as at least *different* from the others.

Then there are the two psycho-killers the film periodically pops back and forth to, about which we know little and care less. They're just there to provide a few respites from the repetitive stalking scenes, and then offer the film's closing "punchline." "I didn't like — and I couldn't fight with [producer/co-writer] Jeff Hogue about it — I didn't like the two guys going around throat-cutting," complained Mikels. "I really wanted to leave that part out. I didn't think it belonged, but Jeff was insistent on it.... That's bad karma to show young people that even such a thing exists — these crazy guys going around shooting and killing people. I had determined even long before that that I would *not* do those things, and yet I couldn't get out of it. Jeff hired me to do the job and I had to do it."[3]

The film's denouement comes off as more nonsensical than ironic. How could Tina possibly know that these two guys offering her a ride are killers? Has her experience with the survivalists colored her outlook on all men? Has being forced to become a brutal Rambette transformed her into a one-woman vigilante force? Has she simply snapped? Neither the screenplay nor Jannina Poynter's (non)acting provides a single clue, so the film ends with a thud — like a joke that's told by someone who really doesn't know how to tell a joke.

Though he didn't have a lot to work with, director Ted V. Mikels should have at least been able to tell the joke. Come to think of it, though, the fringe filmmaker whose best-known works are *The Astro-Zombies* (1968) and *The Corpse Grinders* (1972) shouldn't be expected to pull some cinematic silk purse out of this sow's ear of a screenplay. Mikels throws gas on the flame of ennui, however, with his mundane staging and total non-direction of the actors, further lessening what little emotional impact the sorry script might have made. When talking of the production decades later, Mikels admitted he has very little affinity for the film. "It wasn't my picture," he flatly stated. "I was hired to do the work. That movie belongs to [producer/co-writer] Jeff Hogue."[4] Elaborating further, Mikels concluded, "I'm not pleased with the film.... I just consider myself an entertainer. And that's why in *War Cat* I don't think it's entertaining to see some guy pull a gun and shoot somebody in the face."[5]

Such disaffection no doubt worked against the movie while in production, as Mikels obviously balked at the more exploitative elements of the story. "Hogue wanted all that rough stuff in there. Personally, I wasn't comfortable with it, but he was the one signing the checks."[6] Mikels' "uncomfortable-ness" translates into frequent missed opportunities to make *War Cat* a memorable (or at least watchable) action/exploitation picture. The two executions ("It was too cold and calculated," complained Mikels[7]) are so casually filmed that there's little tension and less bloodshed (just a few post-pop points of stage blood). The pivotal gang-rape scene (upon which the story's second half hinges) is so squeamishly and perfunctorily shot that the viewer can barely tell what happened, much less feel any real visceral or emotional impact. "I didn't even like doing that scene," admitted Mikels, "but there was insistence on doing it. So I said we would do it without showing anything. We'll *imply* that this took place."[8] The sequence begins with a brief shot of Tina (clad in her underwear) tied to a bed. The camera then pans over to one of the soldiers taking off his belt and equipment and putting them on a table where another soldier (Pierre) sits listening to some accordion music! (Note: Mikels is an accordion player who actually performed professionally back in the 1950s before embarking on his filmmaking career.) The first soldier steps out of the scene as the camera stays on Pierre, who idly picks up a wristband from the table and tries it on. The camera cuts to the first soldier returning (presumably from the bed with Tina) to collect his gear from the table, then exit the shack. There's nothing on the soundtrack but what sounds like a tolling bell (and the accordion music, of course) — no screaming, no pleading, no protests ... and no impact.

Apart from the brief death throes of the sticks-in-the-eyes soldier (played by producer Hogue himself, who perhaps demanded from Mikels a bit more "bite" to *his* big death scene), and the hanging-foot gag (which is lit so poorly that it's difficult to see), Mikels shies away from any and all opportunity to make a visceral impact with either blood or breasts (the film offers no nudity, despite ample situations that simply cry out for flesh — not necessarily to titillate, but to drive home the degradation and reinforce the brutality inherent in the scenario). "I'm not really a blood and gore–type person," admitted Mikels. "I may be known for horror, but if it isn't campy I'm not pleased with it.... I'm a family man. I've got six kids, 25 grandkids, 23 great-grandchildren. I'm not in favor of gore, not in favor of violence — other than *campy* violence.... I don't have good feelings about anything that I think is not in good taste for the general public, to kind of steer young people into thinking. But if you're gonna survive in the industry you do what you have to do."[9]

Mikels handles the demise of his lead villain just as poorly — or carelessly. After being pushed into the snake pit by Tina, the Major stands up and looks around, as a few close-ups of rattlesnakes are intercut with the scene. The sequence then abruptly ends with him just standing there, without expression (as usual) — no snake attacks, no frantic efforts to escape, no screams, no curses, no nothing. And "nothing" is what this poor man's PG-level action(less)-exploitation(less) movie delivers.

According to Mikels, *War Cat*'s budget, "as *I* figured it, was $140,000. But when [producer Jeffrey Hogue] talks about it he says $300,000, so he must have spent extra money. I know he made a tour down in South America and went to Cannes; he did some things that cost money and automatically added to the overall figure of the budget."[10] (Mikels personally received a mere $15,000 for directing, line producing, editing, and renting out his camera equipment.) The finished film actually looks even cheaper than Mikels' lowball figure. For instance, the "compound" consists of one small shack, an old trailer (both painted camouflage), and a wooden tower, with a few sandbags in front of the "building" and two strands of barbed wire strung between a few sticks.

It's always a bad sign when several principal actors also receive some form of production credit. (Production manager Carl Irwin plays one of the survivalists; assistant cameraman Jennifer Collins appears as a biker; producer Jeffrey C. Hogue plays the survivalist who literally gets the sharp end of the stick; etc.) And it's an even worse sign when several actors use their *own names* for their characters. Said signs point towards Amateurville, and that is exactly where *War Cat* ends up.

As Tina, Jannina Poynter (who appears to have been chosen more for her big hair and even bigger cleavage than her thespian prowess) does little but spit out her dialogue, looking like she's just finished sucking on a lemon. No emotion other than gross anger ever crosses her face. Apart from her pasted-on look of enraged defiance, her "acting" consists of climbing around rocks and jogging (and jiggling) in her tight black tank-top. "She was very good, and so easy to work with," commented Mikels.[11] Well, perhaps he's *half* right. *War Cat* was Ms. Poynter's acting debut ("she was a waitress on the [Vegas] strip, which is where Jeff [Hogue] found her and asked her if she wanted to be in the movie," recalled Mikels[12]) *and* apparent swan song, as no other credits for her could be found.

David O'Hara, as the Major, has about as much screen presence as a desert cactus. When he yells at his men, his voice offers plenty of volume but no emotion or conviction to go with it. He looks stiff and uncomfortable in front of the camera, and his eyes, body language and facial expression (or lack thereof) frequently fails to match his words. Though the supposed brains of the outfit, O'Hara's "Major," with his bland looks, big hair (it *was* the '80s) and simplistic speech patterns, doesn't appear smart enough to clean his weapon without shooting himself, much less run a military compound (no matter how small-scale and cut-rate). A former Olympic-level track coach, O'Hara left the sporting world to try his hand at acting but only appeared in a few low-budget efforts in the mid-to-late '80s (such as *The Tomb*, *Armed Response* and *Hard Rock Zombies*).

Macka Foley, as Manny, on the other hand, goes overboard with *his* emoting, playing the sexually deviant Manny like some psychotic Lennie (instead of "Tell about the rabbits," it's "Think about the snake pit" — with which he taunts a victim). His slow, goofy speech, wild eye rolling, and manic gestures complete the picture of a mentally challenged sociopath, which, for all its entertainment value (and his performance *is* amusing at times), does little for the story's — and film's — efficacy. (Foley went on to become a regular bit player in films and on television, appearing in small roles on shows like *Perfect Strangers*, *Nurses* and *The Drew Carey Show*.)

The threadbare budget shows through in more than the shabby sets and amateurish non-acting. During the key scene in which Tina baits the Major into hunting her, for instance, the lighting darkens inexplicably and distractingly. Obviously the sun went behind the clouds just at that moment, but Mikels kept rolling, deeming it good enough (or perhaps he simply didn't notice) rather than take the time to redo the shot. And this was no anomaly, for Mikels' indifferent (and downright careless at times) lighting often varies from bright sun to strain-your-eyes shade in the same scene. The big blowout of a climax, in which Tina shoots her captured bazooka and throws her bag of hand grenades to blow up the entire camp (consisting of the three structures and some oil drums) is often difficult to make out, since the dim, twilight lighting obscures much of the details, leaving only the occasional fireball to light up the screen (perhaps intentional on Mikels' part, as he tried to salvage some verisimilitude while torching his cheap and cheesy sets). "I did 117 camera set-ups in one day with only one camera," boasted Mikels, rather tellingly. "That has to be some sort of a record!"[13]

Production

Filmed in 1986 in the mountains of Northern California and the desert around Las Vegas, and released a year later, *War Cat* is the last film made by veteran exploitationer Ted V. Mikels to receive a theatrical release (albeit a limited one, as it played mostly in the South). Mikels, the low-budget *auteur* behind such independent drive-in dreck as *Blood Orgy of the She Devils* (1972), *The Doll Squad* (1973) and *Ten Violent Women* (1982), was simply a gun-for-hire on *War Cat*. Practicing attorney Jeffrey C. Hogue wanted to break into the film industry and contacted Mikels (based in Las Vegas) in the early 1980s about a project called *Angel of Vengeance*. When Hogue deemed Mikels' proposed budget of $240,000 too steep, the would-be movie mogul approached another no-budget, Vegas-based filmmaker, Ray Dennis Steckler (*Wild Guitar*, 1962; *The Thrill Killers*, 1964; *The Incredibly Strange Creatures Who Stopped Living and Became Mixed-Up Zombies*, 1964). Steckler said he could bring it in for 20 grand, and started shooting background footage of Las Vegas environs. Hogue, however, quickly became disillusioned with Steckler. As Steckler himself recalls, "I was hired to do a Ray Dennis Steckler movie. Hogue wanted a Jeffrey C. Hogue movie. I gave it to Ted [Mikels]."[14]

Mikels took it and ran — to Northern California for the mountain locations, while filming the desert scenes (and interiors) in and around his own Las Vegas digs. "The scene where Bo the woodcutter gets murdered along with his wife was on my property," recounted the filmmaker. "The buildings where the Major and his men are planning all of their attacks were all mine too."[15] Mikels added, "The inside of that shack was 128 degrees that day. It was terribly hot. We had fans blowing but had to cut off the fan every time the camera rolled. It was tough."[16]

The directorial takeover went smoothly, however. As Mikels recalled:

> On my first day of shooting, after I'd taken over the project, the girl playing Tina literally got on her knees, kissed my hand and thanked me for taking over directing the film. It was the scene where her character begs for a chance to escape by making a deal with the Major to have his men hunt her like an animal, kind of like that movie *The Most Dangerous Game*. Again, I'm not proud of this, as Ray [Steckler] is a friend, but it did happen that way. But I did appreciate the fact that she was pleased to have me as director of the movie.[17]

Too bad the viewer can't say the same (though when one imagines what a Ray Dennis Steckler version might have looked like, perhaps Mikels' involvement worked out for the best).

War Cat was rejected for a United Kingdom video certificate by the British Board of Film Censors in 1987 (during the height of the "video nasties" campaign). One wonders just what the Board objected to, as, apart from the sticks-to-the-eyes incident and the dangling leg moment, the movie offers very little grue (and even those two sequences are brief and, in the case of the latter, poorly lit). Perhaps it was the general tone of the film, highlighted by the execution killings (but, again, apart from a little ketchup splatter, this was filmed in a singularly unspectacular fashion). "The gunshots to the heads of the Thrill Killers," recounted Mikels, "was something that I would not have put into a movie of my own making ... it was too cold and calculated ... but it was Jeff's movie, so I did what he asked."[18] Ultimately, perhaps *War Cat*'s banning in the UK is more a comment on the arbitrariness of censorship than any quality (or lack of same) on the film's part. The PG-level *War Cat* as a video nasty ... the mind boggles. (After the censorship hysteria died down somewhat, *War Cat* did finally make it to the UK but under the film's original shooting title, *Angel of Vengeance*.)

CREDITS: Alternate Title: *Warcat* (video), *Angel of Vengeance* (UK); Director/Cinematographer/Editor: Ted V. Mikels; Producer: Jefferey C. Hogue; Associate Producer: T. Craig Keller; Screenplay: Gary Thompson, Jeffrey C. Hogue, Ted V. Mikels; Additional Dialogue: G. Wayne Caro, Gary Hodge; Music: Charles Dodson, T. Craig Keller; Production Manager: Carl Irwin; Make-up: Mark Williams, Joe Klein; Special Effects: Hollywood Special Effects (pyrotechnicians), Kelley Kerby; Sound: Maria De La Rosa, Jim Mingo; Production Company: Odyssey Pictures II, Ltd.; Distribution Company: Trans World Entertainment; Running Time: 78 minutes.

CAST: Jannina Poynter (Tina), David O'Hara (Major Hargrove), Macka Foley (Manny), Carl Irwin (Ron), Jeffrey C. Hogue (Jake), T. Craig Keller (Craig), Pierre D'Augusto (Pierre), Ron Jason (Don), David Collins (Kid), Gary Hodge (Ace), Pat Kerby (New Guy), Jason Holt (Zach), Ed Walters (Zach's Partner), Linda Eden (Linda), Joe Wilkerson (Motorcycle Gang Leader), Monty Perlin (High Rider).

12

Dangerous Style
Hard Target (1993)

Don't hunt what you can't kill. — poster

Synopsis

A man named Binder (Chuck Pfarrer) flees through the deserted nighttime streets of New Orleans, pursued by a cadre of black-helmeted motorcycle riders and a figure armed with a rifle that shoots metal arrows. "If he makes it to the river, he's won," warns a well-dressed man, Fouchon (Lance Henriksen), who organizes human hunts of homeless combat veterans for his high-paying clients. At this, the hunter takes aim and brings down his prey with an arrow just as the unfortunate reaches the river.

Natasha "Nat" Binder (Yancy Butler) arrives in New Orleans to find her estranged father, whose recent letters to her have abruptly stopped. She learns from her father's friend, a down-on-his luck veteran named Roper (Willie Carpenter), that her father was homeless and hasn't been seen for days. When the police do nothing, she begins searching on her own but falls victim to a gang of muggers. Fortunately, Chance Boudreaux (Jean-Claude Van Damme), a former Marine and Silver Star holder, steps in to stop the assault in a rather emphatic fashion. Natasha soon enlists Chance's aid (for $217 — the amount the out-of-work Chance needs to pay his back union dues so he can ship out as a merchant seaman) in her search, which leads to a sleazy promoter named Randall Poe (Eliot Keener); Poe pays homeless people to hand out sex-chat fliers. Though they get no answers then, it later turns out that Poe helps procure prospective "targets" for Fouchon.

In the meantime, the police have found Binder's body, burned when an abandoned building went up in flames. Wary of Chance's involvement (he's asking too many questions), Fouchon orders "a couple of lads to have a chat with him." Just as Chance discovers evidence that Binder was murdered, Fouchon's thugs surprise him, beat him up, and warn him to leave town. Chance, however, takes the evidence (Binder's dog tag he found at the building site, which was pierced by an arrow) to Detective Carmine (Kasi Lemmons), who reopens the case and orders a new autopsy.

Fouchon, after talking with the panicked police doctor on his payroll, decides that tonight's hunt will be their last in New Orleans. "Looks like we've outstayed our welcome," he tells the nervous medico — just before Fouchon's right-hand man, Van Cleaf (Arnold Vosloo), puts a bullet through the doc's brain. The target for this next and final hunt? Roper. The desperate Roper accepts Fouchon's offer of $10,000 to "get to the river, 10 miles through the city," and tries to shake his pursuers in a nearby cemetery. Turning the tables and killing his hunter, Roper makes it to the safety of the crowded French Quarter, but no one will help the wounded man before Fouchon and his human "dogs" show up to riddle his body with bullets.

After this public killing, Detective Carmine accompanies Chance and Nat to see Poe, arriving just after Van Cleaf has paid the sleazemonger a fatal visit. Van Cleaf and his goons engage them in a gun battle, then a car chase, resulting in Carmine's death, and Chance and Nat escaping by jumping from an overpass onto a moving freight train.

Fouchon and Van Cleaf, along with their small army of thugs, pick up the couple's trail near the train tracks and are soon joined by five invited hunters. "We are stalking an exceptional opponent," Fouchon tells them, "truly a world-class trophy; the price for participating in this little excursion is $750,000 each." The group tracks Chance and Nat into the bayou swamplands to the house of Chance's Cajun uncle, Douvee (Wilford Brimley). But Douvee has rigged his shack and homemade still to explode, taking out a handful of Fouchon's men. Having collected a shotgun and a horse from Douvee, Chance leads his surviving pursuers away through the bayous.

Chance makes it to an old factory/warehouse housing decrepit Mardi Gras floats, with Fouchon and his men in hot pursuit. At this "Mardi Gras graveyard" there ensues a battle of guns, grenades, fists and feet, as Chance (with a little help from Douvee and Nat, who eschew going to the Sheriff in order to come to Chance's aid) takes out his hunters one by one, culminating in a final showdown with Fouchon.

How "Dangerous" Is It?

Hard Target was consciously crafted upon Connell's framework (or at least the first cinematic translation of same — the 1932 *The Most Dangerous Game*). As Universal producer James Jacks recalled:

> *Hard Target* was a script that we were developing at Universal for [Jean-Claude] Van Damme. And so I sat down with this writer Chuck Pfarrer. And we thought about both variations of *The Naked Prey* [and] *Most Dangerous Game*. And first we tried *The Naked Prey*, but that didn't really work, and we also did a kind of *Aliens* which Chuck turned into a comic book called *Virus* for Dark Horse Comics. And the third thing was this *Most Dangerous Game* thing.[1]

Still, scripter Pfarrer took very few specifics from Connell's story, and those he did utilize went through significant transformations.

Lance Henriksen as Fouchon, the Zaroff-by-proxy of *Hard Target*.

Van Damme springs into action for *Hard Target* (a production that employed 30 stunt players and expended over 25,000 rounds of ammunition).

Rather than Zaroff's private tropical island, Fouchon's "hunting ground" consists of the deserted nighttime streets, back alleys, levees and cemeteries(!) of New Orleans. Though this nullifies the "outdoor chess" aspect of one hunter stalking another—making it more of a chase scenario than a woodland "hunt"—Connell's "your woodcraft against mine" conflict finally comes into play when Chance leads his pursuers into the surrounding bayou country. There, in this jungle-like environment, he lays a trap for his hunter(s), like Rainsford before him. Of course, Chance's trap is no Burmese tiger pit or Malay man-catcher but a uniquely inventive (albeit extremely unlikely) snare involving a trip wire and a live rattlesnake!

In place of the sophisticated, hunting-obsessed General Zaroff stands the equally urbane ex-mercenary Fouchon, whose obsession isn't necessarily the hunt but *money*—gleaned through setting up these human hunts for his high-paying clients (at half-a-million dollars a pop), making Fouchon something of a Zaroff-once-removed. On the other hand, like any professional safari guide, he evinces respect for the import and sanctity of the hunt (and prey), preventing one over-eager client from firing too soon at his fleeing quarry, for instance, and even disdainfully reprimanding Van Cleaf for wanting to shoot Chance from a helicopter: "Any pinhead can take him from the air; I want to take him from the ground!" Obviously the significance of the hunt itself holds sway in this man's warped sense of honor and sport. And once he deems it necessary to eliminate Chance, Fouchon dons the mantle of hunter himself, relishing the stalk through the bayou and even demanding at the warehouse, "Seal off this place, the son of a bitch is *mine*!"

Fouchon employs the same twisted reasoning as Zaroff, taking his task to what he considers the logical extreme. As Fouchon tells a prospective client, "It has always been the privilege of the few to hunt the many — soldiers, policemen, fighter pilots. Men who kill for the government do so with impunity. All we do is offer the same opportunity for private citizens such as yourself."

Like Zaroff, Fouchon also seeks the most challenging prey for his Dangerous Game. While Zaroff relies on the natural dangers surrounding his island (the treacherous swim through shark-infested waters after a ship has struck Zaroff's concealed reef) to ensure that only the strong make it to the hunt, Fouchon utilizes a very careful screening process to pick his quarry. "We pride ourselves in only hunting combat veterans," explains Van Cleaf, "men who have the necessary skills to make our hunts more interesting." Fouchon himself adds, "The same government that has made murder their sole preserve, they train our targets."

In place of Connell's solitary hunt, *Hard Target* offers not one, not two, but *three* human hunts. The first is a startling and shocking introduction to the concept, the second an atmospheric pursuit in which the worm most satisfyingly turns (though ultimately ending in bloody tragedy even when it appears the prey might make it to safety), and the third a no-holds-barred, all-out actionfest involving a myriad of secondary stalkers and their demise.

During these hunts, rather than using trained dogs, these modern-day Zaroffs employ black-clad motorcyclists to track and run down their human quarry. It makes for some exciting visuals, not to mention myriad opportunities for impressive stunt work, as these human bloodhounds astride their metal machines block their prey's path or knock them aside. Screenwriter Chuck Pfarrer's original script called for the use of traditional tracking dogs but ultimately took a more high-tech and mechanized turn through its various rewrites.

Critique

On a dark and wet New Orleans street, infused with a foreboding bluish light, the mobile camera fluidly follows a desperate figure vainly seeking sanctuary behind closed shutters and locked doors. Moving smoothly but almost desperately, the camera anxiously turns toward a sound — revealing a horse-drawn carriage driving by on the street, illuminated by a sinister flash of lightening. As if in a panic, the camera abruptly spins around, looking over its shoulder. Suddenly the point of view changes and the camera takes flight, accompanying a spinning arrow in close-up as it slams into a wall next to a man's head, drawing blood by grazing his terrified countenance. With this, even before the credits roll, we have stepped into the stylish and dangerous world not only of the Most Dangerous Game, but the cinema of John Woo. Veteran Hong Kong director Woo is perhaps the most accomplished, and certainly the most stylish, filmmaker to tackle the Most Dangerous Game theme, and definitely the one most qualified to wear the mantle of "auteur." Though with *Hard Target* (his twenty-second feature but his first in America) he was working off a script penned by someone else, the amazing action, fluid visuals, and heroic character portrayals all bear the John Woo stamp. As the director himself said, "The story is less John Woo, but the visual aspects are very John Woo."[2] Lance Henriksen went even further, enthusing, "It's downright, full-out John Woo," and added that he accepted the role of Fouchon because of his respect for Woo's body of work. "Those movies to me were so creative, so balletic, and had this incredible philosophy in them. The violence was only a container for the philosophy."[3]

Given the fact that Woo had far less control on *Hard Target*, his first Hollywood film, than on his previous Hong Kong features (which he generally co-wrote and co-produced as well as directed), the filmmaker's "philosophy" appears to have taken a back seat to the action and violence of *Hard Target*. Though Woo succeeds in making his antagonists and protagonists both human and heroic through his use of roving camera, slow motion, and symbolism (largely centered on birds taking flight — for Woo, symbols of purity and of the soul), he cannot create the near-symbiotic, emotionally resonant fusion of antagonist/protagonist found in his best Hong Kong films, like *A Better Tomorrow* (1986) and *The Killer* (1989).

That said, Woo still manages to bring his trademark style to bear, enhancing nearly every aspect of *Hard Target*, not least of which are the striking visuals and amazing action set-pieces. Woo's constantly moving cameras (sometimes breathtakingly so, at other times far more subtly) brings a sense of fluidity to the story, creating a visual cohesion that flows from one scene to the next and one action set-piece to the next. Often setting up multiple roving cameras placed on dolly tracks, the *Hard Target* crew laughingly renamed the dolly "the Woo-woo Choo-choo." As key grip Lloyd Moriarty said during production, "We've surely laid more dolly tracks than any other movie. I'd say we've laid at least five miles this time." Moriarty explained how they'd set up "multiple dolly moves, three cameras on three dollies, minimum moves anywhere from sixteen up to one hundred foot, and that's consistently, all day long. In fact, I don't think we've run one single camera at any point in this movie, and this is around day fifty, but this is a very unusual movie. For all of us it's very exciting."[4] Such enthusiasm, and loyalty, is well-earned by Woo, who puts his crew through their paces for a definite purpose. As veteran cinematographer Russell Carpenter related:

Hong Kong filmmaker John Woo (right) directs Belgian-born action star Jean-Claude Van Damme (not an easy task, by all accounts) on the streets of New Orleans.

Because of the sheer amount of pyrotechnics and the complexity of many of the stunts, multiple camera coverage was a must on this film. But this is not just a matter of randomly setting several cameras with various lenses on the action.... There might be four or five cameras, manned and unmanned, on a variety of different focal lengths and running at different speeds. Now, to top it all off, as many as two or even three cameras may be on dollies, somehow miraculously missing getting into each others field of view.... John knows that each camera is going to contribute a bit of energy to the whole, and that when all that energy from those cameras comes together it's like nuclear fission. The scene explodes with an energy that's twenty-five times more than what those five cameras contributed. I'm convinced that he has all these sequences edited in his head before he comes to the set. There aren't many people you can say that about.[5]

While definitely going big in the action sequences (the production employed thirty credited "stunt players"), Woo, working off Pfarrer's script, offers a number of small touches that enhance a scene and underscore a character. For instance, when Nat goes to file a missing persons report on her father, she interrupts the female detective at her desk lighting a candle on a foil-wrapped danish. She resignedly sighs, "Happy birthday to me," before hurriedly placing it, candle still lit, in her desk drawer when she sees Nat approaching. Such clever attention to detail suggests that even relatively minor characters are real people with intriguing back stories. And at the end of the sequence, after Nat leaves (with little satisfaction), the detective takes the cake out of the now-smoke-filled drawer and in slow motion blows out the candle, causing the screen to go black and transition into the next shot of an early morning cityscape which pans to show Chance idly waiting at a dock, the melancholy mood carrying over from — and linking — one scene to the next. So while *Hard Target* may lack the emotional complexity Woo brought to his earlier films, making it more of a straight-ahead action movie, Woo's careful crafting of even the minor moments make it a far more nuanced straight-ahead action movie than most.

"Chuck Pfarrer did a good job with the script for *Hard Target*," praised Woo. "It is a simple but powerful story, with a lot of feeling underneath. For a good action film you need a solid structure. Chuck gave me that."[6] Some of that "feeling underneath," though sitting quite close to the Dangerous Game surface, involves class conflict, the haves vs. have-nots subtext adding resonance to the screenplay. By making the "targets" homeless veterans, the film shows the manipulative, jaded rich literally preying on the disenfranchised poor. Fouchon underlines the overemphasis on money in today's society with his offer of $10,000, telling the down-and-out Roper, "You can get new clothes, clean yourself up, look men in the eyes when you pass them on the street. This money could make you a man again instead of the shadow of your former self." To these hunters-of-men, it is money that defines not only one's worth but one's *self*-worth. And those lost souls on the streets buy into this, becoming the human prey of the monied few. As Fouchon arrogantly explains to a prospective client, "It has always been the privilege of the few to hunt the many." And at the very end, the script even mines this topical subtext for a quick laugh. Keeping Chance at bay by holding an arrow to Nat's throat, Fouchon says, "You see, Miss Binder, you I can understand. It was a matter of family. [To Chance] *You* had *nothing* in common with these people. What made you want to complicate my life like this?" Chance's response: "Poor people get bored too."

Chuck Pfarrer's screenplay creates one of the most fully-fleshed Most Dangerous antagonists since the original 1932 film's Count Zaroff, painting Fouchon in colors of arrogance, disdain, camaraderie (hinting at a deeper relationship with his partner Van Cleaf) and even honor. Via illuminating dialogue, the forceful yet subtle playing of Henriksen, and the near-balletic presentation of Woo, Fouchon becomes one of the most intriguing, appealing, and even heroic Zaroff figures in the Most Dangerous canon. From the opening hunt sequence, when Fouchon observes to his client, "It's like a drug, isn't it — to bring a man down," the menace of the man shows through. Later, when Roper's hunter wounds his prey in the cemetery, the hunter loses his nerve, deciding he does not want to kill a man after all. At this, Fouchon becomes enraged. "Finish him!" he hisses. "Don't make me look bad in front of my dogs. You know why you're here — you paid us half a million dollars to find out if you're alive or dead. Now finish him!" The dialogue, coupled with Henriksen's barely-held-in-check rage, displays both the arrogance of the man (who considers his underlings his "dogs") and his sense of twisted respect and responsibility — the hunt must be finished, and wounded prey must be dealt with. Fouchon sees the hunter as almost a surrogate for himself, so that the hunter's actions reflect his own. Fouchon obviously calls the shots, and his image, his authority, his power over life and death, must remain intact and unsullied. The dialogue also reveals Fouchon's warped sense of self-worth — only by dominating another man fully (hunting him down) can anyone be considered truly "alive."

Busy character actor Lance Henriksen (*Aliens, Near Dark, Pumpkinhead*), with his craggy face, intense eyes, and deep, resonant voice, was the perfect choice for Fouchon. Coupled with his fashionable suits, long cashmere coat and luxurious Jaguar convertible, he exudes elegance and menace in equal measure. This extends even to his choice of weapon — a visually grand and powerful pistol called the Contender, which requires reloading after every shot. According to the production's "Weapons Specialist," Robert "Rock" Galotti, "Lance came up and he said, 'I need something really classy — you know, this guy wears Armani suits and he drives a Jag convertible. I got to have something that just shows *class*....' And I thought, a Contender would be pretty cool."[7] Indeed, this weapon fit perfectly with the character, even down to the idea that Fouchon eschews the practicality of machine guns, grenades, and automatic pistols employed by his men and clients for a far more challenging single-shot, breach-loading weapon, making the hunt that much more dangerous and intimate. Henriksen's subtle expressions and movements underline his character at every turn. When the film's first kill is made during the opening hunt, the camera shifts to focus on the observing Fouchon's face. Henriksen lifts his chin, moves his jaw ever so slightly, and lets out an almost inaudible sigh — of satisfaction perhaps, or of momentary longing and regret that it was not *his* hand, but that of his monied client, that dealt the death blow. And when he turns to said client and delivers the line, "It's like a drug, isn't it — to bring a man down," Henriksen's satisfied tone almost smacks of post-coital languor. Later, after Chance escapes Fouchon and his men by leaping onto a moving train, Fouchon turns to Van Cleaf and says, "It appears we'll have one last hunt after all," the slight half-smile on Henriksen's face revealing that he may very well be secretly pleased. But Henriksen's most impressive and revealing scene comes, surprisingly enough, when Fouchon sits at a grand piano at his luxury mansion playing Bach. Henriksen stares straight ahead, his mouth hard, his shoulders moving subtly but almost violently as he plays. Striking the keys with a forceful intensity that reflects a dangerous suppressed anger, his head dips slightly as his mouth hardens further and his eyes stare into nothingness. Henriksen creates a frightening juxtaposition of high culture and beauty (the music) with base, animal emotion barely held in check under a "civilized" veneer. More than in any other sequence, Henriksen's subtle playing (no pun intended) in this scene reveals the beast lurking beneath the sophisticated surface.

Rather than offering the usual snarky one-liners thrown out by the likes of Schwarzenegger, Stallone, or Willis in innumerable action movies, Pfarrer inserts humor into *Hard Target* in a more subtle — and clever — manner. For instance, Natasha's introduction to Chance includes this amusing exchange:

> Natasha: What's your name?
> Chance: Chance Boudreaux. What's *your* name?
> Natasha: It's Nat.
> Chance: Nat? Your parents named you for a — bug?
> Natasha (annoyed): No, actually, its short for Natasha. What kind of a name is "Chance"?
> Chance: Well, my mama took one.

But it's not only the hero who offers the occasional amusing *bon mot*. The calm and always-professional Van Cleaf (played with studied efficacy by actor Arnold Vosloo, whose harsh-yet-melodious South African accent, sinister grin and thousand-yard stare bring his character to full, menacing life), after losing half his men in the confrontation with Chance, turns to his boss and dryly observes, "It appears your trophy is ripping us a new orifice."

New Orleans was an inspired choice of location for this Most Dangerous Game. Producer James Jacks related, "We decided to set it in New Orleans because it would give an explanation for Jean-Claude's accent."[8] That it does (Chance was raised Cajun) — not to mention providing a rather exotic and visually arresting environment in which to set this shocking tale of human sport hunting. Taking a page out of the *Avenging Force* playbook (though the studio would never admit it, inaccurately claiming in the film's official presskit, "For the first time, major action sequences were staged in the heart of the French Quarter,"[9]), Woo makes excellent use of the locale, from the atmospheric deserted nighttime streets, to the "Mardi Gras graveyard" warehouse filled with decaying, cobwebbed decorations, to the forbidding cemetery filled with above-ground tombs and mausoleums. For this last location, Woo opens with a nighttime overhead crane shot showing an overview of the shadowy mausoleums, many spotlit by lighted candles at their base. The camera then swoops down in among the tightly-packed tombs to glide along the narrow rows, moving among and around them to follow the panicked prey, Roper. At one point the primary hunter takes aim at the fleeing Roper and shoots, blasting the head off an Angelic statue — and revealing the frightened face of Roper hiding behind it.

Though given a more, shall we say, simplistic actor in the form of Jean-Claude Van Damme than he was used to in his Hong Kong films (such as the accomplished Tony Leung or Asian superstar Chow Yun-Fat), John Woo manages to paint Van Damme with more depth than that seen in any of the "Muscles from Brussels'" previous portrayals. First off, Woo takes full advantage of Van Damme's undisputed physical grace (not only a martial artist, Van Damme also trained as a dancer) to imbue a noble, even balletic quality to his actions. "I knew from the beginning that John Woo would be a wonderful director for me," said Van Damme. "He is great with action, of course, but what I also notice is that he is very good with actors. He always makes actors look good."[10] And not only does Van Damme look good in *Hard Target*, he also displays more acting ability than he had heretofore. In the film's quieter moments, Van Damme, under Woo's guiding hand, manages to make Chance seem almost introspective. For instance, at one point Chance comforts Nat, grieving over the death of her father, by telling her that being on the streets "is hard, I've been there myself.... And because he loved you so much," he continues, his eyes lowering slightly as he looks inward, the irises moving as if seeing some inner tableau replayed, "he didn't want to pull you into it." Quiet moments like this add more depth to his usual action persona and shows that perhaps when under the guidance of a sensitive director, he was a better actor than given credit for (something borne out years later when Van Damme made the courageously self-reflexive — and self-reflective — 2008 film *JCVD*). Van Damme's fellow actor Willie Carpenter (who played Roper) gives much of the credit to Woo:

> I just think as a persona, what John did lifted Jean-Claude quite a few levels up. John slows the camera down, and Jean-Claude suddenly looks like the biggest, baddest dude. I think he just raised him up, he made him bigger than life — talk about film magic, it was just absolutely wonderful stuff.[11]

Woo doesn't *always* make the best choices, however. For instance, when Chance grabs a rattlesnake by the neck as it's about to strike Nat, he punches it in the head with his fist — looking more than slightly ridiculous. And the subsequent "snake-trap" he constructs makes little sense, with a tripwire somehow rigged to make the reptile leap from a branch to latch onto the face of a clumsy hunter. Of course, this leads into a choice bit of dialogue from an annoyed Fouchon. "If you would die quieter," he tells his startled men, his eyes flashing, "and pick up the pace, Boudreaux would have less time for these little surprises."

But the biggest misstep comes in the form of some impossible pyrotechnics. When Van Cleaf and his men shoot at the horseback-riding Chance from a helicopter, the bullets hitting the ground around him ludicrously spark and flare like cheap Fourth of July fireworks. Later, in the warehouse, Fouchon shoots at Chance but hits a barrel, which literally launches high into the air like a rocket! And huge papier mache Mardi Gras heads and figurines literally explode in a shower of *sparks* from shotgun blasts. Festive, perhaps, but absurd.

Despite the presence of Detective Carmine in a couple of sequences, the police remain largely unseen in *Hard Target*, and appear completely impotent when they do appear. When Nat comes to the station to file a missing persons report on her father, Carmine, preoccupied with her own miseries (working on her birthday, alone in the squad room), can barely be bothered. Later, when Carmine becomes involved in the investigation, she's quickly shot and killed by Van Cleaf and his men, leaving Chance and Nat to fend for themselves and run for their lives. The only other "official" presence comes in the form of the corrupt police doctor, who, in the pay of Fouchon, "helps with the autopsies" to cover up their activities. Even when Roper is shot down in the middle of a crowded street to close out the second hunt, the killers have no fear of the law, with Van Cleaf slowly and deliberately walking up to the body and retrieving their $10,000 before sauntering off. So it's little wonder that Nat decides to leave the police out of it at the end and, rather than going to the Sheriff, rides with Douvee to help Chance. Of course, though transforming this final confrontation into a simplistic battle of good vs. evil, with no holds barred and no official interference, the total non-presence of the police in a city the size of New Orleans requires more than the viewer's fair share of suspension of disbelief. Fortunately, Woo's stylistic and sometimes outrageous portrayal of the nearly non-stop action readily distracts and enraptures the viewer just enough to make such things as logic and reality seem almost trivial.

Production

"*Hard Target* was born," stated a studio publicity piece, "when producer [James] Jacks endorsed screenwriter Chuck Pfarrer's suggestion that the 1932 film *The Most Dangerous Game* was ripe for an update. From the beginning, they had one director in mind: John Woo, whose smash hit *The Killer* had opened to rave reviews on the North American festival circuit after breaking all box office records in Hong Kong."[12] Well, not exactly, as other filmmakers were considered by Universal first. For instance, Andrew Davis (*Under Siege, The Fugitive*) was offered the director's chair but turned it down. In fact, John Woo was something of a hard sell for the studio executives. As producer Jacks recalled:

> [It] became a process of trying to convince the studio to do the movie with John. They really just didn't want to hear about it. Every time I mentioned I was thinking about doing it with John Woo they said, "Well, gee, John would be great. Can he speak English?" I just couldn't get the studio to consider him because it was another Chinese director. [T]he drama in those movies tends to be somewhat over the top, and they were a little concerned about the language, and they had a lot of justifiable concerns. And also they just hadn't seen the movies. But finally [studio chairman] Tom Pollock looked at the movie [*The Killer*] and said, "Well, he certainly can direct an action scene. So if Jean-Claude will approve him, I'll do it with him."[13]

Though he built his career on violent gangster films like *A Better Tomorrow* (1986), *Bullet in the Head* (1990), and *Hard Boiled* (1992), even earning such sobriquets as the "Master of Bullet Ballets," Woo is a very quiet, soft-spoken, and even spiritual man. In fact, he has never fired a gun himself and refuses to do so. Actor Nicholas Cage, who starred in Woo's *Face/Off* (1997), surmised about the filmmaker, "Maybe the more violent your art is, the more peaceful your life is because you're getting that [expression] out. It's sort of a weird contradiction. What you hate can actually become something very interesting to you artistically. You get power over it."[14]

Universal saw *Hard Target* as a vehicle for Jean-Claude Van Damme, with whom they had a multi-picture deal. Born Jean Claude Van Varenberg in Brussels, Belgium, in 1960, he began studying martial arts at the age of 12, making the Belgium Karate Team at age 16 and competing successfully for six years. Simplifying his last name to Van Damme (because it had a "tougher sound"[15]), he went to Hong Kong and then to America to break into the movies. After serving as a sparring partner for Chuck Norris, Norris secured the fledgling young actor a small role in *Missing in Action* (1984). Nothing came of that until an "impromptu display of martial arts prowess for a startled [Cannon Pictures producer] Menahem Golan in the middle of a crowded chic restaurant won the determined performer his kick-off role in *Bloodsport* [1988]."[16] Though the low-budget picture was shelved for two years, it made $30 million on its eventual release, and Van Damme's film career finally took off. In quick succession he starred in a string of financial hits like *Cyborg* (1989), *Lionheart* (1990), *Double Impact* (1991) and *Universal Soldier* (1992). Post–*Hard Target*, Van Damme scored his first $100-million breakthrough with *Timecop* (1994), but his films soon began declining in both box-office and budget. Down but never entirely out, Van Damme starred in some worthy smaller films (such as *JCVD* in 2008) and made for an engaging villain in the overblown action star retirement project *The Expendables 2* (2012).

John Woo was none-too-enamored of the studio's choice of Van Damme for *Hard Target*. In fact, Woo actively sought Kurt Russell for the role, but Russell was already booked. (Screenwriter Chuck Pfarrer envisioned Armand Assante as the hero.[17]) Capitulating, Woo still felt uneasy about his star. "Van Damme wanted some changes," recounted Woo. "He wanted to prove himself as a serious actor and he thought this movie might do it for him if he were able to dictate certain things early on."[18] And dictate the very vocal action star did; apart from demanding script revisions to cast him in a more heroic light, he'd sometimes even question Woo's direction. But Woo persevered, and both Van Damme and the film itself were well served. (Note: Back in 1987 Van Damme was almost on the *other* side of the Most Dangerous fence when he was originally hired to play the titular creature in *Predator*. Van Damme wore the alien hunter-of-men suit until the original design was deemed unacceptable and scrapped. Stan Winston completely revamped this now-classic creation, and the 5-foot-10-inch Van Damme was replaced by 7-foot-2-inch Kevin Peter Hall. Van Damme reportedly had no regrets about being replaced, as he was unhappy that his face wouldn't be shown, and was uncomfortable in the alien suit, even passing out once due to heat exhaustion.)

Screenwriter Chuck Pfarrer, a former Navy SEAL, took the title *Hard Target* from the military term for a well-protected objective (as opposed to an easy "soft target"). Pfarrer (whose previous produced scripts were *Navy Seals* and *Darkman*, both 1990, and whose subsequent work included *The Jackal* [1997], *Virus* [1999], and *Red Planet* [2000]) also appeared onscreen, playing Natasha's father who falls victim to Fouchon's hunters in the movie's opening sequence. Pfarrer utilized his personal military experience to enhance the film's realism, even "tutoring several actors in proper techniques for stalking human beings, and giving lessons in the care and handling of the advanced weaponry used in the film." Said Pfarrer, "This is one movie where you'll never have to ask yourself, 'Just how many bullets does that gun hold, anyway?'"[19]

After shooting for 65 days, Woo worked with editor Bob Murawski to create his final cut. Said Murawski, "A lot of directors just shoot, almost at random, leaving this mass of footage that we then have to hack and carve into a scene. With John, I'm never in doubt about what he intended with each sequence. One of his sequences has 357 cuts in it — and every one of them was in his head before he started shooting. His footage just melts together."[20] Unfortunately, his footage failed to melt the hearts of the MPAA. Contractually obligated by Universal Pictures to deliver an R-rated film, Woo had to trim and trim and trim when his initial cut came back from the MPAA ratings board slapped with the dreaded NC-17 rating (tantamount to an "X"). The board judged it to be too violent and too intense (admittedly, the movie did expend more than 25,000 rounds of ammunition). So Woo re-cut *Hard Target* and submitted it again — a total of *eight times* before finally earning the coveted "R." (At one point Van Damme himself even took a crack at creating an edit of his own, but the result proved laughable when he excised entire characters in order to make room for more close-ups of himself. When asked about this, Van Damme angrily retorted, "People pay their money to see me, not to see Lance Henriksen."[21]) Woo ultimately had to make 20 cuts to his movie, including seven to the opening sequence (such as a shot of Binder agonizingly removing an arrow from his shoulder, and Binder throwing a gas-filled can at a motorcycle rider, resulting in a fatal explosion). Most of the edits, however, came from the climactic battle at the Mardi Gras warehouse, including a number of bullet hits, a man dying with an arrow through his throat, and an arrow tearing through a character's knee. Curiously, Woo was also forced to excise part of the innocuous-but-revealing scene in which Fouchon plays Bach at his piano. Originally, Woo intercut shots of wild African animals preying upon one another with shots of Fouchon's aggressive piano playing — unsubtle, perhaps, but effective. But the ratings board said no. "I don't think it was the amount of blood that the MPAA had a problem with; I think it was the number of deaths," opined producer James Jacks.[22] Writer Chuck Pfarrer commiserated with Woo, saying, "In Hong Kong he can shoot whatever he wants and they will release it and generally audiences will go and see it and decide for themselves if it is any good or not. Here he was put in a position of having his abilities and his vision second guessed by people who had the power but who had no vision or ability of their own."[23] Woo ultimately became frustrated with the board, who would not, or could not, tell him exactly what needed to be excised to their satisfaction. "We were really doing the cutting just by guessing what they wanted or what they didn't want," Woo said. "By the sixth time when one of them told me, 'I don't like the violence,' I got mad and said to him, 'If you don't like the violence, don't go to the movie.'"

On a budget of $19.5 million, *Hard Target* took in over $31 million domestically on its theatrical release, with a worldwide tally of over $71 million, making it both the most expensive and the biggest grossing full-on MDG adaptation to date (though several films, including the original 1932 version, enjoyed a larger cost-to-earnings ratio).

CREDITS: Director: John Woo; Producers: James Jacks, Sean Daniel; Screenplay: Chuck Pfarrer; Cinematographer: Russell Carpenter; Co-Producers: Chuck Pfarrer, Terence Chang; Line Producer: Daryl Kass; Executive Producers: Moshe Diamant, Sam Raimi, Robert Tapert; Music: Graeme Revell (featuring Kodo); Editor: Bob Murawski; Production Designer: Phil Dagort; Production Companies: Alphaville, Renaissance; Distribution Company: Universal Pictures; Release Date: August 20, 1993; Running Time: 92 minutes; MPAA Rating: R; Panavision and Eastman Color.

CAST: Jean-Claude Van Damme (Chance Boudreaux), Lance Henriksen (Fouchon), Yancy Butler (Natasha Binder), Arnold Vosloo (Van Cleaf), Wilford Brimley (Douvee), Kasi Lemmons (Carmine), Willie Carpenter (Elijah Roper), Eliott Keener (Randal Poe), Marco St. John (Dr. Morton).

13

Wilderness Hunt
Surviving The Game (1994)

The Thrill Is The Kill — poster

Synopsis

Surviving the Game opens on a very different scene of "surviving," with a dreadlock-sporting African-American homeless man, Mason (Ice-T), digging through back-alley garbage cans for something to eat. After his dog is killed and his only friend, an elderly homeless vet named Hank (Jeff Corey), dies, Mason has nothing left to lose ("I had a wife and a kid and they're dead," he laments) and decides to step in front of a truck. Cole (Charles S. Dutton), a part-time soup kitchen volunteer, saves him at the last minute, and then offers him a job. "My business partner and I, we need someone to help us as a survival guide with our hunt out in the wilderness." Mason, a former mechanic, is reluctant at first ("I don't know shit about the wilderness," he admits), but takes the business card offered him and goes to see Cole's partner, Burns (Rutger Hauer), at "Hell's Canyon Outfitters." After a fitness test on a treadmill, Burns hires Mason, and they fly in Burns' private plane up to the company's remote cabin in the Oregon wilderness, where they're soon joined by their four paying clients, arriving via another private plane. The clients are Mr. Wolfe, Sr., (F. Murray Abraham), "one of the most feared men on Wall Street"; his son Derek (William McNamara); Dr. Hawkins (Gary Busey), a psychiatrist who works for "the Company — that's the C.I.A."; and Mr. Griffin (John C. McGinley), a tough Texas oil man.

After a rather uneasy pork dinner (with the freshly slaughtered pig's head making up the centerpiece), Mason wakes the next morning to a gun in his face. Burns tells him, "We like to play a game," while Cole explains, "It's very simple. You see, the hunt begins now. We're the hunters and you're the hunted. You leave here now, with a head start of as long as it takes us to eat a nice, leisurely breakfast." Burns concludes, "If you make it to civilization you live. If you don't, maybe God will have mercy." Though Derek, thinking he was on just another animal hunt, protests, "He's a human being!" his father and the rest persuade him to go along.

Mason flees into the woods. Then, after breakfast, the six hunters pursue on motorcycles and ATVs. Initially eluding them, Mason makes it back to the cabin. When Burns and Cole realize that he's doubled back, they seem pleased with their prey's ingenuity ("No one has ever done that before," Cole observes, smiling). At the cabin, Mason breaks into a locked room, but instead of finding weapons, he discovers shelves full of human heads preserved in jars — as well as one standing empty labeled "MASON."

DVD cover (featuring the same design as the "Style B" theatrical poster). Pictured (clockwise from top left) are Gary Busey, Rutger Hauer, and Ice-T.

Mason sets the cabin ablaze just as the hunters arrive and search the house. While the rest help rescue Wolfe, trapped upstairs by the fire, Hawkins bursts through the back door and tackles the retreating Mason. The vicious fight ends with Mason pushing Hawkins through a window back into the blazing cabin just before the propane tanks explode. Mason flees into the woods again, and the remaining five hunters give chase, cornering Mason on a clifftop. As they fire, Mason leaps into the raging river below and makes his escape.

Later, setting a trap by using a lit cigarette stuck into a tree trunk as a decoy, Mason leaps down and subdues the isolated Griffin. Now armed with Griffin's shotgun, as well as his radio gear, Mason stashes the bound Griffin in an old mine and radios Burns, demanding he fly him back to civilization or he'll let Griffin die. Burns, however, who knows the region like the back of his hand, surmises Mason's whereabouts; but when the hunters come to the mine in the morning, all they find is Griffin, unharmed. Griffin decides he's done with hunting men. "Mason could have killed me last night easy, but he didn't. Gotta let him go." But Burns and Cole think otherwise, and, after a tense confrontation, Cole shoots Griffin right between the eyes.

The hunt resumes, and Mason leads them down the river before cleverly doubling back and rigging one of their ATVs to explode (by placing a sparking starter wire in the gas tank), mortally wounding Cole. Burns, visibly affected by this, finishes the job.

Mason comes to a gorge and, using the last shells from Griffin's shotgun, blasts through a tree at the edge, causing it to fall across the span to bridge the ravine. When the three remaining hunters begin to cross in pursuit, Mason, having hidden on the near side, begins throwing rocks at them, dislodging Derek, who falls to his death. Burns gets a shot off at the fleeing Mason, wounding him in the stomach.

Burns and Wolfe now decide to sit and wait for Mason to come to *them*. Just before dawn, Mason sneaks into their camp. After the grief-stricken and hate-maddened Wolfe frantically empties his pistol into the darkness, Mason attacks Wolfe, snapping his neck. Burns, realizing the tables have turned, takes the opportunity to flee on his motorcycle, with Mason giving chase on Wolfe's ATV.

Mason arrives back at the cabin just as Burns is revving up the clients' plane. Mason runs toward it but finds the cockpit empty — it was a trick. From the trees, the hidden Burns takes aim and shoots at the plane's gas tank, exploding the aircraft and presumably killing Mason. But Mason had spotted the ruse just in time.

In Seattle three days later, Burns is in his office, having changed his appearance and disguised himself as an Orthodox priest(!). He intends to shut down his operation and disappear with a new identity. But when his car won't start, Burns realizes *he* is being hunted now, and he's in Mason's territory this time. In a deserted back alley, Mason attacks and the two fight, with Mason ultimately getting the upper hand and Burns' weapon. "Ok, do it," says Burns, cowering before him. "Finish the game." "Bang!" shouts Mason and walks away. Mason takes the clip from Burns' gun and drops the weapon in the alley. Startled and relieved, Burns retrieves the weapon and finds a lone bullet. Loading the gun, he takes aim at Mason's retreating back. But Mason had jammed the barrel, and the gun explodes in Burns' hands, killing him. The game is now truly over.

How *"Dangerous"* Is It?

Refreshingly, New Line Cinema comes right out and says in its publicity materials that *Surviving the Game* "was inspired by Richard Connell's classic short story 'The Most Dangerous Game.'"[1] An obviously modern updating, the film takes enough from Connell's tale to mark it as a worthy adaptation, yet deviates in a number of significant ways. Apart from the obvious change of Zaroff's private Caribbean island hunting grounds to a patch of remote Oregon mountain wilderness, and the solitary hunter becoming a pack of *six*, there's also a little matter of money. Unlike in the original story, Burns (the primary Zaroff stand-in) takes a more practical approach to the "pure" notion of hunting man for sport. From a comment Wolfe makes, we learn that Burns and Cole charge each man $50,000 for their human hunt. So, in addition to the sport (which Burns obviously relishes, even calling it "therapy" at one point), cold hard cash remains a motivating factor for Burns and Cole. For the rest, however, it's all about the "thrill."

It's a testament to Eric Bernt's screenplay, Ernest Dickerson's direction, and the actors' talents that the six hunters-of-men all remain distinct personalities that reflect different facets of the iconic Zaroff persona. Burns remains the cool, rational, sophisticated leader who, like Zaroff, has set himself apart from — and above — the rest of humanity. "I don't read newspapers anymore," he says. "They're like the mirror of the world's ugliness. I like beautiful things." Cole is the enforcer, almost an Ivan-like figure; though more of a partner than a servant, he nonetheless follows Burns' lead. It is Cole who shoots Griffin in the head when Burns balks at Griffin's intention to abandon the "game." Hawkins, though a man of science (a psychiatrist), reflects the animal side of Zaroff, with his barely-held-in-check impatience to begin the hunt and his enthusiasm for intimate violence ("What really excites me is [the prospect of] breaking his neck with my bare hands," he enthuses at the hunt's start). Griffin's intense, tortured "Texas cowboy" reflects the inner torment found in every killer (his lust to kill stems from the pain of losing his daughter to a murderer a few months before), with the weakness inherent in a killer's reasoning made metaphorically manifest by his reliance on his asthma inhaler. Wolfe is arrogance personified, as he sets himself above his prey, and indeed even above his fellow hunters (challenging and threatening more than one of them on various occasions). His timorous son Derek, however, more accurately mirrors the horror and disgust felt by Rainsford in the short story, though Derek proves too weak to stand up to his father and the rest.

Equally varied are the motivations of these distaff Zaroffs. Rather than Zaroff's hunting humans as balm for ennui and to recapture a zest for life, the cruel and calculating Burns and Cole do it for the money, though they certainly appear to enjoy themselves as well ("I enjoy fuckin' with him," Burns gleefully tells Hawkins at one point). Burns even hints at his philosophy when he offers that "I spent some time in third world countries. Changed my point of view. It's a cliché to say that life was cheap there, but life was way beyond cheap." Life, for Burns, is just a matter of dollars and cents, with little human consideration. For Hawkins, after relating his revealing story of "Prince Henry Stout" (the beloved bulldog he'd raised from a pup that his father forced him to fight and kill when he was 13 in order to become a "man"), it's perhaps a Freudian case of violently proving his manhood over and over again to his now-absent father. (This would certainly explain Hawkins' lust for hand-to-hand killing, culminating in him even throwing his knife away before grappling with Mason, announcing, "We're going bare hands.") For Griffin, hunting down and killing a man serves as an outlet for the rage and impotence he feels in losing his daughter to an unknown murderer who hasn't been caught. For the arrogant Wolfe it's about asserting his superiority — something he intends to transfer to his son Derek, attempting to make him over in his own heartless image by forcing him to participate in this human hunt.

In choosing their prey, Cole "vets" Mason by observing how he handles himself on the street (nodding in satisfaction when he sees Mason turn the tables on a brutal security guard) before sending him to Burns. And Burns, when he notices Mason smoking, almost dismisses him out of hand ("The job needs someone with endurance; I'm afraid your lungs couldn't handle it"). Even the clients themselves are concerned with the quality of their prey. The first thing Hawkins asks when he arrives and spots Mason is "Does he have courage?"; while Wolfe admonishes, "This one better last long enough to make it a challenge." So these hunters-of-men, like Zaroff, seek the most physically fit and challenging prey; they just employ more deliberate, even scientific screening methods (like Burns having Mason run on a treadmill to evaluate his stamina) rather than the screen-by-attrition method employed by Zaroff's shipwreck-survivor strategy.

At one point during the hunt (*before* his beloved partner Cole is killed) Burns takes aim at Mason riding away on a stolen ATV. With Mason's back right in his crosshairs, Burns abruptly swings his rifle to shoot out a tire instead, causing Mason to tumble off the careening vehicle. Though not aping Zaroff's actions exactly, this definitely mirrors Zaroff's *intent*. In Connell's story, when Zaroff first catches up with Rainsford after successfully following the intricate and confusing trail Rainsford had left, he stands below his prey's place of concealment, smiles and simply walks away. At this, Rainsford realizes, "The general was playing with him! The general was saving him for another day's sport!" Like Zaroff, Mason intentionally lets his prey escape in order to prolong the hunt — much to his eventual regret.

Similar to Connell's story, an early dialogue exchange explores the ethics of hunting for sport:

Mason: I still don't understand what it is about hunting animals that gets you off.
Burns: It's not about killing, it's not about death. It's about *life*.
Mason: You tell that to the animal.
Burns: The animal knows it too. This is going to be quite the learning experience.

Unlike so many Dangerous Game adaptations, *Surviving the Game* includes the all-important trophy room. Admittedly, Connell never took his readers into Zaroff's death chamber (or "library," as Zaroff labeled it), but the horror of the notion hung over the story like a ghastly pall. After disclosing his secret of hunting "the most dangerous game" and inviting Rainsford to join in, Zaroff is intent on showing his guest his latest trophies. "'And now,' said the general, 'I want to show you my new collection of heads. Will you come with me to the library?'" A shocked Rainsford begs off, however, answering, "I hope that you will excuse me tonight, General Zaroff. I'm really not feeling all that well." In *Surviving the Game*, director Ernest Dickerson and company brings this queasy notion to full gruesome light by having Mason break into the locked room at the cabin, revealing row upon row of jars containing preserved human heads, each neatly labeled with the "trophy's" name. (This, of course, leads to the deliciously dark "Mason jar" pun when he spies an empty jar standing at the ready, his own name on it.)

Also like in the original story, Mason sets a trap for his pursuer(s). But he being a self-confessed city boy with little knowledge of "woodcraft" (much less a "Malay man-catcher" or "Burmese tiger pit"), he employs a lit cigarette stuck into a tree as a decoy so that he can take a hunter (Griffin) by surprise. And like in Connell's tale, it works, but the "trap" claims not the intended Zaroff (Burns) but one of his followers (Ivan in the story, Griffin in the film).

Surviving the Game takes a key scene from Connell's story when the hunters track Mason to a clifftop, only to have their prey leap into the water below (though here it is a raging river rather than the roiling ocean of Connell's tale) to escape his pursuers. And in the film it comes not at the end, like in the short story, but as a second-act interlude, with more hunt (and violent action) to follow.

Connell's "The Most Dangerous Game" concludes with Rainsford, thought dead by his hunter, making it back to Zaroff's lair (his jungle castle) to engage the general in mortal combat. So too does *Surviving the Game*, though Mason, thought by Burns to be killed in the plane explosion, escapes the wilderness hunting ground to arrive in Seattle. There he confronts Burns just outside the hunter's office—the place where it all started. Just as in Connell's story, the tables have turned and the prey becomes the hunter at the place where it all began.

Critique

"The great action adventure films were always my favorites," said *Surviving the Game* director Ernest Dickerson. "They had such rich characters. The audience always got to see how these people changed and responded to the stress around them. I made *Surviving the Game* as a combination of an adventure and a suspense film in the tradition of *Deliverance*."[2] And rich characters and stressful situations, set against a beautiful—and dangerous—wilderness backdrop, is what this Most Dangerous tale is all about.

It all begins with the well-constructed and richly thematic screenplay by Eric Bernt (amazingly, his first) that not only touches on the obvious issues of hunting for sport, but of class and even race conflict (not to mention suicide and its ethical conundrums). "So often in films," continued Dickerson, "the homeless are portrayed as these psychopaths. A lot of people who are homeless today had jobs two or three years ago and a driveway with a car in it. But factories and companies go out of business, and people find themselves without jobs. It's important to show that a lot of homeless folks, like the people in our movie, are trying to maintain some kind of structure and dignity in their lives in order to survive."[3] Apart from this obvious haves-vs.-have-nots subtext (something also underlined in the previous year's *Hard Target*) that arises when a cadre of rich men hunt a poor one for fun (crystallized by Wolfe's comment that Mason is "a homeless piece of shit, he's nothing; he's *less* than nothing"), there lurks beneath the story's surface the notion of race as well. Is it an accident that these wealthy killers are all white and their prey a black man? Granted, Cole is black, but Mason obviously sees him as an Uncle Tom (albeit a deadly one) for Cole's aligning himself with these rich Caucasian killers (with an angry Mason calling Cole a "punk sell-out motherfucker"). Adding power to the racial undercurrent is the fact that director Ernest Dickerson is African-American himself, and previously worked as cinematographer on a number of Spike Lee films.

Another intriguing and involving theme focuses on how Mason, a man "with nothing left to lose" (as he himself puts it), and who even attempts suicide at one point, changes through these dire circumstances into a man who'll battle to the death to save what he earlier sought to discard. (When asked by Cole why he'd want to kill himself, Mason angrily, and perhaps presciently, answers, "Maybe I like the idea of choosing when I die instead of having somebody else choose for me.") "I really like the idea that Mason is a homeless character," commented Dickerson. "He's a man who finds strength and a will to survive within himself that he never knew he had. He's alone in an alien environment and overcomes this situation on his own. I was really fascinated by that and by the idea of people hunting people."[4] So be grateful for what you have (even when all you have is your life), the film might be saying, as only when it's threatened do people really begin to appreciate it. With such thematic depth, *Surviving the Game* offers more food for thought than most action movies (including many of its Most Dangerous compatriots).

But a script is only as good as the actors and crew that bring it to life. Fortunately, *Surviving the Game* features arguably the best cast (including an Oscar-winner and another nominee) in any MDG film, and sports the sure-handed direction of a former class-A cinematographer, meaning the visuals are always on the mark.

Working with editor Sam Pollard (*Mo' Better Blues, Jungle Fever, Clockers*), Dickerson sets the fast-paced, emotional and innovative standard from the opening scene. Like a number of Most Dangerous Game adaptations before it (*Avenging Force, Slave Girls from Beyond Infinity, Hard Target,* multiple TV episodes), *Surviving the Game* opens with an initial hunt in which some unknown, disposable character runs for his or her life until brought down by a pursuer; only then are we introduced to our primary protagonist and his/her part in the general set-up. But *un*like those other variations, *Surviving the Game* cleverly intersperses scenes of Mason (eating from a dumpster, offering his dog some of his found food, and watching helplessly as his canine friend is hit by a car) with shots of the hunters in the wilderness stalking their prey and making the kill—thereby introducing the main character concurrently with, and visually linking him to, the hunt itself. The sequence concludes with a rapid series of quick edits showing: Mason's dog giving chase to a cat; a startled deer fleeing through the forest; four hunters on the move; Mason chasing after his dog; one hunter taking aim and firing; Mason reacting with horror as we hear tires squeal and a dog yelp; and—shockingly—a man in the woods clutching his bloody shoulder and turning to look back, his eyes wide, terrified. Here we realize that the hunters are not after the deer but a *man*. It's a brilliantly conceived and executed opening sequence that deftly sets up the main premise while delineating both the protagonist's circumstances (dire) and character (kind), as well as foreshadowing the terrors to come.

Dickerson, alongside his cinematographer, Bojan Bazelli (*Pumpkinhead, King of New York, The Sorcerer's Apprentice*), utilizes his mastery of the camera to generate mood, excitement and suspense through his choice of angles, movement and even point-of-view shots. The main hunt begins when Mason wakes with a gun pointed at his face. Dickerson shows it from Mason's point of view so that Cole towers over him—over *us*—the gun barrel looking disproportionately huge and threatening in the foreground. Burns, leaning against the wall behind Cole, steps forward and looks down, looming over us as he smilingly intones, "We like to play a game..."

Then they open the bedroom door and push Mason through into the cabin's main room, only to be greeted by the rest of the hunters, shouting and jeering in a kind of derisive gauntlet. The camera again takes Mason's point of view, as Hawkins gets in his (our) face, with the camera tilting and whirling in confusion and panic. The hunters' mocking visages loom large, with the intense Griffin's angry countenance coming into view as he literally spits, "I want you so bad I can taste it!" Next the condescending Wolfe steps into frame, mock-offering, "Let me get the door" just before Cole and Burns toss Mason through it to start the hunt. The point-of-view shots bring an immediacy to the scene, placing us in Mason's bewildered and panicked shoes, while the hunters' faces thrust forward, looking animalistic and terrifying, adds a chaotic, almost lunatic feel.

As Mason flees through the woods, the amazingly mobile camera moves alongside him as he runs, keeping him in focus while the trees passing behind, and even in front, go by as a blur, enhancing the sense of panicked flight. For marked contrast, Dickerson juxtaposes shots of the hunters back at the cabin, calmly enjoying a leisurely breakfast, with shots of Mason running, first with the the camera in front of him, then behind him, tracking as he leaps over fallen logs and sprints in terror. Breakfast over, we see the hunters take off on their motorcycles and ATVs before a shot of Mason shows him deep in the woods, exhausted and panting for breath. The camera suddenly swoops towards Mason as he abruptly turns, startled by the menacing mechanized sound of the vehicles. The swift camera movement towards Mason, coupled with its off-kilter, tilting angle, visually underscores his renewed sense of panic at the approaching danger. The sequence closes as the camera, like the hunters, pursues Mason when he sets off again, continuing his headlong flight.

Dickerson's careful handling of the pivotal "trophy room" scene makes what could have been merely a cheap and cheesy gore sequence into a memorable and shocking central set-piece. When Mason breaks the lock and opens the door, we initially see only a darkened room, the eerie greenish light filtering in through the drawn window shades revealing the merest outlines of some standing shelving. But when Mason hits the light switch, the camera abruptly zooms in to reveal in shocking close-up a human head suspended in liquid in a glass jar, lit from below with a hellish glow. Then come rapid shots of other heads in jars, and finally a long shot revealing the three shelving units and their horrible contents in all their gruesome glory. A reaction shot shows Mason gagging and covering his mouth in horrified disgust before uttering, "Sick motherfuckers!" The camera then moves back into the room and into a brief close-up of a head, then sidles upward to show another on the shelf above, before spinning away, ever so wobbly (like Mason — and the viewer — himself), to reveal an empty jar with an engraved base plate reading "MASON." It's a powerful and disturbing scene, with the horror of it all brought home by the woozy camerawork, atmospheric lighting and judicious editing.

Bringing the well-delineated characters to life is a cadre of fine, experienced actors. Even rapper-turned-thespian Ice-T, a relative newcomer to film (making only his fourth significant screen appearance), overcomes his urban gangsta, expletive-spouting persona to imbue Mason with emotional depth (particularly during his impromptu recollection, steeped in guilt and self-loathing, of how his family died in a tenement fire that he feels he should have prevented). Though few viewers can truly identify with the dirty, dreadlocked, dumpster-diving character of Mason, Ice-T's tough-but-tormented performance provides for a sympathetic, multi-layered protagonist.

Rutger Hauer brings the complicated depth and off-beat qualities that made him a go-to villain for so many films — from *Blade Runner* (1982) to *The Hitcher* (1986) to *Salem's Lot* (2004) — to bear fully on Burns, making him a worthy overseer for all these ruthless hunters-of-men. Hauer's intensity of expression and intelligent, measured dialogue delivery make it clear that something is always going on — the wheels are always turning — behind Burns' deceptively innocuous eyeglasses. (Note: These glasses were a deliberate and important prop for Hauer. Said the actor, "I made Mr. Burns still wear glasses, which turns out to be a vulnerable side and metaphor. He is a master of disguise. Just like the devil. He does not wear his horns on his sleeve. He is a very quick thinker."[5]) About his penchant for villainy, the Dutch-born Hauer said (a year after the film's release):

> [Hollywood producers] always want to put me in bad guy boxes, but playing villains comes easy to me. I find that people are fascinated by evil. They're totally paralyzed by it and, as an actor, I'm not. Part of the freedom you have as a bad guy is that you can go anywhere, especially if it's a psychotic bad guy. You can do anything you want. I think in my darker characters I go a little

further than most American actors.... Maybe it's because I'm not afraid of that side myself. If I can get to play a monster on the inside I like it a lot. Because a lot of us are monsters on the inside.[6]

Amusingly, this "monster on the inside" lived on a potato farm in Holland at the time.

Few actors are as adept at portraying a disturbed, violent man working mightily to keep from going off the rails as Gary Busey (whose subsequent real life might just mirror that description a little too closely). An Oscar nominee (for 1978's *The Buddy Holly Story*), and in 1994 still a decade away from becoming a human caricature, Busey's Hawkins effectively encapsulates the animal within us all, struggling to be set loose. Before dinner, Hawkins proposes, "Here's a toast to the hunters—and a prayer for the hunted." At this, Busey's eyes subtly yet hungrily slide sideways toward Mason. Then, during their repast, Hawkins turns the pig head on a platter towards Mason and instructs, "While you're eating the flesh from the pig, look into its beady little eyes. That way you will be devouring his soul." At this, Burns bemusedly comments, "Doc, sometimes you even scare *me*." Hawkins replies, still gazing intently at Mason (as if wanting to devour *his* soul, perhaps), "Good," and smiles—with his mouth but not his unwavering eyes. Busey's smooth voice, intense gaze—cold but with a fire burning just behind his eyes—and toothy grin (which fades ever so slightly at the end) speaks volumes about his dangerous character.

Busey's finest moment comes with his telling of how he acquired his facial scar, which he calls his "birthmark." It occurred when he was 13 years old and his overbearing father decided it was time he became a man—by inciting his beloved bulldog to fight him to the death. This three-minute "Prince Henry Stout" monologue, with Busey's gesticulations and disturbing expressions conveying the confusion and the terror of the situation as he subtly acts it out while sitting in his chair, rivals Karloff's riveting "The Appointment in Samarra" recital from *Targets* (1968) in its rapt intensity, and very nearly equals Robert Shaw's spellbinding tale of the USS Indianapolis from *Jaws* (1975). By the time Busey finishes his story, he's breathing heavily, his eyes staring intently as he relives the horrific experience in his mind. Briefly closing his eyes with the faintest of grimaces, Busey gives one final sigh and opens them again, as if reborn. It's a powerful sequence, with Busey's storytelling skills making it both shocking and enthralling—not least because of his obviously suppressed emotion that makes him seem like a coiled spring. A *dangerous* spring. The scene concludes on a near-comical note (designed, no doubt, to relieve the nearly unbearable tension) when Mason, dumbfounded, carefully asks Doc Hawkins, "Do your *patients* know about this story?" But just as the viewer's mouth begins to twitch into a smile, Busey responds with a level "No..." and then chokes the welling laughter in our throats by ominously adding, "but you do." Chilling.

According to Busey himself, this scene was primarily improvisational:

Surviving the Game! That was fantastic and when it came time to do the story about how I got into this game of surviving the game, the line was about three inches long. I told the director, Ernest Dickerson, I said, "Ernest, this is not enough to tell the people why I'm here. Can I enlarge this?" And he said, "Yes you can." And I said, "You have just watered my garden! Thank you." So out came the story about me fighting Prince Henry Stout, the bulldog—life and death. And all that was improv. It's used in film studies now at colleges and universities to talk about the power of improvisation and spontaneity. And here is the key to spontaneity. This is a quote. Spontaneity comes from an invisible idea that is there before the creation begins—end quote. We all have it. We all have it in us, this natural gift.[7]

The remaining cast acquit themselves well, too, from Charles S. Dutton's humor-loving yet dangerously imposing Cole, to John C. McGinley's intense, tortured, almost Aspergerlike Griffin. But special mention should be made of Oscar-winning actor (for 1984's *Amadeus*) F. Murray Abraham. Known for being an "actor's actor," Abraham has admitted, "I'm both intense and serious when it comes to acting, but I'm so much more."[8] Indeed, Abraham brings that intensity to bear fully on his character of Wolfe, Sr. His barely-held-in-check interactions with his son, whom he desperately wants to mold in his own image (yet sees as an obvious disappointment, at one point hissing, "You're too much like your mother!"), speaks volumes. And though perhaps the least prepossessing character both physically and in terms of his background (he's a stockbroker!), he more than holds his own with the other, more rough-and-tumble (and more overtly psychotic) characters. Thanks to Abraham's "intensity" and "seriousness," one readily believes that he can — and would — go toe to toe with any of them. (Incidentally, for years people have speculated about what the "F" in F. Murray Abraham's name stands for. The *Internet Movie Data Base*, for instance, claims that he was born Fahrid Murray Abraham. Not true, he says. In fact, the "F" doesn't mean anything. "I made it up," he admitted. "Actually, I did it in honor of my father, whose first name was Frederick.... The 'F' does not stand for Fahrid.... The 'F' is just an 'F.'"[9])

Abraham suffered a serious injury during the shoot, but, being a consummate professional, the Oscar-winner didn't let it slow him down. Recalled Dickerson:

> He really was a big inspiration because he almost lost his life making the film. We were four days into shooting and we had been shooting the dinner scene at the cabin. All of our locations were about an hour away from the hotel.... One night ... a drunk driver ran a stop sign and slammed into his car.... The driver in the other car was killed, and the two passengers had to be airlifted out to a hospital because we were four hours away from Seattle.... Murray had three broken ribs, a broken hand, and his face had hit the steering wheel, so he was really banged up badly. He was in quite a bit of pain ... [but] Murray insisted on coming back to work after three days.... God bless him, he was a real trooper and a good friend. He came back and completed his role with quite a bit of discomfort to himself because we were in pretty rough terrain.[10]

Unfortunately, like many a film before and since, *Surviving the Game* sometimes glosses over such minor considerations as reality and logic. When Mason comes to a high gorge, how does he fell a large tree growing at its edge in order to bridge the chasm? Why, he repeatedly shoots it with a shotgun, of course. Later, pursued by the two surviving hunters, Mason trips, rolls down a hill and goes over a cliff. Amazingly, there's a tree growing horizontally(!) out from said cliff face, which Mason manages to grab onto to save himself. Of course, this begs the question: In what forest do trees grow parallel to the earth rather than upwards toward the sun? Then Mason climbs back up the side of the cliff (serious abdominal wound and all, having been shot in the stomach by Burns), only to find that the two hunters have foolishly scampered off. Worse than this bit of plot contrivance is the fact that when Mason finally drags himself over the rim at the top to lay flat on his back with relief, we distinctly hear on the soundtrack loud wheezing and snorting noises — just like a bear would make. Mason then abruptly rolls over to stare at something off-screen as the camera zooms in on his suddenly alarmed countenance. But *there is no bear*, and the scene simply ends, moving on to Burns and Wolfe deciding to stay put somewhere and let Mason come to them. Perhaps the bear handler was sick that day, or maybe Dickerson and editor Sam Pollard felt the (comical) wolf encounter earlier (when Mason nearly stumbles over a snarling wolf before backing away and telling it, "I'm get the fuck out your woods, ok? Just cool out. Chill. Nice wolf") was enough fauna and so cut the bear scene. If so, then why leave in those few seconds of bear-breathing and Ice-T's startled reaction? It only raises questions — and hopes — that go frustratingly unfulfilled.

Then, of course, there's the issue of just how Mason got out of that deep wilderness (accessible only by private plane) and back to Seattle, alone and gut-shot, in just three days. (Adding careless insult to locational injury, it's actually the *Philadelphia* skyline that appears onscreen rather than Seattle's!) And once back in the city, why did he not go to the police? More to the point, why did he not at least seek medical attention (Mason still sports the same tattered shirt from his earlier confrontation with Burns — with the blood inexplicably looking just as fresh as three days ago)?! Instead, seemingly none the worse for wear (despite a still-untreated bullet wound to the stomach), he decides to engage Burns in a vigorous back-alley battle.

Bernt, Dickerson, et al. obviously succumbed to the Action Movie Syndrome for the film's final act. It starts when Wolfe, who's proven himself to be one mean hombre afraid of nothing (including his fellow killers, whom he slaps down and challenges on several occasions), is so easily spooked by simple sounds in the night, resulting in his blindly firing his pistol into the darkness. Such behavior remains completely out of character. The scene even includes a seriously cliched moment when Wolfe shouts, "Take a look, Mason, I got no gun"— right before he hears a twig snap and frantically fires blindly. Now out of bullets, Wolfe hysterically screams, "I don't need this fucking gun! C'mon Mason, show yourself." Wolfe turns, and suddenly Mason is right there — to smash him in the face. So what had been a taut, intelligent, character-driven and eventful Most Dangerous Game abruptly goes into cliched Action Mode for its final 15 minutes, with Mason even painting his face and going all Rambo (complete with suddenly sleeveless shirt). It's a disappointing finish to an otherwise excellent adaptation.

Despite this concluding misstep, *Surviving the Game* still remains a fast-paced, well-acted, entertaining update that offers enough of Connell's core to satisfy any Most Dangerous fan. And you just gotta love a movie sporting a closing credit that reads: "Human Trophy Heads Created and Designed By..."

Production

The *Surviving the Game* cast and crew shot on location for two months in and around the Wenatchee National Forest, and the town of Wenatchee, in Eastern Washington. Star Rutger Hauer thoroughly enjoyed the location, reportedly taking up residence in a remote cabin where he would hike and motorcycle during his time off. "I lived in a city for 25 years," said Hauer, "and then I moved to the country. I will never move back to the city again. I grow my own vegetables when I have time, and I cut my own grass. I love it."[11] Hauer was pleased with the script as well. Said the actor:

> The story of *Surviving the Game* is not new. I have not seen the other films it was based on. It is a survival story of one man.... What a nasty and cruel story. A man's game. A manhunt. The homeless — again — chosen because no one will miss him quickly or dearly, and no one who would will be believed. It is a story which I found to be one of the most cruel. Fascinating to work on such sinister and cynic material.[12]

Hauer enjoys his villainy, commenting, "I take great, great pleasure and pride in trying to make these characters as sinister as possible, and my joy in doing so may just add another touch. I happen to believe that I know parts of the devil, so to speak, and I dig creatively for space, size and room to get the wings out."[13] After running away from his Amsterdam home at age 15 to work for a year on a merchant freighter, Hauer returned to the Netherlands to toil as a laborer while attending acting classes. After appearing in such films as Paul Verhoeven's *Turkish Delight* (1973) and *Soldier of Orange* (1977), he made his American movie debut in *Nighthawks* (1981) opposite Sylvester Stallone. Since then he's carved a successful international career by alternating between villain and hero in such films as *Ladyhawke* (1985), *Flesh and Blood* (1986), the 1988 telefilm *Escape from Sobibor* (for which he won a Golden Globe Award), *The Blood of Heroes* (1990), *Confessions of a Dangerous Mind* (2002), and the cult oddity *Hobo with a Shotgun* (2011).

"Rap superstar Ice-T is one of the few performers to make the successful transition from rap to acting," begins a *Surviving the Game* publicity piece.[14] Born Tracy Morrow, he grew up among the gang culture of Los Angeles, aligning himself with the Crips and perpetrating petty crimes until joining the U.S. Army for four years. ("I've already lived past my life expectancy," he observed during production on *Surviving the Game*, "so I have to be ready to risk it all if I'm going for something I want."[15]) After leaving the military, he forged a successful career as a DJ and rapper (attaining his greatest fame—or infamy—with his controversial song "Cop Killer"). After two brief film appearances (in the terrible *Breakin'* and its equally vapid sequel *Breakin' 2: Electric Boogaloo*, both 1984), he hit it big by appearing in the 1989 Mario Van Peebles film *New Jack City*, and his acting career took off. Since 2000, he's enjoyed a recurring role on TV's popular *Law and Order: Special Victims Unit*. Ice-T returned to the Dangerous Game fold twice more, making him the Most Prolific Actor in the Dangerous Game subgenre. Three years after he *Survived the Game* he looked down the *other* side of the gun barrel when he starred in the direct-to-video feature *Mean Guns*, an "*Almost* Dangerous Game" entry in which he orchestrates a most dangerous free-for-all among a band of gangsters and killers. Then in 2012 he appeared in a Most Dangerous episode of *Law and Order: Special Victims Unit* called "Hunting Ground."

African-American cinematographer-turned-director Ernest Dickerson made his name during his long-time pairing with filmmaker Spike Lee, for whom he shot such favorites as *School Daze* (1988), *Do the Right Thing* (1989), *Jungle Fever* (1991) and *Malcolm X* (1992). Dickerson turned full-fledged director on *Juice* (1992), with *Surviving the Game* being his sophomore directorial effort. Attracted to the horror, science fiction and action genres, Dickerson helmed such films as *Tales from the Crypt: Demon Knight* (1995), *Bones* (2001) and *Never Die Alone* (2004), his last theatrical feature to date as director. "I like unusual stories, you know," said Dickerson. "I'm not the kinda guy to do a romantic comedy. The older I've gotten, the more I've embraced more off-the-wall genres. And I love when you take a few different genres and mix them all together."[16] In the mid-00s Dickerson turned to television, overseeing episodes of edgy and popular series like *The Wire*, *Dexter*, and *The Walking Dead*.

Neophyte screenwriter Eric Bernt, though creating a work of significant depth and characterization in *Surviving the Game*, felt his first produced script was far from perfect. For one thing, he lamented his decision to kill off the Hawkins/Busey character so early on. Said Bernt in 2013:

> It's something I think about and regret every day. I mean, in retrospect, I put in all that work developing his back story, even giving him a three minute monologue to tell the story of his self proclaimed "birthmark" [scar] that he received when his father made him fight Prince Henry Stout to the death. After giving viewers that kind of window into the character, he should have been kept around much longer.... If I had the chance to do it over again, I would alter the order of deaths drastically. But I was so wet behind the ears that I didn't think about the big picture, and I have to live with that.[17]

When prompted further about what he would change in his screenplay, Bernt responded:

> Without question, F. Murray Abraham's character (Derek Wolfe, Sr.) should have died first. That would have made it easier for the character's apprehensive son (played by William McNamara) to get over the fact they were hunting another human and dive headlong into the hunt. Plus, I could have had Busey [Hawkins] step in to become a father figure to McNamara, and that quasi father/son dynamic would have slowly morphed McNamara's character into a second Busey. If I had done that, I'd probably have an Oscar on my mantle right now.[18]

Bernt was also asked which character deaths he got right, and he offered:

> I think I really nailed the deaths of John C. McGinley's character [Griffin, killed by Cole after trying to quit the hunt] and Charles S. Dutton's character [Cole, mercy killed by Burns after being mortally wounded in an ATV explosion precipitated by Mason]. To get to those, I really tried to put myself in the shoes of a group of guys hunting another human, and I wasn't let down.[19]

Regrets aside, Bernt showed that he has what it takes to survive in the movie business game, as to date six of his subsequent screenplays since *Surviving the Game* have been made into films, including 2000's *Romeo Must Die* and 2007's *The Hitcher*.

Upon its domestic theatrical release, *Surviving the Game* barely broke even, domestically grossing less than three hundred thousand dollars over its reported $7.4 million budget. Which is a pity, as the film deserved better, standing as it does as one of the best Most Dangerous adaptations extant.

On a lighter (and perhaps tastier) note, while watching the film on DVD, you and your friends can play the *Surviving the Game* drinking game.[20] According to the fine folks at *drinkingcinema.com*, you take a drink whenever (among others):

- Someone needlessly assaults or de-personifies a street person. Seriously, Ice-T's dog gets run over, and *he's* the one who gets punched?
- You see a stuffed head (human or animal). Human is the *ultimate game* and why *wouldn't* you want to show off your human head trophies? Oh, because it's beyond illegal and completely psychotic. No, you're right. Put them in the guest room.
- A hunter enlightens you with some nice, creepy hunter zen. Like how you should always eat the head of an animal and stare into its eyes so that you ensure you are devouring its soul as well as its flesh. Maybe that's not zen so much as crazy, but who are we to judge those who hunt people for sport.
- Someone shares way too personal of a story. The stories are usually unprompted and go on *much* longer than you thought they would. Just like your grandpa's ... except your grandpa never hunted you for sport afterwards.

CREDITS: Director: Ernest Dickerson; Producer: David Permut; Screenplay: Eric Bernt; Cinematographer: Bojan Bazelli; Co-Producer: Fred Caruso; Executive Procuder: Kevin J. Messick; Costumes: Ruth Carter; Production Design: Christiaan Wagener; Music: Stuart Copeland; Editor: Sam Pollard; Production Companies: New Line Productions, David Permut Productions; Distribution Company: New Line Cinema; Release Date: April 15, 1994; Running Time: 96 minutes; MPAA Rating: R.

CAST: Rutger Hauer (Burns), Ice-T (Mason), Charles S. Dutton (Cole), Gary Busey (Hawkins), F. Murray Abraham (Wolfe, Sr.), John C. McGinley (Griffin), Jeff Corey (Hank), William McNamara (Wolfe, Jr.).

14

Comedy Game
The Pest (1997)

> What kind of freakazoid would let someone hunt him just to collect $50,000?
> Next question.— poster

Synopsis

In Miami, Latino delivery boy-cum-self-styled scam artist Pestario "Pest" Vargas (John Leguizamo) owes "the Scottish Mob" $50,000 after his bets "turned south." At the Little Havana Calle Ocho Festival, German hunter Gustav Shank (Jeffrey Jones) cruises the crowd for a prime "specimen," but his assistant Leo (Tim McCleister) misunderstands and chooses Pest, whose blind-man shell game ruse is interrupted by kilt-wearing gangsters wanting their money. Slipping through the Scottish thugs' grasp, Pest ends up at Shank's mansion, where he's duped into thinking he's won a "$50,000 scholarship." Says Shank, "We have a little tradition that all the winners join me for a little gentlemanly hunt on my private island."

After arriving at the island aboard Shank's helicopter, Pest meets Shank's effeminate son, Himmel (Edoardo Ballerini), who finds Pest rather attractive and warns him that *Pest* will be the prey in his father's hunt. Literally tumbling into Shank's trophy room (lined with human heads from all the ethnic groups save one—Latino), Pest realizes it's true. Refusing to play Shank's sick "game," Pest quickly changes his tune when offered the $50,000 if he can stay alive for 24 hours. ("Oh my god, why didn't you say so?" he squeals. "Hunt away, you great white hunter.") Off Pest goes into the jungle, with Shank and his reluctant son (who'd rather be a hairdresser than a hunter) in hot pursuit. After being temporarily waylaid by a trap set by Pest (resulting in Himmel hoisted in a net), the two hunters spot Pest "doing his business." Before they can take aim, Himmel's rocket launcher accidentally goes off, resulting in an explosion that leaves only Pest's shoes behind. "Looks like your hunt is over," observes a relieved Himmel. "I'm going back to the house before I miss *Hogan's Heroes*." But Pest is not dead after all, and sneaks back to the house. There Pest convinces Himmel to help him escape in Shank's speedboat (where they both become woefully seasick). But when Himmel is temporarily incapacitated by some seagull poop to the eye, Pest jumps overboard and swims to Miami, arriving just in time to join his friends at a pool party.

Shank soon crashes the party in his helicopter and resumes the hunt. A tracking device he'd slipped into Pest's underwear leads Shank to Pest's African-American girlfriend's house, where Pest (sporting an outrageous afro wig and African garb, and talking nonsensical "jive")

14. Comedy Game

"Pest — is that your name or a personality trait?" asks the annoyed Shank (Jeffery Jones, right) of Pest (John Leguizamo) before taking him to his private island for a Most Dangerous Game.

has gone to meet her parents; then to a synagogue, where Pest attempts to pass himself off as an Hasidic rabbi; and finally to a nightclub where Pest disguises himself as a karaoke-singing Japanese businessman. Finally, a frustrated Shank takes the slippery Pest's family, girlfriend, and even the girlfriend's family all hostage at a shipping dock. After much shenanigans, Pest manages to get the drop on Shank. But Shank tells him, "You remember our little toast on our island, Pest? I poisoned your drink. The poison kills in exactly 18 hours. You've got 15 seconds, Pest. Enjoy." Pest collapses. When Shank goes to the bank the next morning to retrieve the $50,000 from a safety deposit box, he finds it empty. The phone rings, and it's Pest:

> Surprise! ... I puked up all the poison on that thrilling boat ride with your Himmel. And with the help of my close personal friend the German Ambassador, I was able to liberate all your money. And you know, there was a lot more than $50,000 in there. Oh, and the Ambassador spoke to the authorities about your — how shall I put it — extensive hunting activities.

The police burst in and arrest Shank. On the way out, however, they bump into Pest — dressed as the "German Ambassador" — for a final round of slapstick humiliation (with a concluding "goose" for good measure) before Pest happily drives off with his girlfriend and homeys.

How "Dangerous" Is It?

Taking into account that *The Pest* plays its Most Dangerous Game hand for cheap laughs and gags (it *is* a comedy after all, if a woefully unfunny one) rather than horror and suspense, it still holds a few ostensibly Connell-like cards. Like Zaroff, the haughty Shank (though a nasty Nazi rather than a crazed Cossack) seeks the most "challenging" game for his sport. While cruising Pest's Latino neighborhood, Shank admonishes his impatient assistant, "A good hunter must always remember — the most challenging prey is often the most difficult to find." And where Zaroff orchestrates shipwrecks to screen out the weak, leaving only the fittest for his prey, Shank screens *his* intended targets via a battery of physical tests. "We have to administer a few small tests to see if you qualify," he tells Pest (who thinks he's applying for a "scholarship"). Ridiculously, these tests involve a spinning table (causing Pest to vomit profusely); a leg-press machine (resulting in Pest doing the painful splits), and a *squash court* (on which Pest knocks himself out with his racket). But I suppose it's the thought that counts...

Shank, just like Zaroff, has his own private Caribbean island upon which to hunt his most dangerous game. As seen from the air, it's much smaller, though, which is perhaps the reason Shank's time limit for his "game" is 24 hours rather than Zaroff's three days.

Just as Rainsford does, Pest lays a trap for his pursuer(s). And it's even something along the lines of Rainsford's "Malay man-catcher," in which a trip-wire/vine causes a huge log to fall (or, in this case, swing down). Here, rather than catching Shank/Zaroff a glancing blow on the shoulder (like in the story), it hits Himmel full on, tossing him through the air into the nearby river and onto a net laid just under the surface that closes up and hoists him into the air, suspending the young man like a ripe, er, fruit (no pun intended). Just how Pest managed to rig such a Rube Goldberg-esque man-trap (much less from where he acquired all the rope and netting) remains a mystery, but it's all for laughs in any case. And it does lead to one of the film's few truly amusing exchanges, this between the haughty Shank and his sensitive son:

> Himmel (hanging in net): "Get me down."
> Shank (ignoring Himmel and marveling at the trap): "Oh, this Pest is *good*!"
> Himmel (angry): "Get me down!"
> Shank (dismissively): "Oh, don't be such a sissy."
> Himmel (calmly): "I don't know if you've noticed lately, father, but *I am a sissy!*"

Then, of course, there's the trophy room. Though Connell never takes his readers inside Zaroff's den of death, the grotesque implication hangs over the tale like a pall. Shank's trophy room offers (questionable) chuckles to go along with its shudders, as the mounted human heads lining its walls feature labels like "Filipino," "Chinese," and an empty plaque that reads "Latinus Spicticus" just waiting for Pest's noggin.

Screenwriter David Bar Katz, like Connell before him, gives *his* Zaroff figure a significant speech about his motivation for hunting the most dangerous game — though, short and (not so) sweet, it lacks the poetry and power of Connell's monologue. "By the time I was thirty," explains Shank, "I'd hunted nearly every animal there was to be hunted. I was bored, I was depressed. I needed a challenge." At this, Pest interrupts with, "Have you tried Parcheesi? It *is* a game of skill as well as chance." Ignoring him, Shank continues, "Here on this island I have successfully hunted every ethnicity except one." Pest again interjects, with, "Oh my god, haven't the Jewish people suffered enough?!" (A cheap shot, perhaps, but given Shank's militant Germanic leanings, an ironically funny one.)

Katz must have seen *Surviving the Game*, for *The Pest* borrows a couple of innovative ideas from that relatively recent MDG adaptation (released less than two years before *The Pest* was shot). The first comes when Pest meets Himmel, and the young man revealingly recounts how his father had tried to make him a man — just like Gary Busey's character did

14. Comedy Game

with his shocking "Prince Henry Stout" soliloquy in *Surviving the Game*. "Do you know what he used to do to me when I was a child?" asks Himmel. "He would lock me in a room with a boa constrictor and tell me I couldn't get out until I *killed* it. He kept me in that room for six weeks. I loved that snake!" Though it ain't a patch on Busey's riveting — and revealing — monologue, it nonetheless offers an easy explanation for Himmel's fascination with snakes (both of the literal and metaphorical type), leading to the occasional humorous reference later on. (And, of course, Pest gets to conclude the scene with the obvious-yet-still-droll comment, "You share too much.")

The second "borrowing" from *Surviving the Game* is the father-son dynamic between Shank and Himmel. Just as Wolfe, Sr., wants to introduce his son Derek to the joys of hunting humans (and thus molding his offspring in his own image) in *Surviving the Game*, so too does Shank want to turn his effeminate, snake-loving son into a hunter-of-men, forcing the reluctant lad to accompany him on the hunt, and even insisting he take down the prey. (To this, Himmel humorously replies, "I don't want to make the kill; I want to be a hairdresser and write musicals.") This leads to another of the film's all-too-rare funny bits. After spotting the pooping Pest in the jungle, Shank tells Himmel, "I want you to take him out." "Why me?" asks the lad. Shank replies, passionately, "I want you to experience the utter ecstasy that comes from feeling the *hot, throbbing* force of a man's life when it's in your hands." Obviously thinking along more carnal lines, Himmel eagerly answers, "I'm sold!"

Critique

I'd love to be able to tell you, gentle reader, that I've saved the best for last. But that simply is not the case. In fact, it's the exact opposite. When a film opens with John Leguizamo performing a rap song ("The Pest [Voodoo Mambo]") while dancing in the shower, complete with bad impersonations of everyone from Edward G. Robinson to Jerry Lewis, and pop-culture references to everything from *Dracula* to *I Love Lucy*, you know you're in trouble. And with lyrics like "I'm ridica-lica-liculous / Like a booger I stick to this," it's best to simply run screaming from the room.

"I thought the script was very funny, demented and strange, while verging on being totally tasteless," said

Edoardo Ballerini as reluctant hunter Himmel in *The Pest*, who named his pet snake "Cocteau" — not for the French playwright but "after my two favorite body parts."

Pest co-star Jeffrey Jones.[1] In the manic, undisciplined hands of John Leguizamo, however, most of the "funny, demented and strange" devolves into "stupid, painful and offensive." And no "verging" about it, *The Pest* is indeed totally tasteless.

"We believe in John [Leguizamo]," enthused co-producer Sid Sheinberg, "and wanted to give him a chance to make the movie he wanted to make. He is an enormously talented writer/comedian and a proven actor. This story is a great platform to let him go crazy."[2] And go crazy he did, tossing in everything but the kitchen *shtick*. One moment emulating a Jerry Lewis pratfall, the next performing a patented Three Stooges "nose-grab," Leguizamo's manic, unoriginal antics grow more wearisome by the minute. Silly slapstick abounds, typified by Pest's encounter with a jungle snake in which Leguizamo whips the reptile around, plays it like a base fiddle, uses it as a jump rope, and even rides it like a pony—all shown via sped-up, Keystone Cop–like photography.

Pest manages to insult nearly every minority group imaginable over the course of this puerile picture, from epileptics (throwing a faux "fit" to distract some Scottish thugs) to Asians ("Me love you long time"). Admittedly, such an approach *can* be funny (Don Rickles made an entire career out of this), but Leguizamo's efforts appear stupid and mean-spirited rather than clever and biting. Still, at least he's an equal opportunity offender, leaving no group unscathed.

When Pest spies all the trophy heads—each sporting labels like "African American," "Hindi," or "Japanese"—he exclaims, shocked, "This is the most *disgusting* thing I've ever seen!" before elaborating, "Those heads haven't been dusted in months, hahaha. I'm just gonna get a nice little wet rag and I'll be right back. Buh-bye." It's like something from a bad *Get Smart* episode, except Leguizamo lacks the hilarious deadpan delivery that made Don Adams so brilliant with ludicrous lines like these. Another brief exchange obviously inspired by that classic '60s sitcom comes when Angus warns Pest, "Today's Monday, and without the money you owe me by Wednesday, I'm going to kill your whole family." At this, Pest suggests, "How about Thursday, and you just take out a cousin"? Ugh. The *Get Smart* Most Dangerous Game episode "Island of the Darned" offers five times as many laughs in its scant 24 minutes than *The Pest* does in all of its 82 (which, by the way, feel much, *much* longer).

"'Pest'—is that your name or a personality trait?" asks Shank at one point. Leguizamo described his character as a "wily super genius Latino scam artist running around Miami Beach and taking advantage of everyone: his friends, his loved ones, strangers—he has no boundaries."[3] Indeed, Pest remains so unlikable and lacking in any redeeming qualities that he not only annoys but ultimately *repulses* the viewer, who can only nod vigorously when Shank later says, "I can't think of anything I would rather do before returning to the Homeland than ridding the earth of this *creature*!" The character of Pest changes not a whit over the course of his nerve-wracking adventure. "[Pest has] got hubris coming out of every pore," observed Leguizamo. "he's the man. And then, once he becomes prey instead of predator, he realizes that maybe he's been doing something wrong. Maybe in some obscure way he asks for this."[4] If Pest does indeed gain such insight, he plays it close to the vest, for he remains the same obnoxious, self-centered, manipulative creep in the final scene as he was in the first. As a result, the movie lacks any real character center and devolves into little more than a string of unfunny, tasteless jokes.

Said Leguizamo, "I love silent films and broad slapstick, while [screenwriter] David [Katz] loves verbal films, Woody Allen, literary stuff. In this story we just combined all that stuff together."[5] From the finished product, one wishes that Katz had won out more often than Leguizamo, since the vast majority of Leguizamo's unoriginal slapstick comedy (much of it based on the Three Stooges) is about as funny — and enjoyable — as a poke in the eye (of the *real*, non–Stooges variety). His constant hyper-kinetic, frantic antics are exhausting at best and excruciating at worst. Most of the (few) witty moments in the film come when Leguizamo is nowhere to be seen, and primarily involve the genuinely jocular Jeffery Jones, whose haughty demeanor and exasperated expressions bring his character to comedic life. Shank's acerbic exchanges with his effeminate son remain the film's all-too-infrequent highlights. For instance:

> Himmel: Father, I don't want to participate in this; I think it's wrong.
> Shank: You have to learn some time.
> Himmel: Why would I ever have to learn to hunt *people*?
> Shank: The hunt is just a metaphor for that *glorious* cycle of endless life and rebirth. And remember — always, always, always shoot 'em in the head.
> Himmel: I hate you.
> Shank: Shut up.
> Himmel: I'm getting more tea.

The superb timing and deadpan delivery of Jones and Ballerini inject genuine humor into the absurd interplay, making it seem like they're bickering over some mundane chore rather than hunting down a man for sport.

Another entertaining exchange comes when Shank senses something amiss during the hunt (just before he inadvertently springs Pest's trap):

> Shank (pondering): Something is wrong.
> Himmel (sarcastically): What could be wrong? We're hunting a human being. Most fathers take their sons to baseball games. But *no*, you —
> Shank (dismissively): Tell it to Ricky Lake.
> Himmel (again sarcastically): Ja, I can see it now — "Nazi fathers and their snake-obsessed sons!"

Of course for every once-in-a-blue-moon moment of genuine amusement there are dozens of cringe-inducing gags — the "gag" part sometimes threatening to become literal — such as not one but *two* visually explicit vomit scenes, not to mention a lengthy sequence of Pest *defecating* in the woods (during which he recites part of Hamlet's famous soliloquy, reads the paper, and uses his sock for TP)! But I suppose that's par for the course in a film that opens with a rap song featuring an entire verse about flatulence.

Regarding the film's message, "It's pain and suffering," joked director Paul Miller, "because we find humor in that."[6] *If* it's done well, we might. With a comedy as poor as *The Pest*, "pain and suffering" is generally all the viewer gets.

Production

The Pest evolved from an idea developed by screenwriter David Bar Katz and actor/comedian John Leguizamo, who had been collaborating on a number of screenplays. "We were working on a black comedy," said Leguizamo, "and David said, 'Let's do something really simple and really broad.' I said, 'Four characters, homeys in a jeep, one's a scam artist and he owes money to the mob,' and then David put it all together and said, '*The Most Dangerous Game* — you're being hunted!' — and it was born."[7]

According to Leguizamo, said newborn script reached full maturity in a mere *three days*. "I really wanted to make a movie, so my best friend at the time, [Katz,] we wrote a treatment together, and I bet him $1,000 that he couldn't write the screenplay for it. Then he had it written in three days. Maybe that shows a little. And then I wrote a lot of the gags, the opening shower sequence, the tortures, a lot of stuff."[8]

"John Leguizamo has established a career that defies categorization," begins a *Pest* publicity piece. "With credits in television, film and theater, his work encompasses a variety of genres." And, fortunately, his work in those genres is generally *far* better than what he exhibits in *The Pest*. Born in Bogata, Columbia, and raised in New York since the age of four, Leguizamo started out as a stand-up comic, garnering significant attention — and praise — in 1991 as the writer/performer of his one-man off–Broadway show *Mambo Mouth*, in which he played seven different Latino characters (earning various critics' awards and an HBO special). Significant TV and film roles (including a break-out performance in 1995's *To Wong Foo: Thanks for Everything, Julie Newmar*, which earned him a Golden Globe nomination) and a whole series of one-man shows followed. Among Leguizamo's many movies are *Spawn* (1997), *Summer of Sam* (1999), *Assault on Precinct 13* (2005), *Land of the Dead* (2005), and the popular *Ice Age* animated films.

When interviewed six years after its release, Leguizamo said about *The Pest*, "[Now] I'd probably do things a little differently, like not having it be written in three days. You know, maybe it'd be more like a month. A month would be cool. I kinda fucked up."[9] Indeed.

Screenwriter/co-producer David Katz wrote the role of Gustav Shank with Jeffrey Jones in mind. "I've always thought he was a comic genius," said Katz of the veteran actor of such films as *Ferris Bueller's Day Off* (1986), *Beetlejuice* (1988), and *Ed Wood* (1994). "When we were initially negotiating with Jeffrey to do the part I told John I wanted to call Jeffrey personally and ask him to please do it because I wrote the part just for him. John told me not to because that's what producers always say to get actors to take parts, but in this case it was absolutely true!"[10] Jones contributed exemplary work to such films as the much-lauded *Amadeus* (1984), the excellent and underrated *Ravenous* and *Sleepy Hollow* (both 1999), and the critically acclaimed cable television series *Deadwood* (2004–2006). Jones reveled in playing the Germanic caricature that was Gustav Shank in *The Pest*. "I worked out a German accent," recalled the actor, "that's not quite Colonel Klink from *Hogan's Heroes*, but more of a Marlene Dietrich-French accented German. You're not exactly sure if this guy speaks this way or if he just speaks this way because he insists on being German. Either way, my character is going to offend the entire country of Germany. And that's what I appreciated about doing this movie is the sort of 'bash-on-regardless attitude' of the people who were involved."[11] Though an excellent character actor and comedian, Jones proved to be less than exemplary in his private life. In 2002 he was arrested for hiring a 14-year-old boy to pose for sexually explicit photographs, and for possessing child pornography. He initially pleaded not guilty but eventually changed his plea to No Contest, earning five years probation and a place on the sex offender registry.

Filming of *The Pest* began in April 1996 on a 30-day schedule in and around Miami, Florida, and Los Angeles. With an estimated budget of $17 million, *The Pest* grossed a paltry $3.5 million upon its domestic release. But that's *still* a lot of people left wanting their money back.

CREDITS: Director: Paul Miller; Producers: Sid, Jon and Bill Sheinberg; Screenplay: David Bar Katz (story: David Bar Katz, John Leguizamo); Cinematographer: Roy H. Wagner;

14. Comedy Game

Executive Producer: Robert A. Papazian; Co-Producers: John Leguizamo, David Bar Katz; Music: Kevin Kiner; Editors: Russ Albert, David Rawlins; Production Designer: Rodger E. Maus; Production Companies: Tri-Star Pictures, The Bubble Factory; Distribution Company: TriStar Pictures; Release Date: February 7, 1997; Running Time: 82 minutes; MPAA Rating: PG-13.

CAST: John Leguizamo (Pest), Jeffrey Jones (Gustav Shank), Edoardo Ballerini (Himmel), Freddy Rodriguez (Ninja), Tammy Townsend (Xantha Kent), Aries Spears (Chubby), Joe Morton (Mr. Kent), Charles Hallahan (Angus), Tom McCleister (Leo), Ivonee Coll (Gladyz), Pat Skipper (Glen Livitt).

15

DTV Danger

This chapter focuses on those "The Most Dangerous Game" adaptations that bypassed a theatrical release and went direct to video (DTV) or were produced expressly for television broadcast. Also included are foreign productions that never made it to English-speaking theaters. In other words, if an MDG movie did not receive a North American theatrical release, it will be detailed here, listed alphabetically.

Bet Your Life (2004; GRB Entertainment/NBC) Airdate: August 4, 2004. Director: Louis Morneau; Producers: Steve Richards, Alan Schechter; Teleplay: Jeff Welch, Louis Morneau (story: Jeff Welch); Cinematographer: George Mooradian. Cast: Sean Carrigan, Corinee Van Ryck de Groot, Billy Zane.

Starring in this made-for-TV actionfest was the "prize" for the two winners (one male, one female) of the little-seen-and-soon-forgotten 2004 NBC reality show *Next Action Star*, in which a group of wannabe action actors were put through their stuntwork and acting paces to show they have what it takes to become America's next Big Thing in the action-movie arena.

"Ever read any Hemingway? It's fascinating, the carnal behavioral patterns during the thrill of the hunt, the love of the hunt — even for the prey." So begins Joseph (Billy Zane), the wealthy owner of an exclusive Las Vegas private club/casino, before making a very odd proposition to down-on-his-luck former pro quarterback and compulsive gambler Sonny Briggs (*Next Action Star* winner Sean Carrigan). "Quite simply," says Joseph, "I want to hunt you down like an animal, Sonny. I want to match my wits against yours. If I catch you I kill you. But if you can outmaneuver me, stay alive for the next 24 hours, you will win $2.4 million dollars." Sonny, on the run from a loan shark's bounty hunter, Carmen (fellow winner Corinne Van Ryck de Groot), reluctantly accepts Joseph's bizarre offer. Through a series of unlikely events, Sonny escapes to Cleveland, where Joseph and his team track him via high-tech equipment (as well as private jet and helicopter), engaging in all manner of chase sequences before Sonny and Carmen (now teamed up against Joseph) make it back to Vegas for the final showdown.

Given the gimmicky nature of *Bet Your Life*'s production, it's little wonder the finished telefilm failed to set the (small) screen afire and disappeared without a ripple into the ratings void. Nor is it surprising that the two "Next Action Stars" have more or less vanished as well (Carrigan, a competent newcomer with at least a modicum of charisma, has only appeared in a few small television roles; while the disappointingly one-dimensional Van Ryck de Groot rightly abandoning acting for stunt work). What *is* surprising, however, is that *Bet Your Life* stands as an intermittently entertaining modern update on the hunting-humans-for-sport concept, thanks largely to an amusingly smug turn by well-traveled actor Billy Zane (*Dead Calm, Tombstone, Titanic*) and a relentless pace sprinkled with some inventive action sequences.

On a relatively small budget of only $5 million, director Louis Morneau (a direct-to-video B-movie veteran with credits like *Carnosaur 2*, *Bats*, and *The Hitcher 2*) offers some unique locations (such as a bridge that raises its entire deck a hundred feet in the air) and exciting action set-pieces (including an inventive, if admittedly unlikely, use of a fireboat's water hose aimed at a helicopter) involving trains, planes and automobiles (as well as trucks, moving bridges and boats). Unfortunately, he simply can't overcome the superficial script's shortfalls, which include a ridiculous amount of impossible scenarios (how many times can one shoot incendiary grenades from a helicopter, engage in destructive vehicle chases through the streets of two major cities, and fire off automatic weapons for minutes at a time without the police ever putting in an appearance?!) and a complete lack of character text (don't even *think* about *sub*text). This latter is most disappointing to the Most Dangerous Game fan, as the screenplay offers nothing to explain Joseph's obsession with hunting humans. Worse, the script actually *brings it up* on several occasions, only to drop it like a hot incendiary device. Early on, an incredulous Sonny asks Joseph, "Why do you do this?" His answer: "I'm a gambler, like you." Which is no answer at all, of course (and gives one the urge to shout, "Then go play the slots, you nutjob!"). Towards the end, Carmen spits out, "What kind of sick freak hunts down a man for sport?" At this, an impatient Joseph quips, "Beats playing golf." Again, no answer. Even one of Joseph's underlings gets in on the act when he queries, "GPS tracking devices, automatic weapons, grenade launchers — where's the sport in that?" receiving merely a cold stare in reply.

Granted, Billy Zane's disarming smile and cool, calm, bemused demeanor goes a long way toward making this modern-day Zaroff at least an *entertaining* villain, and his innate charm overcomes the occasional clunkiness of his frequent one-liners. For instance, at one point Joseph deadpans "I love carpooling"— just before leaping from the back of his moving Humvee onto the hood of Sonny's car. Zane's infectious smirk and cool enthusiasm nearly sells it. Still, while Zane offers abundant personality (including a quick Elvis impersonation and some bluesy harmonica playing), the script provides him little real depth. So while his portrayal appears intermittently entertaining, in the end it seems shallow and ultimately unsatisfying. And that pretty much sums up the film as a whole, as *Bet Your Life*, like most things in Vegas, stands as a sucker's *Bet*.

Big Game (1980; MB Diffusion; Spain/France) Original Language Title: *Big Game: La chasse aux noirs*. Alternate Title: *Mad Mex the Blackfighter*. Director/Screenplay: Max H. Boulois; Producer: M.B. Diffusion, Inc. (Max H. Boulois); Cinematographers: Antonio L. Ballesteros, Roberto Ochoa. Cast: Max H. Boulois, Tom Hernandez, William Anthon, Virginia Mataix, Dan Forrest, Emilio Higuera.

Big Game was completed in 1980 but not released theatrically until 1987, and then only in Europe, including France (writer/producer/director/star Max Boulois' home country) and the former Yugoslavia. As far as can be determined, *Big Game* never even enjoyed a legitimate video release in the U.S., though it made it onto the shelves in several European countries, including Greece and the Netherlands (where it was inexplicably — and amusingly — retitled *Mad Mex the Blackfighter*).

This Most Dangerous Obscurity begins in "North Vietnam, April 1975" as escaped P.O.W. Jo Johnson (Max Boulois) literally carries an army buddy to safety. Back in New York after the war, Jo, a former professional football player, tries to save his floundering gym business by borrowing $25,000 from some loan sharks. When payment comes due, so does a bizarre offer: "You have been selected to participate in a big game hunt. You will be the prey.... We offer you a million dollars to escape the hunters." Desperate, Jo agrees and is taken, blindfolded, to an isolated woodland and given a 12-hour head start. But this is only half the story. After Jo disables the two primary hunters (one with a sharpened-stick spring trap) and dispatches several of their support men, he goes to collect his money, resulting only in the death of his friend (who Jo sent to pick up the cash supposedly left in a locker). Then begins a vendetta in which Jo pursues the wealthy, "respectable" hunters (and their corrupt F.B.I. contacts) to both retrieve what's rightfully his and exact vengeance for his buddy's death.

After the production company's credit, the first words flashed on the screen are "THIS PICTURE IS BASED ON REAL FACTS." Of course, this begs the question: Are there *un*real facts? Poor verbiage aside, about the only verifiable "real" fact in this vanity project is that Max Boulois did everything in his power to make himself look good as the big, bearded, black ex–Marine sergeant/football star who is always three steps ahead of his adversaries and seemingly never breaks a sweat even when mowing down bad guys or taking out a pursuing helicopter with nothing more than a pistol(!). This last action-movie conceit reveals the production's minuscule budget (if the underexposed filming from doorways, lack of ambient sound, and various guerrilla shooting techniques used to capture the "gritty streets" of New York hadn't already given this cheap Game away). Unable to afford real pyrotechnics or even miniatures, the 'copter, after being hit by Jo's bullet, simply flies behind a hill and out of frame, with the subsequent explosion signified solely by a flare-up on the film stock. Add in random narration by several different characters to try to explain things as they happen, and the cheapjack feel is complete.

Also disappointing, Most Dangerous Game-wise, is the (real) fact that the hunt itself lasts a mere 10 minutes. But Boulois manages to at least make those 10 minutes eventful. First he pulls the old hide-underwater-while-breathing-through-a-reed trick to surprise the hunters' tracker, taking the man's boots (Jo had been relieved of his shoes at the start of the hunt) and hunting knife. This leads to one of the few real shocks of the film when the tracker staggers back to his companions, and Simpson (Tom Hernandez), the lead hunter, calmly takes aim and shoots the tracker, concluding, "A warrior guide who lets himself get captured is worthless to himself." Ironically, Simpson himself is later surprised by Jo, who drops out of a tree and knocks the hunter unconscious—just as a trap set by Jo launches a sharpened stick into his companion's chest. Then it's a matter of Jo taking out the hunters' second unit (a jeep and its four men) and the support helicopter, and hightailing it back to NYC to collect his dough. Of course, there's still half a movie to go, and after Jo's double-cross the remainder focuses on Jo's discovery of the culprits' identities (humanitarian that he is, he left the two hunters alive), his learning of the corrupt FBI agents' involvement, and his locating the villains and taking them down (culminating in a shoot-out at Simpson's well-guarded Florida compound). Unfortunately, Jo so obviously out-fights, out-shoots and out-smarts everyone he meets that there's never any real suspense (even at the end, when it seems Simpson finally has the drop on him, things miraculously turn in Jo's favor).

Besides suspense and believability, also missing is any real characterization, which is doubly disappointing when it comes to Simpson and his companion Gary (with the only thing revealed about the latter being his status as an ex–Army colonel). At the film's beginning, the two hunters, dressed in elegant white hunting togs, walk through some grasslands, take aim and shoot a fleeing black man in the back. At this, Simpson, sporting a fashionable cravat, complains, "Too easy. My next target must be challenging and choice materials." (Cue the recruitment of the tough-as-nails Jo.) No further exploration of Simpson's motivations for hunting humans arise, and all we learn about him is that he's cultured, rich, powerful — and apparently a racist. Sipping champagne in a posh drawing room, the tuxedo-wearing Simpson admonishes his companion:

> My dear Gary, I simply can't share your opinion. You say the black man is like a wild bear. That he's not very intelligent, and he's only dangerous when he's hurt. Well let me tell you, the black man is the real king of the jungle. And I'll tell you why. His black skin is a natural camouflage. He can make a weapon out of any tree branch. He's agile as a monkey. He knows the ways of the white man and can figure out his intentions. The black man is the only animal that can swim below and above water, leap from tree to tree, jump huge crevasses, and run the savannah.

Adding uninformative insult to impoverished injury, Simpson has no trophy room. So much for the Most Dangerous Game.

One-man wrecking ... er, filmmaking crew Max H. Boulois continued his auteurship after *Big Game* (his directorial debut) by going on to direct, write and star in the nearly unwatchable *Black Jack* (1981; co-starring a blink-and-you'll-miss-him Peter Cushing) and the slightly-more-(but not much)-palatable *Othello the Black Commando* (1982, in which Boulois gave co-screenwriting credit to none other than William Shakespeare!). Neither of these fared any better in distribution than *Big Game*. Besides his failed bid at becoming the French Orson Welles, Boulois made several music albums — as "Max-B" — released in Spain (his adopted country) in the 1970s, including *Sex Revolution* and *Super Afro*. They were filled with electronic funk/soul tracks with titles like "Jungle" and "Super Bwana." And yes, as well as writing, directing and starring in *Big Game*, do-it-yourselfer Boulois provided all of the film's music as well.

Clown Hunt (2012; Big Shoes Productions/Seminal Films) Director/Screenplay: Barry Tubb; Producers: P.K. Munson, S.L. Weinert, Barry Tubb; Cinematographer: P.K. Munson. Cast: David Keith, Brendan Wayne, Tuff Hedeman, Robert Earl Keen, Savannah Welch, Eloise DeJoria, Matthew Posey, Joe Williams, Barry Tubb.

Yes, this is exactly what it sounds like — a satirical jab at the Most Dangerous Game theme with circus clowns taking the brunt of the sardonic roundhouses (though the hunters themselves receive their fair share of derisive body blows). Shot in Texas in 2010 and released directly to video in 2012, the obviously low-budget *Clown Hunt* posits that clowns have become big game for Texas rednecks, who buy hunting licenses and join (semi)organized hunts to bag their limit of clowns out on the open range. In this particular chuckle-filled universe, clowns apparently live together in herds out in the wilds, performing random clown tricks as well as partaking in such odd activities as bouncing kittens off trampolines(!) and smashing baby chicks with their oversized shoes(!!). A group of rednecks run the gauntlet of "Save-the-Clown" protestors (whose activities are appropriately chronicled by KLWN-TV) to descend on local landowner B.J.'s (David Keith, the only "name" actor in the film — obviously there for one day and a quick paycheck) "Chuckle Ranch" and set up camp for the start of Clown season. "First week of the season is Happy clowns only," one hunter reminds the group. "Sad clown season doesn't start till the second week." As the band of hunters prepare for opening day, they drink, mud-wrassle (an hilarious homoerotic homage), and scout the local clown fauna. They also recall the legend of "Albino Willy," a famous clown who's "been seen all over the world, but nobody's been able to cap his ass." As the hunt begins, Albino Willy shows up and leads an impromptu clown revolt, so that the hunters soon become the prey.

Clown Hunt offers more gags and pratfalls than story and characters, the latter of which are pretty much ciphers, though one hunter (played by the film's writer/director/co-producer) appears more sensitive than the others (even offering the politically-correct observation that "they really don't like to be referred to as 'clowns' anymore; they would prefer to be called 'laugh-makers'"). In a clever riff on the notion of intolerance, he turns out to be a closeted clown himself (he retires to his tent each night to don clown makeup). When he finally "comes out" as a clown, the nonplussed expressions on the faces of his heretofore unsuspecting backwoods buddies speak volumes.

It being basically a one-joke movie, *Clown Hunt*'s entertainment value comes from the variations that branch off from said joke. Some are clever ("I was readin' *Big Shoes Big Guns* the other day..."; or the clowns dying in character, complete with comical feet in the air for their death throes), some are tasteless (such as Albino Willy placing a shovel under a hunter who's defecating into a hole, resulting in the drunken man's confusion when he finishes and finds nothing there), and some are tastelessly funny (when one clown becomes so frightened by the sound of a gun going off, he drops a load of jelly bean scat before running away). How much a viewer will enjoy this film stems from how one reacts to the various gags that come fast and furious throughout the 70-minute running time.

Writer-director Barry Tubb foregoes any exploration into what kind of a society evolved (or *de*-volved) into hunting clowns, nor are there any explanations as to why clowns seem to behave like herd animals (given that they are indeed just *people* in make-up and oversized shoes, as demonstrated by the closeted clown hunter in the group). Consequently, Tubb sacrifices myriad opportunities for social or political satire, focusing instead on a stream of sight (and sound) gags (yes, there are fart jokes) that tend to become both puerile and repetitious over time. And Tubb obviously had difficulty coming up with a suitable ending for his Bozo bonanza. The climax begins well enough via an amusing, small-scale *Road Warrior* homage (as the few remaining hunters, driving an odd assortment of vehicles, try to run Albino Willy, riding an ATV decked out with a giant clown head[!], to ground), but deteriorates into the firing of a giant rocket-missile (complete with clown nose) and a nonsensical final shot of Willy's white wig floating in New York Harbor(?!). *Clown Hunt* might have done better as a concise comic short or even a faux trailer. As is, it comes dangerously close to wearing out its big-nosed welcome.

Director-producer-screenwriter-actor Barry Tubb forged a career appearing in supporting roles on television in the 1980s in such series as *Hill Street Blues* and the *Lonesome Dove* telefilms, and movies such as *Mask* (1985) and *Top Gun* (1986). Becoming disenchanted with Tinseltown, however, he worked on Broadway and then moved to France in the '90s, appearing there in a Wild West show (born and raised in Texas, Tubb was a champion bull rider at age 15). He eventually turned to the production side of filmmaking near the end of the decade, helming *Blood Trail* (1997) and *Grand Champion* (2002) before tackling the trials and tribulations of red noses and oversized shoes with *Clown Hunt*. Said Tubb, "I wanted to make my own movies because Hollywood just wasn't cutting it for me. The movies I was reading weren't as good as the stories I knew growing up."

While a tale of "clown hunting" may not qualify as a "good" story (and certainly wasn't something Tubb "knew growing up"), it at least makes for an intermittently amusing one that comes off as a unique pie in the face to Connell's concept.

Coplan Saves His Skin (1968; France/Italy) Original Language Title: *Coplan suave sa peau*. Director: Yves Boisset; Producer: Robert de Nesle; Screenplay: Claude Veilot, Yves Boisset (based on the novel *Coplan paie le cerceuil* by Paul Kenny [Jean Libert and Gaston van den

Panhuyse]); Cinematographer: Pierre L'homme. Cast: Claudio Brook, Margaret Lee, Klaus Kinski, Jean Servais, Bernard Blier.

In the wake of James Bond's immense success, a number of French writers created several series of Gallic counterparts to Her Majesty's secret agent in book and film, some of which remain popular even today. Of these, Francis Coplan was the brainchild of Paul Kenny, a pseudonym for two Belgian writers, Jean Libert and Gaston van den Panhuyse. The character is remarkable for the fact that in a series of five films released between 1964 and 1968 he was played by five different actors (Dominique Paturel, Ken Clark, Richard Wyler, Lang Jeffries and, finally, Mexican actor Claudio Brook). *Coplan sauve sa peau* (Coplan Saves His Skin) is the last film in the series and the directorial debut of Yves Boisset, who also co-wrote the script. Over the subsequent years Boisset became one of France's foremost directors of police thrillers and action movies. In 1983 he went to the Most Dangerous well once more with the excellent Dangerous Game Show entry *The Prize of Peril.*

Following a request for help from Mara (Margaret Lee), a former lover, Agent Coplan (Claudio Brook) arrives in Istanbul to unearth a plot to annihilate the city. Unable to protect Mara from being viciously beaten and killed, he discovers her sister (also played by Lee), a dancer, who leads him to their brother (Hans Meyer), a megalomaniac scientist with a fortress in a remote part of the country. When Coplan refuses to participate in the madman's schemes, he is forced to take part in a cruel game of hunt-the-human.

Coplan sauve sa peau is clearly a film of two halves. The first is more of a standard Eurospy story in which the secret agent tries to unravel the mystery behind an international conspiracy. Strangely, most of these scenes have Coplan awkwardly going about his business with his arm in a sling (due to an injury received during the early fight in which he failed to protect his old flame). Drawing a gun, unlocking doors or chasing baddies doesn't come easy with such a handicap. Furthermore, his tendency to whine about lost loves and forgotten promises, not to mention his walking into arrests and even getting harassed by a tractor salesman in a bar, seem rather emasculating for a suave secret agent. The highlight of the film's first half are three rather incongruous but highly entertaining scenes with a barechested Klaus Kinski as a mad sculptor, in which he conducts a séance to contact the spirit of the Marquis de Sade, caresses his erotic sculptures, poses his nude models, smokes incessantly, and lasciviously undresses Barbie dolls while lying on the floor of a Turkish bath just seconds before being killed (drowned in a toilet bowl!).

Despite these few intriguing moments, and though filmed in authentic exotic locales, the film's first half ultimately fails due to an overabundance of chatter and pseudo-philosophical ramblings, and some slow, awkward chase sequences. At one stage we watch a fat man (Bernard Blier) being chased by another fat man. Slowly.

The minute Coplan loses his sling, however, the pace ratchets up a few notches and brings us into "The Most Dangerous Game" territory. The film changes its narrative style, and the newly introduced characters prove far more interesting than most of those seen in the preceding hour.

In the middle of the Turkish wilderness, Eva and Mara's brother Hugo has set up shop in an ancient fortress. A disillusioned and facially disfigured scientist, he intends to teach the world a lesson about ignoring his warnings. He and his female sidekick Carole (Nanna Michael), a black leather-clad blonde model with a fetish for whips, reign over the dwarves and wrestlers that populate the castle, capture damsels in distress just to string them up in cages, and invite everyone who happens to disagree with their plans to a Most Dangerous Game–style hunt. Enter Coplan, who finally manages to show what he's made of.

The entire hunt section (lasting about 15 minutes) is shot virtually free of dialogue or music, with just the sound of nature accompanying Coplan through rocky mountain ranges where he's chased by dogs, falcons and men (and women) armed with bows, knives and bolas in this centuries-old manhunt. One of the film's most memorable scenes sees Carole step out off her black Dominatrix-style clothes to reveal pristine white bra and panties prior to diving into the water for an all too brief battle with Coplan, resulting in her being mourned by a dwarf and a pair of howling dogs.

Ultimately *Coplan sauve sa peau* can best be described as an interesting but flawed production. The film offers the occasional intriguing moment and ingenious set-piece, but as a whole suffers from a rambling plot and slow first half, not to mention a somewhat less-than-suave International Man of Mystery.

Author's Note: No evidence was found that this film ever received an English-language release (more's the pity). I was able to view a German-language print under the title *Der Teufelsgarten* (The Devil's Garden), but, given my less-than-competent command of the language, I imposed upon my friend, German film historian Holger Haase, to assess the picture. Vielen Dank to Herr Haase for providing the preceding review.

Death Ring (1992; Trans Atlantic Entertainment) Director: R. J. Kizer; Producers: Gary M. Bettman, Philip Steuer; Screenplay: George T. LeBrun (story: George T. LeBrun, Mike Norris); Cinematographer: Glenn Kershaw. Cast: Mike Norris, Billy Drago, Chad McQueen, Don Swayze, Elizabeth Fong Sung, Isabel Glasser.

A better title for this low-budget, straight-to-video Dangerous Game riff would be *The Most Dangerous Relatives*, given that the prey consists of Mike Norris (son of Chuck) and Don Swayze (brother of Patrick), with some help from Chad McQueen (offspring of Steve). While such second-generation casting offers a definite gimmick value, that's the extent of what *Death Ring* has going for it.

Ex-Special Forces soldier Matt Collins (Mike Norris) has just won the "Survival of the Fittest" iron man–style race. Still, he's at loose ends with what to do with his life, putting a strain on his relationship with rich girlfriend Lauren (Isabel Glasser). Meanwhile, wealthy hunter Danton Vachs (Billy Drago), aided by his devoted assistant Ms. Ling (Elizabeth Fong Sung), seeks a new subject for his next round of paying "guests" (to the tune of $100,000 each) arriving on his private island to play hunt-the-human. Vachs hires a couple of lowlifes to kidnap and deliver both Collins and his girlfriend (the latter to be used as "incentive" for the former) for the next round. After one of his five guests complains a bit too vociferously about the failure of the last hunt (when the prey apparently met his end in quicksand rather than at the hands of the hunters), Vachs abruptly silences the complainer with a fatal clubbing. Vachs then sends his four remaining clients into the island jungle, armed with a few simple weapons, to track and kill Collins. As the ex–Special Forces man faces off against — and bests — his pursuers one by one, he stumbles across the survivor of the previous hunt (Don Swayze), who only faked his death. The duo decide to storm the house, taking out Vachs' guards with their own machine guns before Collins goes one-on-one with Vachs and his samurai sword. Collins' pilot-buddy Skylord (Chad McQueen), who'd tracked down his missing friend to this mysterious island, arrives in a helicopter to facilitate the final rescue.

Filmed in and around the environs of L.A., *Death Ring* oozes So-Cal plasticity, with the Hollywood hills and a manicured Beverly Hills estate unconvincingly standing in for the remote island hunting grounds. There's even a sequence shot in the "caves" at Bronson

Canyon (an overused L.A. location seen in everything from TV's *Batman* to countless sci-fi films of the 1950s) to add a whiff of low-rent familiarity. Production-wise, this formula actioner sports that over-bright, artificial look so common to early–90s straight-to-video productions.

George T. LeBrun's meandering script (apparently his *only* produced screenplay) offers up equal parts banality and cheese. "You Americans were always too weak with women," Elizabeth Fong Sung sneers at Mike Norris as they fight, whereupon he throws her out the window and comments, "Ladies first." Toss in a going-nowhere subplot involving a group of devil worshippers ("Skylord" tracks down one of the thugs that nabbed his pals and learns that he belongs to a cult of Satanists, who take Skylord hostage, tie him up, and then *answer his questions* about his missing friends before letting him go!), and *Death Ring*'s scenario, er, rings hollow. Further filler includes Skylord's attempts to interest a police detective in the case, and his unfunny comic interludes with his impatient (and gratuitously topless) girlfriend.

Acting-wise, Mike Norris possesses no more charisma than his far-more-famous father (himself by no means the most dynamic of Hollywood's "action stars"), and far *less* of Chuck's likable, unprepossessing demeanor. The apple didn't roll far from the tree in the Norris family, even though it appears to be all downhill for Mike, whose stiffness in front of the camera is all too apparent. His appearance and demeanor is more that of an elementary school teacher than a trained killer. Norris (Jr.) also receives co-credit for *Death Ring*'s story, though given the results, that's a feather he may want to leave *off* his resume cap.

Even more disparity exists between Don Swayze and his older brother, the late Patrick Swayze (*Dirty Dancing, Ghost*), as the lesser Swayze has forged his "career" out of TV spots and grade-C movies like *Beach Babes from Beyond* and this one. Surprisingly, Don Swayze's brief turn in *Death Ring* is the most naturalistic of the bunch — a rather strong indictment of the film's level of thespian artistry.

Then there's Chad McQueen, son of screen icon Steve McQueen. As the helpful friend Skylord, who shows up at the end to drop grenades and rescue his compadres with a helicopter, McQueen, Jr., offers only generic, strained affability in place of his father's intensity and "cool."

Even the "real" actors let the side down. Of course, none of the thespians (whether poor relation or pro) are well-served by the script's sketchy characterizations. Of primary disappointment is Vachs, the obvious Zaroff character, as played by veteran B-villain Billy Drago. Drago, who's perhaps best known for playing the killer Frank Nitti in *The Untouchables* (1987), appears to be doing his best John Hurt impression, but he lacks the depth and presence of that far-superior British actor. Drago's attempt to forge a memorable villain consists of little more than whispering his dialogue and frequently smoothing back his wavy blonde locks. Of course, Drago isn't helped by the fact that the script offers *no* back story — or even simple motivation — for Zachs' hunting-humans scenario. With such a disappointing central antagonist, the mantle of villainy falls to Drago's four guests, who do all the real work in this human hunt. Unfortunately, the four hunters appear anything but formidable (one's even a middle-aged lawyer who looks about as deadly as, well, a middle-aged lawyer). And given the fact that the quartet is sent out armed with nothing more than a knife, a spear, three throwing stars and a garrote between them, it's little wonder the Special Forces veteran ("the best soldier in the outfit") takes them out so easily.

Death Ring director R.J. Kizer was an editor and soundman who took charge of the megaphone only three times in his career. His first turn in the directing chair (sort of) was on *Godzilla 1985*, for which he helmed the U.S. inserts (with Raymond Burr). He next directed the micro-budgeted *Hell Comes to Frogtown* in 1988 (an audacious and intermittently entertaining post-nuker). *Death Ring* was his final feature as director — and his least interesting.

As a crumb thrown to MDG fans, the "Very Special Thanks" section at the close of *Death Ring*'s end credits concludes with "...and Ernest B. Schoedsack," indicating that Kizer and company had at least a passing familiarity with (and acknowledged their debt to) the first cinematic adaptation of *The Most Dangerous Game*, directed by Schoedsack in 1932. Of course, the *exclusion* of Richard Connell's name no doubt indicates ignorance of the original story, which goes a long way towards explaining Kizer's and LeBrun's frequent poor choices and missed opportunities.

Dogboys (1998; Showtime) Airdate: April 4, 1998; Alternate Title: *Tracked*. Director/Producer: Ken Russell; Screenplay: Rob Stork and David Taylor; Cinematographer: Jamie Thompson. Cast: Bryan Brown, Dean Cain, Tia Carrere, Ken James, Sean McCann, Richard Chevolleau.

This made-for-cable-TV adaptation employs Connell's general concept of humans hunting humans for sport, but virtually nothing else (and, of course, gives no credit to the original story). Julian Taylor (Dean Cain), a young ex–Marine, is sent to prison for assault and, after defending himself against some brutal inmates, finds himself assigned to the prison's dog kennels(!). The head guard, Captain Brown (Bryan Brown), trains dogs to track men by sending prisoners (labeled "dogboys") out into the fenced-in woodland surrounding the prison for the hounds to hunt. Eventually, Taylor stumbles upon the fact that Captain Brown and his paying cronies periodically hunt a prisoner for sport, later claiming they killed him as he was trying to escape. Along with a concerned female district attorney (Tia Carrere) who's stumbled upon the truth, Taylor must run for his life in one final hunt.

Though it offers a novel, prison-set take on the humans-hunting-humans concept, *Dogboys* fails to deliver on any front. It's 68 minutes in before the Most Dangerous Game aspect rears its ugly head, and 75 minutes before the (disappointingly perfunctory) first hunt! There are no traps, no close calls, no confrontations — just Taylor and the pretty D.A. tricking their hunters far too easily into believing they'd escaped. And Captain Brown makes for one of the most disappointing Zaroff stand-ins in the history of cinema. While the heroine refers to him as a "psychopath," Aussie actor Bryan Brown (*Breaker Morant*, 1980; *F/X*, 1986; *Cocktail*, 1988) offers a stern tone and little else — nothing quirky or mildly interesting, much less psychopathic. His motivation? He thinks all convicts are scum because one raped and killed his daughter (and beloved dog), and so has no compunction about hunting them (or letting others do the same — for cash, of course). Also, while the sadistic Captain has his "lair" (a furnished shed out in the woods), there's no forbidding, gruesome "trophy room." His only "trophies" consist of polaroid snapshots of the victims — no heads mounted on the wall or bobbing in tanks, no bodies preserved in their posture of death. And what's worse, we never even *see* any of the kills, as the only hunt consists of the brief, unsatisfying run by Our Hero and Heroine, who use mace to throw the Captain's dog off the scent, then a shred of torn clothing to make him think they've made it over the perimeter fence.

The production values and acting are all of the typical small-screen/small-scale variety — adequate but no more. The script spends far too long getting to the meat of the matter. The hero is the hero because he's clean-cut, hunky and kind. A former marine champion boxer convicted of aggravated assault, he's in prison because, in his words, "I beat up a redneck in a bar." Dean Cain (star of TV's *Lois and Clark: The New Adventures of Superman*) has little presence and even less personality as said Hero.

The biggest shock offered by *Dogboys* comes during the opening credits when the name Ken Russell appears as director. How the iconoclastic filmmaker of such quirky, controversial, thought-provoking, and often downright disturbing films as *The Devils* (1971), *Tommy* (1975), *Altered States* (1980), *Gothic* (1986) and *The Lair of the White Worm* (1988) could have churned out such a nondescript endeavor as this is beyond understanding.

In the end, the film comes off as more of a dull prison drama — or *faux* drama, considering the artificiality of it all (with its impossible dog kennels and warehouse-like spaces for its prisoners) — than a horrific Dangerous Game. The humans-hunting-humans concept, though integral to the script, seems almost an afterthought as presented. It's too little and too late to save *Dogboys* from being anything other than a forgettable cinematic dog.

Fantasy Island (1977; CBS Television) Airdate: January 14, 1977. Director: Richard Lang; Producers: Leonard Goldberg, Aaron Spelling; Screenplay: Gene Levitt; Cinematographer: Archie R. Dalzell. Cast: Ricardo Montalban, Bill Bixby, Sandra Dee, Peter Lawford, Carol Lynley, Hugh O'Brien, Eleanor Parker, Victoria Principal, Dick Sargent, Christina Sinatra, Herve Villechaize.

"Welcome to Fantasy Island." With this simple phrase smilingly delivered by the debonair, mysterious, and apparently omnipotent Mr. Roarke (Ricardo Montalban), pop culture saw the birth of one of its most beloved television shows. This made-for-TV movie began it all, laying the groundwork for the series that came a year later (also called *Fantasy Island*, 1978–1984) in which Roarke and his midget assistant, Tatoo (Herve Villechaize), ostensibly fulfill the fantasies of their paying guests while teaching them important lessons about life. In this first movie-length outing, however, Roarke comes off as far less benign a puppeteer than on the subsequent show, and the trio of stories detailed here remain far darker and more serious than most of the fluff that followed. Roarke's forceful comment to one misbehaving player, for instance — "I make the rules on this island, *all* of them, *all* of the time; only *I* break them!" — and Montalban's sometimes sinister smiles and occasional hard looks smack of megalomania and secret, even menacing manipulation (something decidedly toned down for the regular series).

Three guests arrive by sea plane on Roarke's "Fantasy Island," each paying "$50,000 for a three day stay." The film then moves back and forth between the three separate tales of fantasies wished for and fantasies fulfilled (though not necessarily in the way expected). One story focuses on a wealthy businesswoman (Eleanor Parker) who stages her own funeral in order to gauge the reactions of her supposed loved ones. Another deals with a lonely old man (Bill Bixby in fairly convincing age makeup) intent on reliving a two-day romance he experienced during World War II. And the third centers on "Paul Henley [Hugh O'Brien], not so long ago the most famous hunter in Africa." As Roarke tells him upon his arrival, "Your fantasy is that we try to kill you; we are ready." Henley's curious response: "Were you able to secure expert hunters?" Indeed he was, as Roarke has hired three "dedicated" hunters, one for each "phase" of the hunt. The first consists of Henley waking up handcuffed to the lovely girl (Victoria Principal) Roarke had provided for his amusement, with Henley and the girl having twenty minutes to cover a hundred yards and reach a red flag, or hunter number one will "shoot to kill." The catch: those hundred yards of jungle are festooned with traps and snares, including arrows triggered by tripwires, a spike-lined pit, and even a live tiger blocking the way. After avoiding the traps and saving the girl just in time, Henley faces phase two. Here he must run a 100-yard gauntlet down a steep hill to reach the safety of a flag while the second hunter fires at will with a high-powered rifle. Ingeniously utilizing a camp table as a toboggan, Henley survives yet again. But the next morning comes the coup de grace: Hunter number three will be tracking Henley with a helicopter, shooting at him from the air with an automatic rifle! "That's not a hunt," protests Henley, "that's murder!" Though Henley wants to end the hunt, Roarke will have none of it, amusingly announcing from a safe distance through a bullhorn, "Sorry, I can't hear you; I have a helicopter in my ear," before signaling for the hunt to begin. Though wounded in the leg, Henley makes it to the safety of the flag — just. But there's a sting in the tale, as we learn that the trio of hunters, all chosen to try to kill him because they'd been wronged by Henley in the past (one was swindled out of valuable land, another had his child injured by Henley's drunken driving, and the third lost his cheating wife to the Great White Hunter), were wrong or even lying about Henley — he was innocent of these supposed sins.

Fantasy Island turns Connell's concept on its head by focusing on a hunter who wants to be hunted. This time the thrill comes not from stalking human prey but from *being* said prey. Or does it? At the end, after Henley has survived all three "phases" of the hunt, Roarke confronts him about his motivation. "You wanted to die for all the killing you did as a hunter — animal killing, trophy killing, *futile* killing. It finally got to you. Right or wrong, Henley?!" Interestingly, Henley remains mute on the subject, but Roarke, satisfied with his conclusion, kindly offers, "You're just not that rotten, apparently. You're not even all bad, or you wouldn't have had that sense of guilt in the first place." It makes for an intriguing twist on an already clever one. Couple this grimly-themed Most Dangerous Game with the other two story lines — which involve attempted murder and death or insanity — and this made-for-television movie stands as a sort of "Monkey's Paw" version of the often lightweight and frequently banal series it started. Be careful what you wish for indeed.

Note: Mr. Roarke oversaw a more straightforward Most Dangerous fantasy two years later in the series' second-season episode "Spending Spree/The Hunted."

The Final Executioner (1984; L'Immagine/Cannon; Italy) Original Language Title: *L'Ultimo Guerriero*. Director: Romolo Guerrieri; Producer: Luciano Appignani; Screenplay: Roberto Leoni; Cinematography: Guglielmo Mancori. Cast: William Mang, Marina Costa, Harrison Muller, Woody Strode, Margi Newton, Stefano Davanzati, Renato Miracco.

Here's a novelty: an Italian post-nuker (a surprisingly large cinematic subset in the early-to-mid '80s) with a Most Dangerous Game twist. Over black-and-white stock footage of A-bomb blasts, followed by (color) shots of erupting volcanoes and pouring lava(!), a narrator intones:

> After the holocaust, the world was divided into two groups — the rich, privileged minority who had avoided any contact with the radiation, and the contaminated masses. And thus the Hunt was born, an entertaining method of cleansing society of the human flotsam that had been classified as *target* material. Then one day one man discovered that the contamination was finished.

That "one man" is Alan Tanner (Austrian-born German TV actor William Mang), who, for his unwelcomed discovery, is reclassified by the remaining powers-that-be as a "target" and sent to the surface to be hunted for sport by the wealthy elite (who live in run-down, heavily-guarded villas). While all of his fellow targets are gunned down, Alan is wounded but escapes, only to be found and nursed back to health by Old Sam (a 70-year-old but still incredibly robust Woody Strode). "I want justice," says Alan and begins training with Sam, a former policeman, in fighting and survival techniques. Now tough as irradiated nails, Alan sets out to take revenge on the half-dozen hunters who slaughtered his ... well, a bunch of people he didn't really know.

Therein lies the problem (one of many, really) with *The Final Executioner*: sketchy motivation for even sketchier characters, resulting in a superficial film with little to distinguish it from countless other sub-par low-budget 1980s actioners (with the feathery hairstyles and ridiculous headbands tying the film to the fashion-challenged *real* 1984 far more firmly than Orwell's dystopian *1984*). The Most Dangerous Game element is utilized merely as an excuse for the occasional substandard slaughter set-piece (in which people are shot down willy-nilly in a *de rigueur* rock quarry—with nary a squib in sight, as the victims simply grab their chests and fall over) and one perfunctory "hunt." Said hunt (with Alan as the prey) not only lacks any palpable tension or suspense, it offers none of Connell's "outdoor chess" excitement—no confrontations, no verbal sparring, no traps set and sprung. After this opening gambit, the film devolves into a standard wronged-hero-trains-for-revenge-and-then-exacts-it scenario. And the only indication this is set in the post-nuclear-holocaust future (besides the narration) is one sequence in which a helicopter drops a load of canned food to be fought over by bands of scavengers. Otherwise, it's just a tale of a group of ill-defined wackos (who receive no back story nor motivation for what has turned them into hunters-of-men) living in a dilapidated villa, bickering among themselves, and occasionally going out to shoot people in rock quarries and abandoned factories.

Though receiving a theatrical release in West Germany and its home country, this Italian import only managed to make it to America (in a poorly-dubbed version) on home video. Production company L'Immagine decided to recycle footage of *The Final Executioner* not once but twice to create two "new" features: *The Bronx Executioner* and *Urban Warriors* (neither of which retain the Most Dangerous Game element). Why they bothered is the *Final* mystery, as both are even worse than the original template.

The Hunt (2012; Full Screen / Jinga Films; France) Director: Thomas Szczepanski; Screenplay: Francois Gaillard, Thomas Szczepanski; Cinematography: Anna Naigeon. Cast: Jellali Mouina, Sarah Lucide, Michel Coste, Mari-Christine Jeanney, Zuriel de Peslovan, Frederic Sassine.

Riding the wave of New Millennium visceral French horror—in the vein of such films as *High Tension* (2003), *Frontiers* (2007), *Inside* (2007) and *Martyrs* (2008)—*The Hunt* offers the gruesome thrills and arresting visuals typical of this Gallic subset. Unfortunately, it fails to bring to the characters the emotional intensity found in the best of them (such as *High Tension* and *Martyrs*).

Tabloid reporter Alex (Jellali Mouina) is on the skids, suffering from writer's block and dipping below even his rock-bottom standards by concocting bestiality stories about women who "love" dogs. When his editor gives him one week to come up with something better (preferably something with lots of violence), Alex turns to his dominatrix girlfriend (Sarah Lucide) for a lead. She directs him to the house of a rich and powerful client, where Alex breaks in and runs across a mysterious bag containing money, weapons, and a cell phone that rings to deliver cryptic instructions. Following said instructions, Alex ends up at a chateau in the deep woods as part of a group of masked hunters, wealthy individuals who wager large sums of money by placing a pile of cash in small lockboxes. Then begins a human hunt in which these hunters track down and kill (with bow and arrow) kidnapped homeless victims to whom the lockboxes have been handcuffed. In making a kill, the hunter wins the wager and claims the cash prize. Of course, nothing says the hunters can't try and take the money from their compatriots ("The only rule is," says the aged leader of this secret cabal, "there are no rules") by any means possible, including murder. During the hunt, Alex must face down several of the killers and then try to make his escape.

While striking to look at — sometimes too much so, as the camerawork (full of handheld shots, low angles, deep focus, arty dissolves, and even slow-motion) often draws attention to itself, and the technique becomes a little too precious for its own good (e.g., running the film backwards as Alex flashes back to his first glimpse of bloody violence, or cutting from a violent kill to a bee struggling on the ground, its wings too wet with blood to function) — *The Hunt* lacks an emotional center. The faceless hunters are interchangeable — almost literally, as they're dressed in identical camouflage uniforms and black hoods, and never utter a word — while the victims are clothed in identical cheap suits and never utter a word either (for the gruesome reason that their tongues have been cut out). Consequently, the only singular presence upon which the viewer can focus is Alex himself, but he's merely a sleazy opportunist with no obvious redeeming features (he even mercilessly manipulates his reluctant girlfriend to further his own disagreeable ends).

It's never made clear to what extent the various hunters are motivated by the hunt itself, the money, or simple sadism, leaving the central concept woefully unexplored. Consequently, the hunt becomes no more than exploitative spectacle, as we know little of, and care less about, any of the characters. And while said spectacle is well-shot and offers a few startling moments (such as when an arrow suddenly slams into the throat of a victim, resulting in a surprising, bloody spray), it can't fully sustain interest even over the course of the film's brief 74-minute running time. It's too bad that cinematographer-turned-director Thomas Szczepanski takes far less care with his characters and story than with his visuals.

Shot in 2010, *The Hunt* premiered at the Razor Reel Film Festival in Bruges, Belgium before being subtitled and released on video in the U.S. and Canada in July 2012.

The Hunted (1998; Paramount) Airdate: February 4, 1998. Director: Stuart Cooper; Producer: Colleen Nystedt; Screenplay: Bennett Cohen, David Ives; Cinematographer: Curtis Petersen. Cast: Harry Hamlin, Madchen Amick, Hannes Jaenicke, Enuka Okuma, Peter Lacroix, Terence Kelly, Fulvio Cecere.

This made-for-TV movie filmed in and around the environs of Vancouver, Canada, stars Madchen Amick as hotshot insurance investigator Samantha "Sam" Clark, sent to the wilds of Alaska to find the pilot of a small plane that crashed bearing $12 million in payroll cash. After wrecking her car on a rough road while trying to reach the crash site, she stumbles upon the mountain cabin of recluse "Doc" Kovac (Harry Hamlin), who agrees to take her to the wreckage the next morning. Instead, Kovac leads her to the pilot's corpse, trussed up in the forest like some decomposing trophy. Kovac gives Sam a pistol and a head start, then hunts her with his deadly bow. Though ultimately wounded, Sam eludes Kovac and makes it back to his cabin before him, turning the tables and then making her escape (with Kovac presumed dead). Back in the big city, Sam recovers from her ordeal, only to have Kovac reappear, intending to complete the hunt.

Apart from its hunting-humans concept, *The Hunted* pays homage to Connell's original story by having a desperate and cornered Rainsf ... er, Sam, choose to leap off a cliff into the sea ... er, river, before unexpectedly making his ... er, her, way back to Zaroff's ... er, Kovac's, lair — just like in the classic tale (and the 1932 cinematic incarnation). While there's no direct confrontation at the chateau ... er, cabin, like in the original story, *The Hunted* offers a clever variation by having Sam lure Kovac into the cabin and then trap him there (via a log dropped over the door) while she sets the structure ablaze. (Of course, this begs the continuity question of how Kovac escapes the conflagration to show up later in the city, given that we last saw him surrounded by flames, futilely hacking at the burning door with a tiny hatchet. And then he turns up shortly afterward with nary a singed eyebrow.)

Like Connell did before them, scripters Bennett Cohen and David Ives offer food for thought upon which their characters (and viewers) can chew. They take it in a slightly different direction, however, by making Kovac something of an anthropologist who has a deep respect for primitive peoples and customs, which he twists into a rationale for hunting the most dangerous game. "Most native cultures," Doc tells Sam early on, "you don't just kill your prey, you honor it. The greater the prey, the greater the honor. The body dies but the spirit lives on." On their way to the downed plane the next morning, a cougar crosses Kovac and Sam's path. "We're being hunted," says Kovac, calm but excited. "It's like a dance. First comes the stalking and the chase, then the kill." Of course, Kovac makes a beautiful shot with his bow to take down the big cat just as it leaps for Sam. When Kovac finally reveals his plan for Sam — to hunt her like an animal — he enthuses, "You're gonna like this, Sam. You have no idea what a gift I'm giving you. You see, most people just *sleep* their life away. But in the hunt — you *live*."

Video box for the made-for-TV *The Hunted*.

The Hunted looks pretty much like what it is — a middle-of-the-road TV production from the 1990s, complete with adequate but unimaginative lighting, professional but uninspired photography, and a plethora of continuity issues and plot holes. For instance, when Sam comes face-to-gruesome-face with the dead pilot, the ominous skies are slate gray and filled with rain. But the shot of her horrified reaction is backed by bright sunshine, as is the subsequent start of the hunt. (Living in the Pacific Northwest, this author knows all about the region's fickle weather patterns, but they don't change *that* quickly.) That lazy screenwriter's helper, Contrivance, rears its ugly head from time to time, such as when Sam smacks Kovac in the face with a rock, temporarily laying him low, but instead of shooting him with her gun she just grabs the pistol and runs. Then, when she's shot in the shoulder with an arrow while crossing a river, she easily swims — using *both* arms — a great distance underwater to temporary safety, seemingly none the worse for wear. And back in the city, when Sam receives an ominous phone call from Kovac and deduces he's waiting for her at the local native art museum, does she alert the police? No, she and her boyfriend go there alone to confront the madman. Fortunately, Hamlin's excellent portrayal, the intriguing concept and characterization, and the film's quick pacing generally keep things interesting and lets the viewer go with the (sometimes less-than-smooth) flow.

TV pretty-boy Harry Hamlin does surprisingly well in his mountain-man Zaroff role, oozing his trademark charm while at the same time exuding an unexpected undercurrent of suppressed menace. Then, when all is revealed, he exercises admirable restraint, going just far enough in his mania to make it believable, while thankfully eschewing whatever opportunities for bombast the role and scenario present. It's a subtle, shaded performance, and one tinged with just the right amount of humor to complement his charming madness, that stands out as one of the better Zaroff stand-in portrayals of the subgenre. Unfortunately, protagonist Madchen Amick (another attractive actor who worked — and works — almost exclusively on the small screen) can't make a similar claim, as she fails to convince as the tough-as-nails, single-minded investigator. Her pretty face (beautified beyond verisimilitude given her extended plight in the wilderness) and too-precious demeanor speaks more of superficial plasticity than underlying grit.

The reveal of the pilot's body suspended off the ground — almost crucified — from a horizontal pole generates a gruesome *frisson*, with the half-decomposed face adding grisly punctuation to the shocking sight. TV veteran director Stuart Cooper adds an obvious but effective visual exclamation point by zooming the camera in on the hideous countenance. Hamlin's half-bemused, half-mocking demeanor as he "introduces" the corpse to Sam ("Sam, meet Harry Augerman," he deadpans) underscores the revelatory moment with a dose of black humor, his callous regard for his prior "prey" making Sam's situation all the more desperate and dire. (So much for "honoring" one's prey, however.) This sequence marks a clever and effective variation on the typical MDG Trophy Room scene.

Of the two hunts, the first (and longest) remains far more satisfying; though, admittedly, the second (in the city) offers some choice dialogue in Doc's pontifications on the kinship of the hunter and the hunted. To wit: "It's the illusion I hate the most. As if we can pave over what's animal in us with concrete and asphalt. The ancients believed that before the hunt was over, the hunter and hunted merged, becoming each other, becoming one." Disappointingly, the big-city lure-and-stalk sequence takes on the mantle of a nineties low-rent "thriller" more than anything, complete with a sub-par (sort of) car chase and crash. But it does make for a nice bookend to both the concept and the characters, since this time around, as Doc says, "We're on your turf now, Sam. This is *your* hunting ground." And when Sam turns the tables once again and begins hunting Kovac, it offers a striking character revelation and comment about the "animal" (and hunter) in all of us.

The Hunters (2011; Lionsgate; France/Luxemburg/Belgium) Director: Chris Briant; Producer: Thomas Malmonte; Screenplay: Michael Lehman; Cinematographer: John B. Aronson. Cast: Steve Waddington, Tony Becker, Dianna Agron, Terence Knox, Jay Brown, Chris Briant.

A European (primarily French) co-production shot in English (for marketing reasons),

The Hunters posits the Most Dangerous Game as an answer to mid-life crisis. The story centers on a pair of middle-aged men disaffected with their life and place in society. One (Steve Waddington) is a schoolteacher who seemingly can't relate to his own kids (or anyone else, as he's plagued by nightmares and schizophrenic auditory hallucinations), while the other (Tony Becker) is a computer technician in a dead-end job and loveless marriage. The latter talks of "Vikings" and "Nature's Way," and sets about living this philosophy by spending his weekends hunting humans with his schoolteacher buddy and two young men whom the duo appears to be mentoring in the ways of the Most Dangerous Game. Enter Le Saint (actor/first-time director Chris Briant), fresh to the local police force after suffering injuries as a soldier in Iraq. Plagued by PTSD, Le Saint is intent on putting the past behind him by throwing himself into his work—namely, the investigation of 22 missing persons from this relatively small town. Though his belligerent boss (Terence Knox) diverts him to another assignment, circumstances bring Le Saint to the imposing Fort Goben, an abandoned complex-cum-game preserve that just happens to be the hunting grounds of the aforementioned hunters. There ensues a cat-and-mouse, life-and-death struggle, with several innocents caught in the crossfire.

Disappointingly, given its subject matter, there really is no "hunt" per se, as we see only one bit-player victim beaten to death by one of the seemingly enraged hunters (rather than witnessing the hunt itself). In fact, it appears that these "hunters" are more interested in merely killing than hunting. Le Saint himself is quickly taken down with a blow-dart(!), then wakes up inside the "trophy room" (featuring a wall of decomposing heads), where he battles one of the young hunters and then goes on the run looking for a way out of the labyrinthine complex and fenced woodland. Consequently, the film eschews any opportunity for stalking, trap-setting, or intellectual contests.

The movie's pace could generously be labeled "leisurely," and a myriad of plot threads fail to weave together into a satisfying whole. A potential love interest, for instance (played by *Glee* TV star Dianna Agron), though featured prominently in the movie's marketing, remains largely superfluous. Likewise, Le Saint's perennially-shouting police chief boss features into a narrative turn that's about as twisty (or surprising) as a bullet's trajectory.

The mix of accents among the actors is seriously distracting, as are the not-fooling-anyone-into-thinking-this-is-America locations. Though several of the principals speak with American accents, the film's hero is obviously French, and a number of supporting characters sport various Euro-accents. While the setting is meant to be the U.S., the ornate buildings used to represent the police station scream Old World Europe, as does the ancient crumbling fort itself.

On the plus side, Fort Goben looks impressive and forbidding—all dank stone rooms and corridors, not to mention the dense surrounding woodlands—and cinematographer John B. Aronson lights them in a suitably malevolent manner (often utilizing candle and torchlight). The gun battles between Le Saint and the hunters come off as far more realistic than most action set-pieces, with both the protagonist and antagonists missing far more often than hitting. The frantic cinematography perfectly captures the panic and intensity of the situation. And for MDG fans there's the added bonus of that trophy room—or at least a wall of shelves containing the severed heads of the victims in various stages of decay. It's a gruesome and disturbing sight, made more so when one of the young hunters takes down a trophy to "play" with. Though not a completely satisfying adaptation, the direct-to-DVD *The Hunters* offers enough variation to create a thoughtful, intermittently entertaining entry in the Most Dangerous Game canon.

Hydra (2009; Cinetel Films/Eagle Pictures) Airdate: February 22, 2009. Director: Andrew Pedergast; Producer: Daniel Gilboy; Screenplay: Peter Sullivan, William Langlois; Cinematographer: Howard Wexler. Cast: George Stults, Dawn Olivieri, Michael Shamus Wiles, Alex McArthur, Texas Battle, Polly Shamon, Dwayne Adway.

What has the legendary Greek myth of the Hydra have to do with "The Most Dangerous Game"? Nothing. Unless, of course, you're the production arm of the SyFy Channel, the same folks who brought us *Frankenfish* (2004), *SharkMan* (2005), and *Rock Monster* (2008), among many other paper-thin slices of small-screen cheese. (To be fair, *Frankenfish*, despite its goofy title, is actually rather entertaining. Too bad the same can *not* be said of *Hydra*.)

An archeological expedition lands on an uncharted island and uncovers a lost Greek temple —*and* the mythological monster that lives there. The titular beast devours nearly all of them, while a storm sinks their boat. Two months later another ship arrives, this one bearing a very different "expedition"— four hunters and their quartet of human prey, whom they intend to stalk and kill on this self-same island. Of course, the Hydra disrupts their little hunt (and eats nearly all of the principals), before the hero (an ex–Special Forces veteran), aided by the first group's sole survivor, finds the "Sword of Hercules" in the temple cave and uses it to dispatch the beast (any other weapon merely causes two Hydra heads to grow back in place of one).

The film adds an intriguing twist to the antagonists' motivations here. While they're characterized as "avid hunters" looking for the "ultimate thrill," a deeper bond unites these four hunters-of-men. "Each and every one of us has dealt with a personal tragedy, the loss of a loved one," announces Camden, the hunt's organizer, to his four paying shipboard guests. "And loss not by chance, but loss — and pain — due to a failed system." One man's wife was killed by a drunk driver, another man's daughter was raped and murdered, etc. "There's only one way to ease the pain," pronounces Camden. And that is to hunt down and kill four convicted criminals who've committed similar crimes. As Camden later proclaims, "It's a game. And you know what the game is? It's 'Hunt the Felon.'" Of course, such an elaborate form of grief therapy doesn't come cheap, and the four men are paying $10 million dollars each for the privilege. (This begs the question — how does one find four billionaires with not only a deep personal tragedy in their recent past and a thirst for vengeance so strong they're eager to commit murder, but who are also extreme hunters. Camden has a bright future as a corporate headhunter.) Unfortunately, a dearth of characterization — of both hunters and hunted — weakens such clever innovation, leaving the principals as mere ciphers.

Plot-wise, the monstrous Hydra is not the only fly in this game's ointment. The ship's captain (and Camden's partner) has substituted his own candidate as one of the prey — Nolan (George Stults, who looks and sounds like a second-rate Bill Paxton), an ex-soldier who was under the captain's command in Iraq, and who took umbrage at his former commander's callous killing of civilians and tried to take him down. On the island, the resourceful Nolan leads his three fellow victims-to-be (a rapist, a yuppie D.U.I. perp, and a woman who shot her abusive husband) to construct a trap for their hunters, catching one with a spring-loaded spike through the leg. Though the Hydra does the rest of their dirty work for them, at least these prey prove to be proactive. This is the only significant confrontation between hunter and hunted, however, which means the remainder of the film must rely on the Creature Feature angle to carry it through — which proves to be a big mistake.

Reportedly made for a mere $700,000, *Hydra* looks even cheaper, despite shooting aboard the authentic World War II vessel *SS Victory Lane* at the Maritime Museum in Long

Beach, California. While the production's lighting, staging and acting are about on par with the superficial characterizations (adequate yet uninvolving), the all-important special effects of the titular terror makes it look like a two-dimensional cartoon come to (sort-of) life. Never convincing, the cheap CGI Hydra inspires more guffaws and groans than chills and thrills. And adding ridiculous insult to ludicrous injury, the victims' screams are sometimes heard *after* they've been torn apart and consumed! So while many of the Hydra attacks appear gruesomely disturbing in concept (as the toothy, multi-headed beast literally rips its prey to pieces, with CGI bood flying everywhere), they frequently fall flat in (ahem) execution. Unsatisfactory in both the Most Dangerous Game aspects and its monster mayhem, the made-for-cable *Hydra* demonstrates that two (or three or four) heads are not always better than one.

King of the Hill (2007; Telecine/Dimension; Spain) Original Language Title: *El Rey de la Montana*. Director: Gonzalo Lopez-Gallego; Producers: Juan Pita, Juan Manuel Arance, Miguel Bardem, Alvaro Augustin; Screenplay: Javier Gullon, Gonzalo Lopez-Gallego; Cinematographer: Jose David Montero. Cast: Leonardo Sbaraglia, Maria Valverde, Thomas Riordan, Andres Juste, Pablo Menasanch, Francisco Olmo, Manuel Sanchez Ramos.

Unfolding in the the mountainous Castilia y Leon region of Northern Spain, *King of the Hill* follows lone driver Quim (Leonardo Sbaraglia) on his way to visit his girlfriend (or "ex," since, as he says, "it's complicated"). At a gas station he's seduced and robbed by a girl, Bea (Maria Valverde). When he spots her car on the road and follows her up into the mountains, he's shot at by snipers and forced to take to the woods after his car is disabled. Running across Bea, the two must try to trust each other as they flee for their lives through the forest from the unseen hunters.

Director Gonzalo Lopez-Gallego (who, beckoned by Hollywood, went on to make the excellent *Apollo 18* in 2011) alternates expansive shots of the rugged, mountainous countryside that cruelly dwarf his protagonists with intimate hand-held camerawork and varied angles (both from above and below) that bring home the claustrophobic immediacy of their plight. Unexpected things happen, terrible choices must be made, and an air of danger permeates the film, as the distant crack of a rifle shot can (and does) send bullets whizzing towards them at any time. The two leads (Sbaraglia and Valverde) brilliantly convey the confusion, panic, and sheer terror experienced by their characters, as well as displaying an uneasy chemistry that reflects both their attraction and wariness. Javier Gullon and Lopez-Gallego's script refuses to follow the typical Hollywood trope by portraying Quim not as some ex–Special Forces badass but as a regular, flawed human being who is ofttimes weak and afraid (becoming tearful and even lashing out at Bea), and doesn't always act particularly "heroic." His actions keep the viewer wavering, as at times he does the right thing, while at others he succumbs to fear—no doubt exactly how most people would react in this impossibly horrific situation.

Just after the film's hour mark comes a startling revelation that remains so shocking, so unthinkable, that it changes the very tone of the picture. In fact, from this moment the camera switches from focusing on the prey to following the hitherto-unseen hunters, not only disclosing and exploring their characters and competitive "game," but even linking the viewer visually to them by employing a "rifle-cam" as they stalk the remaining protagonist, Quim. Thus the viewer has now switched from prey to hunter.

Spoiler Note: For those readers who have yet to see this unique film and intend on doing so, I suggest you stop reading this entry RIGHT HERE. Not only is this particular twist critical to any discussion of the picture and its Most Dangerous implications, it is essential that the viewer have no prior inkling in order to experience its full impact. And this development definitely leaves its mark, growing more unsettling as the film continues, leading to a powerful conclusion that raises all sorts of moral and sociological issues, and stays with the viewer long after the screen goes dark. So, Gentle Reader, you've been warned...

At one point Bea becomes trapped in a natural pit she's fallen into during their headlong flight. Quim searches for the means to get her out, but at the sound of the approaching hunters, he must make a choice. Quim chooses to run. It's a powerful scene, made more so by the distraught playing of both actors. But this emotional distress pales in comparison to the moment when, from down in the pit with Bea, the camera (and viewer) looks up to see the faces of the two hunters finally loom into view—the faces of two pre-teen boys. These hunters-of-humans are *children*—children who take careful aim and fire, then smile and marvel at how high the blood spattered. For most of the rest of the film the camera (and viewer) stays with them as they stalk "the last one." It's merely a game to them, with one even quietly taunting the other at one point, "You're gonna miss, you're gonna miss," as his playmate sights Quim in his crosshairs.

Unique among Most Dangerous Game films, these young Zaroffs are motivated not by ennui or adrenaline or the feeling of power that comes from taking life, but by a child's instinct for competitive play. To them, it's merely a matter of points on a tally sheet, along with the fun of hunting in the woods and seeing the blood spray. Chilling in its abstractness, stalking and killing human beings for them is merely a childhood pastime, complete with rules (over which they argue like any squabbling siblings) and score card. These hunters-of-humans have no concept of the consequences or morality of their "game," which culminates in a tense and terrible final confrontation that remains terrifying in its emotional and sociological implications. Impactful on the level of the 1976 Spanish classic *Who Could Kill a Child?*, *King of the Hill* stands as a unique, enthralling, and oh-so-disturbing Most Dangerous variation that, once seen, is not soon forgotten.

Maneater (1973; Universal Television/ABC) Airdate: December 8, 1973; Alternate Title: *Evasion* (UK); Director: Vince Edwards; Producer: Robert F. O'Neill; Screenplay: Vince Edwards, Marcus Demian; Cinematographer: Haskell B. Boggs. Cast: Ben Gazarra, Sheree North, Kip Niven, Laurette Spang, Richard Basehart.

Here's a unique twist on Connell's concept—a man using a pair of *tigers* to hunt his human prey. In this made-for-TV movie, Richard Basehart plays Carl Brenner, a former circus animal trainer who now runs a dilapidated roadside attraction on a disused highway. When two vacationing couples have Winnebago trouble, Brenner ostensibly offers aid but ultimately decides to give his two man-killing cats some exercise by allowing them to stalk the quartet. "You against my tigers," Brenner tells them. "It's the challenge that's important—a true opportunity to show what you're made of." There ensues a, er ... cat-and-mouse game as the four flee through the countryside, tracked by the hungry beasts.

"WHEN INSTINCT IS THE ONLY THING THAT STANDS BETWEEN SURVIVAL AND DEATH" shouts the UK video tagline. For the two tigers, yes; but for the hunted humans it's intelligence rather than instinct that proves to be their best hope. In one of the film's disappointingly few suspenseful scenes, they temporarily throw the tigers off their scent by hiding in a river, breathing through hollow reeds. And in the movie's one truly exciting action set-piece they construct a rope lure to trap and violently deal with one of the vicious cats. As Brenner puts it, "Instinct versus intelligence—it's a very interesting situation." Unfortunately, director/co-writer Vince Edwards (who spent most of his career in *front* of television cameras as a journeyman actor rather than behind them as director) fails to generate much of said interest through his slow pacing, poor handling of actors, and hasty non-ending.

Ben Gazarra, as the far-too-assured and emotionless leader of the four protagonists, sleepwalks through his role, offering little depth or conviction — which stands in stark contrast to the too-earnest and amateurish overplaying of fellow huntees Kip Niven and Laurette Spang. On the plus side, safari togs–sporting Richard Basehart is as charismatic as ever, stealing every scene he's in — even upstaging the tigers — with his jovial bearing and courteous manner broken by sudden bouts of near-maniacal laughter. But he's left off-screen for far too long at a stretch. In support, Claire Brennen, the *She Freak* (1967) herself, turns in a brief but memorable cameo as Brenner's odd-yet-sympathetic wife.

The hunt takes place over the course of one night, and the frequently dim lighting generates more annoyance than atmosphere as the viewer strains to see what is happening. It almost makes one long for a little of that never-convincing-but-at-least-visible day-for-night photography. Ironically, such a wish is ultimately granted on several occasions, as Edwards intermittently resorts to that self-same technique, which only serves to call attention to the obvious mismatching.

The film ends on an abrupt and unsatisfactory note when two rangers suddenly appear out of nowhere to sort it all out with a high-powered rifle. Despite the title, nobody gets killed, much less eaten; and the obviously mad Brenner receives only the most perfunctory of wrap-up speeches. It's a disappointing denouement that fails to do justice to the clever concept, Basehart's talents, or even the two gorgeous animals, which Edwards deigns to photograph to full advantage. Categorically, this tame *Maneater* belongs to the good idea/bad execution phylum.

Manhunt (2008; Norsk Filmstudio/Euforia Film; Norway) Original Language Title: *Rodvyr*. Director: Patrik Syversen; Producer: Torleif Hauge; Screenpaly: Nini Bull Robsahm, patrik Syversen; Cinematographer: Havard Byrkjeland. Cast: Henriette Bruusgaard, Nini Bull Rebsahm, Jorn-Bjorn Fuller-Gee, Lasse Valdal.

The date "17 July, 1974" flashes onto a blood-red background to set the stage for *Manhunt*, a Norwegian backwoods horror film patterned after *The Texas Chainsaw Massacre*, with a dash of *Deliverance*, a pinch of *The Last House on the Left* (*Manhunt* even borrows *Last House*'s folk song "Wait for the Rain," written and performed by *Last House* star David Hess, for its opening), and a helping of "The Most Dangerous Game." The movie begins with a disheveled girl sprinting through a forest in a panic, only to step into a bear trap. As she painfully struggles to free her mangled leg, a shot rings out and she falls forward, dead. Startlingly, her body is then violently yanked out of frame by an unseen hand, and the film's title comes up. It's a hard-hitting beginning to the tale of a quartet of young adults who set off on a hiking trip, only to encounter the Scandinavian version of hillbilly locals who kill one and knock the others unconscious. Awakening in the woods to the sound of a hunting horn, the trio must run for their lives as these hunters-of-humans stalk and kill them one by one.

It's no coincidence that this *Manhunt* takes place during the same year that saw the release of *The Texas Chainsaw Massacre*. The set-up is virtually the same, with a group of young people in a VW microbus (just like in *Texas Chainsaw*) picking up a disturbed hitchhiker (just like in *Texas Chainsaw*) before running afoul of three backwoods psycho-killers (just like in ... well, you get the picture). But more importantly, *Manhunt* cannily captures the gritty, grimy, anyone-can-die-at-any-time tone of that seminal classic from three decades earlier. *Manhunt*'s is a simplistic plot but a disturbing one nonetheless.

Director/co-screenwriter Patrik Syversen, making his feature debut, shoots in a guerrilla style, utilizing hand-held camerawork and close-ups to generate a claustrophobic immediacy, even in the woodland surroundings. Said forest appears dark, dreary, and menacingly inhospitable thanks to cinematographer Havard Byrkjeland's largely muted color schemes. Syversen never shies away from the brutal reality of his story's violence. Apart from bloody stabbings and bullet wounds, there's a victim graphically shotgunned in the heel, a man tied to a tree with his tongue cut out, and a gory evisceration. It's graphic, it's dirty, and it's frighteningly realistic.

Syversen, however, along with co-scripter Nini Bull Robsahm (who also acts in the film, playing the first of the quartet to die), fails to take full advantage of his tale's Most Dangerous Game aspect. The victims can do little more than run blindly (with only one fighting back with any efficacy), providing little in the way of challenging game. Like in Connell's story, traps are laid (the bear trap, some nasty barbed wire strung between trees to snare its victim like some rusty spider's web, and a lethal pressure-plate booby trap) — but they're set by the hunters, not the prey. More importantly, the three hunters-of-humans remain woefully unexplored characters and are completely interchangeable. They even look alike. Hulking, scruffy, and dirty, they cut menacing figures, but are little seen and *never* heard (none of them utters a single word). Though their deadly but largely unseen and silent presence permeates the picture and ramps up the tension — so that every snap of a twig or bird call becomes just as frightening as the terror inspired by the more obvious sounds of a nearby gunshot or the dreaded hunting horn — it leaves their motivations unexplored and their characters a complete blank.

As of this writing, *Manhunt* (its U.K. video title) has yet to see any kind of U.S. release, even on DVD, which is a shame because while *Manhunt* may give short shrift to the Most Dangerous Game concept, it successfully recaptures the spirit of gritty 1970s horror cinema without the usual self-reflexive "cleverness" seen in most like-minded efforts.

The Most Dangerous Game, (2001; Arrowhead Productions) Director/Screenplay: Daniel Lee; Producer: Cindy Blyther; Cinematograhper: Stephen Kozlowski. Cast: Aldo Bilingslea, Daniel Malony, Zahra C. Langfoal, Michael McGee.

Running just under half an hour, this shot-on-video adaptation, "based upon the short story by Richard Connell," by commercial and trailer editor Daniel Lee is a semi-faithful rendering of Connell's tale, with some changes obviously dictated by the budget and others the result of a search for novelty. The film opens on various generic "nature" shots — seagull, caterpillar — as soothing piano-and-flute music plays on the soundtrack and a narrator quietly intones: "Where does it lie, the line between man and beast? I'd always believed that experience was the fabric from which a great hunter was woven, the summation, the view of the dying stars, the way the world should be." Said introspective narrator turns out to be big-game hunter Robert Rainsford, who wakes up on an island beach (looking none the worse for wear) after his boat sinks. Making his way through the jungle (re: California woodlands), he finds a large house (with perfectly manicured lawn) owned by the Russian Count Zaroff. (Note: While crediting Connell's short story, writer-director-editor Lee cribbed the minor character name changes made by Ernest B. Shoedsack's 1932 film adaptation.) After introductions (Zaroff is a fan of Rainsford's hunting books), the two engage in a philosophical discussion of hunting and Man's place atop the food chain. "What are we if not gods walking this earth?" asks the haughty Zaroff. "We have the history, we have the ability, we have the experience, and therefore we have the right." Reflecting Connell's character's sentiments, if not exactly his words, the Count continues: "It's true I have respect for creatures of *instinct*, but I have grown tired of hunting them. There is so little challenge, so little skill required.... Here I have imported a new kind of game—the most dangerous." Before retiring to bed, Zaroff teases, "Think outside the box, Mr. Rainsford. I know you can do it." Rainsford wakes in the night only to discover Zaroff in his trophy room, gloating over his latest kill—a man strung up from the ceiling. (The trophy room offers nothing more shocking than a deer head on one wall and two human bodies stretched out on gurneys, limned by some candles and red lighting.) Rainsford is suitably shocked, but Zaroff counters, "Man, Mr. Rainsford, [is] the only creature on this globe with consciousness, and therefore the only creature worth hunting." Unlike in Connell's story, Zaroff doesn't try to convince Rainsford to join him as a partner in his sadistic sport but instead immediately casts him in the role of prey. "At last an opponent of equal skill and cunning," he enthuses. "At last a challenge." Filmmaker Daniel Lee then tosses in one of Connell's most famous lines when Zaroff continues, "Think of it, outdoor chess—your skill against mine, your woodcraft against mine." After the hunt begins, Rainsford constructs a "Malay mantrap" (just as in Connell's story), but it fails to stop the pursuing Zaroff. (Actually, this version's Rainsford digs a "Burmese tiger trap," as described in the original story, but filmmaker Lee mislabels it, confusing it with the "Malay man-catcher" deadfall that Rainsford constructs from a leaning log.) As Rainsford flees, panic-stricken, he trips over a log and falls—his hand landing in a steel bear trap. Rainsford then cuts off his own hand (off-screen, of course) to escape! Cornered on a clifftop, the wounded Rainsford leaps into the sea below (paralleling the events of the original story). Later, Rainsford returns to the house, having miraculously survived the fall (one-handed and all), and engages in a sword duel with Zaroff, fatally stabbing the sadistic hunter (a ludicrous moment, as they're battling with flexible *fencing foils*). As Zaroff dies, he proclaims, "You—are a real hunter now." The story closes with Rainsford standing atop the cliff, thinking, "What have I become?" This angst-driven question offers a far different take on the self-satisfied victorious hero of Connell's original.

Though an intriguing effort, this *Most Dangerous Game* is hindered by its poor production values and amateurish acting. Hulking African-American actor Aldo Bilingslea (a colorful—if unconvincing—departure from Connell's hero) looks more like a linebacker than a great white ... er, black hunter, and he emotes more like one as well. As Zaroff, Daniel Malony employs an accent that's more Bela Lugosi parody than authentic Russian, and he makes for a decidedly *un*imposing opponent. But filmmaker Lee deserves credit for taking it all seriously (perhaps too much so at times, as the central "conversation" sequence teeters on a precipice of pretension). And the physical loss of Rainsford's hand (though no more convincing than the rest of the impoverished production) makes for a nice juxtaposition with the spiritual loss he suffers after becoming a "true hunter" like Zaroff.

While it may not be the most effective take on Connell's story, Daniel Lee's *The Most Dangerous Game* at least (like the original tale) offers some food for thought. And at less than 28 minute it doesn't outstay its welcome—*too* much, anyway.

Naked Fear (2007; Cinetel Films) Director: Thom Eberhardt; Producer: Ronald S. Dunas; Screenplay: Christine Olivia Vasquez; Cinematography: John Grace. Cast: Daniella DeLuca, J. D. Garfield, Aaron Shiver, Joe Mantegna, Kevin Wiggins, Jenny Marlowe, Rima Miller.

Though its title and packaging advertises this as something of a sexploitation film, the direct-to-DVD release *Naked Fear* is a half-disappointing, half-riveting modernized (and uncredited) take on Connell's tale that deftly sidesteps the exploitation trap to become an effectively disturbing variation on its timeless theme. The disappointment comes during the film's first 45 minutes, in which soap opera-ish plotting vies with amateurish acting to set up the scenario of a small desert town in New Mexico plagued by an inordinate amount of missing persons — most of them down-and-out strippers from the local clubs. While the feature offers plenty of nudity (in its second half, anyway), it is decidedly non-erotic in nature, stemming naturally from the terrifying turn of events (a local hunting legend drugs his female victims, then drops them naked in the middle of the wilderness to hunt them down like animals). After a brief (and admittedly disturbing) credit sequence in which a man shoots a terrified nude woman with a crossbow, wounding her and then finished the job with a pistol shot to the head (like he was finishing off a wounded buck), little of interest happens as we're introduced to our clichéd lead character, the naïve Diana, who was lured from her small town and trapped into becoming a "dancer" at a strip club.

Finally, at the 45 minute mark, the hunt begins. From that point onward, however, comes one suspenseful sequence after another, as the desperate Diana tries to elude the Hunter. With varied camera angles (even shooting from above at times to show the close proximity of the two antagonists) and effective editing, director Thom Eberhardt builds the tension, and often places the viewer in Diana's shoes (or feet, since for most of it she has no clothes), inspiring an involving "what would *I* do" reaction in the viewer.

Eberhardt pulls no punches. While he avoids excessive blood and gore, he cleverly captures the impact of the brutality and violence by use of editing and suggestion. For instance, when two boys out camping with their father try to help Diana but are killed for their trouble, we first see Diana hiding while we hear a shot, then see the younger boy fall into her field of vision, his eyes open and staring, a small red hole in his forehead. It leaves its brutal mark without having to resort to spattered brains and exposed viscera.

As Diana, Daniella DeLuca's acting could charitably be labeled "uneven" during the more mundane introductory scenes, but once the hunt begins she effectively conveys the terror, bewilderment, hopelessness, desperation, and, ultimately, animal madness her character experiences. Of course, it doesn't hurt that she looks very good naked as well.

As the Hunter (a character based, no doubt, on real-life Alaskan hunter/serial killer Robert Hansen), J.D. Garfield brings a likable charm to his underwritten role. Disappointingly, the script allows him no real back story nor explanatory moments that might convey why he's become what he has. There are no diatribes on hunting or the "ultimate sport," no verbal inklings of the obsessive madness lurking beneath the southwestern surface. All we know of him is that he's been written up in sportsmen magazines and enjoys hunting women. More characterization could have added further dimension to the tale and created a character worthy of Connell's concept.

All in all, while *Naked Fear* suffers from its dull opening and lack of significant characterization, the patient viewer will ultimately be rewarded with an involving and intermittently thrilling Most Dangerous Game variation.

New Town Killers (2009; NTK Distribution, Ltd., UK) Director/Screenplay: Richard Jobson. Producers: Luc Roeg, Richard Jobson; Cinematographer: Simon Dennis. Cast: Dougray Scott, Alistair Mackenzie, James Anthony Pearson, Liz White, Charles Mnene.

"*New Town Killers* was inspired by working with a charity in Edinburgh called Circle," declares director Richard Jobson in the DVD featurette *New Town Killers: The Story*. "And

15. *DTV Danger* 169

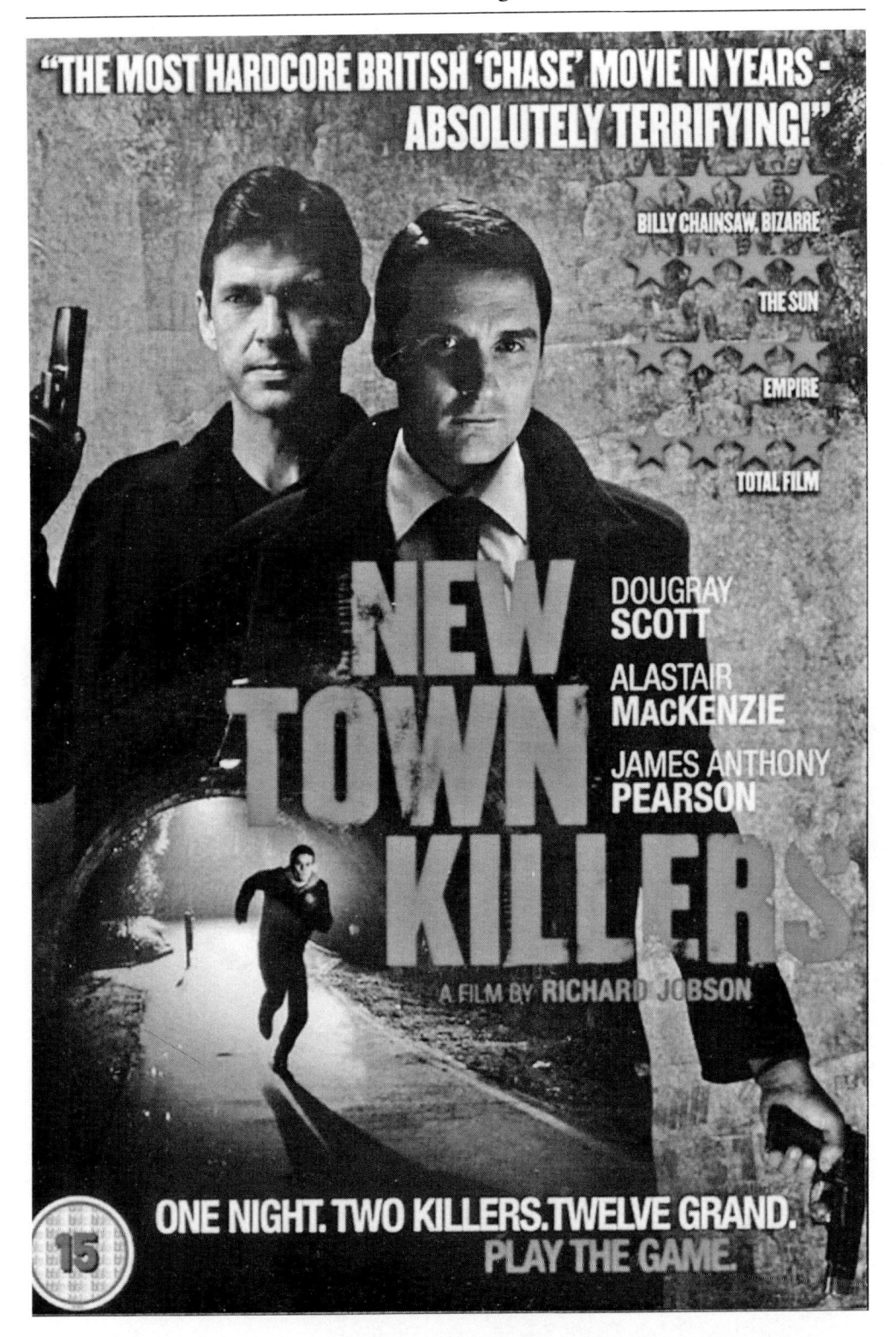

An Edinburgh-set Most Dangerous Game.

I was working with a lot of kids whose parents were alcoholics or junkies, and the kids had all but been forgotten." Once you've seen this gritty, suspenseful, and socially-relevant Edinburgh-set Most Dangerous Game riff, one is not soon likely to forget *New Town Killers*. "Edinburgh is the home of Burke and Hare," continues Jobson, "and this is a Burke and Hare for the 21st century." Not exactly, as it's more like a Zaroff and Rainsford for the new millennium.

Alistair Rashoinikow (Dougray Scott), successful CEO of the Edinburgh banking firm "Ethical Finances," manipulates the financial circumstances of council flat teen Sean MacDonald (James Anthony Pearson) so that his older sister, with whom the orphaned Sean lives, ends up 12,000 pounds in debt to some very bad people. Rashoinikow then approaches Sean with a proposition: Play a game of "hide and seek" over the course of one night; if Sean can elude Rashoinikow and his protege James Stewart (Alistair Mackenzie) for one night, 12 grand is his to keep. Of course, it soon becomes clear that Rashoinikow is playing this "game" for keeps — with Sean's death as the ultimate prize.

While brutal and action-filled (Rashoinikow has no compunction about beating — and even killing — anyone who gets in his way), the real name of this Game is social relevance. In Edinburgh, the "New Town" is a Georgian enclave where the super-rich live, powered by financial institutions and Old World money. Rashoinikow (and Stewart) personify this monied elite who take advantage of the city's poor. In the case of Rashoinikow, the Haves *literally* prey on the Have-Nots. The lack of police presence, or any authority figures, as Sean flees through the nighttime city, is summed up by Rashoinikow's observation that his victims (there have been many earlier "games") are "invisible" (i.e., poor and lower-class), and "nobody cares what happens to them." Director Jobson cleverly underscores this bit of politicking by having the same two cops who had hassled Sean at the film's beginning (simply for being out of place in a posh part of town) fail to even recognize him later when he's wearing a stolen suit and sitting behind the wheel of Stewart's Maserati. In fact, the now-obsequious coppers helpfully point out that there's a bit of shirt sticking out of the car's trunk (a garment worn by Stewart's dead body).

While occasional credibility problems arise (the normally-busy Edinburgh streets are often simply *too* empty; and the way an undereducated teen from the Council Estates so readily hacks his way into the financial genius' personal computer screams "plot contrivance"), the film's engaging characters, gritty tone, fast pace, and sudden stabs of realistic violence help to smooth out the rough edges. With its approachable protagonist (a good kid who loves his older, irresponsible sister, is kind to his elderly neighbor, and asks only for the opportunity to work a decent job), well-played by the likable James Anthony Pearson; its merciless modern sociopath of an antagonist ("I did it because ... because I could," states Rashoinikow when asked why he hunts people), brought to realistic life by the calm, assured and downright malevolent playing of veteran actor Dougray Scott; and its novel ending (a truly satisfying resolution that replaces the clichéd action set-piece with modern realism), *New Town Killers* is a rare worthy Dangerous Game for the New Millennium. It's a shame that it failed to secure a theatrical release and went straight to DVD.

Overkill (1996; Tanglewood Entertainment/Vidmark) Director: Dean Ferrandini; Producers: Carrie Chambers, Andy Howard; Screenplay: Ron Swanson, Jerry Lazarus (story: John Langley, Jerry Lazarus); Cinematography: John M. Stephens. Cast: Aaron Norris, Michael Nouri, Pamela Dickerson, David Rowe, Kenny Moskow.

What is it with the Norris clan and Dangerous Game movies? Here's the second direct-to-video Most Dangerous Game flick to star a Chuck Norris relative — his younger brother Aaron this time. (Less than four years earlier, Chuck's son, Mike Norris, played the prey in *Death Ring*. Is it only a matter of time before Chuck himself makes his own humans-hunting-humans entry?)

Overkill begins with a well-staged and excitingly-edited police raid on a drug hideout, during which L.A. uber-cop (and karate expert) Jack Hazard (Aaron Norris) takes out many a bad guy — as well as the department's own undercover operative. Oops. Ordered to take a vacation or resign, Hazard flies to a remote South American resort for some much-needed R&R. Unfortunately, he runs afoul of the local federales when he reluctantly saves nebbish accountant Gary Steiner (Kenny Moskow) from a beating. It turns out that Steiner's assailant is the police chief(!), who's in the pocket of American millionaire developer Lloyd Wheeler (Michael Nouri). Steiner had stumbled upon Wheeler's black market dealings and intends to blow the whistle on his illegal (and murderous) activities. Wheeler has both Steiner and Hazard captured and thrown in prison. But Wheeler has further plans for them, as he intends to allow the two to escape, then hunt them down for sport. As Steiner relates, "[Wheeler] is the great white hunter, only he gave up on *animals* a long time ago. I think we're next on his list. I never thought I'd die like this — a hunted animal." Hazard escapes on his own (taking Steiner and a native Indian cellmate with him) and flees into the jungle. Wheeler, bemused by his prey's "initiative," mounts his "hunting party" and takes off in pursuit, confident that he will soon bag his prey. But he hadn't counted on the resourceful Jack Hazard...

In comparing the two films, *Overkill* towers, er ... over *Death Ring* in every respect. First, brother Aaron not only resembles his far-more-famous sibling physically, he packs a much meaner roundhouse kick than Chuck's son Mike. (The fact that Aaron holds two black belts in his own right might have something to do with it.) And while Aaron is no more expressive than Chuck, he at least ably apes the solid stoicism of his elder brother and offers a modicum of Chuck's likability and gravitas — traits that young Michael simply can't muster. As a consequence, Aaron's action/fight scenes in *Overkill* appear far more realistic than the stagey choreography seen in *Death Ring*.

Second, while the budgets of the two DTV (direct-to-video) productions may not have been worlds apart, the *look* of the two films are — as the *Overkill* team, headed by director Dean Ferrandini (a veteran stuntman and second-unit director), took the initiative to shoot on location in and around Puerto Vallarta, Mexico, adding a far more exotic look to its jungle hunt than *Death Ring*'s supposed island setting (unconvincingly played by the tousled Hollywood hills and manicured environs of L.A.).

Third, *Overkill*, while not exactly faithful to Connell's story, at least borrows the author's more potent elements, including the all-important trap-setting and the focus on an obsessed antagonist (a big-game-hunter-turned-evil-developer who relishes the idea of "the hunt"). *Death Ring* dispensed with the whole notion of traps, electing instead to simply detail the chase and subsequent tables-turned scenario, while foolishly keeping the Zaroff character literally stuck behind a desk for the entirety of the hunt (with four sketchy "clients" out in the brush doing his dirty work).

With *Overkill*, sometime-actor, stuntman, and second-unit director Dean Ferrandini stepped behind the camera for his first (and only, to date) solo directing credit. As might be expected, the film's strongest sequences are its action set-pieces and fight scenes, which Ferrandini stages with a sure hand and exciting urgency. Unfortunately, the movie's other elements, including characterization and story, don't fare as well. The characters never expand beyond their two-dimensional cardboard fronts (tough good guy, charming bad guy, tight-jawed toady, hapless comic relief tag-along, spiritual local Indian). And the story's thematics remain superficial at best. For instance, Wheeler's obsession with hunting is stated but never explored, with the viewer simply having to take it on faith. Missing are any explanations or scenes detailing *why* he's become a man-killer. And the film's ending, in which the wounded Wheeler (shot by his own right-hand man, who finally becomes fed up with Wheeler's constant denigration) stumbles into the shrine of the mysterious jungle-inhabiting "Shadow People" (only to be confronted by the Indian shaman his men had previously killed), attempts to add a touch of poetic justice that comes off as more muddled than mystical. And by having Wheeler's personal assistant/girlfriend, who has enthusiastically accompanied Wheeler on the "hunt," turn out to be a CIA plant seeking to secure Steiner alive smacks more of kitchen-sink desperation than smart scripting.

Still, *Overkill* does its best to Overcome its shortcomings with a fast pace, enthusiastic action, and even some humor (Aaron, while no closer to the Academy Awards podium than his stone-jawed brother, at least acts appropriately bemused at his haplesss companion's ineptitude and occasional wisecracks), making it a mildly diverting modern take on Connell's concept.

The Perverse Countess (1974; Comptoir Francais; France) Original Language Titles: *La Comtesse perverse*; *Les Croqueuses* (The Munchers); Alternate Titles: *Sexy Nature* (hard-core version); *Countess Perverse* (U.S. DVD). Director: Jess Franco (as Clifford Brown); Producer: Robert de Nesle; Screenplay: Jesus Franco Manera (dialogue: Elisabeth Ledu de Nesle); Cinematographer: Gerard Brissaud. Cast: Alice Arno, Robert Woods, Howard Vernon, Tania Busselier, Lina Romay.

Spanish filmmaker Jesus Franco Manera, né Jess Franco, made well over 150 movies (some put the figure closer to 200) over a five-decade career. After making a name for himself with a handful of worthy horror films in his native Spain in the 1960s (such as *The Awful Dr. Orlof* [1962], *The Diabolical Dr. Z* [1966], and *Venus in Furs* [1968]), Franco relocated to France in the '70s to take advantage of an increased laxity in cinematic sex and violence. The result? He slid further and further into the sexploitation realm as his films became bizarre, fetishistic fever dreams. In among the often weird and disturbing soft- (and eventually hard-) core eroticism are a handful of horror-tinged nightmares (in both the thematic and *cinematic* sense of the word). *The Perverse Countess*, one of eleven features Franco completed in France in 1973 alone, is one of these. By this time Franco had become the kind of director that would just as soon zoom in to a close-up of a crotch as to a face. Consequently, *Perverse Countess* owes as much to the Marquis De Sade (whom Franco directly adapted for such films as *Justine* [1969] and *Eugenie* [1970]) as to Richard Connell, with the Perverse Countess' (and Count's) cruel debauchery taking center stage for most of the picture. Franco abandons much of the horror of Connell's tale in favor of leering sleaze and some morbid humor (centering on knowing winks at the central couple's cannibalism). Apart from a few brief shots of a pair of (unconvincing) human heads on the wall, the film only enters its Most Dangerous territory during the final fifteen minutes.

The story (such as it is) posits a pair of modern-day libertine aristocrats, Count and Countess Zaroff (Howard Vernon and Alice Arno), luring naive young beauties to their remote island in order to seduce, hunt, and then eat them. Bob and Moira (Robert Woods and Tania Busselier), an attractive, amoral couple, aid the Zaroffs in their procurement, with the trusting Sylvia (Lina Romay) next on the (literal) chopping block.

The first thing to strike the viewer are the gorgeous settings Franco found for his film, including expansive beaches, daunting rock cliffs and coastline, and an amazing post-modern mansion that seems like a massive puzzle box with rooms jutting from every surface (complete with an interior that looks like something from an Escher drawing). Franco (whose earlier work proved that he *did* know his way around a camera) utilizes low angles, forced perspective, and even a fish-eye lens (generating an unsettling, "off" feeling) to suggest the potential melancholy and even malevolence of the striking settings.

But the viewer soon comes to realize that Franco so languorously focuses on said locations — as well as the bodies of his beautiful actresses (with the camera ranging all over their undraped forms like the eyes of a sex-starved teenager) — that very little actually takes place in these stunning surroundings. Franco spends an inordinate amount of time and footage showing the principals puttering about in boats, walking to and from the beach up to the (admittedly imposing) house, and dining on their "favorite meat."

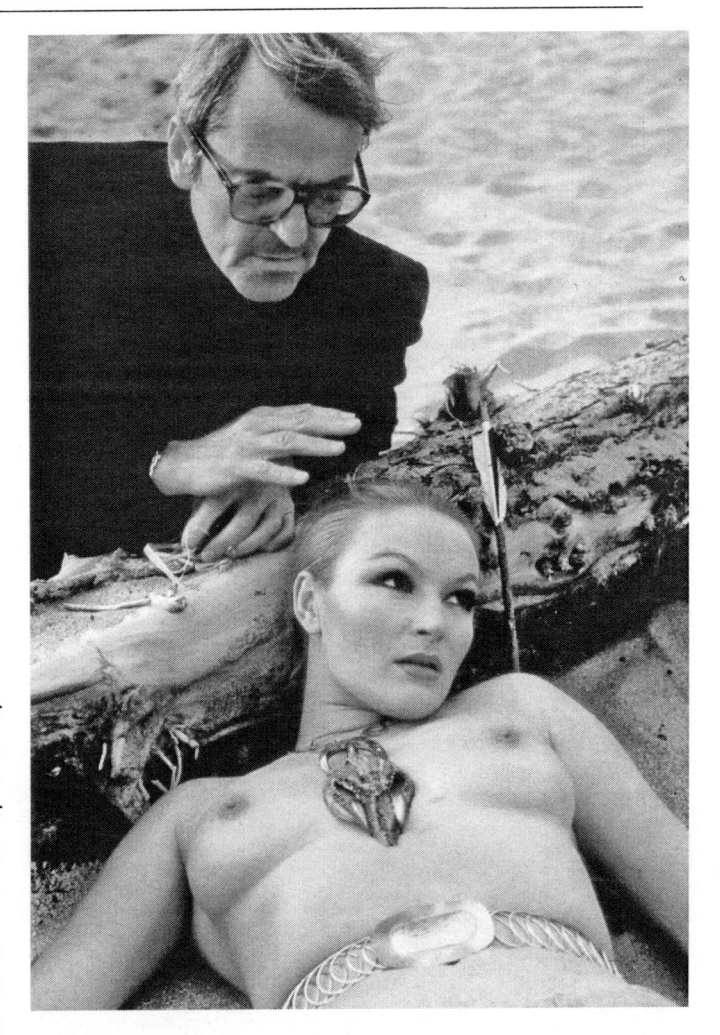

The Perverse Countess (Alice Arno) receives her comeuppance, while the perverse Count (Howard Vernon) looks on ... hungrily.

Then there's the sex scenes, in which Franco moves beyond the realm of eroticism into that of boredom by, for instance, lingering on two women kissing for well over a minute, then offering another full minute of the one noodling the other's nipple — all in excruciating close-up.

After an hour, the hunt finally commences. And it's nothing if not novel, for not only is the prey (Sylvia) completely naked as she flees through the well-manicured grounds and tries to hide among the beach grass, so is her huntress. Clad in nothing but a gold amulet and belt, the starkers Countess advances through the brush, brandishing her bow like some eroticized Diana, Greek goddess of the hunt. (And yes, Countess Zaroff *is* a natural strawberry blonde.) The cannibal Countess thinks of she and her husband as "artists" who would never simply kill a victim — no matter how hungry for her "favorite meat." As she tells, Sylvia, "I, Countess Zaroff, am incapable of killing in cold blood. I love the hunt — the game of life and death. I always give my prey a chance to escape."

Lina Romay, soon to become Franco's muse and life-partner (appearing in over 100

Franco films), provides a welcome presence as Sylvia, with her blank-slate beauty, wide-eyed terror, and naïve innocence (somehow remaining intact even during the sex scenes) helping to raise the movie above the level of unpleasant sexploitation. Aiding the cause is the assured, enigmatic, and oh-so-malignant demeanor of Swiss-born veteran actor Howard Vernon (who wound up making over 50 movies with Franco) as the sinister Count. When Sylvia stumbles upon the Count and Countess hacking up a previous victim for their "meat," Vernon calmly instructs the horrified Sylvia, "You know, it's no easy task to cut off a human head; it's hard work," with just the right level of banal malevolence. Though the Countess often takes the lead, with Vernon's Count sometimes relegated to the background (*literally* at one point, as he watches through gauze curtains while his wife seduces Sylvia), Vernon's vulture-like presence permeates the picture. (In fact, it is *he*, rather than his huntress wife, who finally flushes out Sylvia during the hunt.) And, of course, his spider-like, black-clad Count receives the last, ironic word as he eyes his wife's freshly-killed corpse: "I've waited for this moment so long, my love; for me, you will be the best meal of my life."

When Franco's producer, Robert de Nesle, received Franco's work print for *The Perverse Countess*, he was none too pleased (feeling it too dark and disturbing). He remained even less so when the film failed to generate much interest during its initial release. So he asked Franco to shoot several hard-core sex sequences to splice into the movie, transforming it into a full-on porno picture. De Nesle retitled it *Les Croqueuses* (The Munchers), and in a slightly altered form released this hard-core version in Italy as *Sexy Nature*. The original *Perverse Countess* didn't receive a legitimate English-language debut until Mondo Macabro put out an official "Director's Cut" DVD in 2012 under the title *Countess Perverse*.

Piranha (2006; Rekun TV; Russia) Original Language Title: *Okhota na piranyu*. Director: Andrei Kavun; Producers: Valeriy Todorofskiy; Screenplay: Dmitriy Zverkov; Cinematographer: Roman Vasyanov. Cast: Vladimir Mashkov, Svetlana Antonova, Yevgeny Mironov, Viktoriya Isakova.

A Russian blockbuster-style action movie in the Bruce Willis/Sly Stallone/Chuck Norris mold (though with a decidedly Russian bent), *Piranha* stars Vladimir Mashkov as veteran commando Kirill Mazour of the Piranha Special Ops unit (the sole reference justifying the film's title) who, along with beautiful bio-chemist Olga (Svetlana Antoyoya), is sent on a mission to deactivate and destroy a secret military storage installation at the bottom of a lake in the Siberian Taiga wilderness. Thirty years before, the facility housed a deadly bio-chemical warfare lab until an accident killed everyone there and flooded the installation. The lone survivor was an 8-year-old boy (son of one of the chemists), who grew up to become Prokhor (Yevgeny Mironov), a ruthless gangster lording over the area. Prokhor also keeps a hunting camp nearby, from which he periodically plays "a very entertaining game"—hunting humans for sport. Kirill and Olga fall into Prokhor's clutches and, along with four others, become the prey for the gangster and his men in their latest hunt. If this were not bad enough, Prokhor has recovered two vials of a deadly bio-weapon from the secret installation and intends to sell them. Can Kirill turn the tables on his hunters and stop the madman from disseminating the deadly agent?

With some evocative scenery (lakes, swamps, rivers, and grimy, impoverished settlements); two attractive stars with good onscreen chemistry; a strong, self-reliant and sardonic hero; a charismatic villain with a poignant back story; intriguing secondary characters; and fast-paced, realistic action, *Piranha* has all the ingredients for an entertaining action movie. And with a well-realized Most Dangerous Game theme at the film's core, *Piranha* offers plenty of, well ... bite. The film wisely takes its time with the hunt, which (like in Connell's story) extends over multiple days. Like Zaroff, Prokhor wears a cultured mantle to hide his inner beast, speaking calmly and with caustic humor at times, and even reciting poetry. Enthusing about the hunt, he mock admonishes his six prey before turning them loose to flee for their lives: "Why are you so dull, pals? It is a real adventure. You'll live your lives to the fullest. A man can really breathe freely on the verge of his death." Like Zaroff, Prokhor seeks a challenge in his "game," even giving Kirill a selection of knives. "I want to level out our chances," he beams, "I'm not a villain." Well, in fact he is — and a duplicitous one at that — since Kirill soon discovers that Prokhor has hidden electronic tracking devices within the knives' hilts. During the exciting hunt (the film's centerpiece), Kirill not only ingeniously fashions his own weapons (a bow and arrow — using entwined strands of human hair for the string; an axe made of bone), he sets multiple traps for his pursuers, including a spike-lined pit (like Rainsford's Burmese tiger trap), a tree snare, and a spectacular spring-trap that launches deadly spears.

Unfortunately, director Andrei Kavun too often emulates the Bag 'o Tricks school of filmmaking by employing look-at-me slow-motion, awkward skip-frame sequencing, and caffeine-fueled camerawork that calls attention to *itself* rather than the story. But at least he keeps the action gritty and on a more realistic level than most overblown Hollywood product (that is, until the somewhat over-the-top saber battle atop a moving train at the finale).

Though obviously a well-funded production with well-established Russian stars, the film has received no English-language release to date, either theatrical or on DVD, and can be found only on foreign DVD (thankfully *with* English subtitles). Which is surprising, as *Piranha* stands as an entertaining, well-acted, amusing and exciting Most Dangerous Game entry (and, incidentally, the only one produced by General Zaroff's home country).

Season of the Hunted (2004; Alexis Entertainment/Lions Gate Home Entertainment) Director: Ron Sperling; Producers: Ron Sperling, Philip "Chick" Faicco; Screenplay: Philip "Chick" Faicco; Cinematographer: Ben Dolphin. Cast: Muse Watson, Timothy Gibbs, Matthew Cowles, Raynor Scheine, Tony Travis, Wass Stevens, Lou Martini, Jr.

Take one part *Deliverance*, one part *Texas Chainsaw Massacre*, and one part "The Most Dangerous Game," stir and serve straight to video, and what do you get? In the case of *Season of the Hunted*, something far less satisfying than its raw ingredients might indicate. Five New York City friends — Steve, Frank, Charlie, Lenny and Al — drive to an upstate hunting lodge to go bow hunting. "A rifle is for attacking an armed opponent," espouses one of them during a tediously protracted breakfast sequence before their journey. "It's only appropriate if your target is shooting back — otherwise it's pussy shit. If you want to experience the raw, medieval rush of the hunt, you gotta bow hunt." It turns out that experiencing said "medieval rush" won't be a problem for these boys — though not in the way they thought, as the hillbillies (apparently upstate New York is hillbilly central) running the lodge are a group of cannibals who lure sportsmen to their private woods and hunt them down before butchering them for meat. Once Steve and Frank discover their three friends' demise, they must turn the tables and take out their pursuers in order to survive.

The first thing to strike the hapless viewer is *Season*'s amateurish look, with its obvious shot-on-video photography giving the homemade game away from the outset. Flat outdoor lighting alternates with dim indoor scenes, while a distracting black shadow intermittently appears at the corners of the frame — as if the filmmakers used the wrong lens at times. First (and last) time director Ron Sperling sets his foot wrong at almost every step, from the poor pacing and obvious camera "techniques" (including slo-mo black-and-white 'Nam flashbacks that look like they were filmed in the producer's backyard) to repetitive transitions, abrupt cuts and garden-shear editing that takes the viewer right out of the story. The hunt itself doesn't begin until after 37 excruciating minutes, during which we're subjected to lengthy scenes of the five protagonists' "conversation" (consisting primarily of lame jokes, insults and waitress harassment), driving, and card-playing. It's like a low-rent *Deerhunter* gone bad. Rather than developing character, these annoying sequences simply make us impatient to see these putzes hunted down like dogs. But even *that* is woefully mishandled.

"They're hunting us just for fun!" exclaims Frank (veteran character actor Muse Watson, one of the few involved who doesn't embarrass himself). Unfortunately, it's not much of a "hunt" after all, but more like a turkey shoot. Apart from a pair of hillbillies taking away Charlie's bow, counting to ten, then setting their dog after him, the rest of the protagonists are simply ambushed by the cannibal hillbillies. Apparently, Charlie kills the vicious dog chasing him — not that the viewer actually *sees* this potentially exciting action but instead learns of it when one of the hillbillies *says* so. And later, Steve wails, "They killed Charlie," but again we're only *told* this — which the viewer finds doubly disappointing, as the blowhard Charlie is the most obnoxious of the five protagonists, so seeing him die would have been one of the few pleasures this poor picture might have offered.

A brief nod to Connell at the drawn-out conclusion (in which Frank and Steve hobble to the highway, are picked up by a local, taken to his house, then engage in protracted wound-treating) comes too little and too late. "You have discovered hunters of a different kind," drawls their supposed rescuer, tipping his cannibalistic hand, "hunters that hunt the most dangerous game of all — man." But he (and the film) should have quit while ahead, as he quickly veers off into the nonsensical: "Think of it — man is the greatest animal on the face of the earth. No other animal equals his *passion*. We're all part of an instinct to hunt and survive. The ancient races, they knew it. Cannibals, they knew it. Man was designed to eat his own kind." Er, yeah...

Tender Flesh (1997; One Shot Productions; Spain/U.S.) Director/Screenplay: Jess Franco; Producers: Kevin Collins Hugh Gallagher, Peter Blumenstock; Cinematographer: Benjamin L. Gordon. Cast: Lina Romay, Monique Parent, Aldo Sambrell, Alai Petit, Analie Ivars, Mikel Kronen, Amber Newman.

In the 1990s prolific Spanish filmmaker Jess Franco (with over 150 films to his credit — though many think most of them less than credible) found it hard to find backing for his outre cinemaventures. With a few American dollars provided by One Shot Productions, Franco updated an earlier project, *The Perverse Countess* (1974), to make *Tender Flesh*. Updated, perhaps, but not improved. In fact, the nihilistic, degrading, and impoverished *Tender Flesh* may very well be the worst MDG movie to date.

Filmed in Malaga, Spain, the "story" has a stripper, Paula (Amber Newman), and her sleazy boyfriend paid by a rich couple and their aristocratic friends to come to a private island for a weekend of sexual excess. But soon the real reason for Paula's presence becomes clear: They intend to hunt her for sport and then serve her up as the centerpiece for their degenerate feast ("Breast or leg?" asks the chef at film's end).

Opposite: Amazingly, Jess Franco's 1997 direct-to-video sex film/"Most Dangerous Game" adaptation (a loose remake of his earlier *Perverse Countess*) received a "photo comic" tie-in. "Pray for Paula, for Paula is the prey!"

15. DTV Danger

The first 80 minutes of this 93-minute feature offers nothing but bizarre sexual situations and scenes. Among them: a woman getting up on a table to explicitly urinate into a bowl (which then serves as a *cooking ingredient* for the excited cook!); a woman on all fours under a table orally servicing the guests during lunch; a four-minute "erotic" massage whose drawn-out repetitiveness negates its eroticism; nude whipping and sexual assault with a riding crop; assorted crotch zooms; a mid-forties overweight Lina Romay fondling her own breast while a sex slave fellates her stiletto heels; a woman hand-feeding her nipple into the mouth of an old man; and a 12-minute sequence in which a nude Paula "dances" around and fondles the giant penises of a pair of papier mache statues. If the viewer has made it through all this, he/she is "treated" to the climactic hunt — which lasts seven meager minutes.

For said hunt it is the two *women* who serve as the Zaroff-like predators, with their husbands relegated to the role of "hunting hounds" ("mere dogs at our orders"). Unfortunately, this gender-bending notion is undercut by the fact that these supposedly lethal ladies handle their bows so poorly it's a wonder one is able to wound Paula, even from just a few yards away. During this half-speed human hunt Paula triggers two booby traps, the first being a jokey balloon spider that drops down to startle her, with the second being a *real* one that catches her foot in a snare (from which she's able to cut herself free).

Every once in a while Franco attempts to dress up his sick fetishist fantasy with odd, pseudo-arty touches, like using refracted images, blurring the lens, or adding an incongruous *laugh track*(!) for the duration of the hunt, but these just appear inexplicable and desperate among the film's porno-level sensibilities. The lack of redeeming characters (even Paula comes off as a money-hungry degenerate), a poor soundtrack, and accents so thick (it was shot in English) that much of the dialogue remains unintelligible, complete the inept unpleasantness. Towards the film's end, Lina Romay's character says after two women's deaths, "Oh Lord, we are stickin' it to you this time, sending you these two bitches at once." It's not the Lord above, however, but the viewer below that Franco is "stickin' it to" with *Tender Flesh*.

Whatever one thinks of Franco the filmmaker, Franco the man commanded respect and even loyalty from those who knew him. After his death in 2013 at age 82, *Tender Flesh* co-star Analia Ivars said of the man:

> He is my "father in film," the first director with which I worked and, of course, with which I learned more about acting.... Jesus, like almost all artists, was special. Sometimes weird, selfish, a blackmailer with strong and an often dominant character. But he was also fun, a great conversationalist with an exquisite taste for music, both to listen to it as well as to play it. We fought many times over these 30 years of professional relationship (we both have a strong character) but the next encounter was always tinged with nostalgia.

These are pretty positive words for a man who made her pee on-camera...

With quotes from: "An Invisible Cord: Analia Ivars on Jess Franco," by David Zuzelo, *Tomb It May Concern* (http://david-z.blogspot.com).

16

Almost Dangerous Games

So what constitutes an *Almost* Dangerous Game? Those films in which hunting humans for sport remains merely a minor subplot (e.g., *The Twilight People* and *Bitter Feast*). And those movies in which the hunting humans angle is significant but which fails to fully qualify in the motivation department (such as *Johnny Allegro* and *Run for the Sun*). And those pictures in which the hunted are not altogether human (the werewolf in *The Beast Must Die*). Basically, if a movie offers a Most Dangerous Game element that's not quite full-on people-hunting-people-for-sport, then it will be included here.

The Beast Must Die (1974; Amicus/Cinerama Releasing; U.K.) Alternate Title: *Black Werewolf* (video). Director: Paul Annett; Producers: Max J. Rosenberg, Milton Subotsky; Screenplay: Michael Winder (based on the novella *There Shall Be No Darkness* by James Blish); Cinematographer: Jack Hildyard. Cast: Calvin Lockhart, Peter Cushing, Charles Gray, Anton Diffring, Marlene Clark, Cairan Madden, Tom Chadbon, Michael Gambon.

Here's a real novelty in the Most Dangerous Game subgenre: A wealthy big game hunter is obsessed not with hunting fellow humans, but with hunting a *werewolf*. To this end he gathers half a dozen suspects — one of whom is a lycanthrope — at his palatial estate (the wild grounds of which he's rigged with all manner of cameras and sound devices for tracking purposes) to ferret out the hairy culprit in order to hunt him (or her) down like a ... well, like a dog.

Such a clever premise not only combines "The Most Dangerous Game" with various horror movie tropes, it turns Connell's characters on their ears by transforming his obsessed antagonist into an obsessed *protagonist* (in the form of big-game hunter and millionaire businessman Tom Newcliffe). This synthesis of the Zaroff and Rainsford icons into one figure is so rife with possibilities that it becomes almost criminal to see it wasted so badly in the hands of neophyte director Paul Annett and blaxploitation actor Calvin Lockhart (*Cotton Comes to Harlem*, 1970). Lockhart can't seem to say his dialogue without shouting and posing, as if he's playing some low-rent dinner-theater Othello. His wide-eyed, forced delivery of lines such as "In this world you're either the hunter or the hunted," "One of you sitting here in this room is a werewolf," and "[I] dream of hunting and facing what no man has ever trapped before" rings more of strained desperation than the intended intensity. Lockhart lacks anything remotely resembling charisma (and cuts a pretty poor physical specimen as well, with his slight frame sheathed in a black leather pantsuit), so that his pivotal Zaroff-Rainsford melding carries no weight. (Note: Reportedly, Robert Quarry [*Count Yorga, Vampire*, 1970] was originally set to play the lead, but the producers went with Lockhart instead to capitalize on the then-current blaxploitation craze. Pity.)

Two other major issues keep this *Beast* from becoming a true beauty. First is the mean-

One-sheet poster for one of the most unusual Dangerous Game variations ever filmed — in which the prey is not merely human, but a *werewolf*!

dering and repetitive script, which, when not forcing its players into repeated parlor games of pass-the-silver-candlestick or breathe-the-wolfsbane-fumes (as Newcliffe tries repeatedly — and unsuccessfully — to learn the identity of the lycanthrope), offers three tiresomely repetitive "hunts" on the three successive nights of the full moon, utilizing everything from security cameras seemingly mounted on every tree to a helicopter equipped with infrared camera and machine gun (so much for "sport"). The other major blunder comes in the form of the monster itself. Rather than a slavering man-beast straight out of a nightmare, this werewolf looks no more menacing than what it really is — a shaggy-maned German Shepherd straight out of a kennel. For the scene in which it supposedly rips out a victim's throat, the man merely clutches the beast upright to his chest, making it look more like a doggy dance than a life-and-death struggle.

One of the film's few memorable moments comes not during any attack but in its *aftermath*, when the camera reveals a victim's gruesomely bloody face — complete with a hole where his left eye should be (with the camera zooming in for grisly effect). Oddly enough, this shocking bit of grue was only included *because of* the censors. In some bizzarro-world scenario, co-producer Milton Subotsky — and U.K. distributor British Lion — were desperate for *Beast* to earn an "X" rating in the U.K. (their equivalent of America's "R"), but the British Board of Film Censors passed the picture with an "AA" rating for all audiences (not so marketable for a purported horror flick). Subotsky went to the Board:

> I said I didn't want to put unnecessary material in the picture and would they please give me an "X," but they refused. The Board said that audiences expected certain things from an "X," so I had to put outtakes of werewolf attacks Paul Annett had shot that I didn't like into the print to get the rating. The gore was redundant.

Well, said redundancy went a long way towards providing what few thrills and bits of excitement the film could muster.

Also injected into the movie at the last minute was the (in)famous "werewolf break," added by Subotsky as a William Castle–style gimmick intended to beef up viewer enthusiasm for this lycanthropic "detective story" (as the narrator labels it). With about 15 minutes to go, the film freezes and an unseen narrator announces: "This is the werewolf break," and invites the viewer to guess the beast's human identity. Over shots of the various suspects, he asks, "Is it Paul Foote, Jan, Davina, Dr. Lundgren, Caroline? You have 30 seconds to give your answer.... Made up your mind? Let's see if you're right." And the film resumes. While such a cheesy ploy can't fail to bring a smile to the face of the seasoned horror fan, the hoary device brings the already creaking carriage of a scenario to full stop.

One of the few joys of the picture is (with the one obvious exception) its cast. Such wonderful character actors as Charles Gray, Anton Diffring, and the inimitable Peter Cushing go a long way towards grounding this outrageous premise in some manner of believability. Unfortunately, Diffring and Gray are literally the first to go, and Cushing, as the werewolf "expert," is saddled with too much expository claptrap. Still, ever the professional, Cushing brought something special to his difficult task. Said director Paul Annett to interviewer Jonathan Sothcott:

> I have never before or since worked with an actor so diligent in his preparation for a role. Before filming started and whilst he was still on another picture, envelopes containing little color crayon drawings arrived for my approval. He was playing a Norwegian professor of lycanthropy and had worked out exactly how he would like to appear, from the sandy crew cut wig to the colors in his knitted sweater. "But only if you approve, my dear." Approve? I loved him for it.

Cushing was equally beloved by his fellow actors. "The first day I was on the set," recalled Marlene Clark, "Peter Cushing came over to me, and he was holding something behind his back. It was a nosegay [a flower]! He gave me a nosegay to welcome me to the film, and to England. It was such a wonderful gesture. He really was a gentleman." In addition to cultivating friendships by delivering flowers, Cushing went the extra mile to cultivate his character's Norwegian accent by studying language tapes. While a testament to his professionalism, he really needn't have bothered, given the caliber of the production—though, admittedly, the viewer is truly grateful whenever Cushing is onscreen (and Lockhart is not).

The final horror movie produced by the English film company Amicus (best known for their many portmanteau horrors, such as *Tales from the Crypt* and *The House That Dripped Blood*), *The Beast Must Die* took the company rather limply over the finish line with this unique but disappointingly tepid combination of blaxploitation horror, Agatha Christie's *Ten Little Indians* and Connell's "The Most Dangerous Game." Audiences thought so too. In the U.K., *The Beast Must Die* was released on a double bill with Brian DePalma's far superior *Sisters* (retitled *Blood Sisters*)—and *Die* it did at the box office, both in Britain and America.

With quotes from: "Scream and Scream Again: The Uncensored History of Amicus Productions," by Philip Nutman, *Little Shoppe of Horrors* 20 (June 2008); "Slinking Through the '70s," by Chris Poggiali, *Fangoria* 191 (April 2000).

Bitter Feast (2010; Glass Eye Pix/Dark Sky Films) Director/Screenplay: Joe Maggio. Producers: Brent Kunkle, Peter Phok, Larry Fessenden. Cinematographer: Michael McDonough. Cast: James Le Gros, Joshua Leonard, Amy Seimetz, Larry Fessenden, Megan Hilty, John Speredakos, Mario Batali.

This unique *Iron Chef*-meets-*Saw* addition to the New Millennium's torture-porn obsession finishes with a flourish via a brief detour down the Most Dangerous Game road. Peter Gray (James Le Gros) is a celebrity chef with his own TV show and high-end restaurant job. J.T. Franks (Joshua Leonard) is an acerbic food critic with an influential blog. When Franks lambasts both Gray's show and his restaurant, Gray loses both and decides to do what so many creative-types would *love* to do—mete out retribution to his criticizer. To this end Gray kidnaps Franks and chains him up in his deep-woods country home. There, like some demented Iron Chef, Gray gives the beaten and bloodied Franks a series of cooking challenges, including frying the perfect egg, barbequing the perfect steak, or choosing which wild rabbit dish contains mulberries and which contains deadly belladonna. Of course, should he fail in any of the tasks (which he inevitably does), there will be punishment...

After Gray has had his fun and it's time to get down to brass tacks, he decides to don his hunting togs, give Franks a 3-minute head start, and hunt him down like the deer and rabbit he regularly shoots in the surrounding forest. This Most Dangerous Game interlude comes only after 90 minutes and lasts barely a few more. But it adds zest to this tasty cinematic dish (particularly given that Gray intends to butcher Franks and literally feed him to his unwitting wife, whom Gray also holds captive in his basement!).

During one segment of Gray's cooking show (*before* he loses it—along with his sanity), he cooks up a venison steak from a deer he shot and butchered himself—to the mock dismay of his flighty female co-host, Pam, who labels it "Bambi." To this the annoyed Gray responds, "Hunting is one of the most fundamentally human acts. We've been doing it for thousands of years." "It's gross," retorts Pam. "It is organic; it is sustainable," insists Gray. And, as we shall see, he practices what he preaches—to the Nth degree.

Though the hunting humans concept remains more of a side dish than the main course of this *Bitter Feast*, there's plenty of meat on this cinematic bone, as director-screenwriter Joe Maggio ratchets up the tension all the way to the satisfyingly ironic conclusion. Maggio provides enough back story on the two principals to make them multifaceted, while the naturalistic acting of James Le Gros and Joshua Leonard, as Gray and Franks, allows the viewer to identify (and even empathize) with both these generally unlikable figures (one for his pomposity and the other for his bitter meanness). It all serves to make *Bitter Feast* not only the subtlest of celebrity chef parodies but an engrossing, character-driven thriller that, like the first *Saw*—and *un*like the myriad sequels and knock-offs that followed that groundbreaker—presents its torture-porn elements in a rather, er, tasteful manner that only increases the impact.

Deadly Game (1991; Paramount Television) Director: Thomas J. Wright; Producer: Johanna Persons, Thomas J. Wright; Screenplay: Wes Claridge; Cinematographer: Frank Beascoechea. Cast: Michael Beck, Abdul Salaam, El Razzac, Fredric Lehne, Steven Leigh, Roddy McDowall, Soon-Teck Oh, John Pleshette, Mitchell Ryan, Jenny Seagrove, Marc Singer.

Seven people (including a professional dancer, Yakuza boss, disgraced former football player, and Vietnam vet), all strangers to one another, are lured to the remote Pacific Northwest island home of the powerful and mysterious Mr. Osirus, only to discover that they are to be hunted by their host and his trio of murderous henchmen. Why? "Each of you," one underling announces, "at some moment in your lives, have crossed paths with Mr. Osirus—and he has a long memory." As seven flashbacks—one for each victim—gradually reveal each of the protagonists' connection to Osirus, what initially appears to be a straight variation on Connell's story becomes a tale of revenge.

The mossy trees and dense undergrowth of Oregon's Mt. Hood National Forest, accompanied by an almost constant downpour, make for an appropriately oppressive setting for the "hunt." The intriguing scenario features several deadly traps—set by the hunters this time, rather than the prey—resulting in some startlingly realistic and gruesome effects (courtesy of the veteran Kurtzman, Nicotero and Berger EFX Group), with the highlight being an unexpected and disturbingly effective decapitation.

With so many different protagonists, however, the characterizations remain sketchy at best, but veteran thespians like Roddy McDowall, Mitchell Ryan and Soon-Teck Oh manage to put some meat on their characters' cardboard bones. *The Beastmaster* himself—Marc Singer—even makes his weasely ex-jock character almost three-dimensional (and without benefit of pet eagle, tiger or ferrets this time).

Unfortunately, the two romantic leads, hero Michael Beck (who made his mark in 1979's *The Warriors* before slipping into television and direct-to-cable purgatory) and heroine Jenny Seagrove, offer little screen presence and no chemistry. In addition, the repetitive flashback structure works against the story building any real tension; while further distraction comes (along with a chuckle) when the frequently shouting Osirus starts sounding like Gilbert Godfried! But a truly unexpected twist puts a memorable sting in this Almost Dangerous tale, so that this made-for-cable *Game* remains not only *Deadly*, but fairly entertaining as well.

Deadly Prey (1988; Action International Pictures/Sony Video) Director/Screenwriter: David A. Prior; Producer: Peter Yuval; Cinematographer: Stephen A. Blake. Cast: Cameron Mitchell, Troy Donahue, Ted Prior, Fritz Matthews, David Campbell, Dawn Abraham, William Zipp, Suzzane Tara.

Made by direct-to-video specialist David A. Prior, the man who brought us *Killer Workout* (aka *Aerobicide*) two years earlier, *Deadly Prey* does for "The Most Dangerous Game" what *Killer Workout* did for dancercize. As an unintentionally hilarious take on the Rambo subgenre, *Deadly Prey* works a treat; as a serious action film, however, it generates about as much suspense as a Jane Fonda workout video.

A group of mercenaries grab random people off the streets and take them to their training camp "seventy-five miles southeast of Los Angeles." "The Colonel don't believe in war games," explains an underling, "he likes to use the real thing." (Note: Since they hunt not for "sport" but for training, *Deadly Game* qualifies as an "*Almost* Dangerous Game" entry.) Then they grab the wrong "runner," hunky ex–Special Forces and Vietnam vet Michael Danton (Ted Prior), as he takes out the trash at his suburban tract home!

What results is 88 minutes of the most absurd Rambo-esque action ever put to VHS tape, as the blonde-mulleted Danton, stripped to his cutoff short-shorts and brandishing a knife like a suburban Tarzan, decimates the entire paramilitary outfit, killing soldiers with sharpened sticks, deadly traps (of elaborate-tripwires-and-wall-of-spikes complexity), and his bare hands. Among his amazing feats are: (1) outrunning an artillery barrage from a tank, then racing back to take out the metal monster with a grenade; (2) digging a pit and constructing a trap door through which he can spring and mow down his pursuers — who in the previous shot were *right behind him*!; (3) pushing over a conveniently stacked pile of Styrofoam rocks to rain down on his tormentors; (4) jumping out of trees, watering holes, and beds of leaves to take his hunters by surprise; (5) dropping a grenade down a soldier's pants; and (6) slicing off the lead henchman's arm and, before scalping the man as the *coup de grace*, beating him into unconsciousness with the bloody appendage!

Apart from the two cameo appearances by Cameron Mitchell (as Danton's retired-cop father-in-law who goes searching for him) and Troy Donahue (as the wealthy executive-type financing the mercenary operation), the no-name cast comes off as amateurish at best and ridiculous at worst. As Danton, Ted Prior's performance alternates between staring blankly and spitting out his dialogue with melodramatic venom, befitting a former *Playgirl* centerfold model (and brother of the director).

The script itself is about as witty as the hunk-o-beef hero (whose snappiest "kill-line" is a toneless "You're dead"), with the various plot holes perfectly in keeping with the risible dialogue. (Staring into said holes, one can't help but ask: how does Danton's father-in-law find the "secret" camp so easily?; why doesn't Danton ever take any of the automatic weapons from the dozens of soldiers he kills, preferring instead to rely on his knife and sharpened twigs?; why didn't Danton's wife — or her ex-cop father — call the police when he was kidnapped?; why does the Colonel keep sending out more of his valuable trained men to be killed in small batches [we never see more than eight soldiers together]?) Poor Cameron Mitchell's "big scene" comes when he faces down the outfit's moneyman and must deliver this barely coherent rant: "Who am I? A little man who spent 27 years of his life as a cop trying to put big shots like you away. Twenty-seven years in the filth and the dirt of the street — and there ain't no music down there. You watch the people in the streets killing, raping each other, pumping dope through their veins while big men like you sit in the fancy penthouses and let the poor slobs rot in hell!"

Couple all this ineptitude with a shockingly brutal and surprisingly effective ending (Prior definitely saved the best — the *only*, really — for last), and *Deadly Prey,* with its mullets, head bands, waterbeds and generic synthesizer soundtrack, becomes the 1980s' own *Rambo-Meets-Plan Nine*.

16. Almost *Dangerous Games*

The Game of Death! (1974; Topaz Film Productions; Philippines) Alternate Title: *Games of Death* (South Africa). Director: Jun Gallardo; Producer: Jun Dominguez; Cinematography: Ricardo M. David. Cast: Ramon Zamora, Evangeline Pascual, Eddie Garcia, Panchito Alloa, Roldon Aquino Rayvann, Max Alvarado, Edna Diaz.

You know you're in trouble when a film opens with a "Karate Championship" bout between an average-looking fellow in a Bruce Lee haircut and a portly opponent with curly hair and moustache—set in a cramped room occupied by a handful of extras sitting on folding chairs. But when you factor in the lackluster fight choreography, the over-the-top foley sound work for the various punches and kicks, and the high-pitched howls emanating from the hero's mouth, this pre-credit "hook" falls flatter than a Bruce Lee opponent after a roundhouse kick. An incongruous ballad-type theme song ("The game you play / Is not an ordinary game / You'll find that on your way... So be-waaaare of the game of deeeaaath...") playing over the credits does little to raise one's hopes for this Filipino knock-off of the previous year's Bruce Lee vehicle *Enter the Dragon*.

The story has a mysterious businessman luring this new Karate champion, Charlie (the decidedly less-than-dynamic Ramon Zamora, billed in the film's advertising as "Philippines' Bruce Lee"), and his manager Pancho to the private island of wealthy recluse Colonel Von Stouffer (*Beast of Blood*'s Eddie Garcia) for a special tournament of champions. It soon comes to light that Stouffer (after his first introduction, the characters inexplicably drop the "Von") is a megalomaniac who rules his small island like a king and populates it with kidnapped women and karate-practicing henchmen. After a number of fights between the various champions Stouffer has collected on his island, we learn that Charlie and Pancho are actually secret government agents searching for some missing socialites (whom Stouffer has kidnapped). More karate duels, broken up by scenes of Charlie and Pancho sneaking about trying to learn the truth, finally leads to a rebellion of sorts and two distinct chase sequences, one of which takes a Most Dangerous Game turn. As Charlie leads four women and one male captive to the relative safety of the island seashore, Stouffer announces his arrival by sending a crossbow bolt into one of the girls. "I told you," he intones from a bluff above them, "no one escapes from this island. But I'm giving you another chance. I want you to run for your lives. For an exciting game has started—the game of death!"

This human hunt comes only after 80-plus minutes of sub-par karate fights (choreographed by star Ramon Zamora himself, who receives an additional "Fight Director" credit for his troubles) and dull plotting, and then lasts for a mere five minutes, as it's periodically interrupted by scenes of the hero's comical sidekick Pancho fleeing with a gaggle of women from a pack of Stouffer's lackeys. Within those scant few minutes, Stouffer manages to dispatch three of the six protagonists in Charlie's group before wounding Charlie, running out of arrows and coming after him with a medieval flail! Like the rest of the disappointing action, however, this final confrontation between hero and villain lasts for only a few seconds before Charlie lands some karate blows, kicks Stouffer between the legs(!) and dispatches him with a piercing Bruce Lee yell and killer punch—*out of frame*.

With such a cut-rate, copycat scenario (had this obscure *Game* received any kind of decent international distribution, no doubt the producers of *Enter the Dragon* would have set their legal eagles upon it), one can only hope to glean a bit of quirky fun from the possibilities on hand here. Unfortunately, not only does *The Game of Death* fail to provide any development of, or insight into, the villainous Von Stouffer—or even add anything to the hunting humans angle—it remains curiously circumspect about its exploitative elements by offering no nudity (not even some salacious suggestion) or significant bloodshed (despite several battles "to the death," it's all handled in an oddly sterile manner). Instead, the viewer must make do with scene after scene of interminable and interchangeable faux karate fights.

This *Game* does feature a few moments of levity, one of them even *intentional* (when Charlie practices his karate on the roof of Stouffer's "castle," his punches and kicks soon devolve into a series of dance moves—much to his embarrassment when caught by the watching Pancho). More common, however, are the few moments of *un*intentional humor, such as Stouffer's welcoming Romanesque banquet reception featuring as entertainment a quartet of impossibly inept tumbling midgets in polka-dot outfits! But nothing inspires more derisive guffaws than the first sight of Stouffer himself—poor Eddie Garcia sports a glittering gold headband over a blonde Prince Valiant wig while clad in a yellow dressing gown and blue cape! Garcia (who, still going strong with over 500 credits, must be the Philippines' busiest actor) had enacted a similar villainous hunter role in the full-on Most Dangerous Game entry *Woman Hunt* the previous year—though, thankfully, in a far less undignified outfit.

The few "hunt" scenes offer a modicum of suspense, as Stouffer shows up at the end of whatever trail our protagonists take, loosing another arrow to either spur the little band to continue their flight or to bring one of them down. But it's too little and too late. And its out-of-left-field abruptness makes this "twist" a mere curiosity rather than a thematic statement—that is, *if* the viewer has had the patience to stay with the dull scenario for the previous 80-plus minutes (which is about as likely as, well, a ridiculous cape-wearing madman battling a second-rate Bruce Lee clone).

Whatever you do, don't confuse this Filipino turkey with either the 1945 *A Game of Death* or the Bruce Lee starrer *Game of Death* (completed and released posthumously in 1978). You've been warned.

The Hunting Party (1971; United Artists) Director: Don Medford; Producer: Lou Morheim; Screenplay: Lou Morheim, William W. Norton, Gilbert Ralston; Cinematographer: Cecilio Paniagua. Cast: Oliver Reed, Gene Hackman, Candice Bergen, Simon Oakland, Ronald Howard, L. Q. Jones, Mitchell Ryan.

"You're invited to a party," reads the tagline for this bleak, early-seventies Western. "We'll play the deadliest game of all ... hunting 20 men and 1 woman!"

Outlaw leader Frank Calder (Oliver Reed) kidnaps the wife (Candice Bergen) of wealthy cattleman Brandt Ruger (Gene Hackman) simply because the bandit wants to learn to read. Brandt and his cronies cut short their traveling-by-train hunting party and pursue the outlaw gang, using the newest weapons technology (rifles that accurately fire up to 800 yards) to pick off the bandits one by one from distance. Though rescue and revenge are ostensibly the motivating factors in this human hunt, it quickly becomes something more for the increasingly unhinged Brandt. At one point, as Brandt energetically collects and lines up the bodies of the men he's shot at a watering hole, his friend Matthew protests, "Jesus Christ, Brandt, stop it! They're not game we bagged!" But that is exactly what they are to the obsessed Brandt. Several times Brandt has Calder dead to rights in his gun sights, but chooses not to fire and lets him go so that the hunt can continue.

The film's cast of consummate professionals—Reed and Hackman, of course, but also reliable character actors like L.Q. Jones, Simon Oakland and Mitchell Ryan—manage to overcome the story's occasional awkwardness, such as the lack of back story given the criminal gang, the near-nonexistent motivations for many of the characters, and the unbelievable twist of the kidnapped wife suddenly falling in love with her outlaw captor, even though the man has just *raped* her! Director Don Medford, who worked almost exclusively in television over his nearly four-decade-long career, makes good use of the expansive wilderness settings and keeps things moving at a brisk pace, while peppering the proceedings with some startling Peckinpaugh-esque bloodshed, making *The Hunting Party* a memorable treatise on the power and danger of obsession.

Hunting Season (2000; SnJ Productions) Alternate Title: *Grave Vengeance*. Director/Cinematographer: Jeff Leroy; Producer: David Sterling; Screenplay: Sybil Cummings, Tim Sullivan, Ron Ford. Cast: Cindy Pena, Ken X, Chris Lerude, Robert Croker, Michael Walker, Gergory Van Gorder, Jack Sparacio.

This shot-on-video (in Nu-View 3-D, though it was also released flat) no-budgeter from director-cinematographer (well, videographer anyway)-editor Jeff Leroy begins auspiciously enough with an onscreen written quotation: "There's no hunting like the hunting of armed men.—Ernest Hemingway." Unfortunately, it's all downhill from there.

The first thing to strike the viewer of this one-step-away-from-backyard production is the cheap camcorder photography during a long scene of two hikers walking and walking (and walking) over some unattractive hillside just beyond a busy freeway(!). But, to his credit, Leroy jumps into the action fairly quickly, as within 10 minutes the camping couple are attacked by a trio of mask-wearing hunters who brutally beat the man and gang-rape the woman, Sarah (Cindy Pena). With her boyfriend in the hospital and the local sheriff proving neither sympathetic nor effectual, Sarah takes matters into her own hands by donning a leather outfit and taking her crossbow into the woods to seek out the perpetrators (she is a former champion archer and bow hunter). She finds her prey (recognizing the hunting license number displayed on one of their jackets) and begins a cat-and-mouse hunt in which she terrorizes them with narrowly-missing arrow fire and strings of skinned rabbits (one representing each of her human quarry), before picking them off one by one in gruesome fashion (including the use of woodland booby traps).

Though revenge-inspired, the human hunt seems to take on more relevance than simple vengeance, as Sarah could have easily and simply dispatched the villains right away if that were all she sought. Though there's disappointingly little extrapolation on her reveling in the hunt, the script does provide a tiny window of insight at the beginning when she answers her boyfriend's query about the appeal of hunting with, "You have to experience the thrill of the hunt to understand and appreciate it." While this makes for a clever twist on the Connell concept—having the *protagonist* serve as the Zaroff character—it's disappointing that the script does so little with it.

Also disappointing is how the story devolves into long stretches of walking (and running) through the woods, amateurish acting, even poorer dialogue, and cheesy gore effects (including a ridiculous-looking severed hand, a casaba-melon squashed head, and a floppy dummy tossed off a cliff).

Since the cut-rate special effects prove none-too-special, Leroy (who made a whole slew of shot-on-video obscurities with titles like *Psychon Invaders*, *Rat Scratch Fever*, and *Werewolf in a Women's Prison*) offers some typical titillation to go with the gore by including a plethora of scenes showing off Pena's silicone breasts and fetishist outfit. The video camera lovingly lingers on her stripper's physique as she transforms herself from victim into would-be avenger by donning high lace-up black boots, black leather jerkin and sexy lip gloss. Toss in a gratuitous flashback sex scene, repeat several times, and the seemingly requisite T&A requirement is complete.

Though Leroy attempts to add some artistry to the exploitation by periodically including low-angle shots, tilted camerawork, and even rifle- and arrow-cam sequences, he's constantly undermined by his lack of resources and poor decision-making. For instance, the skinned rabbits used to unsettle and ultimately panic the antagonists are obviously fairground-bought stuffed bunnies covered in red paint! And Leroy unwisely focuses on them again and again by repeatedly superimposing the childish props over shots of the spooked hunters.

While the acting is almost uniformly bad, one bright spot is lead Cindy Pena. Obviously game for not only displaying her body but using it, she athletically sprints through the woods, impressively dodging and weaving. She runs the gamut of emotions as well — from terrified, humiliated victim to rage-filled, obsessed avenger — with at least a modicum of conviction. Pena, who appeared in half a dozen no-budget video features before dropping from sight in the mid-00s, seems deserving of better vehicles than this.

On the plus side, an ironic twist puts a clever sting in this tale, while the final coda does its best to live up to its '70s-inspired rape-revenge roots. Unfortunately for the viewer, however, the ideas in *Hunting Season* prove far better than the shaky (ahem) execution.

Johnny Allegro (1949; Columbia; b&w) Director: Ted Tetzlaff; Producer: Irving Starr; Screenlay: Karen DeWolf, Guy Endore (story by James Edward Grant); Cinematographer: Joseph Biroc. Cast: George Raft, Nina Foch, Geroge Macready, Will Geer, Gloria Henry, Ivan Triesault, Harry Antrim, William "Bill" Phillips.

Counterfeiter and big game hunter Morgan Vallin (George Macready, with bow) double-crosses his foreign partners with the help of *Johnny Allegro* (George Raft, second from left).

"I like this — it's a new experience; it's exhilarating, hunting man." So states the bow-and-arrow-wielding villain towards the end of this George Raft gangster vehicle, which only detours into "Dangerous Game" territory in literally the last five minutes. Raft plays Johnny Allegro, an ex-gangster and prison-escapee-turned-flower-shop-owner(!) who is drawn into the web of criminal mastermind (and big-game hunter) Morgan Vallin (George Macready) via Vallin's femme fatale wife (Nina Foch). Pressed into service by the Treasury Department, Allegro goes "undercover" to expose Vallin's organization. Taken to Vallin's private island off the coast of Florida, Allegro discovers Vallin's plot, backed by a foreign power, to flood the U.S. with counterfeit currency. Unfortunately, Vallin discovers Allegro's duplicity and hunts him down with his favored weapon — the bow.

Johnny Allegro boasts an excellent noirish tone (all fatalism and world-weary, conniving characters), night-edged photography and solid production values (courtesy of cinematographer-turned-director Ted Tetzlaff, whose 20 years operating the camera saw him lens such classics as *My Man Godfrey* [1936] and Hitchcock's *Notorious* [1946]), and intriguing characters (with "been-around-the-block-a-few-times" Raft as the likable and intelligent reformed crook counter-balanced by the arrogant urbanity of Aryan-styled villain Macready). Add in the suspenseful (if brief) Connell-inspired finale, in which Allegro must try to elude Vallin's deadly arrows and outwit the man himself, and *Johnny Allegro* becomes one of the best "*Almost* Dangerous Games" in town.

Jumanji (1995; TriStar) Director: Joe Johnston; Producers: Scott Kroopf, William Teitler; Screenplay: Jonathan Hensleigh, Greg Taylor, Jim Strain (story: Jim Strain, Greg Taylor, Chris Van Allsburg); Cinematographer: Thomas Ackerman. Cast: Robin Williams, Kirsten Dunst, David Alan Grier, Adam Hann-Byrd, Bonnie Hunt, Jonathan Hyde.

Based on the children's book by Chris Van Allsburg, *Jumanji* tells the story of a magical (and malevolent) board game that materializes dangerous elements from its alternate reality with the roll of its dice. A boy, Alan Parrish, who was sucked into the game's jungle vortex 26 years earlier, is finally released (as a now-grown Robin Williams) and must help a pair of pre-teens survive the travails of the game. Among the dangers are a troupe of nasty monkeys, man-eating mobile plants, a wild animal stampede, giant spiders, and a determined pith-helmeted 19th-century hunter named Van Pelt. "You might have told us there was a man with a rifle in there that hunts people," complains one protagonist after they escape Van Pelt's initial assault. As Alan says, "He's a hunter. He kills things — that's what he does. Right now he wants to hunt me and kill me." But this hunter has no interest in hunting anyone besides Alan, and Alan has no idea why Van Pelt wants to kill him — except that it was Alan who "rolled the dice." Taking up only a fraction of the film's running time, Van Pelt's hunt for Alan is played more for laughs than menace, with the kids even stopping the hunter at one point via a Rube Goldberg–type trap involving some liquid detergent, compressed air tanks and a canoe!

A decidedly juvenile-targeted adventure film, *Jumanji* comes off as a sometimes cloying Disneyesque adventure with a few clever gags and the occasional thrill, but there's very little here for either the adult viewer or the Most Dangerous Game fan.

Lethal Woman (1988; Independent Network, Inc./Film Ventures) Alternate Title: *The Most Dangerous Woman Alive*; Director: Christian Marnham; Producers: John Karie, S. D. Nethersole, Josh Spencer; Screenplay: Michael Olsen, Gabriel Elias; Cinematographer: Vincent G. Cox. Cast: Merete Van Kamp, Robert Lipton, Shannon Tweed, James Luisi, Deep Roy.

Though not a direct adaptation of "The Most Dangerous Game," and straying far from Connell's story, this low-budget, late-eighties direct-to-video action entry is one of the few films to directly reference the author's famous tale. When the hero begins to suspect the truth, he observes, "Funny, it reminds me of a story I once read about a hunter that lived alone on an island. He also imported game. You see, he'd lure these ships onto rocks surrounding the island, and then he'd hunt the survivors of the wrecks." Said observer is Major Derek Johnson (Robert Lipton), a reluctant undercover Army operative sent to investigate the disappearance of a dozen officers and enlisted men over the last few years, all of whom answered an ad for a mysterious "erotic adventure" vacation. Not-so-coincidentally, all 12 missing men were involved in the kangaroo-court military trial of Colonel Maxim (James Luisi), who raped beautiful enlisted woman Christine (Merete Van Kamp) but got off Scott-free. Christine has changed her name to Diana (goddess of the hunt), bought a private island, taken in a group of like-minded (and equally gorgeous) rape victims, and set up a hunting preserve of sorts — luring the culprits to her island in order to exact her revenge by hunting them down. When one of Diana's underlings (Shannon Tweed) falls for the Major ("We agreed on revenge," she argues, "not murder"), the prey gains the upper hand on the huntress.

Filled with such exploitable elements as brutal catfights (disguised as "training"); gruesome kills (including one particularly memorable earrings-to-the-eyes moment); stylish war-paint and skimpy outfits; a *From Here to Eternity*-style beach frolic showcasing a topless Tweed; a group bathing scene; and gratuitous midget shenanigans during an animalistic feast scene in which diminutive actor Deep Roy (*Big Fish*, 2003; *Charlie and the Chocolate Factory*, 2005) — in drag(!) — prances around on the table offering the girls hunks of meat, *Lethal Woman* rarely outstays its welcome. Unknown director Christian Marnham (whose only other notable credit is a 1985 episode of *Dempsey & Makepeace*) keeps things moving at a brisk pace, tossing in a hunting/action sequence whenever the film's threadbare production values and/or thespian shortcomings threaten to derail the entertainment train. One particularly effective scene involves a nighttime (and nightmare) discovery of Diana's "trophy room," which features a host of decayed severed heads dangling from the ceiling on chains. Of course, *Lethal Woman* requires far more than its fair share of suspension of disbelief, given the film's ludicrous premise (Diana dupes her 12 victims — career Army all — with some cheesy magazine ad; while the military sends *one* agent — a reservist, no less! — into the lioness' den to investigate all on his own), mismatched footage (in one kill scene Diana dispatches a victim in broad daylight, but the close-up reveals a nighttime background, then it's day again, then night...), a never-dissipating supply of sun-drenched woodland *fog*; and less-than-Academy-worthy acting. Danish-born former model Merete Van Kamp makes for a statuesque but too-delicate-to-be-convincing she-wolf, while hero Robert Lipton never seems to take things seriously, trying altogether too hard to adopt a devil-may-care secret agent–type persona. The most impressive thespian onboard (and the only pseudo-"name") is Shannon Tweed, soon to become the queen of direct-to-video "erotic thrillers," who not only gets to display her obvious charms but a few acting abilities as well.

With its odd mix of feminist attitude and exploitative delivery, *Lethal Woman* remains a unique and generally entertaining Dangerous Game variation. And one can't help but smile at the closing theme song, "The Most Dangerous Woman Alive": "Let them chase me in vain, I'll survive / When those hunters are hunted / By those who most wanted / Then certainly it's most likely to be the most dangerous woman aliiiiiive..."

16. Almost *Dangerous Games*

The Man with the Golden Gun (1974; United Artists) Director: Guy Hamilton; Producers: Albert R. Broccoli, Harry Saltzman; Screenplay: Richard Maibaum, Tom Mankiewicz; Cinematographers: Ted Moore, Oswald Morris. Cast: Roger Moore, Christopher Lee, Britt Ekland, Maud Adams, Herve Villechaize, Clifton James, Bernard Lee.

Even James Bond, arguably the most popular personage in pictures, got in on the Most Dangerous Game act at one point (though in a rather minor and ultimately disappointing fashion). In this ninth entry in the long-running series (and the second with Roger Moore as the intrepid British secret agent 007), Bond is apparently targeted by the world's greatest hit man, Scaramanga (played with urbane relish by Christopher Lee), who uses a golden gun and bullets to complete his million-dollar assassinations. With the McGuffin of a tiny device that can unlock the secrets of solar power (this *was* 1974, after all, the height of the Energy Crisis), Bond tracks Scaramanga to his private island off the China coast, where the villain is preparing to sell said device to the highest bidder. Welcoming Bond as a near-compatriot ("We have so much in common, Mr. Bond ... ours is the loneliest of professions"), Scaramanga proposes that they duel. "You see, Mr. Bond, like every great artist I want to create an indisputable masterpiece once in my lifetime. The death of 007 — mano a mano, face to face — will be mine." At this, Bond retorts, "You mean stuffed and displayed over your rocky mantelpiece." What begins as a "gentleman's duel" on the beach becomes a human hunt when Scaramanga slips away and lures Bond into his funhouse-like killing ground, where the assassin stalks the agent through a maze of mirrors, concealed panels and life-sized wax figures (including one of Bond himself, which 007 takes the place of in order to lure Scaramanga into the open and shoot him).

The character of Scaramanga from author Ian Fleming's original novel *The Man with the Golden Gun* is very different from that of the film (as was the plot itself, which was far more straightforward in the book). Recounted Scaramanga himself (Christopher Lee), "It was much to their credit that [the screenwriters] radically altered the figure Ian visualized, and replaced the lurid thug with a more diverse character, some ambivalence about his own compulsive sexuality (mysteriously linked to his third nipple, which my doctor surprised me by saying is not uncommon), an edge of humor, and a sense that he is indulging himself in a great game."

When Roger Moore stepped into Sean Connery's shoes for *Live and Let Die* (1973), the Bond films took on a very different tone. Gone was the tough-as-nails, cold-blooded determination of Connery's Bond, replaced with the smooth-talking charm and winking humor of Moore's. (As Christopher Lee observed, "One sensed that Roger's Bond was just as happy talking his way out of a bad situation, but Sean's would kill you!") Typical of this new tongue-in-cheek tone direction is the unfortunate — and ludicrously unlikely — return of the embarrassing character of Louisiana sheriff J.W. Pepper (Clifton James) from *Live and Let Die*. This good ol' boy cartoon just happens to be sitting inside a car that Bond steals from a showroom in order to pursue Scaramanga. Adding awful insult to this slapstick injury, the filmmakers ruin what may be the most impressive car stunt in cinema history (in which Bond jumps his car across a river via a ruined bridge, doing a full barrel roll[!] before touching down on the opposite bank) by adding a comical slide-whistle sound effect.

But perhaps the most disappointing aspect of the film is its brief (anti) climax. The Bond-Scaramanga hunt through the funhouse is a near shot-for-shot repeat of the film's pre-credit sequence (in which Nick Nack, Scaramanga's assistant, orchestrates and oversees a deadly confrontation between Scaramanga and a gangster as a kind of hunting "exercise").

Even the most popular film franchise in history went to the Dangerous Game well, as Scaramanga (Christopher Lee) and Agent 007 (Roger Moore) get set to launch their own dangerous game in the James Bond opus *The Man with the Golden Gun* (German lobby card).

This seen-it-before reprise offers a disappointingly perfunctory demise for what was one of the better Bond villains. Lee himself agreed: "The weakest part of the film was the death of Scaramanga." So despite a well-fleshed out antagonist and the added spice of the human hunt, the mishandled conclusion, the misguided comical injections, and the unnecessarily convoluted plotting mark *The Man with the Golden Gun* as a decidedly lesser Bond.

Note: Scaramanga's right-hand man, Nick Nack, was played by dwarf actor Herve Villechaize, who went on to achieve pop-culture stardom as Tattoo on television's *Fantasy Island*. On that series, Villechaize presided over not one but *two* more instances of human hunts. Unfortunately, the 3'11" actor "had the reputation of a complete monster" (according to Lee) and committed suicide in 1993 at age 50.

With quotes from: Lord of Misrule, by Christopher Lee; *The Christopher Lee Filmography*, by Tom Johnson and Mark A. Miller; *The Films of Christopher Lee*, by Robert W. Pohle, Jr., and Douglas C. Hart.

Mean Guns (1997; New City Releasing) Airdate: November 21, 1997. Director: Albert Pyun; Producers: Tom Karnowski, Gary Schmoeller; Screenplay: Andrew Withem; Cinematographer: George Mooradian. Cast: Christopher Lambert, Ice-T, Michael Halsey, Deborah Van Valkenburgh, Tina Cote.

"This is the deadliest game—a true test of your skills, either real or imagined." So explains Vincent Moon (Ice-T), the "Syndicate" representative who gathers together about two-dozen (though the film's ad-line lays claim to "100") "employees" who've betrayed the organization in one way or another. Summoning them to a brand new, yet-to-open prison facility built by the Syndicate (who won the building contract by hook and by crook, of course), Moon sets the numerous criminals against one another (literally dumping boxes of weapons over the crowd of killers), with a promised 10 million dollars to be split between the final three survivors. There ensues bloody mayhem until the herd is culled and the remaining human beasts split up into small groups to hunt each other throughout the high-tech prison.

Full of forced tough talk ("Reality is a cold, hard thing when it comes up and bites you in the ass") and even tougher (at times ridiculously so) ciphers ... er ... characters, *Mean Guns* sets out to become a B-movie action fan's dream. While it tries hard with sheer volume, it fails in that lofty goal when the continuous gunplay quickly becomes repetitive. And the abundance of long black coats and two-fisted pistol-handling mercilessly exposes the plagiaristic roots of the film's John Woo dye-job. As a result, it all starts to grow tiresome, with the violence losing much of its impact (particularly since we know little, and care less, about the myriad characters falling beneath the hail of bullets and baseball bats). The film's soundtrack, however, a bizarre mixing of Spaghetti Western riffs (employed to heighten the tension during the quieter hunting sequences) and jaunty mambo dance music, lends a blackly comic tone to the proceedings, making the underdeveloped characters and nondescript acting of the principals (including the usually wooden Christopher Lambert taking a rather more "limber" turn) far easier to digest.

In the end, though, like several of the characters themselves, *Mean Guns* tries rather too hard to be "cool," relegating this made-for-cable *Almost* Dangerous Game to the *Almost* Entertaining category.

My Son, the Hero (1962; Vides Cinematografica/United Artists; Italy/France) Original Language Title: *Arrivano i titani*. Alternate Titles: *The Titans*; *Sons of Thunder* (UK). Director: Duccio Tessari; Producer: Alexandre Mnouchkine; Screenplay: Ennio De Concini, Duccio Tessari; Cinematographer: Alfio Contini. Cast: Pedro Armendariz, Giuliano Gemma, Antonella Lualdi, Serge Nubret, Jacqueline Sassard.

"Smarter than a fox! Braver than a lion! Cuter than a pussy cat!" This silly tagline on the *My Son, the Hero*'s cartoonish American poster rather overstates the case for this unique take on the Italian muscleman movie (or "peplum"). While it does offer a lighter tone than most peplums, and spotlights a hero who relies more on his wits than his biceps (though he still holds his own in the palace guard–tossing department), it's no mere live-action cartoon. In fact, *My Son, the Hero* is refreshingly rife with often-creepy supernatural elements (many right out of Greek mythology), making it one of the more entertaining entries in this generally moribund subgenre. *And* it offers a brief Most Dangerous Game interlude...

When Cadmus (Pedro Armendari), the evil king of Crete, murders his wife in order to marry his mistress, the gods take notice and send an oracle to warn him that he will die once his infant daughter grows to womanhood and falls in love. (As insurance, they stipulate that should he kill his child, his heart will cease to beat when hers does.) Some 18 years later the sequestered princess has never seen a man. Now the gods decide to release from hell the youngest (and smartest) of the demi-god Titans, Krios (Giuliano Gemma), to exact (belated) vengeance on Cadmus. Krios is made mortal and instructed to bring about the demise of Cadmus. Krios subsequently insinuates himself into the king's court, and even falls in love with the forbidden princess, before he's aided by his fellow Titan brothers in a final battle against the king and his invincible soldiers.

Unlike most musclemen heroes, such as Hercules, Maciste, Goliath, et al, Krios utilizes his brain more than his brawn, and displays a definite sense of humor about things (which peplum purveyors like Steve Reeves, Kirk Morris and Gordon Mitchell generally lacked). As a result, the classical storyline takes on a breezier tone, which serves to bring the darker elements into sharp relief when they arise. And arise they do, in the form of such supernatural horrors as two separate trips to hell (complete with classical Greek torments), a cadre of invincible soldiers (bloody, mortal sword wounds miraculously disappear as they rise to continue the fight), and a tense confrontation with a Gorgon. (Despite the mythical monster's disappointingly mundane appearance — looking like nothing more than a mildly unattractive woman with a few garter snakes woven into her hair — director Duccio Tessari generates some horrific atmosphere and genuine suspense through low-angle camerawork and clever editing.)

Giuliano Gemma (né "Montgomery Wood") makes for a far more engaging hero than the standard Muscle Beach denizens generally cast in peplums. Gemma, who traded in his leather loincloth for a pair of six-guns a few years later to become a staple in Spaghetti Westerns (including several *Ringo* titles), possesses not only a pleasing screen presence but genuine acting ability, as demonstrated over his nearly five-decades-long career in Italian cinema. His natural charm, relaxed demeanor before the camera (many peplum purveyors look stiff and uncomfortable on-camera, even the supposed sword-and-sandal "king," Steve Reeves) and surprising litheness (including some impressive trampoline-type acrobatics on market awnings as he amusingly eludes pursuing soldiers) helps make *My Son, the Hero* one of the more enjoyable Euro He-Man movies of the decade.

Connell's concept enters the story when the king decides to provide a little amusement for himself and his court — by going hunting. "What kind of animal do we hunt?" asks Krios, now one of Cadmus' favorites at court. "The most formidable, the most difficult to kill — Man," answers the king. Krios goes along with the brutal game and employs his reasoning ability to lead the king right to his prey (a muscular prisoner who's managed to elude his pursuers and their tracking dogs). But just as the king takes aim with his bow, Krios turns the tables to reveal that he's in cahoots with the victim-to-be and intends to take Cadmus to Hades for the Gods' punishment. The king has the last laugh, however, when his men arrive and force Krios and his cohort to flee. The entire episode lasts barely five minutes, remaining a mere mini-subplot in the greater scheme of things, but it provides a novel environment in which to see the Most Dangerous Game play out, however briefly.

The Naked Prey (1966; Paramount) Director/Producer: Cornel Wilde; Screenplay: Clint Johnston, Don Peters; Cinematographer: H.A.R. Thomson. Cast: Cornel Wilde, Gert Van der Berg, Ken Gampu, Patrick Mynhardt, Bella Randles.

"Stripped, weaponless, alone and only ten desperate seconds ahead of the killers!" touted the ads for *The Naked Prey*. Producer-director-star Cornel Wilde originally intended to film the true-life tale of trapper John Colter's arduous escape from Blackfoot Indians in 1809 Wyoming, but lower shooting costs, tax breaks, and promised assistance from the South African government prompted him to adapt Clint Johnston and Don Peters' script to an African setting. And fortunate this was, as the incredible African locations (captured brilliantly by cinematographer H.A.R. Thomson's panoramic color photography, all orange-red earth, green and brown junglescape, and deep blue sky) and amazing wildlife footage sprinkled throughout the film greatly enhanced this tale of a man pursued across the wilderness by vengeful warriors. (The revised script also netted Johnston and Peters an Academy Award nomination.)

Cornel Wilde (designated only by the generic "Man" in the credits) plays a big-game hunter in Colonial-era Africa leading an Ivory-gathering safari. When they encounter a band of native warriors expecting gifts for allowing them to pass through their territory, the boozing, bigoted safari financier (South African actor Gert Van der Berg) refuses and insults the warriors. Later, the disgruntled tribesmen attack the safari camp, killing many of the bearers and bringing the party's three white men back to their village. There they torture and kill them in various ways until it's "Man's" turn. They strip him naked, give him a few hundred yards head start, and then come after him at intervals one by one. When the Man manages to kill his first pursuer with the tribesman's own spear, a band of eight warriors gives chase into the bush, so that it becomes not only the task of the Man to keep himself alive in this hostile environment, but also elude and/or kill those hunting him.

Falling into the *Almost* Dangerous Game category by dint of the hunters' motivations (it's not for sport that they hunt the Man, it's a punishment for perceived wrongs inflicted, and then vengeance for the killing of their fellow tribesman), *The Naked Prey* nonetheless stands as one of the most engrossing, tension-filled and impressively mounted human hunts ever committed to celluloid. Realism takes center stage, not only in the actual, often hostile environment (complete with genuine, sometimes savage animal footage), but in the actions of both the hunted and hunters (who occasionally argue among themselves — refreshingly, in their native Bantu tongue rather than the pidgin English of so many other African-set movies — and display emotions like grief, anger and fatigue). One never doubts the hardships endured by Wilde's character (and Wilde himself, for that matter — the 52-year-old actor reportedly was ill throughout much of the shooting but soldiered on, feeling that this added to his performance). The trials and tribulations of merely staying alive become just as absorbing as his efforts to elude his pursuers, be it desperately digging for roots only for them to make him sick, and successfully spearing a gazelle only to have his kill taken from him by a lion; or carefully laying a false track in order to get the drop on his pursuer, and starting a brush fire in order to create a wall of flame between himself and the hunters.

The picture refuses to pull its punches, detailing not only the harsh savagery of nature (with myriad shots of predators stalking and killing their prey mirroring the human drama playing out) but that of man. The film includes unflinching footage of elephants being slaughtered and then butchered, with men literally crawling inside of a bull elephant's slit belly to do their work. The tortures of the captives are appalling in their cruelty and inventiveness. The first man (the lead bearer) is covered in clay and roasted alive over a fire; the next (the safari overseer) is trussed up like a chicken (complete with mocking feathered headdress) and forced to hop for his life, pursed by the village women who fall upon him with sharpened sticks; and the third (the financier) is tied to the ground in a ring of fire with a cobra at his *face*.

Of Cornel Wilde, filmmaker Martin Scorsese said, "He was a pleasant actor, but you would never guess from his performances that he would develop into such a good filmmaker. *The Naked Prey* is his best film, I think (I'm also fond of *Storm Fear*), and it was quite unlike anything else made in 1966, a sort of throwback to the Ernest Schoedsack–Merian C. Cooper productions of the early '30s, particularly *The Most Dangerous Game*." It was indeed, and Wilde makes an excellent everyMan. When his callous companion casually comments, "After this I'd like to go into the slave trade — very lucrative," Wilde gives a subtle but revealing

EXTRA! **DAILY MIRROR** **SPECIAL!**

From Paramount Pictures — In Panavision-Technicolor

FIERCELY HUNTED AS "NAKED PREY"

Stripped, Weaponless, Alone And Only Ten Desperate Seconds Ahead Of The Killers!

'NAKED PREY' STAR BATTLES TRIBESMEN MAN-EATING BEASTS AND AFRICAN TERROR FOR RIGHT TO LIVE

Newspaper-styled herald for perhaps the best Almost Dangerous Game ever filmed, *The Naked Prey*.

look of disdain in response. Later, after they spend the day shooting elephants for their ivory, Wilde reacts to his companion's excessive, indiscriminate killing with angry contempt ("What the hell, so I shot some for sport," counters the lout). (Wilde's concern for animal life was genuine, as he was determined not to harm the animals used in his film whenever possible. During a scene in which a large monitor lizard battles a python, when it became apparent the lizard was going to succumb, Wilde himself intervened, resulting in the monitor biting his leg and refusing to let go until the crew killed it. Wilde had to be taken to the local hospital for treatment.)

As a pressbook article pointed out, "Authentic African music, sung by tribesmen to the tune of their native instruments, provide the musical score for *The Naked Prey*." Apart from this occasional tribal chanting and some evocative percussion drumming, the film's soundtrack primarily consists of a constant buzz of animal and insect noise, adding aural authenticity to the visual verisimilitude. It all adds up to one of the greatest adventure films ever made.

Apart from the usual lobby displays, library tie-ins, and radio-TV spots, Paramount offered a couple of rather unusual ballyhoo suggestions in its exhibitors manual. One was to "invite a [Boy Scout] troop to see the picture [and] have them put on a 'survival' demonstration — how to live in the woods or wilderness without weapons." But the most imaginative was, "Tie in with one of the 'live' [dance] studios to show relationship of 'modern' dances like the 'Frugue,' the 'Monkey,' and the 'Watusi' to the ancient primitive tribal dances of Africa." Indeed, what could be a more natural match than *The Naked Prey* and jiving juveniles?...

With quotes from: Martin Scorsese, "*The Naked Prey* (1966) and *Apocalypto* (2006) Review"; *The Naked Prey* pressbook (Paramount, 1966).

Piranha (1972; American National Enterprises; Venezuela/U.S.) Alternate Title: *Piranha, Piranha!* (video). Director: Bill Gibson; Producer: L. Guillermo Villegas; Screenplay: Richard Finder; Cinematographer: Luis Jacko. Cast: William Smith, Peter Brown, Ahna Capri, Tom Simcox, Joahn Villegas.

Not to be confused (either in terms of plot *or* quality) with the like-named 1978 Roger Corman-produced/Joe Dante-directed exploitation classic (nor its 1995 and 2010 remakes), *or* the Russian-made, full-out "Dangerous Game" entry from 2006, this *Piranha* follows the adventures of Terry (Ahna Capri), a pretty wildlife photographer, and her fun-loving brother Art (Tom Simcox), who hire nice-guy guide Jim (Peter Brown) to take them on a photo safari in the Venezuelan jungle. There they run across Caribe (William Smith, who had co-starred with Peter Brown five years earlier in the TV series *Loredo*, about a group of Texas Rangers), the local Great White Hunter. Circumstances bring them to his jungle compound, and while the men are away, Caribe sneaks back and rapes Terry, then kills Art with a machete and feeds him to piranhas in the nearby river (the only time the titular terrors make an appearance — sort of, as we never actually see the little maneaters, their presence represented solely by some bloody clothing swirling around on the river's surface). Jim and Terry make a run for it, but Caribe hunts them down, overpowers Jim and takes Terry back to his compound. But Jim is not dead, and the tables are about to turn.

Piranha offers only tangential ties to Connell's story via a few dialogue exchanges and the "Great Hunter" aspect of Caribe's character. While Caribe appears to enjoy tracking the fleeing couple (even laughing heartily as he sets fire to the straw huts in the native village where the two have taken refuge — the film's one truly effective and suspenseful set-piece), he doesn't necessarily hunt them for sport, but ostensibly to retrieve the girl. The best screenwriter Richard Finder can deliver is a brief dialogue exchange on hunting in which the anti-gun Terry (an obvious spokesperson for the then-fashionable pacifist movement of the early 1970s) takes issue with Caribe's profession and lifestyle, demanding, "As a hunter, don't you feel the blood, the terror and the pain of the animal? Don't you care about the motherless offspring that won't live to survive?" Caribe answers, "A hunter feels only the excitement, the chase, victory." Terry, outraged, presses, "Why do you do that?" to which Caribe responds, "Instinct — better the predator than the prey" (this last being a variation of Connell's "the hunters and the hunted" soliloquy).

Low-budget, small scale, and slow moving, with only the occasional glimmer of interest (generally sparked by man-mountain William Smith, who, though doing little real "acting," oozes arrogant charisma and menace), the film's running time is eaten up by Venezuelan travelogue and nature photography, protracted motorcycle racing (between the macho Caribe and the posturing Jim), diamond mining footage, and even a sappy falling-in-love montage sequence (complete with tepid song) when Art temporarily hooks up with a woman in Caracas. The four principals do well enough in their respective roles, but the threadbare script barely even scratches the surface of their cipher characters (compassionate liberal woman, happy-go-lucky charmer, serious-minded good-guy, and macho loner villain). Unlike the real fish, this poor-man's *Piranha* is more dull than dangerous.

Prey for the Hunter (1993; Anchor Film) Director/Cinematographer: John H. Parr; Producer: Lindsay Kaye; Screenplay: Paul S. Rowlston. Cast: Todd Jensen, Andre Jacobs, Michelle Bestbier, Evan J. Klisser, David Butler, Alan Granville.

Cinema doesn't get much worse than this. When American journalist Simon Rush (Todd Jensen) ends up stranded in the middle of nowhere in Africa, he hooks up with a party of four businessmen ("the last of the Great White Hunters," one jokes) on a hunting trip. The quartet, bored with stalking dumb animals, suggest they make Rush their prey — using paint guns. Rush agrees to join the fun, but when he turns the tables on the hunters and soundly beats them at their own game, the group's leader, Eric DuPont (Alan Granville), snaps and decides to replace the harmless paint guns with real weapons. With his companions at first reluctant to play "the most dangerous game," circumstances soon escalate into an all-out war between Rush and the businessmen.

Small of scale (there's only six characters) and bereft of original ideas (they do little but loiter at their makeshift campsite or skulk through the "African" bush), *Prey for the Hunter* adds nothing to the Most Dangerous Game canon — particularly since it turns out that DuPont has set the whole thing up as a ruse to dispose of his partners and so make a killing (pardon the pun) on an upcoming defense contract without having to share the spoils. A cheesy synth soundtrack, banal photography (with a few poorly-matched stock shots of wild animals the only thing to indicate they're in Africa rather than some overgrown vacant lot), brainless characters, no-name actors with about as much appeal as a muddy watering hole (though Alan Granville amusingly overreacts — and overacts — as the ostensibly crazy DuPont), and an absolutely awful, seen-it-coming-an-African-league-away denouement make *Prey* a pointless exercise in tedium. Forget *Prey for the Hunter* and instead Pray for the Viewer who's unlucky enough to run across this torpid mess.

Punishment Park (1971; Sherpix) Director/Screenplay: Peter Watkins; Producer: Susan Martin; Cinematographer: Joan Churchill. Cast: Patrick Boland, Kent Foreman, Carmen Arganziano, Luke Johnson, Katherine Quittner, Scott Turner.

The Most Dangerous Game for the era of Mi Lai and Kent State, *Punishment Park*, a fictional film shot like a documentary, details the workings of Punishment Park, "described by the U.S. Senate Subcommittee on Law and Order as 'a necessary training for law officers and the national guard of the country in the control of those elements who seek the violent overthrow of the United States government and the means for providing a punitive deterrent for said subversive elements.'" In other words, after a perfunctory hearing, a group of antiwar protestors and draft dodgers are given the choice of long prison terms or a 3-day ordeal in Punishment Park, in which they must flee 53 miles through the searing desert and "evade capture by pursuing law enforcement officers" to reach an American flag. Though the police coordinator tells the participants that "your capture, should that occur, will be as peaceful as you want it to be," it generally ends in violence and death, thanks to the trigger-happy pursuers (comprised of various policemen, U.S. marshals and national guardsmen).

Director Peter Watkins (who also serves as the film's unseen narrator, the director of a supposed documentary crew filming the proceedings) cuts back and forth between the grueling ordeal of one group of dissidents, and the hearing, set in a large army tent right there in the desert, of another group, in which the anti-war protesters, modeled, according to Watkins, on such real-life figures as Abby Hoffman, Bobby Seale and Joan Baez, rail against the Vietnam War, government corruption, and the Establishment in general (with "pig" seemingly the epithet of choice). Filmed in three weeks in August–September 1970 at the El Mirage dry lakebed in the San Bernadino desert, and shot with a hand-held 16mm camera by a small (less than 10) film crew, *Punishment Park* possesses a cinema verite–like aura that adds gritty realism to the disturbing scenario. Watkins allowed his cast of mostly non-actors and unknowns to improvise during the tribunal scenes, which results in more naturalistic confrontations, with some members lucidly articulating their points while others engage in expletive-filled shouting matches. Such volatile verbal battles, juxtaposed with the grueling scenes of the exhausted, water-deprived runners; the escalating tensions among both the hunted and hunters; and the seemingly inevitable sporadic violence and death, make *Punishment Park* a powerful polemic on the misuse of authority.

According to Watkins, he could not secure any major studio distribution because the usual Hollywood players feared "retribution from the Federal authorities." Consequently, *Punishment Park* received only spotty independent release (though it enjoyed a number of college campus showings) and no exposure on American television. Critics labeled it "paranoid" and "masochistic." Amusingly, when showed on Danish television, the Danish press reacted angrily against the U.S. Government, thinking the film was a *real* documentary, and had to issue retractions once they learned it was a work of fiction (or a "metaphor," as Watkins labeled it).

In his introduction to the picture's 2004 DVD release, Watkins asked, "With all [that is] happening in the world today, can the film *Punishment Park* remain dismissed as a so-called paranoid fantasy?" It's a very good question indeed.

Pure Race (1995; Cornerstone Films of America) Director/Producer/Cinematographer: Rocco DeVilliers; Screenplay: Fred Hunting, Rocco DeVilliers. Cast: Fred Hunting, Gregg Haynes, Marvin Payne, Katherine Willis, Derek White, J. Todd Adams, Dan Urness.

Two University of Washington students, white nerd Tony and black athlete Carl, share a ride back to their home state of Colorado for the summer break. These two suburban *Defiant Ones* instantly bond, with Tony being totally won over and shown the error of his mildly-prejudiced ways by Carl's friendly charm and super-nice demeanor. When their car breaks down on a lonely stretch of road in Idaho, they seek help at a nearby farmhouse and stumble upon an Aryan Nation meeting (complete with a recently-lynched body hanging in the barn). The Supremacists decide to set the duo free in the woods, give them a half-hour head start, and hunt them down like animals. "This is not a game," says their leader.

"We will hunt you, and we will kill you." These "hunters" are not hunting for sport (though some appear to truly relish the idea), but to exterminate the black Carl and his traitor-to-his-race friend in an effort to promote "pure race." And they do so in a method that will train their "soldiers" for the race war they anticipate will come.

There ensues one of the most frenetic, fast-paced, emotionally-charged Most Dangerous Game chase sequences in cinema, as Tony and Carl find their inner strength and prevail over the five automatic weapons–carrying bigots on horseback. The brutal and realistic fight scenes, the emotional turmoil of the protagonists, and the harrowing adrenaline rush of riding a river's rapids *without* a raft highlight the film's final third. And as all the best "hunt" scenarios do, *Pure Race* inspires the viewer to ask, "What would *I* do in this situation," effectively involving the audience in the characters' perilous plight.

The video for *Pure Race* opens with this written coda: "The film you are about to see is an extraordinary achievement. Twenty-one year old director Rocco DeVilliers brought *Pure Race* to the screen with no crew, performing most of the film's dangerous stunts himself." This "extraordinary achievement" (it truly is) by South Africa–born one-man-band DeVilliers (who not only produced, directed, co-wrote, shot, and edited this nearly two-hour feature, but acted onscreen [as Tony's cereal-spilling roommate], served as the makeup artist, and performed most of the impressive stunts himself) completely belies its meager $15,000 shooting budget. Looking for all the world like a professional action movie, *Pure Race* is only let down by the sometimes amateurish acting (it was populated by the filmmaker's friends), and the somewhat simplistic characters and occasional sledgehammer-styled "message" moment.

Though marred by its treacly getting-to-know-you opening, as well as a drawn-out denouement which is about as subtle as a burning cross (hammering home the point that you can take down a gaggle of over-the-top racists but still fall prey to the little bigotries of "normal" society), *Pure Race* is pure gold in the action department, and a fantastic testament to what one can accomplish through sheer dedication, determination, and talent.

Run for the Sun (1956; MGM/United Artists) Director: Roy Boulting; Producer: Harry Tatelman; Screenplay: Dudley Nichols, Ray Boulting (story: Richard Connell); Cinematographer: Joseph La Shelle, A.S.C. Cast: Richard Widmark, Trevor Howard, Jane Greer, Peter Van Eyck, Juan Garcia, Jose Antonio Carbajal, Jose Chavez Trowe.

Though "From a Story by Richard Connell" (as the screen credits claim), and often cited by film historians as another "Most Dangerous Game" adaptation, this glossy but overlong action/romance has disappointingly little to do with Connell's classic story. Rather than a madman hunting humans for sport, *Run for the Sun* features a very sane British turncoat and ex–Nazi sympathizer hiding out with his cronies in the Mexican jungle who must track and kill the two protagonists that have stumbled across their secret. Trevor Howard is memorably charming as the cultured British traitor ("I shall be sorry," he says when he decides his two visitors must die; "I've enjoyed having them around — it's been a pleasant change"), but Richard Widmark fails to convince as the Hemingway-styled writer who (along with his duplicitous reporter love-interest) crash-lands his plane near Howard's remote jungle estate. The film spends two-thirds of its running time building up the rocky romance between the reclusive writer and the female reporter (Jane Greer) sent to get his life story, and only kicks into "Dangerous" gear when the duo go on their run for the sun (or at least run through the jungle), which offers the occasional moment of excitement (and even a "death trap" set by Widmark — the picture's one direct borrowing from Connell).

The Savages (1974; ABC-TV) Director: Lee H. Katzin; Producers: Lee Goldberg, Aaron Spelling; Screenplay: William Wood (based on a novel by Robb White); Cinematographer: Tim Southcott. Cast: Andy Griffith, Sam Bottoms, Noah Beery, Jr., James Best, Randy Boone, Jim Antonio.

In this made-for-TV movie, Andy Griffith plays a big-game hunter (complete with safari hat and outfit) after big-horned sheep in the desert who accidentally shoots and kills an old prospector and then must hunt his own conscience-stricken guide (Sam Bottoms) when the young man refuses to keep silent about the accident. Griffith isn't hunting for sport, and he doesn't really intend to kill the boy himself; he's relying on the desert to do his dirty work for him. Still, he stalks the boy (after relieving him of his shoes, shirt and supplies), and fires periodic warning shots when the young man gets too close to anything that might aid him in his desperate trek (such as water).

Both Griffith and Bottoms are quite good in their respective roles, and veteran television and film director Lee H. Katzin (*Whatever Happened to Aunt Alice?*, 1969) makes the most of the searing desert and dusty small-town locations. The story takes a surprising turn when both men make it back alive, and it becomes a your-word-against-mine scenario in which the honest young man becomes almost hysterical when the rich, respected and powerful older man (here Griffith turns on his patented southern charm) twists the story to make it seem that *he* is the injured party.

The Savages was Griffith's follow-up to the same year's *Pray for the Wildcats*, the TV movie that first portrayed Griffith as the bad guy. For *Gunsmoke* and *The Killer Shrews* (1959) fans, the friendly but doubting local sheriff in *The Savages* is played by James Best.

Scream of the Wolf (1974; ABC-TV) Airdate: January 16, 1974; Director/Producer: Dan Curtis; Screenplay: Richard Matheson (story: David Case); Cinematographer: Paul Lohmann. Cast: Peter Graves, Clint Walker, Jo Ann Pflug, Philip Carey, Don Megowan.

This *ABC Movie of the Week* entry produced and directed by TV horror specialist Dan Curtis (*Dark Shadows, The Night Stalker, Trilogy of Terror*) focuses on a Malibu, California, community terrorized by a rash of brutal killings in which the victims are torn apart by a wolf-like creature. Big-game hunter-turned-adventure novelist John Weatherby (Peter Graves), called in to consult by his friend the sheriff, remains puzzled. "The tracks go from four feet to two feet to nothing, period!" Soon the press begins printing headlines like "'WEREWOLF' KILLER STILL AT LARGE," and Weatherby seeks out his reclusive friend and former hunting partner Byron (Clint Walker) for help in stalking the beast. But Byron (who, incidentally, had earlier been bitten by a wolf himself) isn't interested. "In a way, these killings may be of benefit to everybody," Byron opines, believing that the anger and fear in the community will make its all-too-civilized citizens "feel alive—perhaps for the first time in years." It turns out the disturbed Byron keeps a wolf in his basement that he has trained "to kill another kind of prey," after which he places altered footprints at the scene to suggest a werewolf attack. Why? "To give these rustic clods some reason for existence. To fill their empty minds with so much terror that even *they* come alive. And to bring my old friend back to me again." Byron then gives Weatherby a choice: re-join him in his hunting adventures or be hunted himself by Byron and his vicious beast. With Weatherby given a 5-minute head start, the hunt is on.

Western film and television star Clint Walker (*Cheyenne*) brings a chilling arrogance and air of superiority (not to mention a menacing physical presence, with his hulking 6-foot-6-inch frame) to the disturbed Byron. His icy smile and calm, condescending manner as he talks of hunting reveals the human animal beneath the turtle-neck sweater and sports coat. "I give life as well as take it," he reasons. "The animals I kill are never more alive than in that instant before my bullet strikes them. And I'm never more alive than in that instant when they could kill *me* just as easily." He's the kind of hunter who, while tracking a man-killing wolf in Canada, sits and waits for the beast with only a single bullet in his gun to even the odds.

Curtis handles the "werewolf" attacks well, generating tension with p.o.v. camerawork for the stalk through mist-shrouded woodlands and shadowy home invasions. We never see the beast—the camera abruptly rushes in, glass shatters, the victim screams, and the screen fades to black. Foggy nights, key lighting, and low angles generate tension. Unfortunately, theses sequences come few and far between, with the majority of the telefilm's running time taken up with Weatherby puzzling over the mystery, the sheriff searching for clues, and repeated visits to Byron to try to talk him into helping. But with the periodic attacks, the werewolf mystery angle (Byron's quietly suspicious manservant serves as a likely suspect), Walker's menacingly creepy portrayal, and the various twists and turns (including the exciting—if brief—concluding hunt), *Scream of the Wolf* holds one's interest better than most made-for-TV movies from the 1970s.

Seven Women for Satan (1974; France) Original Language Titles: *Les Week-ends maléfiques du Comte Zaroff; Sept femmes pour un sadique.* Director/screenplay: Michel Lemoine. Producer: Yves Witner; Cinematographer: Philippe Theaudiere. Cast: Howard Vernon, Michel Lemoine, Martine Azencot, Joelle Coeur, Sophie Grynholc, Robert Icart, Stephane Lorry, Patricia Mionet, Emmanuel Pluton, Nathalie Zeiger.

A nude woman flees through the countryside, pursued by a huge black dog and a man on a horse. Cornering her on a cliff-top, the rider lashes out with his whip, causing her to fall to her death. He then rapturously closes his eyes as the camera zooms in on his satisfied countenance—only to pull back again to reveal the same man sitting behind an office desk, daydreaming. "Sorry, I was lost in my thoughts," he tells his secretary. So begins the misnamed French obscurity *Seven Women for Satan*, a unique slice of sexploitation/Eurohorror with a Most Dangerous Game bent.

Despite its English title, there's nothing "Satanic" about the film (its alternate French moniker, *Sept femmes pour un sadique*—"Seven Women for a Sadist"—is far more accurate a description), as the story centers on Boris Zaroff (Michel Lemoine), son of Connell's famous hunter-of-men. Outwardly a mild-mannered Paris businessman, he fantasizes about torturing and killing women, and ends up putting said fantasies into practice at his weekend chateau, encouraged and aided by his family servant, Karl (Jess Franco regular Howard Vernon). Years ago Karl made a deathbed promise to his father, faithful servant of the original Count Zaroff. "My spirit cannot rest," Karl's dying dad intones, "until you rekindle in his descendent the taste for torture." And rekindle he does, though Karl's efforts are complicated by the beautiful ghost of a woman somehow connected to the original Zaroff—or is it all in Boris' tortured mind?

Seven Women for Satan is only superficially a Most Dangerous Game derivation, since the only "hunt" remains the one in Boris' fantasy that opens the film. This Zaroff doesn't seek the challenge of the hunt but rather the thrill of the kill (and torture). He's far more of a sadist than a hunter (he doesn't even carry a weapon). And his victims are not the most "dangerous" game but the *sexiest*—beautiful naked women.

"I love horror and fantasy films," stated writer-director-star Michel Lemoine. With

Seven Women for Satan, it shows, as Lemoine takes the time and effort to invest this slightly-plotted Eurotrash with unusual, even artistic touches to generate an offbeat and otherworldly ambiance. Odd camera angles, well-framed and carefully composed shots, excellent use of the old-world chateau setting and surrounding mist-laden woodlands, inventive use of mirrors and reflections, and clever transitions mark this Eurohorror as a cut above many of its contemporaries. For instance, in one scene the light fades from Karl's face, transforming him into a shadow figure as the film transitions into his father's deathbed flashback; then, as the sequence ends, the light comes up again so that Karl's visage materializes out of the darkness and we're once more in the present day. In another sequence, as Zaroff interviews a new secretary/victim at his office, his arm rests on a glass tabletop in the foreground. The camera peers down over his shoulder so that it looks like his hand rests on the woman's shapely legs as she sits in the chair opposite. When his restless fingers move ever so slightly, it creates the illusion that he's stroking her calves—a visual metaphor if ever there was one. Though *Seven Woman* brings to mind the works of prolific Spanish horror/sexploitation specialist Jess Franco (for whom Lemoine worked as an actor on several occasions) via its sexploitative subject matter (Franco even made his own sexualized Most Dangerous Game variation this same year with his *The Perverse Countess*) and almost surreal sensibilities, *Seven Women* remains superior to most of Franco's output, as Lemoine invests far more directorial care than Franco generally did.

As an actor, Lemoine's odd, almond-shaped eyes, long face, and angular frame makes him both an intriguing and menacing presence. His glassy-eyed, penetrating stare completes the picture of a man with sinister secrets. Yet he never completely loses an air of vulnerability, which the story bears out by making him something of an anti-hero as well as villain, exploited by the nefarious Karl (with several of the deaths seemingly more Karl's doing that Zaroff's) and tormented by visions of—and longing for—the ghostly Anne (Jean Rollin regular Joelle Coeur). An early sequence highlights Lemoine's skill at portraying a man confused and conflicted, with violence bubbling just beneath the surface. Taking a walk in the woods, Boris begins to kiss a beautiful hitchhiker he's picked up, and she responds in kind. Slowly he wraps his hands about her neck and begins to strangler her. When she struggles, he releases her and abruptly apologizes, "I wanted to feel your life run through my fingers." Apparently forgiven, he continues his seduction but suddenly bites her breast, then flips her over and smashes her face into the earth! When he lets her up and she (understandably) demands to leave, he becomes impatient and viciously kicks her in the thigh!! She flees, and he chases after her in his car, all the while shouting apologies and sincerely promising he'd never hurt her—just before he inadvertently runs her over. Looking at her crumpled body, he sadly observes, "You're only a rag doll. And I thought you were a woman." Strange, disturbing and sad, this sequence inspires both fear of and pity for the torturing—and tortured—Zaroff.

Not everything in the film works, however, including the rather jarring ending (complete with a laughably amateurish skeleton). And, this being a sexploitation as well as horror picture, the frequent softcore interludes and bump-and-grind sequences sometimes slow the pace. But even these scenes of nude writing and dancing frequently feature something strange enough to play into the macabre mood (such as a statue seemingly come to life to fondle an ecstatic beauty, or a mirror suddenly reflecting back the image of a previous victim rather than the present subject).

Seven Women for Satan was dealt a death blow by the French censors, who slapped it with an X rating, effectively banning it from regular cinemas in its home country. Michel

Lemoine had a great deal of his own money tied up in the production, as he could only find a producer that would put up half the cash ("Sadly, when I started to direct, it was hard to make such a film here [in France]"). Nearly ruined financially, Lemoine turned to making sex comedies and then hardcore films (using various pseudonyms). Barely released during the 1970s (and given minimal distribution in English dubbed form in the U.K. only), *Seven Women for Satan* had to wait nearly 40 years to make it to America, when Mondo Macabro resurrected it on DVD in 2003.

With quotes from: "Formidable! The Michel Lemoine Story," *Seven Women for Satan* dvd, Mondo Macabro, 2003.

Superbeast (1972; United Artists/MGM; U.S./Philippines) Director/Producer/Screenplay: George Schenck. Cinematographer: Nonong Rasca. Cast: Antoinette Bower, Craig Littler, Harry Lauter, Vic Diaz, Jose Romulo, John Garwood.

This U.S.-Filipino co-production combines *The Island of Dr. Moreau* with *Dr. Jekyll and Mr. Hyde* via Connell's "The Most Dangerous Game" by way of Manila. With so many tried-and-tested literary concepts, not to mention the uber-photogenic setting of the Filipino jungle, one would think that such a melding couldn't possibly go wrong. However, one would not have counted upon the stolid script and poor pacing of first-time triple-threat director/producer/screenwriter George Schenck. Schenck came from a background in television writing — and quickly returned to same after this one misstep into cinematic territory.

The story has female pathologist Alix Pardee (Antoinette Bower) journeying to a remote jungle in the Philippines to investigate the mysterious case of a crazed mutant killer that ended up on her autopsy table. After her canoe goes over a waterfall, she washes up at the mid-river island compound of young American researcher Dr. Bill Fleming (Craig Littler), who's working on a drug formula that will "rehabilitate even the most hardened criminal." After much wandering to and fro (and about an hour of the film's running time), Alix finally learns that the doc has been experimenting on human subjects — "convicts remanded to my custody," admits Fleming. And worse, that the formula works for only about 10 days, "then they go through a physical and sociological metamorphosis. They revert to the primitive [and take] an evolutionary step backwards." Worse still, Fleming's financier, rich businessman and big-game enthusiast Stewart Victor (Harry Lauter), has a deal with the doc to "dispose" of these primitive-mutant failures by hunting them for sport. It all leads to one final hunt, with the now-transformed Fleming (tricked by Alix into imbibing his own formula) as the prey.

Schenck handicaps this *Superbeast* from the get-go by beginning his opus in Manila, then quickly switching to Guam, then Venezuela and then back to Manila — all within the first 10 minutes and before the viewer has any idea of who is who or what is what. Not only does Schenck start his story in scattered fashion, he quashes viewer interest at the outset via too many filler scenes of (unknown) characters boarding airplanes, exiting airplanes, getting in cars, getting out of cars, etc. Once things finally become a little less murky, Schenck offers very little characterization but lots of handheld camerawork, courtesy of low-budget cinematographer Nanong Rasca (*Night of the Cobra Woman*, *The Thirsty Dead*). Unfortunately, rather than generating any cinema verite–like immediacy, the (un)steadycam photography (perhaps employed more for expediency than artistic reasons) simply becomes annoying, since far too little happens apart from people taking boat rides, taking car rides, walking down the street, paddling a canoe, etc. Finally, half an hour into the movie, some-

Playing big-game hunter Stewart Victor, Harry Lauter (left) threatens Filipino actor Vic Diaz (the Philippines' answer to Peter Lorre) in *Superbeast*.

thing happens when the protagonist's canoe goes over a waterfall — only to inspire guffaws at the obvious dummies involved (figuratively for the characters; literally for the "effects").

To his credit, Schenck managed to secure the services of makeup man John Chambers, renowned for his groundbreaking work on *Planet of the Apes* (1968), to create the Neanderthal visages for *Superbeast*'s mutant humanoids. While these countenances look effectively "primitive," there's nothing particularly frightening or arresting about them — particularly in the perfunctory way Schenck and company light and film them.

Like their producer-director, the film's three leads also came from (and returned to) television. As our heroine, horsefaced Antoinette Bower never changes her blank expression — even when told outright that she's to be killed. She does frequently exclaim "Wow" (but, of course, tonelessly). Craig Littler does somewhat better as the renegade doc, adding some low-rent charm to his character's "hip" demeanor (this brilliant scientist tends to say "dig" and "man" a lot). And Harry Lauter, as the obsessed hunter, at least brings some convincing brutishness to his one-note character and effectively offers a few lines of pertinent dialogue (e.g.: "I hunt because I want to pit my knowledge, my skill and endurance against a wild animal in their own environment. But actually it's the thrill of the stalk.") The best of the thespian bunch is the always-welcome (and seemingly ubiquitous) Vic Diaz, the Philippines' answer to Peter Lorre. Diaz plays ... er, "Diaz," the corrupt local lawman whose sweaty, smarmy, sinister presence adds a welcome layer of verisimilitude to the otherwise ridiculous artificiality of the cast. Unfortunately, Diaz only appears in a few scenes at the movie's beginning and end.

Perhaps reflecting his TV sensibilities, Schenck offers no gore or nudity, and not even a single swear word — which is curious for an exploitation flick from the 1970s aimed squarely at the drive-ins. The only thing to warrant the film's "R" rating is the incorporation of some real-life autopsy footage. While these few shots add a seriously queasy factor (particularly when a cadaver's belly is slit open to display the linked-sausage innards), it does nothing to enhance the story or characters — or excite or engage the viewer (apart from potential nausea).

Though *Superbeast* employs a novel, sci-fi-tinged variation on the Dangerous Game concept, it also relegates it to mere subplot status. The "hunt" isn't showcased until the film's final 10 minutes, and then lasts only half that time (with little suspense raised by its banal staging) before its (anti) climactic confrontation and perfunctory dispatching of the villain. Adding dull insult to boring injury, there follows a drawn-out, unconvincingly "poignant" coda to the whole desultory enterprise.

Further distancing the film from Connell's concept is the fact that this hunter-of-men doesn't even see his prey *as* men, labeling them "wild animals, dangerous creatures, worthless forms of life." Of course, this does lead to a rather amusing dialogue exchange between Alix and Victor:

> Alix: You're killing. You are perverted.
> Victor: Oh, "Bambi, Bambi, Bambi!" You're livin' in a dream world. It's a fantasy. You think every animal is a goddamned "Bambi."

In the end, there's nothing super about this *Superbeast*.

Tag: The Assassination Game (1982; New World Pictures) Alternate Title: *Everybody Gets It in the End*. Director/Screenplay: Nick Castle; Producers: Peter Rosten, Daniel Rosenthal; Cinematographer: Willy Kurant. Cast: Robert Carradine, Linda Hamilton, Kristine DeBell, Perry Lang, John Mengatti, Michael Winslow, Frazer Smith, Bruce Abbott.

What's one part college-set romantic comedy, one part film noir pastiche, one part chase thriller, and one part Most Dangerous Game? Why, it's *TAG: The Assassination Game*. With its alternate title being *Everybody Gets It in the End* (and catchphrases like "The Movie That Sticks to Your Face" and "This time the butler didn't do it," along with the image of a rubber dart stuck to a shapely female posterior, in its advertising), there's little doubt about its comedic leanings. Which makes it all the more startling when *T.A.G.* goes off in a different direction half-way through the film.

After a tense and shadowy pre-credit stalking sequence that ends in a comical payoff (a suction cup dart to the forehead of the stalkee), *T.A.G.* segues into an amusing James Bond–style credits sequence. The story, set on a college campus, revolves around "the game that's sweeping the nation" — T.A.G.: The Assassination Game, which has "kids pretending to be killers, hunting each other like Chicago hitmen [armed with rubber dart guns]," as cigar-chomping college newspaperman Alex Marsh (Robert Carradine) puts it. When beautiful T.A.G. player Susan Swayze (Linda Hamilton) steps into Alex's life by stepping into his dorm room to avoid another T.A.G. player, Alex decides to do a feature on the game for the college paper by shadowing Susan (his real motivation being to simply get close to the captivating beauty, whom the wannabe-hard-boiled Alex likens to Ida Lupino). When a geeky player gets lucky and accidentally shoots five-time T.A.G. champion Gersh (Bruce Abbott) during the course of the game, Gersh snaps and replaces his plastic dart gun with a *real* Beretta pistol, taking out his targets and hiding their bodies in his dorm room. Alex finally puts it all together just as Susan and Gersh, the two finalists, are about to go head to head. But can he stop the crazed Gersh in time? (Note: I've included *T.A.G.* as an *Almost*

Dangerous Game rather than placing it in the Deadly Game Show chapter because it's a first-person, participant-oriented event that lacks the third-party observer component found in the Game Show subset.)

When Alex asks Susan why she signed up for T.A.G., she answers, "It's something to do. Everybody likes to play games.... It's safe, it's a game." It's also a reasonable answer, one that could be applied to everything from playing Dungeons and Dragons and violent video games to watching scary movies. So what motivates Gersh to turn this harmless bit of fun into a campus-set Most Dangerous Game? "Applause," he tells a cornered Susan. "I want to win the game, you silly." Gersh simply loves the adulation that comes with winning. Of course, there's little logic to this (since there's no way he can retain his title once the truth inevitably comes out), which disappointingly turns this BMOC Zaroff into a mere crazy rather than a clever hunter-of-men. But at least he has a trophy room of sorts, which Susan stumbles upon at one point, revealing the partially-wrapped dead bodies of his victims.

T.A.G. starts out with a lighthearted tone, as a romantic comedy with film noir overtones (but more winking homage than serious noir). It then shifts into serial killer territory when Gersch snaps and begins shooting for real. Finally, it goes full-on dark thriller after Susan discovers the bodies in Gersh's room (the PG film's one moment of gruesomeness) before finally coming back around with a humorous (though still blackly-laced) quip at the final scene, with the last shot again referencing noir. It makes for clever shifts and an intriguing rhythm that keeps the viewer slightly off-balance and generates both unease and even shock (enhancing the film's solitary gore scene — the discovery of the bodies — without bloodying it all up too much). Unfortunately, not everything works, including some of the awkward homages and lightweight situations and gags (particularly a sequence involving a black T.A.G. player and his bodyguards — one of whom is future Oscar-winner Forest Whitaker in a bit part! — who speaks in unintelligible noises and bleeps like some ridiculous R2D2-from-the-hood).

Filmed on the UCLA campus (though the college is never named in the movie), *T.A.G.* is obviously low budget ($1.5 million, according to scripter/director Nick Castle), but Castle and company, along with his cadre of up-and-coming actors, show an assured proficiency that translated into busy careers for many of them. Some suspenseful set-pieces intermix with a number of knowing dialogue exchanges that reference everything from classic noir (Hamilton does a decent interpretation of "You know how to whistle, don't you?") to *Serpico* (a long-haired, Army-jacketed T.A.G. player carries around a white rat in his pocket). One office even has a Bogart poster on the wall.

But what really brings this rubber-tipped *Game* to life is the soon-to-be-famous cast. Robert Carradine brings his patented geekish charm (later perfected in the *Revenge of the Nerds* series) to his cigar-smoking, love-smitten, Dashell Hammet-esque character. Linda Hamilton oozes a playful sultriness and hard-bitten assurance that epitomizes the noir heroines of old. And Bruce Abbott offers subtle, disturbing mannerisms and a sly stealthiness that even Anthony Perkins would have been proud of.

Abbott, best known for his lead role in *Re-Animator* (1985), made his film debut here as the unhinged Gersh. And, unlike with the Gersh/Susan dynamic in the film, Abbott really did "get" Linda Hamilton in the end, as the two actors married on December 19, 1982 (they divorced in 1989).

Of course, the biggest star-to-be in *T.A.G.* is Linda Hamilton, just two years from her breakout role of Sarah Connor in *The Terminator* (1984). Co-star Robert Carradine also enjoyed a hit in 1984 with *Revenge of the Nerds*. Robert, part of the Carradine acting clan begun by his father John Carradine, never exactly made it big but carved a steady career in TV and low-to-medium budget films.

Also of interest in the cast is Christine DeBell as Susan's breezy and clever T.A.G.-playing friend. DeBell got her start as a *Playboy* model and entered the movies by playing the title role in the hardcore porn flick *Alice in Wonderland: An X-Rated Musical Fantasy* (1976). However, she soon graduated to mainstream TV (on shows like *B.J. and the Bear*, *Eight Is Enough*, and *CHiPs*) and films, such as *Meatballs* (1979) and *Lifepod* (1981).

First-time director Nick Castle went on to make a career of family-friendly fare with such projects as *The Last Starfighter* (1984), *The Boy Who Could Fly* (1986), and *Dennis the Menace* (1993). The Tom Atkins character in John Carpenter's *The Fog* (1980) was named after Nick Castle. Castle had played Michael Myers/"the Shape" in Carpenter's *Halloween* (1978), as well as working the camera and playing the alien in *Dark Star* (1974), Carpenter's feature debut. Castle also co-wrote *Escape from New York* (1981) with Carpenter. Castle learned much from John Carpenter, and it shows in his atmospheric staging, particularly during *T.A.G.*'s climactic nighttime sequence. "John has a real economy in his directing style," commented Castle, "because he comes from low-budget pictures where you just can't overshoot because you don't have the film. And he likes to work in the dark. The night, I've found from working on his films, is good for hiding potentially bad things. Keep it dark, and if you have lights in the background to bring dimension to the shot, it can look beautiful — and you don't have to spend millions of dollars."

With its complete lack of nudity (but still offering several decidedly sexy scenes) and its violence mostly implied, *T.A.G.* shows that exploitation need not always apply. Story, character, craft and acting can indeed carry a film. Though ultimately its story and outcome remain somewhat predictable, *T.A.G.: The Assassination Game* stands as an amusing and stylish genre blending with an Almost Most Dangerous Game bent.

With quotes from: "Nick Castle: 'How Do You Get Around Star Wars?'" by Brian Lowry, *Starlog* 87 (October 1984).

Transylmania (2009; Full Circle Releasing) Directors: David Hillenbrand, Scott Hillenbrand; Producers: Sanford Hampton, Jenna Johnson, Kim Swartz, Radu Badica; Screenplay: Patrick Casey, Worm Miller; Cinematographer: Viorel Sergovici. Cast: Oren Skoog, Worm Miller, Patrick Casey, Jennifer Lyons, Tony Denman.

In this broad, hit-and-miss horror spoof, a group of American college students spend a semester at a university in Romania (housed in an impressive and forbidding castle) where they run afoul of vampires *and* the mad scientist/dwarf college dean. Taking potshots at everything from *Frankenstein* and *The Hunchback of Notre Dame* to *The Brain That Wouldn't Die* and *Van Helsing*, with some *Animal House* thrown in for good measure, most of the gags (running or otherwise) are too repetitious and puerile to leave an impression, and the stereotypical characters (hot girl, stoners, nerd, etc.) add nothing to the dull mix. Some of the more successful comedy bits feature a student posing as a vampire hunter to impress Romanian chicks, a pair of potheads paying for drinks and lap dances by using "American blue jeans" as currency, and an inspired (but all-too-brief) riff on "The Most Dangerous Game." Two students pay some locals to take them on an illegal hunt, thinking they'll be shooting some exotic game. "I hope it's a panda," enthuses one, "they're so *cute*!" But when the locals open the wooden crate to release their prey, out staggers a fellow student with bullseyes pasted on his forehead, chest and crotch! When one of the would-be hunters gasps, "That's a person," the heavily-accented local answers, "Most dangerous game!"

16. Almost Dangerous Games

This 2009 horror spoof, poking fun at everything from *Frankenstein* to *The Brain That Wouldn't Die*, even takes an amusing potshot at "The Most Dangerous Game."

The Twilight People (1972; Dimension Pictures, Inc.; U.S./Philippines) Director: Eddie Romero; Producers: John Ashley, Eddie Romero; Screenplay: Jerome Small, Eddie Romero; Cinematographer: Fredy Conde. Cast: John Ashley, Pat Woodell, Jan Merlin, Charles McCaulay, Pam Grier, Eddie Garcia.

Made for $150,000 in the Philippines, this John Ashley–starrer continues the tradition of wackiness begun by actor/producer Ashley's previous Eddie Romero–directed Filipino horrors (*Mad Doctor of Blood Island*, 1968, *Brides of Blood*, 1968, *Beast of the Yellow Night*, 1971, *Beast of Blood*, 1971). For fans of this odd little cinematic subset, *The Twilight People* offers up nearly all the requisite ingredients: jungle footage, stilted acting, bizarre premise, outré violence, a smattering of gore, faded American "stars," unknown American starlets, a fistful of Filipino extras, and the always reliable Eddie Garcia. The only thing missing is the expected gratuitous nudity. But what this cheapjack *Island of Dr. Moreau*–wannabe lacks in exposed flesh, it more than makes up for in bizarre characters and situations. To wit: A mad doctor (Charles McCaulay) who believes "the human race cannot survive unless it remakes itself"; a "scholar, soldier of fortune [and] hunter" hero (the impossibly blank-faced Ashley), who retorts, "I'm a little skeptical about building master races — maybe it's the unsavory precedents"; the doctor's chief henchman, an Aryan-styled killer named Steinman (Jan Merlin), who appears to have something of a crush on the hero; the doctor's medical-minded daughter Mary (Pat Woodell, who, along with Ashley, appeared in a full-fledged Most Dangerous Game variation, *Woman Hunt*, this same year), who wears her false eyelashes, heavy eye shadow and bright red lipstick not only in the operating theater but to bed as well; and the cheesy-looking antelope-man (complete with horns), ape-man ("the guy we hired to play the Ape Man, he had that Neanderthal look to begin with," laughed producer/actor Ashley), wolf-woman (who communicates by *barking*), bat-man (who, by film's end, finally masters the art of flight), and vicious panther-woman (a pre-blaxploitation stardom Pam Grier in fangs, whose only lines consist of dubbed-in puma growls).

The story has healthy specimen Matt Farrell (Ashley) kidnapped while scuba diving and brought to Dr. Gordon's private island as a potential subject in his experiments to transform people into animals. Scripters Jerome Small and Eddie Romero borrow a page from Connell's "Most Dangerous Game" book by having Steinman fixate on wanting to hunt Farrell ("I'm a hunter myself," he tells his skeptical prisoner). Steinman finally gets his wish when Mary, prompted by her conscience (and newfound love for Farrell), helps Matt and the various beast-people escape into the jungle, where Steinman and his men hunt them down like ... well, animals.

Though obviously constrained by its budget, *Twilight People* (like all its Philippine-shot brethren) made the most of what little it had. For instance, Jan Merlin reported:

> We went to the studio they had, which was a very small, barn-like structure in downtown Manila. They were preparing a set, the interior of the doctor's house. It was to be an entry hall, and they were gluing newspapers to the wooden floor throughout. At one end, where they had already glued the newspapers down and it had dried, men painted what looked like a marble floor on the papers. They did the same thing with the walls — if they didn't have the wood to create a fancy-looking wall, they'd put up newspapers and they'd *paint* a fancy wall on it. It was remarkable, they way they did so well with so little.

Veteran director Eddie Romero (a prolific and revered filmmaker in the Philippines) knew he wasn't making high art with these exploitation flicks. As he said, "These are not really the kind of films I am longing to make. They were the films I had to make considering what the market had to offer, what the market [re: America] wanted."

"I just remember it was a lot of fun to do," recalled Ashley about the film, "and there weren't a lot of problems on it. And we did it so quickly!" Given the right frame of mind, *The Twilight People*, with its beautiful jungle locations, cut-rate acting, cheesy lab sets (complete with exposed brains under glass domes for no discernible reason), goofy animal-people (the sight of the bat-man gliding through the air, flapping his bat wings, before slashing at the throats of his pursuers is worth the price of admission alone), can be a fairly fun 84 minutes for the forgiving viewer as well.

With quotes from: "Jan Merlin: The Thrill of the Hunt," by Tom Weaver, *Chiller Theater* 20 (2004); *Machete Maidens Unleashed!*, directed by Mark Hartley; *Interviews with B Science Fiction and Horror Movie Makers*, by Tom Weaver.

Walk The Dark Street (1956; Associated Artists; b&w) Director/Producer/Screenplay: Wyott Ordung; Cinematographer: Brydon Baker. Cast: Chuck Connors, Don Ross, Regina Gleason, Vonne Godfrey, Eddie Kafafian.

Given the fact that the most prominent credits of actor-turned-writer-turned-director Wyott Ordung include writing *Robot Monster* (1953) and directing *Monster from the Ocean Floor* (1954), it's amazing that his *Walk the Dark Street* turned out to be such a novel (if minor) "Most Dangerous Game" permutation.

Taking Connell's concept as a jumping off point, *Walk the Dark Street* has Korean War veteran Dan Lawton look up Frank Garrick, the brother of a former Army buddy. Secretly — and misguidedly — seeking revenge for his beloved brother's death in Korea, Frank, an impassioned hunter, makes a proposition to Dan: the two will hunt each other through the city streets — with "camera rifles." The first to get the other in his sights and "shoot" a picture wins the wager. Dan, in need of money, agrees. But Frank replaces the "film bullet" in *his* rifle with a live round...

Both Chuck Connors and Don Ross (who receives a special "introducing" credit for this, his debut film) create convincing, believable characters in this admittedly odd situation. Connors' increasing tension and agitation as time slips away while he hunts for his prey speaks volumes about his character's determination and unhinged mind-frame. Ross' likable and calm demeanor, and initial incredulity when finally faced with the truth, draws the viewer into the situation to step right alongside Dan as he plays this Dangerous Game. And both actors are impressively energetic during their climactic foot race, as they climb and jump fences, careen across rooftops and hurtle down alleyways in an exciting and athletic display.

Don Ross spent the next quarter-century toiling in television in small roles and bit parts without, alas, landing that big break that elevated Chuck Connors to household-name status. For Connors, a former minor (and, briefly, major) league baseball player, that was his starring role as TV's *The Rifleman* (1958–1963), leading to a solid career in both film and television, including highlights like *Old Yeller* (1957), *The Big Country* (1958), and *Soylent Green* (1973), right up until his death in 1991.

By shooting on the streets of Los Angeles, Ordung not only saved on studio rental fees but also added a gritty authenticity to the story, which helps ground the events in a semblance of reality. Of course, this becomes a double-edged sword (or perhaps double-barreled firearm?), as two men with high-powered rifles slung across their shoulders walking about the busy L.A. streets with nary a glance from the locals does give one pause. Admittedly, the weapons are in (gun-shaped) cases, and Connors *is* questioned at one point by a cop; but the idea (and sight) of these two "hunters" in the big city is incongruous at best and incredulous at worst.

Also, Ordung's script offers far too many coincidences and near-misses for complete plausibility, with some of the he-just-stepped-around-the-corner moments becoming almost comical (not to mention a laugh-out-loud sequence in which the two not only just miss

Big game hunter Frank Garrick (Chuck Connors, left) reveals his "camera gun" to Dan Lawton (Don Ross) before inducing him to *Walk the Dark Street* in an (almost) Dangerous Game.

each other but unwittingly exchange rifles!). Still, Ordung generates genuine suspense and empathy for the protagonist's unique plight (with one standout sequence, shot on an abandoned ship, involving Dan unknowingly walking one way on the lower deck while Frank walks towards him on the upper — with the camera viewing both as they pass one another, unseeing). And the fact that for much of the time Dan doesn't even know what's at stake only heightens the tension level.

These days, even with the video/DVD/cable boom, *Walk the Dark Street* has all but disappeared from the cinematic consciousness. More's the pity, as the film stands not only as a relatively taut take on the hunting humans theme, but as an early feather in the cap of one of Hollywood's most dependable character actors, Chuck Connors. Even with its occasional misstep, this *Walk* is definitely worth taking.

Wilderness (2006; First Look International; UK) Director: Michael J. Bassett; Producers: Robert Bernstein, John McDonnell, Douglas Rae; Screenplay: Ryan Hendrick, Dario Poloni; Cinematography: Peter Robertson. Cast: Sean Pertwee, Alex Reid, Toby Kebbell, Stephen Wright, Luke Neal, Ben McKay, Lenora Crichlow, Karly Greene.

"It's not about revenge," reads the film's tagline, "it's about punishment." Well, actually, it *is* about revenge. When a juvenile delinquent kills himself at a Northern Ireland youth detention facility, the warden sends the dead boy's roommates off to an island wilderness on a team-building exercise. They soon find themselves stalked by an unknown killer and his pack of attack dogs. The terrified teens quickly learn that the deadly hunter is the vengeance-seeking, Special Forces–trained father who blames his son's suicide on the torments of his fellow inmates.

Though director Michael Bassett (*Deathwatch*, 2002; *Silent Hill: Revelation 3D*, 2012) takes full advantage of the picturesque setting (putting his cast through their strenuous paces in deep forest, open moorland, and surging beach surf), and executes some truly horrific scenarios (gory dog attacks; fiery cabin siege; forest stalking sequences ending in violent death) with suspenseful aplomb, the script's lack of character focus makes it all a rather empty *Wilderness* exercise. None of the "prey" characters (including the ostensible hero, a self-centered, explosive youth named Callum) are in any way remotely likable, from the stereotypical cynical adult prison officer to the sniveling weasel to the hulking toady to the devious psycho. And the vengeful Zaroff stand-in remains almost unseen until the finale, receiving no dialogue nor characterization apart from one lad noting, "[His son] was scared of him. He loved him, like, but he said he was just crazy." Traps are laid—but these are set by the hunter rather than the hunted. Though the first (involving some strategically placed bear-claw devices taking out a would-be rapist) results in a satisfyingly shocking and gory payoff, the second (a snare trap ending in immolation) seems ridiculously unlikely in its Rube Goldberg complexity. Watching this unlikable little group unravel bit by bit as they're repeatedly chased by the hunter's four trained dogs, shot at with a crossbow, and picked off by a killer who seems nigh on invisible (he employs full-body camouflage to get right next to his victims—sometimes in the most improbable manner) smacks less of the Most Dangerous Game concept and more of slasher movie sensibilities (which is how director Bassett himself describes *Wilderness*—as a "slasher film").

Zombie Doom (1999; Shock-o-Rama Cinema; Germany) Alternate Title: *Violent Shit III: Infantry of Doom*; Director/Screenplay: Andreas Schnaas; Associate Producer: Andrew Teixeira; Cinematographer: Steve Aquilina. Cast: Joe Neumann, Uwe Gruntjes, Winni Holl, Andreas Sroka, Xiu-Yong Lin, Giang Le, Son Le, Dr. Bern, Marc Trinkhaus, Andreas Schnass.

"Audacious," "outrageous," and "over-the-top" are all adjectives that describe this exercise in excess from German backyard "auteur" Andreas Schnaas. Unfortunately, the terms "puerile," "stupid," and "pointless" equally apply to this barely watchable mess of a home movie. When the motor gives out on their sailboat (er ... why not just hoist the sail?), a trio of foul-mouthed "friends" wind up on the island home of "Karl the Butcher" (director Schnaas himself, in silly sheepskin loincloth and facile facial scars) and his skull-faced father, "The Meister," masters of a group of paramilitary soldiers there for no discernible purpose. Also present is mad scientist Dr. Zenius (complete with Hitler mustache), who'll do anything for fresh brains upon which to experiment. When the Meister's cardboard-masked soldiers find the shipwrecked trio, they dispatch one and force the other two interlopers, along with a disobedient guard, to run for their lives, with the soldiers hunting them down ("We're opening up this season's pig-hunt," proclaims Karl, "and these shitfaces are our prey!").

The Dangerous Game angle (with the motivation being more punishment than "sport") is merely a paper-thin framework upon which to hang the many, many, *many* ultra-violent set-pieces. The imaginative outrageousness of the gore effects are matched only by their silly cheapness (which is just as well, since, had they been executed—pun intended—in a realistic or even competent manner, they would be impossible to watch). Among said goofy gruesomeness is: (1) a quadruple guillotine decapitation, complete with Monty Python–esque spurting blood; (2) hooks tossed into a torso, ripping open the ribcage like some meaty trap door; (3) flying chains literally tearing the face off a victim; (4) a woman's teeth broken out with a chisel; and (5) a victim's spine pulled out through his rectum! But wait, there's more nasty wackiness in the form of moldering zombies(!) rising from the earth for no reason (courtesy of Dr. Zenius, one supposes); rogue guards that literally drop from the trees to battle a quartet of ninjas(!!); and an out-of-nowhere throwaway appearance by "the Master of the Flying Guillotine"(!!!). This all sounds far more fun that it turns out to be, however, since the poorly-framed and overlit shot-on-video footage (periodically — and inexplicably — intercut with what looks like grainy 8mm film); the pathetic half-speed action/fight choreography; and the witless, expletive-laden, tinny-sounding dubbing make *Zombie Doom* the *viewer's* doom as well. (Sample dialogue: "The world is full of puke and shit. And now a horde of tin-masked assholes are puking in our faces, full of shit.") Though a film originally titled *Violent Shit III* announces its intentions from the get-go, one wishes that Andreas "hey-let's-put-on-a-gore-show" Schnaas and co. displayed as much talent as misguided enthusiasm.

17

Dangerous Game Shows and Deadly Diversions

Herein is an examination of those films in which people hunt people for the entertainment of *others* (often to the level of national television broadcasts). Begun with the 1965 European production *The Tenth Victim* and carrying through to the 2012 blockbuster *The Hunger Games* (and no doubt beyond), this cinematic subset typically focuses not so much on the motivations and mindset of Connell's classic hunter-of-men (as personified by Zaroff), but on the appeal of hunting humans as third-party entertainment. Note that to qualify for inclusion there must be some form of "hunt" involved (i.e., straight gladiatorial or bloodsport movies don't make the, er, cut).

Battle Royale (2000; Toei Company; Japan) Original Language Title: *Batoru Rowaiaru*. Director: Kinji Fukasaku; Producers: Kenta Fukasaku, Kinji Fukasaku, Kimio Kataoka, Chie Kobayashi, Toshio Nabeshima, Masumi Okada. Screenplay: Kenta Fukasaku (based on the novel by Koushun Takami); Cinematographer: Katsumi Yanagijima. Cast: Tatsuya Fujiwara, Aki Maeda, Taro Yamamoto, Takeshi Kitano, Chiaki Kuriyama, Sosuke Takaoka.

Disturbing, powerful, affecting, thought-provoking, and shocking, *Battle Royale* posits a modern-day Japan where (according to the opening written narration) "at the dawn of the millennium, the nation collapsed. At 15 percent unemployment, 10 million were out of work. 800,000 students boycotted school. The adults lost confidence and, fearing the youth, eventually passed the Millennium Educational Reform Act, aka the BR Act." The result: every year a ninth grade class is chosen by lottery to participate in a "Battle Royale." Isolated on a deserted island, with each given food, water, and a random weapon, these 42 teenage classmates and friends have three days to hunt and kill one another until there's only one left — or they *all* die (metal bands placed around their necks both monitor their activities and ensure their participation, as they can be explosively detonated with the touch of a remote). Symbolic of the adult society's disdain for, and fear of, their youth, the class' bitter former teacher, Kitano (Takeshi Kitano), tells them, "So today's lesson is — you will kill each other off till there's only one left. Nothing's against the rules." Some of the teens embrace their situation and choose to ruthlessly and coldly hunt down their fellows; some try to hide; some pair off or remain in small groups for comfort and protection (a commentary, perhaps, on the cliques and alliances in the dog-eat-dog world of high school); and some opt out altogether from playing the game — by committing suicide.

Though it opens with a scene of almost frenzied media coverage, in which reporters and cameras greet the arrival of a bloodied final survivor of the previous "game" like the coming of a rock star (one TV correspondent noting enthusiastically, "She's smiling!"), *Battle Royale* is a Dangerous Game Show by implication only. Unlike most of its brethren, it eschews scenes of mass viewing and the commentary of third-party observers (present, apart from the sadistic teacher and his attendant soldiers, only as an assumption) to focus strictly on the horrific actions and horrified *re*actions of the (mostly) unwilling participants, some of whom descend into the near-madness of barbarism, while others develop a cold ruthlessness, and still others attempt to desperately hold onto their humanity — for as long as they can.

Viewers that can get past the shock of normal, everyday teenagers perpetrating all manner of violent, gruesome, and lethal acts (and *Battle Royale* refuses to shy away from these, often showing in bloody detail the carnage one human can inflict upon another) are rewarded with a thought-provoking exploration of such issues as respect, loss of innocence, morality, loyalty, and even love, all in a vibrantly disturbing what-would-*I*-do? scenario. It's not every movie that makes one both feel and think, but thanks to a terrifying premise, a brutal, no-holds-barred presentation, and well-drawn and acted characters that fully involve the viewer in their horrendous, hopeless plight, *Battle Royale* stands tall among them.

Though a top-ten box-office grosser in Japan, and released successfully throughout Europe, it took a dozen years for *Battle Royale* to officially find its way to American shores, and then only on DVD, released (perhaps not coincidentally) in 2012, about the same time as the American blockbuster *The Hunger Games*, which handles a similar premise with PG-lined kid gloves.

Battle Royale spawned a horribly inferior sequel in 2003, *Battle Royale II*, that not only plunges the original's thought-provoking thematics into shaky-cam skirmishes and hopeless melodrama, it eschews the Dangerous Game hunting aspect by transforming Battle Royale into "a brand-new war game" in which a ninth-grade class is forced to become soldiers that try to storm a "terrorist" stronghold and take out its leader (a survivor from the first film who's "declared war against every last adult").

The Condemned (2007; Lionsgate) Director: Scott Wiper; Producer: Joel Simon; Screenplay: Scott Wiper, Rob Hedden (story: Rob Hedden, Andy Hedden, Scott Wiper); Cinematographer: Ross Emery. Cast: Steven Austin, Vinnie Jones, Robert Mammone, Victoria Mussett, Manu Bennett, Madeleine West, Rick Hoffman.

WWE wrestling superstar "Stone Cold" Steven Austin made his big-screen debut in *The Condemned* (discounting a bit part in 2005's *The Longest Yard*), and it proved to be an auspicious one — not because it set the box office on fire (it didn't) but because it proved to be a smart, exciting, emotionally-involving and thought-provoking action-fest well tailored to the man-mountain's specific capabilities. Austin plays Conrad, a black ops agent stuck in an El Salvador prison after being apprehended during a mission. Rogue millionaire television producer Ian Breckel (Robert Mammone) "acquires" Conrad for his planned live internet show "The Condemned." As Breckel tells an interviewer, "I pulled 10 contestants from third world prisons. Each was on death row. I will free one of them. Tomorrow I'm gonna bring them to this island, where I will give them a fighting chance at a new life. It's a fight to the death." On his secret New Guinea island location, Breckel and his team have rigged over 400 cameras to capture the action, which will be broadcast live on the worldwide web (for a mere $49.99 subscription fee). The 30-hour hunt begins, and Conrad must elude or fight the other contestants (killers all) while attempting to throw a monkey wrench into Breckel's "show." As the world watches (via 40 million users), the "condemned" hunt down and kill each other until a final battle to the death. But even then it's not quite over...

"You're airing a live snuff film," accuses the shocked journalist. "You're a multimillionaire who may become a billionaire producing *murder.*" Breckel counters, "I didn't create a demand. People like to watch violence, they always have." It certainly provides some food for thought about just where the moral line lies and the consequences of crossing it. The same interviewer reflectively asks near film's end, "Those of us who watch — are *we* the condemned?" Fortunately, *The Condemned* doesn't just make a few simplistic moralizing statements and leave it at that; it explores the topic further through Breckel's various team members staging the show, each reacting to the sometimes hard-to-watch brutality and violence on display (some of it out-and-out torture) according to their conscience and moral compass, cleverly placing the viewer in a similar position.

Director/co-writer Scott Wiper goes for realism in the various fight scenes and action sequences, making these *raison d'etre* set-pieces affecting as well as exciting. Wiper and co-scripter Rob Hedden's screenplay efficiently offers varied traits and back stories for many of the characters, providing an emotional connection and generating pathos even for some of the less-than-savory "condemned." Incredible stunt work and brutal fight choreography (not to mention what may be the most impressive and realistic-looking helicopter crash ever filmed) alternate with intense moments of shock and anguish to raise *The Condemned* above most of its in-your-face action brethren.

One of the film's few missteps comes when Wiper succumbs to the frantically-edited, close-up-reliant, shaky-cam method in a misguided attempt to add immediacy to some of the fight sequences. Rather than making them more exciting, this motion sickness–inducing technique (all too common in the modern action genre) only serves to obscure rather than enhance the action.

And while most of the actors play their roles with realistic vibrancy (particularly the charismatic Vinnie Jones as the sadistic villain you can't help but love to hate), "Stone Cold" Steve Austin generally lives up to his nickname. Bringing an undisputed physical presence to his role, he offers far less in the emoting department. Fortunately, the script casts his character as the strong silent type ("I don't play games," he succinctly states early on), so his limited line deliveries only infrequently detract from his portrayal. In the end, like his character, Austin gets the job done.

The Condemned only grossed eight-and-a-half million dollars worldwide (against a reported $20 million budget), with nearly *half* the total take coming its opening weekend in a saturated 2300-theater booking. After that it sank like a, er ... Stone. Fortunately, this underrated actioner ultimately found its audience via blu-ray and DVD, earning more than $22 million in video sales to date.

Death Race 2000 (1975; New World Pictures) Director: Paul Bartel; Producer: Roger Corman; Screenplay: Robert Thom & Charles Griffith (from a story by Ib Melchior); Cinematographer: Tak Fujimoto. Cast: David Carradine, Simone Griffeth, Sylvester Stallone, Mary Woronov, Roberta Collins, Martin Kove, Louisa Moritz, Don Steele, Joyce Jameson, Carle Bensen, Sandy McCallum.

"One of the things a low or medium budget filmmaker can do," espoused producer Roger Corman to interviewer Leonard Maltin, "is experiment, take chances — such as we did with such a zany idea as *Death Race [2000]*— because you're not gambling that much money." Said zany idea (involving a cross-country road race in which the drivers' aim is not only to finish first, but to run down as many people as they can along the way) cost about $300,000, according to Corman, which was indeed cinematic chicken feed in 1975.

"The year 2000: America is a vast speedway," begins the film's trailer. "People line the streets to witness the greatest drivers on Earth in a race from sea to shining sea." This is not simply an annual transcontinental road race, however, but a *death* race — in which chasing down and killing pedestrians earns you points. A small group of underground rebels intends to sabotage the bloody road race and capture the world's top driver, known only as "Frankenstein" (David Carradine). To this end, one of their own (Simone Griffeth) infiltrates the system by becoming Frankenstein's navigator. But, unknown to the rebels, Frankenstein has become fed up with the carnage and has a plan of his own.

Coming in the middle of the '70s cinematic exploitation explosion, *Death Race 2000* roars ahead of its questionable competition to offer up something besides the expected sex and violence. In amongst the gratuitous massage scenes and (often wittily staged) hit-and-run gore sequences are healthy dollops of social satire poking pointed fun at everything from hero worship to political rhetoric. Granted, none of it is particularly subtle (the leader of the patriotic rebel group is an elderly woman named Mrs. *Thomasina Paine*; and the fawning reporter, whose sycophantic interviews invariably begin with her labeling her subject a "close personal friend of mine," is called Grace *Pander*), but it is no less effective (nor less amusing) for its blatancy. Many moviegoers apparently agreed, for, according to *Variety*, the picture grossed $5.25 million in the U.S. and Canada.

David Carradine is the futuristic race car driver known as "Frankenstein," who here steps away from his souped-up monster auto during the ***Death Race 2000***. Simone Griffeth plays his navigator in this transcontinental road race in which drivers rack up points by hunting down and running over pedestrians.

The movie's unusual (and unusually effective) cast is as offbeat as its attitude. Headed by the rather enigmatic David Carradine playing the rather enigmatic "Frankenstein," it features the likes of cult queen Mary Woronov (*Seizure, Eating Raoul*), a rather blowsy Joyce Jameson (*Tales of Terror, The Comedy of Terrors*), Future *Love Boat*er (and U.S. senator) Fred Grandy, the stern-looking Harriet White Medin (*The Horrible Dr. Hichcock, Black Sabbath*) and, of course, up-and-coming superstar-to-be Sylvester Stallone as the film's chief antagonist. (Corman hired the young, relatively unknown Stallone on the basis of his performance in *The Lords of Flatbush*.) "Sly was a really nice guy back then," recalled Woronov. "He was very funny, but he kept to himself a lot. He told me he was busy writing a script he wanted to star in. That turned out to be *Rocky*."

Corman was apparently displeased with director Paul Bartel's comedic approach to the material, and demanded additional action/violence scenes. "To me," said Corman, "*Death Race* was about gladiator fights in ancient Rome or boxing today—the need the public has to experience vicarious thrills. I wanted to treat it with humor, but what Paul Bartel and [co-scripter] Chuck Griffith wanted to do was make it a silly comedy. A farce comedy. I wanted it to be a smart comedy." The producer got his wish, for *Death Race 2000* is indeed a "smart comedy" about the horror and absurdity of blood sport taken to its ultimate.

Filmmaker George Miller has said that *Death Race 2000* provided the inspiration for his *Road Warrior* films. While those Australian classics admittedly "have a slight edge on *Death Race*" (as Corman himself so dryly put it), *Death Race 2000* remains a watershed in exploitation cinema, offering broad but biting satire along with its nudity and violence to create an entertaining and thought-provoking dystopian vision. So sit back and enjoy the ride, but remember: buckle up for safety—it's the law.

With quotes from: "Interview with Roger Corman," by Leonard Maltin, *Death Race 2000* DVD, Concord–New Horizons Corp., 2001; "The Real Mary Woronov," by Steve Swires, *Fangoria* 51 (1986); *Roger Corman*, by Mark Thomas McGee.

The Eliminator (2004; Artist View Entertainment, Inc.) Director: Ken Barbet; Producer: G. Anthony Joseph; Screenplay: David Neilsen; Cinematographer: Mark Woods. Cast: Michael Rooker, Bas Rutten, Dana Lee, G. Anthony Joseph, Wolf Muser, Marco Ruas, Michael Gregory, Danielle Burgo, Paul Logan.

In yet another voyeuristic variation on "The Most Dangerous Game," seven wealthy patrons each put up $25 million and supply one (unwilling) "contestant" (undercover DEA agent, guerrilla warfare expert, man-mountain psycho, etc.) to be hunted on an unconvincing, computer-generated CGIsland by a group of mercenaries. The "patron" of the last contestant left alive wins the game. Since the hired-help hunters are restricted to stalking at night with a mere two bullets in their guns, it is the contestants who do most of the killing of each other, while the patrons wait around in the luxury of the pink-turreted mansion owned by their host, Miles Dawson (Michael Rooker, of *Henry, Portrait of a Serial Killer* fame).

The Eliminator is similar in concept (though larger in scale) to another, earlier, direct-to-video offering, *Human Target* (1994), except that the wealthy patrons bet on the hand-picked *prey* rather than their hunters. Former Dutch kickboxing champion (as well as Japan's "King of Pancrase" and the 1998 Ultimate Fighting Champion) Bas Rutten plays the unconventional hero. Rutten's charisma and unflappable good humor make for a likable protagonist, but he ultimately cannot put over a script that has Rutten's Dakota Varley ridiculously kickboxing and wrestling just about everyone in the cast (not to mention his rolling-in-the-mud-fully-clothed love scene with the film's token female). Director Ken Barbet relies heavily on time-lapse photography, unsteady cam, psycho p.o.v. shots, a slo-mo CGI bullet effect (used *twice*) and other film school/MTV tricks to make up for the script's lack of characterization, tension, suspense, and inventive traps. Shot in the summer of 2003 in Los Angeles and Florida as *Varley's Game*, *The Eliminator* made barely a ripple in the Dangerous Game pond when released directly to video the following year.

Human Target (1994; Entertainment Securities Ltd.) Alternate Title: *Final Round*. Director: George Erschbamer; Producer: Robert Vince; Screenplay: Arnie Olsen; Cinematographer: Rick Maguire. Cast: Lorenzo Lamas, Anthony de Longis, Kathleen Kinmont, Clark Johnson, Isabelle Jamieson.

Lorenzo Lamas plays a part-time boxer/full-time motorcycle mechanic who, along with his new, one-night-stand girlfriend (Kathleen Kinmont) and a trash-talking ex-football player (Clark Johnson), becomes the "Human Target" of a deadly game in which six hired mercenaries hunt human quarry in a warehouse complex while wealthy viewers watch via closed-circuit satellite and bet on the outcome. Though lacking the overt "gameshow" angle, it's an obvious *Running Man* rip-off, but without the political overtones and social satire, not to mention the glitz, glamour, fast-paced action, big budget or high-priced talent involved (the expressionless Lamas is just as wooden as Ah-nold but lacks Schwarzenegger's undeniable charisma and screen presence). One character even steals Arnie's "Asta la vista, baby" line, while another can't come up with anything better than "Syonara asshole" for *his*.

Human Target offers little more than small-scale, poorly choreographed fights; a claustrophobic warehouse setting; cheap, direct-to-video lighting and photography; subpar acting (with statuesque female lead Kinmont standing tall at 5-foot 11-inches but falling short in the emoting department); and a few unintentional chuckles (particularly when we see Lorenzo strutting about in his powder blue overalls with one strap strategically left undone— apparently considered the height of sexy machismo in the early nineties?). Real-life husband and wife Lorenzo Lamas and Kathleen Kinmont divorced shortly after the completion of this film. Coincidence?

The Hunger Games (2012; Lions Gate/Color Force) Director: Gary Ross; Producers: Nina Jacobson, Jon Kilik; Screenplay: Gary Ross, Suzanne Collins, Billy Ray (based on the novel by Suzanne Collins); Cinematography: Tom Stern. Cast: Jennifer Lawrence, Josh Hutcherson, Liam Hemsworth, Woody Harrelson, Elizabeth Banks, Lenny Kravitz, Stanley Tucci, Donald Sutherland.

Though by far the most expensive (at an estimated cost of 78 million dollars) and the most financially successful entry in this MDG subset (taking in $152 million in the U.S. its opening weekend alone, and going on to gross nearly $700 million worldwide), *The Hunger Games* is not necessarily the most successful thematically or artistically (see *Battle Royale*, for instance, which some claim was the prototype for this blockbuster, though *Hunger Games* author/co-screenwriter Suzanne Collins denies any inspiration from that Japanese groundbreaker and instead cites the juxtaposition of real-life war coverage and so-called "reality" programming on television as the genesis of her novel). Based on Collins' mega-best-selling young adult book of the same name, *The Hunger Games* takes place in a dystopian future in which America has been divvied up into thirteen "districts" where oppressed workers serve the needs of the elite in "the Capitol." Every year the government stages the "Hunger Games." As the opening written scrawl explains: "From the Treaty of the Treason: In penance for their uprising, each district shall offer up a male and female between the ages of 12 and 18 at a public 'Reaping.' These Tributes shall be delivered to the custody of The Capitol. And then transferred to a public arena where they will fight to the death, until a lone victor remains." Before the choosing ceremony, the government enforcers show a short propaganda film (narrated by the President, played by Donald Sutherland) in which the Hunger Games are labeled "a pageant of honor, courage and sacrifice.... This is how we remember our past; this is how we safeguard our future." When her younger sister is chosen to represent District 12 in this year's Hunger Games, Katniss Everdeen (Jennifer Lawrence) volunteers in her place. Then begins her journey to the Capitol, her brief training (under the tutelage of Haymitch, the lone previous winner from her district), and the Game itself, where she must stalk and kill—or be killed—battling both her conscience and her fellow contestants while the whole country watches (and those in power behind the scenes manipulate the outcome).

Well acted, particularly by star Jennifer Lawrence, who displays both a steely resolve and some touching vulnerability, and Woody Harrelson as her cynical and burned-out mentor, *The Hunger Games* deftly sets the stage for the Most Dangerous nightmare to come via some involving characterization (particularly in the relationship between Kat, her sister, and her obviously damaged mother) and the rural District 12 setting that's reminiscent, in both the characters' dress and the dilapidated buildings, of Depression-era America. Unfortunately, the film then takes a turn towards the absurd after Kat is loaded aboard the Art-Deco 200-mph bullet train to take her to the Capitol. There she (and the viewer) are exposed to no end of outrageous technicolor fashions, hairstyles, and set dressings, whose superciliousness is only surpassed by their impracticality. One almost expects the Capitol's wealthy, effete citizens to suddenly burst out singing, "We represent the Lolly Pop Guild..." Though such over-the-top wardrobe and set design provides a jarring contrast to the gritty realism of District 12, it's so outré that it generally appears more silly than sinister. Completing the picture is a blatant attempt to conjure up the decadence of Ancient Rome via a Coliseum-like amphitheater (that includes chariots for the "Tributes' Parade") and a master of ceremonies named "Caesar." (The classic 1975 sci-fier *Rollerball* did the same thing in a far more subtle and effective manner nearly four decades earlier.) In amongst the absurdities are some clever jabs at the shallow voyeurism of "reality" television (including image coaches trying to turn the various Tributes into media darlings to garner sponsors, "which could save your damn life," says Haymitch). But the social commentary is nearly lost among all the Day-Glo glitz and glamour.

Once the Games begin, a number of suspenseful, action-ful, and even emotion-ful (as the excellent characterization and acting makes us care about several of the characters) set-pieces keep interest high, but a reliance on ostentatious film technique threatens to derail the good work of the actors and scriptwriters. Director Gary Ross (*Pleasantville*, *Seabiscuit*) relies too heavily on the hyper-frenetic editing that has become so prevalent in the New Millennium, making it difficult at times to discern what is happening, while resorting to CGI monsters towards the end to inject some magical fantasy (though ostensibly scientific, these conjured-up creatures are something straight out of *Lord of the Rings*) into a scenario that cries out for realism. Of course, this all serves to transform the R-rated concept into a safe-for-sequels PG-13 product—which is oh-so-important for a pre/teen-targeted Hollywood franchise.

Paintball (2009; Spain) Director: Daniel Benmayor; Producer: Julio Fernandez; Screenplay: Mario Schoendorff; Cinematography: Juanmi Azpiroz. Cast: Bendan Mackey, Jennifer Matter, Patrick Regis, Iaone Perez, Neil Maskell, Anna Casas.

This Spanish production (shot in English with actors from the UK as well as Spain) by first-time director Daniel Benmayor begins with a handful of extreme paintballers taken to a secret woodland location for a weekend of paintball warrior "fun." Said fun quickly turns sour, however, when the small band realize that they're being shot at with real bullets rather than paintballs. One by one they're stalked and killed as they bicker among themselves and try to make it to each of the six target flags — spots that hold useful items (such as a machete) and odd bits and pieces, which, when assembled, could create a weapon with which to defend themselves. As their internecine fighting and poor choices lead them to their gruesome deaths one by one, it becomes apparent that a lone hunter stalks their band for the amusement and pleasure of a number of silent observers.

Though containing a promising premise, Mario Schoendorff's underwritten screenplay and Daniel Benmayor's style-over-substance direction shoot *Paintball* in the foot, making it one long string of missed opportunities. The protagonists are little more than ciphers whose characterization consists of shouting obscenities at one another during fits of near-hysteria. Consequently, the viewer has little emotional investment in seeing these people in peril (or even die), so the kills lack both suspense and engagement (apart from maybe some audio relief). Worse still, the hunter remains silent and anonymous (and largely unseen, apart from a hazy outline at a distance), and we've no idea why he does what he does (apart from money, as at one point an unseen overseer radios him instructions about a kill, reminding him that "we pay you to follow orders"). And the "patrons" who finance this operation are likewise left unexplained and unexplored — they are simply nondescript figures who stand behind Plexiglas windows and one-way mirrors to watch the killings. The only explanatory nod comes when the hunt's mysterious organizer states, "You pay to witness death; and that's what you're getting." No further explorations or insights into their mindsets or motivations arise; consequently, neither does much interest for the viewer.

Benmayor begins his film almost immediately with a frantic 10-minute paintball battle sequence at a woodland automotive graveyard in which the newly-arrived group is fired upon by unseen assailant(s) — fellow paintballers. While certainly frenetic, the hand-held camerawork and continual shaky-cam shots generate more nausea than urgency. And despite the desperate visuals, there's no resonance or immediacy to the action because a) you know nothing yet about the characters involved (in some cases not even their names); and b) it's just paintballs whizzing by (at least until the end). So while Our Protagonists are shouting shrill obscenities, frantically ducking and weaving, and doing all sorts of pseudo-military maneuvering, it's all just hollow show, with no heart or real concern. Benmayor further sacrifices substance for style when he chooses to film all the (real) kills in negative image — a hunter-cam p.o.v. Though striking at first, it soon grows tiresome and merely obfuscating, further distancing the viewer from the visceral moments and severing what little emotional connection might be present (as well as saving on more convincing blood and gore effects). Toss in a nonsensical final shot involving the expected Final Girl, and *Paintball* lands with a resounding "splat."

The Prize of Peril (1983; Europe 1; France/Yugoslavia) Original Language Title: *Le Prix du Danger*. Director: Yves Boisset; Producer: Norbert Saada; Screenplay: Yves Boisset, Jean Curtelin (based on the short story "The Prize of Peril" by Robert Sheckley); Cinematographer: Peter-William Glenn. Cast: Gerard Lanvin, Michel Piccoli, Marie-France Pisier, Bruno Cremer, Gabrielle Lazure, Catherine Lachens.

Though not the first of the "Running Man"/game show–styled "Most Dangerous

Game" variations (*The Tenth Victim* preceded it by almost two decades), the French-produced *The Prize of Peril* is arguably the best, and definitely the most realistically hard-hitting. It begins with an ordinary-looking man running through city streets pursued by a pistol-packing group dressed vaguely like security guards. The sequence ends with the desperate suspect jumping into the river to escape, after which his pursuers, in a rowboat, shockingly beat him to death with oars and chains! Captured on film via cameras mounted on motorcycle, helicopter, and even a blimp(!), the events turn out to be staged for a supremely popular television game show called *The Prize of Peril*, in which a contestant must elude his five pursuers for four hours to claim a million-dollar prize. Of course, to date no one has survived to collect the cash. The story then follows the selection of the next "contestant" and his subsequent hunt, while a protest group files suit against CTV (the program's production company). "At a time when the forces of law and order all over the world are struggling to combat the rise in violence, I here and now accuse CTV of deliberately exploiting the public's worst instincts to put money in their pockets," denounces the lead activist before a "Citizen's Committee." Of course, the head of CTV sees it differently, arguing publicly that the program "provides an innocent outlet for violence," and privately that "It's in the national interest—the distraction value. While they're all hypnotized by *The Prize of Peril*, our six million unemployed can't be out rioting in the streets."

The telling difference between *The Prize of Peril* and its obvious progenitor *The Tenth Victim* and subsequent imitators (*The Running Man*, *$lasher$*, etc.) is *Prize*'s realistic (as opposed to camp, glitzy, or over-the-top) approach to its topic. *Prize*'s protagonist and his antagonists all behave as "normal" people would in such extraordinary circumstances. Unlike the muscle-bound fighting machines and over-the-top grotesques that populate *The Running Man* and its ilk, *Prize*'s protagonist, played by Gerard Lanvin, doesn't suddenly develop into an Action Hero; while his five randomly chosen hunters are fairly ordinary citizens (taxidermist, insurance salesman, etc.) who happen to be handed a gun and a license for murder. And far from offering the easy Hollywoodesque happy ending (in which heroics, combined with an appeal to the common people's innate decency, typically topple the evil, exploitative regime sponsoring the game), *Prize* paints a scene far more pessimistic, yet far more realistic, to create a denouement of disturbing resonance.

The Running Man (1987; Tri-Star) Director: Paul Michael Glaser; Producers: Tim Zinnemann, George Linder; Screenplay: Steven E. DeSouza (from a novel by Stephen King [as Richard Bachman]); Cinematographer: Thomas Del Ruth. Cast: Arnold Schwarzenegger, Maria Conchita Alonso, Richard Dawson, Yaphet Kotto, Jim Brown, Jesse Ventura, Erland Van Lidth.

While the high-profile, big-budgeted *The Running Man*, starring action megastar Arnold Schwarzenegger at the height of his popularity, may be the best-known entry in the Dangerous Game Show (sub-)subgenre (at least until *The Hunger Games* came along), it's far from the best. With barely-fleshed out characters (framed Good Guy, helpless Computer Geek, sassy Latino Heroine, smarmy Bastard Showbiz Host); a simplistic plot that leaves too many questions unanswered (not to mention logistical impossibilities); and a cheesy, oh-so-eighties feel (America in 2019 is apparently *still* in love with spandex, big hair, and the Solid Gold Dancers [with choreography by Paula Abdul!]), *The Running Man* pulls up lame as a convincing stab at social criticism. On the plus side, however, it truly lives up to its name by offering plenty of ... well, running, via inventive (if not particularly realistic) action set-pieces and tub-thumping mano-a-mano battles.

Based on the 1982 Stephen King novella (first published under his pseudonym Richard Bachman), which King reportedly wrote in a mere 72 hours, the film has military pilot Ben Richards (Arnold Schwarzenegger) framed for a massacre he tried to prevent, and then forced to become a "contestant" on "the most popular television program in history," *The Running Man*. Hosted by the unctuous but charismatic Damon Killian (Richard Dawson), the show makes convicted criminals run through "400 square blocks of game zone," hunted by various "Stalkers" out to kill them — all for the entertainment of the television audience. Richards has to defeat the Stalkers and then link up with a small resistance group to broadcast the truth about the police state government and discredit the sadistic show.

The Stalkers each have their own individual gimmick and weaponry (everything from chainsaws to flamethrowers to razor-sharp hockey sticks[!]). One Stalker, "Captain Freedom," is played by Jesse Ventura, who appeared with Schwarzenegger this same year in another MDG variant, the Dangerous Alien Game groundbreaker *Predator*. Also playing a stalker was the 6-foot-6, 350-pound Dutch-born actor and opera singer Erland Van Lidth (playing "Dynamo," who sings snippets of Wagner while shooting lightning bolts from his electrical suit at his prey). Tragically, Van Lidth died of a heart attack only a few months after completing work on *The Running Man*, age 34.

Interviewed upon the film's release, Arnold Schwarzenegger boasted, "It's the best work I've ever done. It's the best film that I've ever been involved with. It's the fastest paced, it has the smartest story behind it, it's great action, so I think the world of it." So did the moviegoing public in 1987. The film earned $38 million domestically upon its initial release (on a budget of $27 million). Along with foreign sales and ancillary rights, *The Running Man* proved to be a runaway financial success. Schwarzenegger seems to have drastically changed his tune since 1987, however. Original director Andrew Davis was fired a week into filming *The Running Man* and replaced by Paul Michael Glaser. In his 2012 autobiography, Arnold labeled this a "terrible decision" because Glaser "shot the movie like it was a television show, losing all the deeper themes." A disappointed Stephen King told *Cinefantastique* magazine, "It was totally out of my hands. I didn't have anything to do with making it. They obviously saw it as a book that could be adapted to fit an existing *Rambo-Terminator* kind of genre, where you're able to give Schwarzenegger the tag lines that he's known for, like 'I'll be back.' The biggest thing about that was casting Richard Dawson as the game show host. He was great. But the rest of it is this sort of simplified story. It doesn't have much in common with the novel at all, except the title."

In the film, Schwarzenegger looks, acts and talks tough, with the script giving him plenty of darkly comical one-liners to chew on, including his famous catchphrase "I'll be back" (originated in 1984's *The Terminator* and repeated by Arnie in over a dozen subsequent films). In *The Running Man*, however, Richard Dawson one-ups the comment by cleverly answering, "Only in a rerun." Among Schwarzenegger's sometimes less-than-subtle (or tasteful) quips in *The Running Man* are: "Give you a lift?" before tossing a guard off a catwalk; "What a hothead," after incinerating a stalker; and "He had to split," after chainsawing another in the crotch.

As a simplistic and overblown action movie for a simplistic and overblown action superstar, *The Running Man* crosses the finish line in good time; but as a serious comment on the dangerous appeal of violence via the ultimate "hunt," it trails the pack. (Note: In 2010 a South Korean television show premiered called *The Running Man*, in which participants went on "race missions." Humans were not the targets, however, as the point was to track down and collect as many "running balls" as possible.)

17. *Dangerous Game Shows and Deadly Diversions* 225

Arnold Schwarzenegger is *The Running Man* in what became the prototype for the Dangerous Game Shows subset (German poster).

With quotes from: Interview with Arnold Schwarzenegger at BillBoggs.com; Gary Wood, "Stephen King & Hollywood," *Cinefantastique* (February 1991); *Total Recall: My Unbelievably True Life Story*, by Arnold Schwarzenegger and Peter Petre.

Series 7: The Contenders (2001; USA Films) Director/screenplay: Daniel Minahan; Producers: Jason Kliot, Joana Vicente, Christine Vachon, Kate Roumel; Cinematographer: Randy Drummond. Cast: Brooke Smith, Glenn Fitzgerald, Marylouise Burke, Richard Venture, Michael Kaycheck, Merrit Weaver, Will Arnett.

An eight-months-pregnant woman walks into a convenience store, pulls out a pistol, and suddenly shoots an innocuous-looking middle-aged man point blank in the back. Then, breathing hard, she barks at the stunned clerk, "Do you have any bean dip?!" So begins *Series 7: The Contenders*, a scathing parody of reality television taken to the extreme. "Real people in real danger in a fight for their lives on *The Contenders*," dramatically declares an announcer, and we realize we're watching a reality show in which "six strangers, brought together by the luck of the draw, [are] in a game without rules, where the only prize is the only prize that counts — your life!" Six people are chosen by lottery to kill one another for the benefit of the popular reality TV show *The Contenders*, with cameramen following the participants' every move as they set about offing one another.

Series 7 successfully walks that fine line between biting satire and dramatic impact, subtly aping the subject it parodies to near perfection. The pretentious and preposterous "real-life" interviews provide sublime moments of satire, such as when one 18-year-old female contestant proudly tells the camera, without a hint of irony or self-awareness, "My boyfriend Nathan paid for half of this bullet-proof vest ... I think it shows how much he cares about me." Later, over a shot of her riding in the back of her parents' car, she narrates, "My parents are very overprotective..."—just before her mom turns to her and earnestly asks, "You've got your guns? Rifle?" Another contestant imparts such words of wisdom as, "I don't like the feeling of being hunted. That's when it's time to get proactive. There's much more power in being the hunt-*er*." Then there are the various promo spots in which the announcer spouts such catch-phrases as "*The Contenders*— the game is real" and "These cats don't have nine lives."

Like most reality TV shows, it never appears truly "real," with the drama artificially heightened and the pathetic pathos milked for far more than it's worth. The film cleverly lampoons the manipulative nature of reality TV, showing snippets of one contestant's wedding video and another's baby home movies! Which only points up how spot-on *Series 7* truly is. Unlike its various Dangerous Game Show brethren, *Series 7* never "breaks character," always remaining within the framework of the faux show (a season seven "marathon"). Though initially appearing as a clever conceit, this ultimately becomes the movie's major flaw; without any behind-the-scenes or real-world interaction as contrast, the film becomes repetitive and meandering over the course of its 86-minute running time (just like a stretched-out-for-too-long reality show). Fortunately, the cleverly written scenario and some excellent reality TV–style "acting" from the cast of unknowns keeps interest levels high.

Series 7: The Contenders premiered at the Sundance Film Festival in January of 2001 and received a limited U.S. release three months later. It did well on the festival circuit, receiving nominations at the 2001 Deauville Film Festival, the 2001 Edgar Allan Poe Awards, the 2001 Gijon International Film Festival, and the 2001 Gotham Awards; and winning a "Golden Trailer" at the 2002 Golden Trailers Awards and the "Audience Award" at the 2002 Sweden Fantastic Film Festival.

LAHER$ (2001; Fangoria Video; Canada) Director/Producer/Screenplay: Maurice Devereaux; Cinematographer: Denis-Noel Mostert. Cast: Sarah Joslyn Crowder, Tony Curtis Blondell, Kieran Keller, Jerry Sprio, Carolina Pla, Sofia De Medeiros, Claudine Shiraishi, Chris Piggins, Neil Napier.

"I had seen this Japanese television show called *Endurance*, where people had terrible, inhuman things done to them and survivors won the prizes," recounted Montreal producer-director-writer Maurice Devereaux about the inspiration for *LAHER$*. Though no one ever died on the Japanese series, Devereaux decided to take the concept to the extreme and came up with *LAHER$*, a fictional Japanese game show in which six contestants (on its "first All–American Special") would run for their lives from mask-wearing killers out for blood. Whoever survived to the end of the show would split a multimillion-dollar prize.

Devereaux compared his concept to that of the far more famous *The Running Man* (1987). "In that one," observed the filmmaker, "the contestants were prisoners forced to compete. In *LAHER$* they are all willing competitors.... That's what makes my script different from *The Running Man*." Well, that and about 27 million dollars, since Devereaux had a mere $165 *thousand* to film *his* tale of game shows taken to the extreme. Consequently, his contestants run and fight for their lives in a warehouse interior whose day job is obviously as a paintball arena, and a few cheesy plywood and plastic Halloween funhouse sets. And said stalking and slashing is captured not on film but on *video*, giving *LAHER$* that distractingly cheap visual look so common to daytime television.

Cleverly, Devereaux chose to film the story just like the supposed television series would, with the cameraman following the "contestants" around to catch every moment of suspense, shock and gruesome death on video. And the filmmaker managed to find local actors talented enough (more or less) to flesh out his characters, with each given a fairly thorough back story to encourage viewer interest (in both the faux audience and the real one) and, ultimately, viewer identification. Devereaux also treats his trio of "Slashers"— Charlie Chainsaw, "our favorite inbred redneck"; Preacher Man, "the prophet of pain"; and Dr. Ripper, "the intern of intestines"— with care, providing enough individuality and clever dialogue to bring them to violent, vibrant life. The result: one begins to ignore the obvious cheapness and concentrate on the plight of these characters. Toss in some shocking gore (admittedly, not all of it realistic), some self-reflexive dialogue aimed right at the horror crowd ("In horror movies only the spectators can hear the scary music because the characters don't know they're in deep shit; well, *we* know we're in deep shit"), and some acerbic jabs at reality programming (including an indictment of viewer voyeurism when one near-hysterical protagonist looks directly at the camera and accuses, "By giving your support to this show and their advertisers, *you* are the root of the problem of this sick and inhuman practice"), and *LAHER$* becomes something a little more than the sum of its cheapjack parts. Though unable to completely overcome its low budget, cut-rate sets, and soap opera–level videography, *LAHER$* still manages to engage and hold one's interest via some involving characterizations, a few twists and turns, and some funhouse/house-of-horrors sensibilities.

With quotes from: Bram Eisenthal, "*LAHER$*: Reality Slices," *Fangoria* 215.

The Tenth Victim (1965; Embassy; Italy/France) Original Language Title: *La Decima Vittima*. Director: Elio Petri; Producer: Carlo Ponti; Screenplay: Ennio Flajano, Ernesto Gastaldi, Tonino Guerra, Elio Petri, Giorgio Salvioni, Robert Sheckley (story); Cinematographer: Gianni De Venanzo. Cast: Marcello Mastroianni, Ursula Andress, Elsa Martinelli, Salvo Randone, Massimo Serato, Milo Quesada, Luce Bonifassy.

Spanish poster for *The Tenth Victim*, the original Dangerous Game Show.

In this dystopian satire (set in the near-future in which everyone wears uber-sixties "mod" fashions and lives in garishly-decorated swinging pads), the governments of the Earth sanction murder via the "Big Hunt" game to control population and ease aggressive tendencies towards war. "An elementary study of history confirms the validity of the 'Big Hunt' theory," explains a lecturer at the Ministry of the Hunt. "It is mankind's safety valve. If the Big Hunt had existed in 1940, Hitler certainly would have become a member, and there would have been no World War Two. Indeed, the Big Hunt has done away with war by giving man's violent instincts a competitive outlet." Participants are randomly assigned as either "Hunter" or "Hunted," and must kill their opponent before he or she kills them, receiving cash prizes for every slaying. Those who reach ten kills without perishing receive lifetime political and financial privileges (including a million-dollar bonus).

Ursula Andress plays the icy killer (who dispatched her previous victim via a bullet-barreled bra!) seeking to make her tenth and final kill in front of television cameras as a commercial tie-in for "Ming Tea" (complete with beautiful chorus girls and dancing teacups!!), while Marcello Mastroianni is the world-weary, nerve-jangled mark seeking to turn the tables on his huntress. Love blossoms like bullet hits, and various twists lead to an amusingly unexpected conclusion.

"*The Tenth Victim* is essentially a fantasy told in realistic terms," explained Rome-born journalist-turned-filmmaker Elio Petri. "We are attempting to show what life could be like in the not too distant future in a completely dehumanized society."

The Tenth Victim meanders at times among various tedious subplots and superfluous characters, and the "groovy" sixties lounge music and even groovier threads and furnishings soon become tiresome. Yet, the picture's biting satire (attacking everything from the media and politics to interpersonal relationships and organized religion) and chemistry between the two leads, as they play their deadly cat-and-mouse game, make this a hunt worth watching.

With quotes from: "The Tenth Victim," *Continental Film Review* (September 1965).

The Tournament (2009; Dimension; UK) Director: Scott Mann; Producers: Keith Bell, Gelnn M. Stewart, Gina Fegan; Screenplay: Gary Young, Jonathan Frank, Nick Rowntree; Cinematographer: Emil Topuzov. Cast: Robert Carlyle, Kelly Hu, Ian Somerhalder, Liam Cunningham, Ving Rhames, Scott Adkins.

First and foremost, *The Tournament* is an action flick. Filmed in England and Bulgaria for a relatively inexpensive four million pounds (less than seven million dollars), the movie looks better than much of the overblown Hollywood product costing five times as much. Due to some fantastic fight/action choreography that runs the gamut from modern Hong Kong–style battling to American duke-it-out fisticuffs to French Parkour (Sebastian Foucan, one of Parkour's founders, performs some astounding feats of agility, rapidly climbing, leaping, and even sliding along the ground on his back with his feet braced against the bumper of a speeding car). Toss in a number of convincing physical stunts (thankfully sans CGI) and several thrilling car chases (one involving a double-decker bus and a tanker truck!), and *The Tournament* becomes a Class-A action film in the tradition of *Crank*, *District B13*, and *Shoot 'em Up*.

Every seven years, 30 of the world's deadliest assassins descend on some randomly selected town (this year it's Middlesborough, England) to take part in the Tournament — a 24-hour contest in which they must track and kill one another, with the winner taking home a $10 million prize. By hacking into both closed-circuit and satellite surveillance systems, and using tracking devices implanted in each "player," the contest serves as entertainment for a select few wealthy elite, who watch, applaud and bet huge sums on the killings. Run by a man named Powers (Liam Cunningham) and his team of technicians, the Tournament flies under the public radar by jamming emergency service signals and manipulating the media into blaming the killings (and the vast collateral damage) on such things as terrorist bombings, auto accidents, and lone-gunman rampages. When a series of accidents cause a down-and-out alcoholic priest suffering a crisis of faith (Robert Carlyle) to inadvertently become a Tournament participant, a female assassin with a tortured past (Kelly Hu) becomes his protector, rescuing him time and again from the rest of the killers, including the previous Tournament's champion (Ving Rhames), there to seek revenge (his wife had recently been murdered by a Tournament participant).

If one thinks too hard on the story's premise (not to mention its details), this *Tournament* unravels rather quickly, but first-time director Scott Mann keeps the pace moving so rapidly that it becomes easy to slide into the (twisted) spirit of the "game." Likewise, he squeezes about as much nuance and character development as could be found between the near nonstop action set-pieces (featuring well over 50 onscreen "kills," many of them rather, er, juicy). An engaging and even likable cast, headed by Carlyle (*The Full Monty, 28 Weeks Later*), Hu (the TV series *The Vampire Diaries*), and Rhames (*Pulp Fiction, Dawn of the Dead*), bring their sometimes two-dimensional characters to three-dimensional life. Particularly impressive (and entertaining) is Ian Somerhalder (who went on to co-star with Hu in *The Vampire Diaries*), whose smiling, enthusiastic "Texan" killer gives a whole new dimension to enjoying one's work.

Though filmed in 2007, due to financial difficulties (the production ran out of money twice) and distributor woes, *The Tournament* wasn't released until two years later, in 2009, and then directly to DVD in many territories, including North America. More's the pity, as this *Tournament* is definitely one worth attending.

18

Dangerous Alien Games

Say what you will about our species, humans are top of the food chain. We're also the only species that hunt "lower" life forms for sport (rather than food). But what if we're not actually at the top, at least on a universal scale, and there are more advanced creatures out there? And what if said beings came to Earth for some big game "sport" of their own, with people as their prey? This became the basis for the popular and lucrative *Predator* franchise, begun in 1987 by the Arnold Schwarzenegger–starrer *Predator*.

AVH: Alien vs. Hunter (2007; The Asylum) Director: Scott Harper. Producer/Screenplay: David Michael Latt; Cinematographer: Mark Atkins. Cast: William Katt, Dedee Pfeiffer, Wittley Jourdan, Randy Mulkey.

Made by the opportunistic (or plagiaristic, depending upon one's level of sensitivity) folks at The Asylum (who brought us such opportunistic rip-offs as *The Da Vinci Treasure*, *Mega Piranha* and the immortal *Snakes on a Train*), *AVH* is their no-budget, direct-to-video riff on *AVP: Alien vs. Predator* (2004). Well, more precisely, *Alien vs. Hunter*'s story of a small town beset by rampaging alien beasts tracked by an intergalactic hunter, with various locals caught in the crossfire, steals more from the *AVP* sequel *AVPR: Aliens vs. Predator Requiem* (2007) than the "original."

In *Alien vs. Hunter*, William Katt plays a small-town journalist who, along with a handful of fellow locals, stumbles upon an alien spacecraft, runs afoul of some vicious, spider-bodied creatures, and crosses paths with the armored alien hunter there to stalk the intergalactic beasts. Into the mix steps a small group of survivalist yokels, who become more prey for the hunter.

Utterly dismal in every respect, *AVH* offers only cardboard characters not even fit for alien fodder; both unlikable and unlikely in their behavior, they generate zero interest in whether they live or die. A disjointed story plagued by poor pacing only makes matters worse, with characters continually wandering around the woods or slowly plodding through a system of sewer tunnels that would be overkill for a mighty metropolis, much less this backwater burg. Add in alternately banal and over-strained acting (William "*Greatest American Hero*" Katt, the only "name" in the cast, tries desperately to out-act his mustache and soul patch — and fails miserably), and a couple of cut-rate CGI effects that plops a Giger-esque alien head onto a phony-looking spider body, and the desultory picture is complete. What little enjoyment that can be gleaned from *AVH* comes in the form of a few derisive chuckles at the alien hunter's expense. Sporting second-rate armor topped by a headdress that appears to be part diving helmet and part rice-paddy hat, he looks more like a metallic mushroom than a fearsome otherworldly warrior.

Visual effects man-(*Snakes on a Plane*— the *real* one)-turned-director Scott Harper does a pathetic job not only of telling a cohesive story, but also of staging the all-important alien attacks and hunter confrontations (the hunter-redneck fights are poorly choreographed at half-speed, and nearly all of the creature-caused deaths occur *off-screen*!). Of course, given that Harper reportedly had a mere 12 days to complete principal photography, such action shorthand as having a victim simply duck out of frame and inserting a squelching noise on the soundtrack to indicate his fate might be understandable, if not exactly forgivable.

But hey, at least this digital video travesty pays homage (of sorts) to its source — no, not the *AVP* movies but Richard Connell's story:

> First Girl: "It's a game to him. He's on a hunt.... He's not going to quit until the creature's dead."
> Second Girl: "And us?"
> First Girl: "We're in the way."
> Third Girl: "Unless we're just another trophy."
> Stoner Guy: "Like 'The Most Dangerous Game,' intergalactic style."
> Third Girl: "When did *you* get so literate?"

AVP: Alien vs. Predator (2004; Twentieth Century–Fox) Alternate Title: *Alien vs. Predator*. Director: Paul W. S. Anderson; Producers: John Davis, Gordon Carroll, David Giler, Walter Hill. Screenplay: Paul W. S. Anderson (story: Paul W. S. Anderson, Dan O'Bannon, Ronald Shusett); Cinematographer: David Johnson. Cast: Sanaa Lathan, Raoul Bova, Lance Henriksen, Ewen Bremner, Colin Salmon, Tommy Flannagan, Carsten Norgaard.

This melding of the two ultra-popular sci-fi film franchises started by *Alien* in 1979 and *Predator* in 1987 is something of a Dangerous Alien Game once-removed, as the deadly alien race of hunters known as the Predators stalk not people this time but the far more challenging game of the monstrous Alien, with humans merely caught in the middle and/or used as breeding hosts for the *real* prey. The protagonists soon realized that "the humanoids, the hunters, they brought these creatures here to hunt. And they use us like cattle. We're hosts for them to breed in ... without us there could be no hunt."

A strange "heat bloom" in the Antarctic leads an exploratory crew of archeologists and engineers to a giant pyramid buried 2000 feet below the ice. Once there, they realize that the pyramid is inhabited by deadly Alien monsters that use humans as breeding hosts, and that a second alien species, the humanoid Predators, have arrived to hunt the beasts for sport — with the research team caught in the crossfire. As the pyramid's ancient hieroglyphics reveal, "Every 100 years the 'gods' [Predators] would return.... Humans were used to breed the ultimate prey. The hunters would battle these 'great serpents' to prove themselves worthy."

AVP accomplishes what it sets out to do by pitting the two classic sci-fi monsters in a battle-to-the-death scenario, yet it never rises above the Godzilla-vs.-King Kong mentality of a monster mash-up. As such, it eschews the more hard-hitting, startling (and visceral) qualities of its predecessors in order to secure that family-friendly PG-13 rating, becoming the only film in either franchise not to earn an R. There's no significant character arc or development over the course of the film; it simply puts a handful of poorly-sketched protagonists (including a sorely underused Lance Henriksen) through their action-horror paces until the over-the-top heroic conclusion. The nightmarish terrors of the original films give way to video-game-mentality "thrills" offered by a set of characters trying to make it through a multilevel pyramid that reconfigures itself every 10 minutes, while simultaneously avoiding two different types of monsters. Calculated, competent, and action-filled, *AVP: Alien vs. Predator*, like the 1993 video game that inspired it, ultimately rings hollow, bringing nothing particularly new or innovative to either franchise. Still, its video-game/monster-mash approach worked, as it grossed $172 million worldwide (making it the most financially successful of all the *Predator* films) on a reported $60 million budget, and spawned everything from toys to comic books to more video games.

AVPR: Aliens vs. Predator Requiem (2007; Twentieth Century–Fox) Alternate Title: *AVP: Requiem*. Directors: The Brothers Strause (Colin and Greg); Producers: John Davis, David Giler, Walter Hill; Screenplay: Shane Salerno; Cinematographer: Daniel C. Pearl. Cast: Steven Pasquale, Reiko Aylesworth, John Ortiz, Johnny Lewis, Ariel Gade.

If *AVP: Alien vs. Predator* was a competent but largely soulless exercise in franchise melding, then its direct sequel, *AVPR: Aliens vs. Predator Requiem*, is an *in*competent soulless exercise in going to the well once too often.

Beginning right where *AVP* left off— the body of a dead Predator on his ship disgorges a germinating Alien (this one a Predator-Alien hybrid, complete with the Predator's spidery dreadlocks and crab-like pincer-mouth)—*AVPR: Aliens vs. Predator Requiem* has the Alien run amuck on the Predator ship, causing it to crash near a small Colorado town. Alien facehuggers escape the wreckage and quickly latch onto a pair of father-and-son hunters, who soon becoming father-and-son Alien "chestburster" victims. The town's (extremely roomy) sewers quickly become an Alien den, and the townsfolk begin disappearing. Monitoring the mounting calamity, a Predator leaves his home world for Earth in order to exterminate the Aliens and clean up the mess (he brings a handy blue goo that dissolves everything it touches, leaving no trace of Alien unpleasantness). But the situation has gotten out of hand, and Aliens, including the seemingly unstoppable Pred-Alien, overrun the town, reproducing faster than the Predator can hunt them down. A few locals (the sheriff, an ex-con, his younger brother, a just-returned female veteran, her young daughter, etc.) try to make it out alive after even the National Guard falls prey to the marauding monsters.

Like the first *AVP*, *AVPR* is really a Dangerous Alien Game by proxy, as the solitary Predator (the more expansive and better-produced *AVP* showcased *three*) comes to Earth not to hunt humans (like in the three straight Predator movies) but to eliminate Aliens. Still, at one point the Predator takes down an armed deputy in the woods, and then skins him and hangs his carcass from a tree like a trophy (old habits die hard?). Other than that, however, the warrior-hunter Predator sets his sights firmly on the Aliens, while the human ciphers passed off as protagonists scuttle about trying to stay out of harm's way or blasting at the Aliens themselves (with mixed results).

An unpleasant and eye-straining experience all the way around, the film was shot primarily at night, with the lighting frequently so dim that it becomes difficult to make out what (if anything) is happening. With the local power plant having been destroyed in yet another repetitive Predator-Alien battle, there's even *less* light for the drawn-out, rainy nighttime finale— so much so that the viewer frequently has little sense of *where* or *who* or even *what*. Veteran special effects artists Colin and Greg Strause made their feature directing debut with *AVPR*, and they manage to mishandle nearly every element, from the uneven pacing (too much time spent on fruitlessly trying to develop shallow, uninteresting characters) to the by-the-numbers acting (with future TV actors like Steven Pasquale [*Rescue Me*] and Sam Trammell [*True Blood*] trying to shoulder the load—and failing miserably) to the headache-inducing rapid-fire editing and disorienting, too-tight camerawork that often makes one *glad* the lighting is so poor. It all ends on a pointlessly nihilistic note that leaves a sour taste in the mouth.

Predator (1987; Twentieth Century–Fox) Director: John McTiernan; Producers: Lawrence Gordon, Joel Silver, John Davis; Screenplay: Jim Thomas, John Thomas. Cinematographer: Donald McAlpine. Cast: Arnold Schwarzenegger, Carl Weathers, Elpidia Carrillo, Bill Duke, Jesse Ventura, Sonny Landham, Richard Chaves, R. G. Armstrong, Shane Black, Kevin Peter Hall.

Filmed in eight weeks in the jungles of Mexico, this testosterone-filled sci-fi action film not only ushered in its own franchise (with four sequels to date), but the whole aliens-hunting-humans-for-sport sub-subgenre. (Note: Though *Without Warning* was released seven years earlier, it made little impact at the box office and went largely unnoticed by both the industry and the public at large.) *Predator*'s paper-thin plot has Army major Arnold Schwarzenegger and his elite rescue group dropped into the dense jungles of some unnamed Central American country ostensibly to rescue some hostages. But he's been duped, and he and his men are really there to take out a small army of rebels and derail plans for an invasion into a neighboring country — which they do via an explosion-filled, endless-supply-of-bullets firefight. But this is just the beginning, as soon his men, while making their way to the rendezvous point, are picked off one by one by *something* in the jungle. Said something turns out to be an alien come to hunt the Most Dangerous Game (in this case, Arnie and his armed-to-the-teeth platoon). Filled with clichéd caricatures (Native American tracker-type, Tobacco-spittin' good ol' boy soldier, duplicitous CIA operative, etc.), painful one-liners ("Stick around," deadpans Ah-nold after pinning a rebel to the wall with an oversized knife) and bulging biceps (When Arnie meets his "old friend" Dutch, played by Carl Weathers, they clasp hands and engage in an impromptu bit of arm-wrestling, with the camera worshipfully focused on their straining muscles), *Predator* is a macho action movie-lover's dream.

Nothing was easy for the cast and crew of this cinematic groundbreaker. Shooting consisted of "a lot of 19-hour days in 100-degree heat working with foreign crews whom you had to keep an eye on all the time," related director John McTiernan. "We were seldom on land that had less than a 45 degree angle and were constantly humping

Arnold Schwarzenegger is the prey for the *Predator*. Though not the first Dangerous Alien Game movie, it was popular enough to start its own franchise.

up and down big hills. We had to be cautious when clearing underbrush because of a cousin of the rattlesnake called the Two Step. They call it that because if it bites you, that's how many steps you take before you die."

The Predator itself is a marvel of makeup and imagination, with its ugly, crab-like visage and imposing frame (courtesy of seven-foot-two stuntman Kevin Peter Hall). Truly one of the most unique and imposing humanoid aliens seen on the screen, this "ugly motherfucker" (as Arnold dubs it) was actually a last-minute replacement monster. Richard Edlund (*Raiders of the Lost Ark, Ghost Busters, Fright Night*) was hired to build the first Predator monster. When it arrived in Mexico City, however, director McTiernan was less than pleased. "I turned to my assistant," related the filmmaker, "and said, 'Now we're in trouble.'" So McTiernan shut down production (he'd already shot all the non-monster scenes) while he searched for a new creature maker. And so Stan Winston (an Oscar winner for *Aliens*) ended up creating one of cinema's most memorable alien invaders.

Note: Predator stars not one but *two* future governors — professional wrestler-turned-actor Jesse Ventura became a one-term governor of Minnesota in 1998; while bodybuilder-turned-actor Arnold Schwarzeneggar went on to become governor of California in 2003.

With quotes from: "Predator vs. Schwarzenegger," by Marc Shapiro, *Fangoria* 65 (July 1987).

Predator 2 (1990; Twentieth Century–Fox) Director: Stephen Hopkins, Producers: Lawrence Gordon, Joel Silver, John Davis; Screenplay: Jim Thomas, John Thomas; Cinematographer: Peter Levy. Cast: Danny Glover, Gary Busey, Ruben Blades, Maria Conchita Alonso, Bill Paxton, Kevin Peter Hall.

This first sequel to the popular *Predator* (1987) has an alien hunter (again played by imposing seven-foot-two stuntman Kevin Peter Hall) eschew the previous film's literal jungle to venture into the metaphorical one of a violent Los Angeles (in the "future" of 1997), where drug lords and gangs battle with police in the streets during a scorching heat wave. First targeting the vicious gang members, the Predator ultimately sets his hunter's sights on LAPD cop Lt. Harrigan (Danny Glover) and his team, worthy prey for his trophy cabinet. Shadowing Harrigan's investigation is the mysterious federal agent Keyes (Gary Busey), who knows far more than he's telling.

Predator 2 does what a good action-movie sequel should by further exploring the key character (expanding upon its motivations by having this Predator spare a pregnant police officer, for instance, as well as giving it a whole new range of unique alien weaponry to wield); placing said character in a novel situation (an urban jungle rather than a leafy one); and upping the ante-action (by providing numerous explosive set-pieces and gruesome "kills," and taking the viewer inside the alien's weird ship for the grand finale). Like in the first film, however, the human characters are still drawn in the broadest of strokes (hard-headed police detective; smart-ass new kid partner; ethnic sidekick; sinister government "spook"), though Glover's dogged, Dirty Harry–like Lt. Hannigan (the name even *sounds* like Clint Eastwood's famous "Detective Callahan" from the *Dirty Harry* films) seems a bit more realistic and approachable than Schwarzenegger's steroid-monster commando from the first *Predator*. And Busey's sinister government operative remains far more dangerous-seeming than Carl Weathers' duplicitous "Dillon" from the earlier film. When Busey tells Harrigan, "He's on safari: lions, tigers, bears —*oh my* ... you're the lion; *this* is his jungle," the menacing glint in his eye warns that the alien may not be the only predator to watch out for.

The city setting brings this Dangerous Game to a milieu closer to most viewers' own. As the trailer ominously intones, "This time it's open season *on all of us.*" And the film takes us inside the alien hunter's ship — his lair — with its hellish, organic-looking interior infused with a hot orange light and layered with heat fog. More importantly, it includes a *trophy room*. This grotesque alcove features a variety of mounted skulls, with a number of strange alien craniums sprinkled among the human ones (including a head from *Alien*, presaging the eventual *Alien vs. Predator* crossover).

Twentieth Century–Fox wanted Arnold Schwarzenegger to reprise his role from the first movie, but the actor reportedly balked at the concept of taking the Predator out of the jungle and into the Big City, and chose to make *Terminator 2* instead. In his place, a script revision created the character of Keyes, the mysterious government agent familiar with the Predator. John Lithgow was director Stephen Hopkins' pick for the role, but producer Joel Silver pushed for Gary Busey (making his first film appearance after his near-fatal motorcycle accident in December 1988).

After tracking this Dangerous Alien only to become its prey, Busey went on to hunt humans himself in *Surviving the Game* (1994). Another *Predator 2* cast member, Calvin Lockhart (playing the creepy Jamaican drug lord "King Willy," who falls victim to the Predator), had conducted his own (Almost) Dangerous Game by hunting a *werewolf* for sport in *The Beast Must Die* (1974).

Costing $35 million, nearly twice the first *Predator*'s budget, *Predator 2* grossed $57 million worldwide, little more than *half* what the original made (making it the least financially successful of the five *Predator* films to date). This disappointing showing left the alien hunter-of-men in limbo for nearly a decade and a half until revived by the *Alien/Predator* crossover film *AVP* in 2004. Which is a pity, since *Predator 2* remains one of the more worthy action-film/monster movie follow-ups.

Predators (2010; Twentieth Century–Fox) Director: Nimrod Antal; Producers: Robert Rodriguez, John Davis, Elizabeth Avellan; Screenplay: Alex Litvak, Michael Finch; Cinematographer: Gyula Pados. Cast: Adrien Brody, Topher Grace, Alice Braga, Walton Goggins, Oleg Taktarov, Laurence Fishburne, Danny Trejo.

The most recent *Predator* film to date harkens back to its roots by setting up a group of soldiers and killers as the prey for the alien hunters known as the Predators. The difference this time: The prey are a diverse group of hardened "predators" themselves — from a Sierra Leone Death Squad commando to a Mexican cartel enforcer to a Black Ops–trained American mercenary to "the FBI's Most Wanted" — and the hunt takes place not on Earth but on an alien planet utilized as the Predators' game preserve. The movie opens with an adrenalin rush as Royce (Adrien Brody) awakens in freefall and frantically attempts to deploy what must be a parachute before he plummets to his death. Once on the ground, he finds six others who've similarly been forcibly parachuted in (along with their weapons of choice), and the hunt begins, with the small band stalked by a trio of Predators intent on adding them to their trophy case.

Producer Robert Rodriguez related how for this "direct sequel to *Predator*" (which ignores the two *AVP* entries) they "talked about having this most dangerous game aspect to it," and wanted to make the film "about the chase, about the hunt, and really making [the Predators] scary again. [Director Nimrod Antal] really wanted to bring this fear back into the movie." And that he does, recapturing the impact of the first *Predator* by focusing on the horrific tension and primal terror of people being stalked by a largely unseen hunter — a least for the sequel's riveting first hour. Unfortunately, it then runs out of steam somewhat, with the remainder taken up by interludes with a previous survivor, an encounter with a different kind of alien prey, and various overblown, explosive battles. Still, the production values remain high, the action swift and exciting, the characters better drawn than in most ensemble action films, and the acting first-rate, from the secondary figures of the always-entertaining Danny Trejo and the quirky, half-mad characterization delivered by Laurence Fishburne, right up to the intensity of Oscar-winner and star Adrien Brody, who cuts (and acts) a far more realistic figure than the standard Schwarzenegger clone.

Director Antal had strong feelings about the film's underlying themes. "The Predator, he's the hunter," said the filmmaker, "something that we've lost touch with. Our society now hunts for sport which is almost disgusting compared to eating, feeding yourself, clothing yourself and what hunting was originally supposed to be." Interestingly, the movie takes Connell's theme of duality (Rainsford as the other side of the Zaroff coin, and how the hunter becoming the prey ultimately affects his outlook) and makes it quite explicit. At one point a character concludes that they were all chosen "because *we* are the predators — just like them. We're the monsters of our own world. It's better that we're never going back." A further dialogue exchange raises other intriguing points:

> Isabelle: What made you so fucked up?
> Royce: There is no hunting like the hunting of a man. And those who have hunted armed men long enough — and like it — never really care for anything else thereafter.
> Isabelle (sarcastically): That's very poetic. Did you come up with that yourself?
> Royce: No, actually, that was Hemingway.

(The quote is indeed from a Hemingway short story, "On the Blue Water," first published in the April 1936 issue of *Esquire* magazine. The subsequent line reads: "You will meet them doing various things with resolve, but their interest rarely holds because after the other thing ordinary life is as flat as the taste of wine when the taste buds have been burned off your tongue.")

Predators also features what may very well be the ultimate trap sequence — in which the little band triggers a swinging log, multiple falling sharpened stakes, a spring-loaded wall of spikes, and a pit lined with skewers — all within the space of a few seconds. And like in Connell's story, these booby traps were laid by the prey (albeit an earlier victim whose body rests nearby). As one of them explains, "We triggered a dead man's trap.... This was his last stand." And as a Most Dangerous bonus, like Zaroff before them, the Predators employ hunting dogs for one sequence — or at least an alien facsimile thereof, as these bizarrely spiked and toothy monsters are something out of a hunter's nightmare. After narrowly escaping these horrific hounds (due solely to the Predators calling them to heel), Royce grimly states, "They sent the dogs in ... testing us," which leads to his initial conclusion that "this planet is a game preserve, and we're the game."

On a $40 million budget, *Predators* grossed $127 million worldwide, so perhaps these alien hunters-of-men are not done with us just yet...

With quotes from: "Video Interview: Nimrod Antal and Robert Rodriguez," July 9, 2010, *JoBlo.com*; JimmyO, "Predators Chat with Rodriguez and Antal," July 5, 2010, *iamrogue.com*.

Without Warning (1980; Filmways) Alternate Titles: *It Came Without Warning*; *The Warning* (UK video). Director/Producer: Greydon Clark; Screenplay: Lyn Freeman, Daniel Grodnik, Ben Nett, Steve Mathis; Cinematographer: Dean Cundy. Cast: Jack Palance, Martin Landau, Tarah Nutter, Christopher S. Nelson, Cameron Mitchell, Neville Brand, Sue Ane Langdon, Ralph Meeker, Larry Storch.

Without Warning holds the distinction of being the first alien-hunting-humans-for-sport film. It may also have indirectly inspired its far bigger (and better) brethren. In 1987, while doing a press tour for *Predator*, Arnold Schwarzenegger said, "Did you ever see a little picture called *Without Warning*? A hunter from outer space thing. Well, that's where we are coming from with *Predator*. Even got the same actor playing the monster [Kevin Peter Hall], except we have a production budget that lets us be more realistic."

Indeed. Filmed in three weeks on a tiny budget of $150,000 (with half of that going to its two biggest stars, Jack Palance and Martin Landau), *Without Warning* focuses on a group of teens and backwoods locals facing off against a (largely unseen) alien who kills its prey via pulsing, toothy, living frisbees that it throws through the air to embed tentacles in the skin of its victims. It turns out that the space visitor is a hunter out for sport, and its final prey (the lone surviving teen and a gruff local) must find a way to take down the invader at its lair.

Better than what one might expect from a filmmaker who cut his teeth working on Al Adamson films (*Satan's Sadists, Hell's Bloody Devils, Dracula vs. Frankenstein*) before branching out to make his own low-budget exploitationers (including the outrageous *Black Shampoo* and the fabulously-named *Satan's Cheerleaders*), *Without Warning* impresses for three reasons:

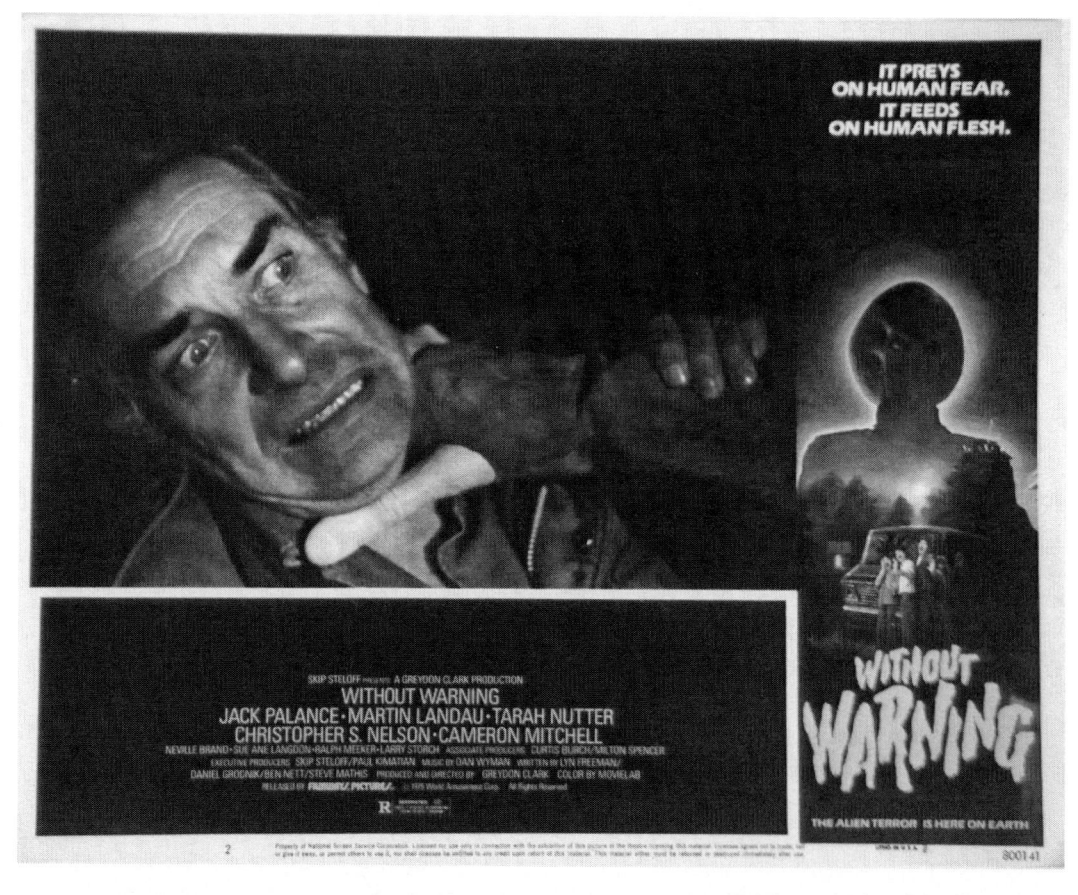

As the unhinged "Sarge," Martin Landau comes face to face with the alien hunter-of-men in *Without Warning*—which is more than can be said for the viewer, as said alien stays off-screen for nearly the entire film (lobby card).

18. Dangerous Alien Games

its cast of Hollywood veterans, the often engaging and atmospheric cinematography, and those grotesque little flying sucker-monsters.

The most striking thing about this low-budget monster flick is its collection of classic players. Cameron Mitchell, Neville Brand, Ralph Meeker and Larry Storch all appear only briefly, but they each make a welcome impression. Leads Jack Palance (as the menacing human hunter who opposes the alien one) and Martin Landau (as the shell-shocked veteran "Sarge," whose paranoia makes him nearly as dangerous as the alien) not only chew the scenery, they devour the local fauna, the cast, and probably even the crew. But their professionalism and charisma shine through the over-the-top playing to bring their characters to enjoyably vibrant life. Palance, in particular, stamps his dangerous edginess on the role of local hunter Taylor. When the two surviving teens ask him to leave his gun with them for protection while he checks out the shack where the alien stores its victims' bodies, Palance just smiles and creepily shines his flashlight up into his own face as he answers, "I ain't the crazy one, remember?" Given his shark-tooth grin and the disturbing glint in his eye, this claim seems dubious at best.

Producer/director Greydon Clark had nothing but respect for his big-name stars, particularly Palance. "I remember going into Jack's trailer," recalled Clark, "and when I walked in he was there working on his scene, working on his character. I looked at his script ... and he had literally pages full of notes on his character. I though, 'My God, here this guy has been a movie star for at least 30 years, and here he is a complete professional, working for me for probably ten percent of what he would get on a normal picture, and really caring about the picture." Of course, Clark may have had a little *too* much respect for his star, as Taylor's climactic charge at the invader while he repeatedly shouts "Alien, alien, alien!" at the top of his lungs borders on high camp.

With cinematographer Dean Cundy (*Halloween, Jurassic Park, Apollo 13*) on board, *Without Warning* at least *looks* good. Filming primarily out of doors and at night ("in the outskirts of the L.A. area at what's known as the Paramount Ranch," recounted Clark), Cundy offers not only some involving fluid camera movement (indicating the alien's malevolent presence) but some otherworldly and atmospheric bluish lighting for the woodland settings.

Another plus is the novel flying-omelets-with-teeth that zip out of the woods to gorily burrow their tentacles into tender flesh. Designed by special effects wiz (and future Oscar-winner) Greg Cannom, they pulsate, gnash their sharp incisors, and ooze grotesquely when cut with a knife. Amazingly, these innovative deadly starfish weren't even in the original screenplay. "When I got involved it was a different script with different elements," recalled Clark. "Then I changed it to add the live creature, frisbee type things that the guy throws at his prey [the original script had the alien hunting with a mundane bow-and-arrow]. I'm familiar with "The Most Dangerous Game," and I would assume the writers read it, but that would be an assumption on my part."

Speaking of the Most Dangerous Game, the subject of hunting comes up fairly early on, when the teens stop at Taylor's back-road filling station. There, in his office festooned with taxidermy trophies, Taylor notices one of the kids' disdain and defends his "sport" in this Rainsford-esque exchange.

> Taylor: You never been hunting before.
> Sandy: No, and I don't plan to start.
> Taylor: Oh, good sport! As long as you follow the rules.
> Sandy: I could never kill an animal.

>Taylor: Depends on the animal and who's doing the hunting. Besides, I eat what I kill. And the sport is in the hunting and tracking, not in the kill.

Unfortunately, *Without Warning* fails in several other (critical) respects — namely, script, pacing and a dearth of alien involvement. The MDG angle is so poorly realized in the script that the hunting-for-sport concept only arises via some strained dialogue (rather than through any alien action). It takes Taylor's periodic suppositions to explain that this extraterrestrial isn't just killing people, it's hunting them for pleasure. "That alien," Taylor theorizes, "he came down here for sport. He wants to pick up a few trophies. And you know what — right now we are the prize game." But there's no real evidence of that, and it's by no means obvious the creature hunts for sport (we haven't even *seen* the alien up to this point — 80 minutes into the film!). Yes, the creature stores its victims' bodies in an old shack, but Taylor had earlier intimated that it kills to *eat*. "This is where the hunter keeps his food," Taylor states, indicating the shack. "Sooner or later he's gotta come back for the bodies. And we'll be waitin'." Consequently, the "sport" aspect of this alien hunter remains a very confused and contrived matter.

Much of the film focuses on the various victims wandering through the woods (or later fleeing through same) to provide targets for the living pinwheel critters. Scene after scene featuring everything from bickering father-and-son hunters to an annoying boy scout troupe, to a quartet of turgid teens driving to the local swimming hole keeps the excitement as sparse as an E.T. sighting. And the time-filling sequence in which the two surviving protagonists take shelter in a woodland house, where they slowly explore the empty structure, change clothes, make coffee, and finally tuck into bed puts the brakes on whatever momentum had built to this point. Granted, the vapid vignette ends with a startling visual shock (stolen from ... er, "inspired by" Hitchcock's *Psycho*) and our first blink-and-you'll-miss-it glimpse of the alien, but it's too little and too late.

More importantly, why make a movie about an alien hunter and never show the alien actually hunting? Nearly 8 feet tall (courtesy of seven-foot-two monster actor Kevin Peter Hall), with a bulbous blue head, angry features and long, webbed fingers, this extraterrestrial looks like it just stepped off an original *Star Trek* set (albeit from one of the better episodes). Perhaps that's why the alien appears in only two scenes, and then simply stands in both, doing nothing more than glaring and tossing a bio-frisbee critter. All the stalking (or "hunting," as Taylor assumes) is implied, suggested by nothing more than a mobile camera and the occasional shadow. And there's no spaceship, either, with the creature storing his "trophies" in a tiny wooden shack labeled "Water Department"! This alien obviously hails from a planet in the galaxy of Missed Opportunities.

Without Warning was very nearly titled *Without Release*. "When I finished that picture," recounted Clark, "we made a deal with [American International Pictures] to distribute it. Literally within less than a month, AIP was sold to Flimways, and the first thing Filmways did after they bought AIP was announce they weren't going to release any more pictures like AIP pictures. I always thought that was amazing. They bought AIP, then turned around and said negative things about AIP!...

"We had to threaten to sue, I guess it was Orion by that time. When we made the picture, we made a deal with HBO for the picture to be shown after a theatrical release, and in the HBO contract it required a certain number of theaters that it had to play around the United States to validate the contract. When AIP was sold and the new owners didn't want to release any AIP-type product, I had to have my attorney threaten to sue them to force them to release the picture."

Upon its eventual release, the *New York Times* labeled it "wretched." While that may be going a bit too far (*Without Warning* has its points — and even a few fans), it could have been so much more. But at least it planted the seed that grew into the far superior *Predator* franchise. Even Greydon Clark agrees, admitting, "*Predator* is a wonderful film."

With quotes from: "High Concepts, Low Budgets: An Interview with Director Greydon Clark," by Brian Albright, *Shock Cinema* 29 (2005); "Late Night Classics — *Without Warning*," by Jason Bene, *Killer Film.com*.

19

Television Games

Here you'll find those television programs that feature a people-hunting-people story in at least one of their episodes. With so many series conducting their own dangerous games, only those episodes that truly adhere to Connell's concept of hunting humans for *sport* are included. (Note: I do also include several series that feature *non*-human, sentient beings as either hunter or prey, since, despite their alien or robotic characters, the underlying concept — and sentiments — remain intact.) Such variations as *The Outer Limits*' "Fun and Games" (in which an alien race pits two humans against two aliens for their own amusement) or *Combat!*'s "The Hunter" (in which a Nazi stalks the protagonist through a ruined winery, bent on revenge) didn't qualify for inclusion. With the world of TV series being so vast, no doubt some episodes have slipped past my purview. I apologize for the inevitable omissions and welcome any suggestions sent via the publisher. In any case, the following are the Most Dangerous television episodes I've found and confirmed.

Airwolf (9/22/1984) "Sweet Britches," Season 2, Episode 1. Creator: David P. Bellsario; Director: Alan J. Levi; Teleplay: David P. Bellsario. Cast: Jan-Michael Vincent, Alex Cord, Jean Bruce Scott, Ernest Borgnine. Guest Stars: Lance Le Gault, Jeff Mackay, Guich Koock, Robert Pierce, James Whitmore, Jr.

Lasting three seasons (1984–87), *Airwolf* follows the adventures of handsome renegade pilot Stringfellow Hawk (Jan-Michael Vincent) and his mechanic sidekick Dominic (Academy Award-winner Ernest Borgnine, largely wasted in a comedy relief role) who go on missions for a secret government agency in the most advanced high-tech battle helicopter in the world, dubbed "Airwolf."

In the season two opener, String and Dom set out to investigate the disappearance of a friend who was being held in a small-town Texas jail. There String runs afoul of the brutal Sheriff Bogan (Lance Le Gault), who's in cahoots with Sam Houston (James Whitmore, Jr., son of veteran character actor James Whitmore), owner of the nearby "African Hunt Club Ranch," an 80,000-acre, fenced-in desert hunting ground stocked with lions, cheetahs and ocelots. When Houston's high-paying hunter clients desire something a little more ... "special," Sheriff Bogan supplies Houston with human prey from his own jail (hitchhikers and drifters he arrests for this very purpose). In trying to help an attractive Texas Highway Patrol chopper pilot investigating the corrupt Sheriff's activities, String ends up as the prey for Houston's latest client.

"Anybody who hunts those beautiful lions ought to be hunted themselves," protests the perky deputy, foreshadowing not only the human hunting about to take place, but the ultimate fate of the greedy mastermind of same, Sam Houston (who charges his clients "$100,000 for a special hunt"). After his jeep is wrecked by String and Dom in the Airwolf, Houston ends up stalked and eaten by the very lions he imports for sport hunting (at least that's the intimation, since, this being Reagan-era television, we're forced to simply *imagine* the villain's fate). While this ending offers some satisfying poetic justice, the human-hunting sequence itself remains woefully inadequate. The hunt, in which Houston guides his client through the desert (in a jeep garishly painted with *zebra stripes*, no less) in pursuit of the fleeing String, lasts a mere two minutes. After a few shots of the sweat-soaked String running for his life, the hunter fires a few rounds from the jeep and misses, allowing String to disappear around an arroyo bend. The next thing we know, the Airwolf rises up over a hill (Dom having picked up String, apparently) and flips the hunters' jeep, killing the client and stranding Houston — just as the hungry lions show up. Both the (nameless) hunter and Houston remain woefully undeveloped, with most of the villainous action taken up by the sadistic Sheriff, so the hunting-humans-for-sport issue rather falls by the wayside.

For an action-adventure series of the time, *Airwolf* sports some impressive production values and stunts, mostly involving the incredible helicopter (kept in a Batcave-like hollowed-out mesa), which in this episode not only knocks over trucks and jeeps from the air, but impressively blasts an entire building to smithereens. Of course, this being 1984, one must also put up with the audio assault of horrible wall-to-wall synthesizer music, something par for the course in the mid–1980s.

Making $250,000 a week for *Airwolf*, Jan-Michael Vincent was at the height of his popularity. Unfortunately, it was all downhill from here for the former Hollywood golden boy (who starred alongside the likes of John Wayne, Robert Mitchum and Charles Bronson), as Vincent spiraled into a morass of alcohol, drugs and domestic violence, serving time in various treatment programs and even jail. After *Airwolf* ended in 1987, Vincent found work in low-budget exploitation flicks for the likes of David DeCoteau (*Deadly Embrace*, 1989) and Fred Olen Ray (*Alienator* and *Haunting Fear*, both 1990), where he'd show up and say his lines (more or less) for anyone who'd pay his $150,000 fee. A near-fatal car accident in 1995 resulted in a broken neck and a partially-ruined voice. Vincent hasn't made a film since 2004 due to health and personal issues.

Jan-Michael Vincent's hefty paycheck aside, the *real* star of *Airwolf* is the sleek, futuristic "Supercopter" (the series' name in France and Italy), looking magnificent and menacing as it threateningly hovers just feet above the ground or zooms through the skies at impossible speeds, guns blazing. After the series was canceled, the "Airwolf" 'copter (actually a Bell 222) was bought by a German company who transformed it into an air ambulance. In 1992 it crashed during a storm, killing three crew members.

American Dad! (9/30/2007) "The Vacation Goo," Season 3, Episode 1. Creator: Seth MacFarlane; Director: Albert Calleros; Teleplay: Josh Bycel, Jonathan Fener. Cast (voices): Seth MacFarlane, Wendy Schaal, Scott Grimes, Rachael MacFarlane, Dee Bradley Baker.

Irreverence oozes like satirical sweat from the pores of this prime-time cartoon skewering the American nuclear family, whose characters include a talking goldfish with the personality of a German athlete and a live-in bulbous-headed alien with aspirations to be "the greatest actor of all time" (at least in *this* episode). The titular right-wing American Dad, Stan Smith, works at the CIA, keeping America safe (though not necessarily sane) for his wife Francine and two teen kids, Haley and Steve.

In the season three opener, "The Vacation Goo," family-focused Francine discovers that all their prior family vacations have been artificial experiences programmed and generated by Stan via some green goo-filled tanks he borrows each year from the CIA so that he can escape to his own perfect vacation — watching football *away* from his family. With the gooey cat out of the bag, Francine demands a *real* family getaway, but when things seem to be going too well, she naturally assumes it's another goo-inspired illusion and jumps off their cruise ship, landing the whole family on a tropical island. There they encounter a psychotic-looking trio who hunt the Smiths for sport ("Ok, here's the deal — they're going to hunt us," Stan informs the rest after returning from the mansion they stumble upon), leading to some family bonding over "long pig" and a clever conclusion.

The hunting-humans-for-sport angle only comes into play toward the very end of the episode and then lasts no more than a minute before a rock slide traps the Smiths in a cave. When the hunters break through the barrier, they shoot all four family members, blood splattering everywhere. But wait, it's not hemoglobin but *paint*, as the hunters are merely extreme paintballers. "No one dies at 'Jimmy Buffet's Most Dangerous Game Family Resort,'" the hunters reassure the astonished (and relieved) Smiths. Brilliant.

Archer (1/26/2012) "El Contador," Season 3, Episode 5. Creator/Teleplay: Adam Reed. Cast (voices): H. Jon Benjamin, Judy Greer, Amber Nash, Chris Parnell, Aisha Tyler, Jessica Walter.

In this decidedly adult animated series (how many cartoons come with "nudity" warnings?), the secret spy organization ISIS does its best to win government contracts and keep afloat in today's modern world, despite its chaotic cast of characters, including the hard-drinking harridan of a head honcho, Mallory Archer; the organization's crass and callow lead field agent (and Mallory's son), Sterling Archer; and various insubordinate subordinates.

A brilliant, scathingly funny riff on everything from James Bond movies to modern-day pirates, *Archer* sets its acerbic sights on "The Most Dangerous Game" with the episode

In the brilliant, adult-oriented satirical spy series *Archer*, Lana (voiced by Aisha Tyler) and Archer (H. Jon Benjamin) become human prey in the season three episode "El Contador."

titled "El Contador." In it, Sterling, his partner Lana, and the newly-minted field agent Cyril (formerly the company's accountant) head to a Central American jungle to take down a drug lord, Calzado, with a million-dollar bounty on his head. When Calzado captures Sterling and Lana instead, he places them in cages next to a host of animals at his jungle compound. They're not in some private zoo, however, but in a private game preserve; Calzado is a hunter who intends to hunt the two agents as "the Most Dangerous Game." To hammer home his point, Calzado coolly takes aim and shoots a caged tiger in the head right before his startled captives' dismayed eyes. Meanwhile, Cyril, who had become separated from his companions in the jungle when he went off to "do his business," passes himself off as a famous criminal accountant ("El Contador") and convinces Calzado to let him partake in the hunt the following morning. During said hunt Cyril manages to aid Lana, and the two interrupt Calzado just as he's about to shoot Sterling, who was baited into a trap by a bottle of booze and now hangs upside-down from a tree.

As a parody of Connell's famous story/concept, "El Contador" gets to the heart of the matter without too much bother about characterization or motivation, and offers only a brief climactic hunt. But it does so with genuine wit, as Sterling appears to go hilariously over the top in his endeavors to evade his hunter (donning a homemade hat of palm leaves, for instance). And it offers a clever twist on the tale by having the hero fall into a trap set by the *hunter*, rather than the other way around. Using a bottle of hooch for bait is just the amusing icing on the comical cake.

Bonanza (1/16/73) "The Hunter," Season 14, Episode 15. Director/Teleplay: Michael Landon. Cast: Lorne Greene, Michael Landon, David Canary. Guest Star: Tom Skerritt.

In the 430th and final episode of the epic Western television series about the Cartwright family, deranged Corporal Bill Tanner (Tom Skerritt) escapes from the Wheaton Asylum, where he was imprisoned for killing women and children. After several more murders he encounters Joe Cartwright (Michael Landon), journeying to Fort Bragg on business for the Ponderosa Ranch. Joe offers Tanner some supper, and the two men engage in an argument about man killing for sport. Suffering from flashbacks and delusions, Tanner decides to make Joe his "prey" the next day, giving him a four-hour head start and then hunting him like an animal. Joe does all he can to throw the madman off his trail, and even wounds him with a sharpened snare trap, but the obsessed Tanner keeps coming, finally cornering Joe in a ghost town. There Joe turns the tables and traps Tanner in the abandoned jail, leading to the insane hunter's death by heart attack as he imagines himself back in the asylum.

Note: This episode was unavailable for viewing by the author.

Buffy the Vampire Slayer (11/3/1998) "Homecoming," Season 3, Episode 5. Creator: Joss Whedon; Director/Teleplay: David Greenwalt. Cast: Sarah Michelle Geller, Nicholas Brendon, Alyson Hannigan, Charisma Carpenter, David Boreanaz, Seth Green, Anthony Stewart Head. Guest Stars: K. Todd Freeman, Jeremy Ratchford, Fab Filippo, Ian Abercrombie, Harry Groener, Eliza Dushku.

A hugely entertaining, clever and popular series (spawning fan clubs, magazines, books, and even a spin-off show, *Angel*) laced with wit and teenage angst, *Buffy the Vampire Slayer* posits a world in which a high school cheerleader becomes "the Slayer," a young girl with superhuman strength charged with protecting humanity from the very real supernatural menaces among us. Buffy (Sarah Michelle Geller), with the help of her friends, and guidance from her adult "Watcher" posing as the school librarian (Anthony Stewart Head), must battle all manner of vampires, demons and dark forces in the town of Sunnydale, California, which just happens to rest on the "Hellmouth."

In the show's third season (of seven), Buffy runs afoul of Connell's concept with "Homecoming"—but with a twist that cleverly slots the hunting-humans-for-sport notion into the Buffyverse. Set up by the dynamically evil vampire Mr. Trick (K. Todd Freeman) is "SlayerFest '98," a hunting expedition for vampires, demons and even humans who want to bag a Slayer. To this end, Mr. Trick arranges for Buffy to be hunted by the likes of a rifle-toting, bear trap-laying hillbilly; a trailer-trash vampire couple; a pair of German psycho brothers sporting high-tech weaponry; and a spiky-headed demon who throws organic knives taken from his own forearms—all on prom night. Circumstances throw the self-centered Cordelia (Charisma Carpenter), Buffy's rival for the title of Homecoming Queen, into the mix as well. Can they elude their deadly hunters, keep their makeup intact, and still make it to the dance on time?

Not one of the series' stellar episodes (of which there *were* plenty), "Homecoming" spends far too much time on Buffy's insecurities and self-pity, as she's dumped by her boyfriend and feels "invisible" at school (which spurs her to campaign for Homecoming Queen, upon which the episode dwells far too long). When the hunt finally arrives ("from the beginning of this tape," explains a video message from Mr. Trick, "you have exactly 30 seconds to run for your lives"), it turns out to be not much of a hunt after all. After avoiding a bear trap and disabling the hillbilly hunter, Buffy and Cordelia hole up in a woodland shack where they fend off and defeat the demon, then retreat to the school library (where Buffy keeps her weapons stash). There they destroy the vampire couple before Buffy cleverly takes down the two Germans in the school hallways.

But true to form, the episode ends on an amusingly ironic high note. Making it back to the dance just in time for the Homecoming Queen announcement, the battered and dirty Buffy and Cordelia (one friend asks if they've been mud wrestling) learns that the contest has ended in a tie—between the two *other* girls who were in the running.

Challenge of the Superfriends (11/4/1978) "Revenge on Gorilla City," Season 1, Episode 9. Directors: Ray Patterson, Carl Urbano; Teleplay: Jeffrey Scott. Cast (voices): Ted Cassidy, Danny Dark, Shannon Farnon, Ruth Forman, Stan Jones, Casey Kasem, Vic Perrin, Stanley Ralph Ross, Olan Soule, Frank Welker, William Woodson.

This Hanna-Barbera superhero cartoon series, which lasted two seasons (for a total of 32 episodes in 1978–79), details the battles between the Justice League of America (Superman, Wonder Woman, Batman, et al.) and the Legion of Doom ("thirteen of the most sinister villains of all time"): "This is the Challenge of the Superfriends," announces the opening narration.

In "Revenge on Gorilla City," the villainous outcast ape Grod utilizes his fellow Legion member Brainiac's "Brainwave Device" to take over the minds of all those in Gorilla City ("an incredible city of advanced super-apes resting peacefully behind the protection of an invisible force field" in Africa). The Legion intends to use the apes to conquer the continent and then the world. The leader of Gorilla City escapes the mind control and alerts the Superfriends, with Batman, Robin, the Flash, and Apache Chief (whose power is to grow gigantic) responding (the rest of the superheroes are away on another mission). At Gorilla City, however, Lex Luthor exposes the quartet to a "power neutralizer" that negates their superpowers. "And now," pronounces Grod, "you'll be given five minutes head start to run free into the jungle. Then we shall hunt you down like animals—for the sport of it." Sinestro and Giganta lead a troupe of mind-controlled gorillas into the jungle after the powerless Superfriends. Though Apache Chief tells his companions, "I still have my Indian tracking abilities—they should help us elude the Legion of Doom," the hunters quickly capture their prey, tie them to a wooden cart, and send them rolling towards a cliff. Only the last-second intervention of the ape leader hiding nearby saves them. "Our only chance for survival is to circle around to Gorilla City and get our powers back," says Batman. This they do, and the Superfriends shut off the mind control device and save the day once again.

With its simplistic stories, stiff characters, poor animation, and wall-to-wall musical bombast, *Challenge of the Superfriends* remains a difficult proposition to sit through for anyone beyond their first decade of life. This episode turns the Most Dangerous Game subplot into little more than a minor incident, spending only a couple of minutes on the hunt, and offering nothing in the way of motivation for the hunters (apart from Grod's solitary line about hunting the Superfriends down "for the sport of it"). No traps are set, and the prey are captured almost immediately. Disappointingly, these Superfriends offer very little "Challenge" after all—and the same could be said for the entire unfortunate series.

Charlie's Angels (12/5/1979) "Angel Hunt," Season 4, Episode 11. Creators: Ivan Goff, Ben Roberts; Director: Paul Stanley; Teleplay: Lee Sheldon. Cast: Jaclyn Smith, Cheryl Ladd, Shelley Hack, David Doyle. Guest Stars: Lloyd Bochner, L.Q. Jones, Paul Sylvan.

This was the show that made Farrah Fawcett the fantasy of nearly every teenage boy in America during the mid–1970s, with *Charlie's Angels* becoming the most popular series on the airwaves. Her famous and iconic bathing-suit poster went up on more walls (this author's included) than any other poster before or since (with a staggering eight million sold). Fawcett, who was married to fellow TV star Lee Majors (*The Six Million Dollar Man*), only stayed with the series for its first year, leaving Cheryl Ladd to take up her tousled blond hairdo. Still, Farrah became forever linked with this sexy series about a private investigation agency run by the heard-but-never-seen Charles Townsend and his three gorgeous former policewomen operatives. By Season Four, another of the original Angels had departed, with Kate Jackson replaced by Shelley Hack, so by the time the series got around to staging its Most Dangerous Game variation, the only original Angel left was Jacqueline Smith.

In "Angel Hunt," Malcolm Case (Lloyd Bochner), a big-game hunter with a grudge against Charlie (Charlie's testimony sent Case to prison 11 years earlier), escapes and lures the three Angels to his family's private island off the coast of Mazatlan, which is stocked with big cats as a "Wild Animal Preserve." He then contacts Charlie, telling him, "I want your head on my trophy room wall. And in order to assure that you'll come to me I've taken three of the people that you care most about." If Charlie doesn't come, Case will "hunt down and kill" the Angels, one per day. As Charlie and his assistant Bosley (David Doyle) scramble to find Case, the madman, along with his two henchmen, begins his hunt. After Tiffany (Shelley Hack) is knocked into a river and presumed drowned, the remaining two Angels set a deadfall trap, which kills one of the henchmen. Tiffany isn't dead after all, but is taken prisoner by Case's other accomplice. The Angels take him out by one luring him down a path and the other swinging from a vine to knock him flat; while Case himself, blindly pursuing the Angels, is attacked by a tiger before he can bring his rifle into play. They find and release Tiffany, and all's well that ends well for these most beautiful game.

MDG-wise, the episode's antagonist, Case, receives little back story or characterization, other than Charlie labeling him "mad" (confirmed by his wide-eyed stare and its maniacal glint). Though a big-game hunter, he's no Zaroff, with his motivation muddled by simple revenge. Still, though he traps the Angels on his island in order to lure Charlie to him, he obviously relishes the "Angel hunt" (he could have simply held them hostage), and excitedly talks of tracking them down for "good sport." And just like in Connell's story, the protagonist(s) set a "Malay man-catcher" trap (which works perfectly to take down one of Case's underlings). Unfortunately, the hunt generates little suspense as it stumbles along to its foregone conclusion, and much of the episode is taken up with the Angels walking around trying to figure out what's going on, building a fire, discovering the scary jungle noises are made by peacocks(!), and reassuring each other with pained smiles and banal dialogue. Far from the series' best episodes, entries like "Angel Hunt" makes one wonder how *Charlie's Angels* remained so popular for so long (five years). But it was the late 1970s, a time of bad hair, bad fashion, bad dancing—and bad television, and *Charlie's Angels* fit the bill perfectly.

That said, "Angel Hunt" is not without its charms, most of them accidental. Though realism was never this lightweight show's forte, "Angel Hunt" turns amusingly absurd in the fact that even after their third day in the jungle without any resources whatsoever (not even their purses), the Angels' hair, makeup and clothes remain absolutely perfect, with nary a smudge to mar their spotless good looks. Even Tiffany looks like she just stepped out of the hairdresser's (or makeup trailer) rather than having been swept downstream to wake up on a sandbank. Such is the amazing world of *Charlie's Angels*...

Cold Case (11/28/2004) "Mind Hunters," Season 2, Episode 9. Creator: Meredith Steihm; Director: Keven Bray; Teleplay: Veena Sud. Cast: Kathryn Morris, DannyPino, John Finn, Jeremy Ratchford, Thom Barry. Guest Stars: John Billingsley.

Lasting seven seasons (from 2003 to 2010), this police procedural show focused on a special division of the Philadelphia PD that investigates "cold cases" (those no longer actively pursued by the department), generally on the appearance of new evidence. In "Mind Hunters," the headless body of a woman who disappeared in 1985 is uncovered in a wilderness preserve. Soon another eight headless female corpses are found nearby, and detective Lily Rush (Kathryn Morris) and her team investigate, learning that these were all victims of a serial killer who "hunts them for hours in the woods, shoots them before dawn, then takes their heads." Deducing that the killer had impersonated a police officer and could only be someone with access to confidential police reports (all of the women were violent crime survivors who fought off their attackers), the team focuses on their own department's reclusive records-keeper, George Marks (John Billingsley). But with no physical evidence linking Marks to the crimes (a search of his home turned up nothing, as "he even wiped his own house" clean), and despite disturbing hints dropped by the self-assured (and very strange) Marks during a series of interrogations, they cannot break him down and have to let him walk, making this one of the few episodes in this—or any—police investigation series in which the perpetrator gets away. "I think I might do some traveling," says Marks as a parting shot, adding ominously, "Beautiful country we live in, lots of empty woods."

Due to the show's very nature, most of the episode details the detectives' investigation and interrogations, limiting the "hunt" scenes to a few brief flashback snippets of underwear-clad women stumbling through the woods at night, and close-ups of terrified victims staring down a rifle barrel. But the evidence gathering, eyewitness flashbacks, and clever deductions paint a fascinating picture of police procedure as the team pieces together details of the crimes, leading inexorably to their suspect. And the subsequent questionings (each and every member takes a crack at the talkative yet clever Marks) lead to some illuminating (and disquieting) exchanges. For instance, when a frustrated Rush heatedly demands, "Tell me who you are in the woods!" Marks responds quietly, almost rapturously, "God." Another revelation comes when a detective asks Marks if he hunts animals, and the suspect scoffs, "Chasing dumb animals in the woods—no challenge," reflecting both Zaroff's boredom with "regular" hunting and Marks' targeting of "battle-tested" crime survivors. Besides the unusual open ending of the episode, "Mind Hunters" also leaves the viewer with the obvious question (one voiced by Rush herself at one point) of "What has he done with the heads?" (i.e. does this modern-day Zaroff have his very own trophy room hidden somewhere?).

Note: George Marks returned a few months later in the same season (episode 23, "The Woods"). And indeed, his trophies—nine buried human skulls lined up in a row—were uncovered in the backyard of his childhood home, staring sightlessly up at the house where his mother had been murdered when he was 12 years old. But this follow-up episode focuses on Marks' obsession with Detective Lily Rush ("I know you, Lily, everything about you," he tells her in his best Hannibal Lecter manner) rather than his hunting of humans. He admits, "Hunting has become a tedious game since I met you, Lily." Instead, it's all about what happened the night of his mother's murder, as the story unravels bit by bit to reveal a scared, disturbed little boy who became a monster.

Criminal Minds (5/2/2007) "Open Season," Season 2, Episode 21. Creator: Jeff Davis; Director: Felix Alcala; Teleplay: Debra J. Fisher, Erica Messer. Cast: Mandy Patinkin, Thomas Gibson, Paget Brewster, Shemar Moore, Matthew Gray Gubler, A.J. Cook, Kirsten Vangsness. Guest Stars: Laura Allen, Jim Parrack, Jake Richardson, Kelly Overton, Larry Sullivan.

Criminal Minds centers on the activities of the FBI's elite BAU (Behavioral Analysis Unit) group, who travel around the country investigating particularly heinous killings or serial murders. In "Open Season," the BAU journey to Idaho when bodies of several missing persons turn up in the Boise National Forest. There they discover that two brothers have been abducting victims and releasing them into the woods where they hunt them for sport with compression bows.

"One man's wilderness is another man's theme park," quotes one of the team members at the episode's beginning. Indeed, these two young men, reclusive brothers raised by a "psychotic uncle" who taught them to hunt and "how and who to kill," see the Idaho wilderness as their own private hunting grounds, with people as their prey. While the brothers' motivation for turning to the Most Dangerous Game remains disappointingly sketchy (as do their characterizations in general), the episode features a resourceful (female) protagonist who does more than just run blindly (at one point she even lays in wait and then leaps from a tree to take her pursuer unawares). It makes for a fairly suspenseful "hunt," and the episode concludes with a decidedly *anti*-hunting coda, as, on the flight back to Virginia, one of the team members intones, "British historian James Anthony Frood once said, 'Wild animals never kill for sport. Man is the only one to whom the torture and death of his fellow creatures is amusing in itself.'"

Criminal Minds (11/3/2010) "Middle Man," Series 6, Episode 7. Creator: Jeff Davis; Director: Robe Spera; Teleplay: Rick Dunkle. Cast: Joe Mantegna, Paget Brewster, Shemar Moore, Matthew Gray Gubler, Kirsten Vangsness, Thomas Gibson. Guest Stars: Robert Newman, Michael Grant Terry, Steve Talley, Jake Thomas, Cherilyn Wilson, Grant Albrecht.

One of the few series to go to the Most Dangerous well a second time, *Criminal Minds* follows the activities of the FBI's Behavioral Analysis Unit (BAU). The sixth-season episode "Middle Man" sees the BAU investigating the murders of exotic dancers in an Indiana farming community. "It is harvest season in Indiana," explains one team member, "and farmers are finding more than corn in their fields." It seems a trio of young men have formed a "pack" in order to abduct strippers, rape them, set them loose in a cornfield at night, hunt them down for fun, and then kill them.

Though less straightforward in its Most Dangerous Game concept than the series' season two episode "Open Season," "Middle Man" (referring to the middle member of the three-man pack, the alpha's "lieutenant" and focus of the story) touches on the hunting-humans-for-sport concept with the agents commenting, "They let them go so they can chase them again," and, "The hunt could be what gets them off." In truth, though, it is the "alpha" leader of the pack who truly drives this "sport"—as he is the one killing the girls, unbeknownst to his two followers. When the lowest member on the totem pole learns of their previous victims' deaths, he protests, "Chase 'em around, have some fun with them—they won't remember [because they've been drugged]. That's what you told me!" As the head of the BAU team tells the local sheriff, "Don't underestimate a pack leader's influence. Each member of the pack is being manipulated into playing his game."

Most of the episode focuses on the "pack" dynamics and how it unravels during the investigation as the FBI tightens their net. The only "hunt" shown comes at the episode's beginning, when a terrified woman runs through a cornfield at night, chased by three men sporting burlap sack hoods in a monstrous pickup festooned with lights. When they finally nab her, one takes her off into the corn to "have some fun." These hunters-of-humans don't brandish weapons; instead, they simply release their female prey into the cornfields, run them down and then have their way with them (with the alpha leader then surreptitiously making the kill).

CSI: Miami (3/13/2011) "Hunting Ground," Season 9, Episode 16. Creators: Anthony E. Zucker, Ann Donahue, Carol Mendelsohn; Director/Teleplay: Adam Rodriguez. Cast: David Caruso, Emily Procter, Jonathan Togo, Rex Linn, Eva LaRue, Omar Miller, Adam Rodriguez. Guest Stars: Jamie Hector, Christian Clemenson, Neil Hopkins.

The immense popularity of the crime drama *CSI: Crime Scene Investigation* (2000–) resulted in not one but *two* successful spin-off series, *CSI: New York* and *CSI: Miami*, the latter focusing on the workings of the Miami-Dade, Florida, police Crime Scene Investigations unit, headed by Lt. Horatio Caine (David Caruso).

In "Hunting Ground," Caine discovers the body of an illegal Cuban immigrant in the Everglades, pinned to a tree with a big-game hunting arrow—as well as another illegal immigrant, Jean (Jamie Hector), who's alive but too fearful to talk. Evidence around the crime scene leads team member Natalia (Eva LaRue) to conclude, "There's humans hunting humans—this is crazy!" Indeed. Finally winning Jean's confidence, Caine learns that someone is importing illegals and then using them as human prey. "We were sold as slaves to be hunted and killed," reveals Jean.

For this episode, the show's producers (of which there are over a *dozen* credited!) handed both the writing and directing chores to longtime series regular Adam Rodriguez. While he keeps things moving and adds some visual flair (including showing the fatal arrow going *through* the victim's tissue in a CGI gorestravaganza), Rodriguez displays his inexperience in the scripting department by piling unlikely contrivance upon ridiculous coincidence. For instance, the team manages to track down one of the hunters by matching DNA found in a *leech* at the crime scene. Unlikely, but possible ... maybe. Next, this supremely self-confident suspect (a successful stockbroker), with little pressure, immediately folds and admits to the killing, confessing everything he knows. Hmmm. Then somehow, with no explanation, the unit conjures up the identity of the human trafficker importing the "targets"; and finally they just happen to be out at the right time and the right place (in the vast Everglades) during the next hunt to round up the bad guys before the kill.

After the brief (admittedly exciting) opening, as the panicked victim flees through the swampland only to end up on the wrong end of an arrow, the show turns primarily procedural, with the team trying to recreate just what happened and discover who pulled the (bow) strings. The climactic second human hunt, when it finally comes, carries little weight, as we know nothing about either of the two generic prey *or* the two nondescript hunters — it's the first time we've seen any of them. And the chase is so brief that it feels perfunctory in any case.

There's little exploration of just why these hunters turn to hunting people. In fact, the script offers no characterization at all, apart from the arrogant stockbroker, whose only explanation is: "You get that rush of adrenaline, it shoots up your spine..." — at which point one of the investigators becomes disgusted and orders him to "Shut up!" (Not the cleverest of detective work to tell a suspect to shut up just as he's launching into his confession.)

But questionable — and downright illegal — police work seems to be par for the course for this Miami Crime Scene Investigation team. For instance, Lt. Caine threatens the illegal immigrant importer with *torture* (coming at the restrained suspect with a white-hot carving utensil!) in order to elicit the name of the man to whom he sells the illegals. And when Caine catches up with the hunt's organizer at the end, instead of simply arresting him, he terrifies the suspect by starting to count down from 15 and ordering him to run — to show him what it's like to be hunted. Adding humiliating insult to terrorized injury, Caine finishes by aiming his shotgun at the prostrate, pleading perp and *pulling the trigger*! — (click, the chamber's empty) — causing the man to wet himself. Now that is *some* police work, and I'm sure a judge would good-naturedly laugh that off in court... Perhaps the show would be better named *CSI: Gestapo*.

Dollhouse (2/20/2009) "Target," Season 1, Episode 2. Creator: Joss Whedon; Director/Teleplay: Steven S. DeKnight. Cast: Eliza Dushku, Harry Lennix, Fran Kranz, Tahmoh Penikett, Enver Gjokaj, Dichen Lachman, Olivia Williams. Guest Stars: Matt Keeslar.

Created by Joss Whedon (*Buffy the Vampire Slayer, Angel*), this TV series lasted only two seasons before low ratings forced its cancellation (Whedon had already planned out a 5-season story/character arc). The science fiction premise has an organization employing a futuristic technique that mind-wipes its subjects, labeled "Dolls," so that false memories and abilities can be programmed into them for the benefit of the organization's high-paying clients. When their assignment ends, the Dolls' memories are erased, and they reside in the eponymous Dollhouse until the next time these human blank slates are called upon to become someone new.

In the series' second episode (the third filmed but the second to air, as the original pilot was never broadcast), a wealthy Dollhouse client (Matt Keeslar) contracts for a "perfect woman" with whom he can spend some quality outdoor time. Unfortunately, this means not only river rafting and rock climbing, but bow hunting — with the beautiful Doll Echo (Eliza Dushku) as the prey.

A serviceable episode with a modicum of action and suspense (Dushku, best known for her turn as "Faith" in the *Buffy the Vampire Slayer* series, makes for an active—and attractive—most dangerous game), it concludes with a tense standoff between hunter (armed with his lethal bow) and hunted (now armed with a pistol). There's little exploration into the hunter's motivation, however, apart from being taught by his father that one must put one's "shoulder to the grindstone" and earn one's place. In effect, as he tells his terrified prey, "see if you can earn the right to live." The episode's coda offers a to-be-continued twist when it's revealed that the client was using a false identity, and that a shadow-figure "hired some nutjob to hunt [Echo] in the woods." The most notable thing about this Most Dangerous Game variation is that said nutjob goes by the alias "Richard Connell." Now *that* is an homage.

Fantasy Island (2/24/1979) "Spending Spree/The Hunted," Season 2, episode 19. Director: George McCowan; "The Hunted" Teleplay: Herman Groves. Cast: Ricardo Montalban, Herve Villechaize. Guest Stars: Kiana Canova, Khigh Dhiegh, Lola Falana, James Shigeta, Doodles Weaver, Stuart Whitman.

This lightweight but extremely popular series that lasted from 1977 to 1984 stars Ricardo Montalban as the enigmatic, smiling, and seemingly omnipotent Mr. Roarke, who, along with his midget assistant Tatoo (Herve Villechaize), runs "Fantasy Island," a tropical paradise where guests' fantasies are made realities. The show's format typically featured a pair of concurrent stories in which guests have their fantasies fulfilled while learning valuable lessons about themselves and what's truly important in life.

In this hour-long episode, the supercilious "Spending Spree" centers on a pair of female friends who were "born to shop," winning a contest in which they must spend half-a-million dollars in a short period of time or lose it all. The other tale, "The Hunted," is an altogether more serious story of "Mr. Charles Wesley [Stuart Whitman], possibly the world's foremost big-game hunter," as Roarke describes him. "An adventurer with formidable credentials, he has lived for thrills, for the chase, perhaps the intangible rapture of risking his life and winning. Now probably bored with lack of new challenges, he's come to us." Wesley seeks "the biggest adventure of his life," continues Roarke. "He's asked me to choose the quarry. His only stipulation is that the hunt be exciting and dangerous." Roarke gives him that in spades when he chooses as Wesley's prey General Lin Sun (James Shigeta) of the Republic of Ching Tu, "an unusual man of many reputations. His supporters call him the George Washington of his country, an enlightened benefactor and force for the future; his enemies call him a corrupt and ruthless dictator." General Sun just happens to be occupying a well-guarded villa on the other side of the island, and it's Wesley's task to shoot him! "If you're asking me to kill him, the answer is no," protests a shocked Wesley. "I don't want you to *kill* him, Mr. Wesley," reassures Roarke, "just shoot him—with this, a camera engineered to fit on your rifle." Taking on the challenge, Wesley eludes the General's guards and lures the man out of his villa to get a clean shot. But just as he bags his photographic prize, a rifle butt smashes into the back of Wesley's head. Waking in the General's villa, the captive Wesley is accused of attempted assassination by the duplicitous General (who has removed the camera apparatus from Wesley's rifle and ordered his execution at dawn). But General Sun has other plans, arranging for Wesley's escape so that the General can hunt him down with Wesley's own weapon—this time loaded with *bullets* rather than film. There ensues a moderately suspenseful stalk and chase sequence (at least by 1970s prime-time television standards) in which the clever Wesley first throws the General's tracking dogs off the scent via some sprinkled gunpowder, then knocks Sun's two accompanying guards out of commission with an ingenious swinging log trap. Finally cornered near some huts, Wesley engages in an energetic hand-to-hand battle with the sadistic General before Mr. Roarke and the General's own people arrive just in time to confront General Sun with his duplicity and lead him away for punishment. A chastened Wesley, who now realizes what it's like to be the hunted, symbolically throws his own rifle away.

While the brevity of the tale offers little time for extrapolation, it's still rather disappointing that there's so little characterization provided for either Wesley or General Sun. Actor James Shigeta plays Sun in a forceful but ultimately bland manner, making him a generic villain with no depth. A dearth of discussion about the General's motivation to hunt Wesley for sport, and nary a word about the ethics of hunting itself (apart from Wesley's observation to Sun, "I'm beginning to see all the worst in myself exposed in you, with a slight difference — I give them a chance") make this *Fantasy* a disappointing one, adaptation-wise. Worse still, thanks to *Fantasy Island*, an entire generation of Americans can no longer spot an airplane in the sky without hearing the immortal line, "De plane, de plane!"

The F.B.I. Files (1999) "A Hunter's Game," Season 2, Episode 6. Director: Stuart Taylor; Writer: Mark Marabella. Cast: James Kallstrom (host), Anthony Call (narrator).

Though ostensibly a "true-life" series that uses reenactments and interviews to detail real F.B.I. cases, *The F.B.I. Files'* "A Hunter's Game," which focuses on the crimes of Alaska's worst serial killer, Robert Hansen, contains enough supposition that it might as well have been some low-budget episode from *Criminal Minds* or *C.S.I.* Hansen, an avid big-game hunter, admitted to taking women by car or private plane into the Alaskan wilderness around Anchorage, where he sexually assaulted and sometimes murdered them. He was convicted of four killings, though he admitted to 13 more. He's currently serving a 461-year prison sentence.

The program, while capturing the gist, gets plenty of the case's details wrong, including portraying the F.B.I.'s involvement as being far more important than it was (all the Bureau did was work up a possible profile and do some ballistics testing; it was the Anchorage P.D. and state troopers who investigated, fingered Hansen, and made the case). More importantly, the show plays up the supposed "hunting" angle for increased sensationalism, taking what was mere speculation on the part of one prosecuting attorney and reporting it as fact. In the episode's initial reenactment we see a young woman (described as "a hopeful young model" by the narrator, when in reality she was a dancer at a strip club), handcuffed and partially blindfolded, stumble through the brush, pursued by a rifle-toting hunter who finally takes aim and fires. The narrator solemnly intones, "He hunted them like animals for his own twisted pleasure." Later, the episode flatly states, "In his confession, Hansen described how he would take his victims into the woods and hunt them as prey." In reality, Hansen *never* confessed to hunting his victims, claiming that he only killed (*not* hunted) them when they fought back or tried to run. Such hyperbole and boldface fabrication points up the powerful fascination we have with the concept of hunting humans for sport (and, of course, the fact that you can't believe everything "true" on television...).

Forever Knight (10/10/1994) "Hunted," Season 2, Episode 7. Creators: James D. Parriott, Barney Cohen; Director: Allan Kroeker; Teleplay: Roy Sallows. Cast: Geraint Wyn Davies, Catherine Disher, Nigel Bennett, Deborah Duchene, Natsuko Ohama, John Kapelos. Guest Star: Gwynyth Walsh.

This Canadian series follows the adventures of Nick Knight (Geraint Wyn Davies), an 800-year-old vampire who works as a homicide detective in Toronto (the night shift, naturally) in order to atone for his past sins and perhaps regain his humanity. In the second-season (of three) episode "Hunted," Nick and his mortal partner Schanke (John Kapelos) investigate a series of killings that appear to be human hunts. "Someone's hunting people" observes the incredulous medical examiner, Natalie Lambert (Catherine Disher). "Hey, why not," responds Schanke," it's instinct. We were born to hunt, it's in our blood. Okay, so it's not necessary anymore. But if you want to understand man's primal self you gotta understand it's all about the hunt. Man against nature." Six have been "hunted" in the last month (with the hunter offering them $2 million if they survive, though none has), and "the killer is escalating the kick" by choosing more and more fit and dangerous prey — culminating in Nick himself. The hunter kidnaps Schanke and leaves a tape-recorded message for Nick: "You have 30 minutes to rescue your partner.... At the end of that time a small but powerful bomb will explode under him.... There will be two ground rules. One, you must do this alone and on foot ... and two, while you're hunting for your partner I'll be hunting you."

"Hunted" dives far deeper into the hunting-humans-for-sport pool than most television episodes, not least by showing the protagonist to be a former hunter-of-men himself. Periodic flashbacks focus on Nick's maker, the 2000-year-old vampire Lacroix, teaching Nick to hunt people not only for food but for sport. As Lacroix asks of a woodland hunter that will soon become the vampires' prey, "Do you not *bask* in the kill, do you not relish the control you have over life and death?" After Nick surprises Lacroix by being the first to bring down their human prey, the master vampire enthuses, "Now you know what it means to truly be a hunter. Now you feel the thrill, the exhilaration, that only death can give." Nick, however, soon comes to realize the pain and grief this "sport" has caused...

Back in the present, the episode allows the modern-day man-hunter ample opportunity to explain herself (yes, this Zaroff stand-in turns out to be a woman). When the captive Schanke asks her, "Why kill all these people?" she responds candidly and enthusiastically, "I like it, feels wonderful. And it's an *exquisite* challenge. Tell me, Detective, what is the one thing that human beings have fought for throughout history? Power. Control. In itself the greatest thrill. And to *kill* is the ultimate control." Once she realizes that Nick is a vampire, this hunter becomes enamored of stalking "a creature designed to hunt, to kill — the perfect adversary." And during the hunt (in which she's armed with holy water, garlic-tipped bullets, and even a cross), she several times confronts Nick and likens herself to him as a "kindred spirit." In some ways she's right, but not completely — which proves to be her undoing. At the episode's conclusion, Nick explains, "She was a hunter.... She could have killed me right there and then. But what's the *thrill* in that? She needed to chase me, to anticipate me, to be *better* than me. That's why a hunter hunts. Believe me, I know."

Get Smart (11/26/1966) "Island of the Darned," Season 2, Episode 11. Creators: Mel Brooks, Buck Henry; Director: Gary Nelson; Teleplay: Buck Henry, William Raynor, Myles Wilder (story: William Raynor, Miles Wilder). Cast: Don Adams, Barbara Feldon, Edward Platt. Guest Stars: Harold Gould, Fabian Dean, Stacy Keach [Sr.], Charles Horrath.

In this second-season episode of the hit 1960s spy spoof comedy TV series, CONTROL agents Maxwell Smart (Don Adams) and 99 (Barbara Feldon) pose as sportsmen to track down CHAOS killer (and former Nazi) Hans Hunter (Harold Gould) after he hunts and kills a fellow agent, shipping the corpse to CONTROL headquarters. Looking at the preserved body at HQ, the disturbed Chief (Edward Platt) exclaims, "Agent 27 has been stuffed!" At this, Max earnestly asks, "Seems a shame to bury him, Chief; couldn't we donate him to a museum?" Thus the comical tone is set for this surprisingly faithful yet funny take on "The Most Dangerous Game," as Max and 99 journey to Hunter's Caribbean island, only to be captured and then hunted for sport. At his trophy-filled home before the hunt (complete with a stuffed saber-tooth tiger head[!] on the wall and an empty mounting plaque that bears the name plate "Maxwell Smart, Killed 1966"[!!]), the comedy riffs keep coming, epitomized by this exchange parodying a pivotal scene from the classic 1932 *The Most Dangerous Game*:

> Hunter [stroking the prominent scar on his temple]: Mr. Smart, have you ever heard of the great white rhino?
> Max [indicating the scar]: That was done by the great white rhino?
> Hunter: No, this was done by a small blue convertible.

With much of the episode shot on location (rather than the show's usual interiors and potted-plant soundstage sets), "Island of the Darned" remains one of the series' more expansive entries. Veteran TV director Gary Nelson (who helmed 23 *Get Smart* episodes, as well as countless others for numerous series over four decades) not only handles the comedy well but fashions a truly exciting and suspenseful hunt sequence via some mobile, hand-held camerawork of the two protagonists fleeing through the brush, sliding down a steep slope, and even going hand-over-hand beneath a rickety rope bridge. In another nod to the story's source, Max and 99 dig a "Malay man-trap"—a pit into which one of Hunter's henchmen falls. Of course, this inspires an angry Hunter to exclaim, "All right, that's it—no more Mr. Nice Guy." (Note that the episode's scripters make the mistake of misnaming this trap, which is actually the "Burmese tiger pit" of Connell's original story; the "Malay mancatcher" that Rainsford constructs in the tale is a dead-fall trap.)

The excellent episode closes with Max and 99 getting the best of Hunter by using the old exploding cigarette trick, leading to the following thoughtful-yet-comedic exchange:

> 99: Oh Max, how horrible.
> Max: He deserved it, 99; he was a CHAOS killer.
> 99: Sometimes I wonder if we're any better, Max.
> Max [incredulous]: What are you talking about, 99? We *have* to shoot and kill and destroy. We represent everything that's wholesome and good in the world.

Indeed.

Gilligan's Island (1/16/1967) "The Hunter," Season 3, Episode 18. Creator: Sherwood Schwartz; Director: Leslie Goodwins; Teleplay: Ben Gershman, William Freedman. Cast: Bob Denver, Alan Hale, Jim Backus, Natalie Schafer, Tina Louise, Dawn Wells, Russell Johnson. Guest Stars: Rory Calhoun, Harold Sakata.

This frequently derided yet much-loved sixties sitcom about seven castaways whose "three-hour tour" turned into a three-year stretch of silly shenanigans on a deserted island went to the Most Dangerous Game well in its third and final season. In "The Hunter" a helicopter brings big-game hunter Jonathan Kincaid (frequent Western star Rory Calhoun) and his man Ramoo (Harold Sakata, the menacing "Odd Job" from *Goldfinger*) to the castaways' uncharted island. When greeted by an excited Gilligan (Bob Denver), who thinks they've finally been rescued, the disappointed hunter learns that there's no big game on the island, just the seven stranded people. This gives him an idea. "I've always wondered what it would be like to track down and kill the most challenging of all game—man," he says. Telling Ramoo, "I want a quarry that will present me with a challenge, somebody that's nimble, agile," Kincaid sets his sights on the bumbling Gilligan. "As added incentive to your participation in this adventure," he tells them all, "if the one I'm hunting can elude me for 24 hours, I'll see that you're all returned to civilization."

Played strictly for laughs, the subsequent hunt offers such comical pratfalls as Gilligan hiding under a pile of leaves to steal a drink from Kincaid's canteen, Gilligan swinging from a vine to inadvertently knock over his pursuer, and Gilligan pulling Kincaid into a water trough, only to have the hunter shoot water from his rifle when he takes aim at his fleeing prey. Gilligan does indeed survive the 24-hour period (just barely — by disguising himself as a tree!). Kincaid leaves but keeps only half his promise (letting Gilligan live); fearing police involvement, he refuses to send a rescue party. The episode concludes with the castaways hearing on their radio a month later that the "famous sportsman" Jonathan Kincaid has won an international skeet shooting contest — only to break down, become violent and end up straitjacketed in a mental hospital. "All the while," relates the broadcaster, "he kept muttering the mysterious words, 'Gilligan, Gilligan, Gilligan.'" Take *that*, General Zaroff!

Highlander (11/9/1997) "Black Tower," Season 6, Episode 6. Director: Richard Martin; Teleplay: Morrie Ruvinsky. Cast: Adrian Paul, Elizabeth Gracen, Peter Wingfield, Jim Byrnes. Guest Stars: Andrew Bicknell, Rochelle Redfield, Alexi Kaye Campbell, Luke D'Silva, Julius D'Silva.

"He is Duncan MacLeod, the Highlander," begins this series' (based on the popular *Highlander* movies) opening narration, "born in 1592 in the Highlands of Scotland, and he is still alive. For 400 years he's been a warrior, a lover, a wanderer, constantly facing other Immortals in a combat to the death. The winner takes his enemy's head and with it his power.... In the end there can be only one [Immortal]. May it be Duncan MacLeod, the Highlander."

For the sixth episode of the final season of this Canadian/French series, Duncan MacLeod (Adrian Paul) is lured into a deadly game when a rival Immortal, Marek (Andrew Bicknell), kidnaps Margo (Rochelle Redfield), MacLeod's new love interest. At the office building housing Marek's toy company empire, the arrogant Marek explains, "It's hide and seek. I hide this gorgeous creature here [indicating Margo], and you try to find her.... Now, of course, while you're looking for her, my friends here [a quartet of heavily armed hunters] will be looking for you.... You have 60 seconds to start running." Thus commences a cat and mouse game as MacLeod tries to elude his pursuers through the building, while Marek gleefully watches the hunt on surveillance monitors. Interspersed are flashback sequences to MacLeod's first encounter with Marek in 1634, which show that even then the pompous, cruel Marek was entranced with hunting humans, as the aristocratic lord releases a poacher into the woods and tells him, "As you hunt the deer, I will hunt you," before chasing him down. Played with over-the-top, almost cartoonish relish by Andrew Bicknell, Marek is fond of spouting lines like, "Now what kind of a hunt would it be if it were over so quickly," and "Run, rabbit, run."

Apart from an unexpected character twist towards the end, "Black Tower" offers little of interest. Small of scale (with only a handful of characters largely confined to one generic office building, and the occasional equally small-scale woodland flashback), it looks cheap, beset with cheesy graphics and primitive videography. The four hunters all employ similar automatic weapons and remain woefully underdeveloped, with little to differentiate them (apart from the one sloppily-dressed killer being a supposed American "hillbilly" bounty hunter). On the Most Dangerous Game front, MacLeod does lay two traps for his pursuers, one employing a mixture of cleaning chemicals to generate an explosion triggered by a trip wire, and the other involving a puddle of water and an electrified door handle. But a sting in the tail and a pair of *MacGyver*-like surprises isn't much to sustain an hour-long television episode.

The Incredible Hulk (12/7/1979) "The Snare," Season 3, Episode 9. Director: Frank Orsatti; Teleplay: Richard Christian Matheson, Thomas E. Szollosi. Cast: Bill Bixby, Jack Colvin, Lou Ferrigno. Guest Star: Bradford Dillman.
  "Dr. David Banner — physician, scientist — searching for a way to tap into the hidden strengths that all humans have," begins the narration opening this popular series based on the Marvel comic book character. "Then an accidental overdose of gamma radiation alters his body chemistry. And now when David Banner is angered or outraged, a startling metamorphosis occurs." Yes, he transforms into a musclebound Lou Ferrigno in fright wig and green body paint. Or, put another way, he becomes *The Incredible Hulk*. "The creature is driven by rage," continues the narrator, "and by an investigative reporter."
  In this third-season episode, the dogged investigator has been replaced by chess-obsessed big-game hunter/millionaire Michael Sutton (Bradford Dillman), who invites David (Bill Bixby) to his private island after the two bond over several games of chess at an airport waiting room. Once there, however, Sutton drugs David, who awakens the next day in an open grave in the woods with a tape recorder around his neck. "I became bored with hunting animals," explains Sutton on the tape. "That's why I prefer to hunt men. You have an intellect, that's what makes you a challenge. Oh, and David, if it helps, think of chess. Like in chess, think twice about everything you do because, unlike chess, when everything is over the board can't be set up again." Armed with a bow and arrow, Sutton begins the hunt on his trap-laden island. David avoids a net snare but falls into a concealed pit. A watching Sutton, disappointed, observes, "You've fallen for the obvious." But when David scrambles to escape the pit, a scorpion sting triggers the transformation, and the Hulk emerges, to the astonishment — and delight — of the big-game hunter. After toppling a tree that temporarily incapacitates Sutton, the Hulk triggers a large deadfall trap, which barely fazes the green-skinned giant. Regaining his human form, David makes it back to Sutton's house — only to be trapped in Sutton's study by steel shutters. There a mini-game begins in which David has five minutes to find the clues to his release — while avoiding several deadly booby traps. When David escapes the house, Sutton shouts after him, "I saw that beast you turned into, David. Incredible. It was magnificent, David, magnificent. Make it come back. Make it come back — and fight." Now obsessed with hunting the Hulk rather than a mere man, Sutton does everything he can to track David and trigger the transformation — to his eventual regret.
  Tapping into Connell's story a bit deeper than most TV adapters, writers Richard Christian Matheson (son of famous scribe Richard Matheson, known for his novels and screenplays like *I Am Legend* and *The Incredible Shrinking Man*) and Thomas Szollosi offer a very Zaroff-like antagonist who goes beyond turning his private island into a hunting preserve to booby trapping even his own house! And though Sutton's brief (taped) monologue about becoming bored with hunting mere animals comes as almost a throwaway moment, it's refreshing to see at least a modicum of motivation borrowed from Connell's antagonist (not to mention the allusion to "outdoor chess" in Sutton's obvious obsession with the game). The hunt itself offers some suspenseful moments, with David climbing a cliffside rope ladder as Sutton's arrows strike the rock around him, or hiding submerged in a river

pool as the hunter stalks past. But it all nearly falls to pieces when the Hulk lumbers onto the scene, doing nothing really except flexing, roaring and toppling the odd tree. (Even Sutton's ultimate demise comes through the man's own clumsiness rather than from anything the simpleton Hulk does.) And the viewer can't help but burst out laughing when the green monster finds a pair of baby birds and lovingly gathers them in his palm to gently stroke the tiny creatures. One almost expects him to say, "Tell about the birdies, George." But such are the vagaries of a series titled *The Incredible Hulk*, as a better moniker might have been *The Incredulous Viewer*.

It's Always Sunny in Philadelphia (9/18/2008) "Mac and Dennis: Manhunters," Season 4, Episode 1. Creator: Rob McElhenney; Director: Fred Savage; Teleplay: Charlie Day, Jordan Young, Elijah Aron. Cast: Charlie Day, Glenn Howerton, Rob McElhenney, Kaitlin Olson, Danny DeVito. Guest Stars: David Hornsby, Jonathan Spencer.

For its fourth season opener, this hip comedy series about a quartet of egocentric friends who own an Irish bar, and whose cavalier, immature outlook leads to all manner of bizarre situations, tosses in a dash of the old Most Dangerous Game to spice up its offbeat flavor. When Mac (Rob McElhenney) and Dennis (Glenn Howerton) learn that Frank (Danny DeVito) is a big-time hunter (having just bagged a 10-point buck), they are less than impressed. "How does hunting a defenseless creature make you a great hunter?" Mac asks. "Yeah, you should go after something that can at least defend itself," adds Dennis. "You know, a *really* great hunter would go after something that can hunt him back — like a *man*." Frank is aghast, admonishing, "Don't even joke about huntin' no man." But it's no joke to the boys, who determine to do just that, setting their sights on hunting down their homeless friend, Cricket (David Hornsby). To that end they dress themselves in camouflage outfits and set up a cardboard "blind" on the street where Cricket usually does his begging. "Hunting is awesome," observes Dennis. "We get to wear sweet clothes and get wasted all day." And what do they intend to do when they catch their prey? Not shoot him (they don't even have guns) but simply "teabag" him.

So it is indeed a joke after all — and a fairly funny one at that. But the biggest laughs come from the concurrent storyline involving Charlie (Charlie Day) and Dee (Kaitlin Olson), who are tricked by Frank into thinking they've eaten human flesh and now have an insatiable craving for long pig. It all combines to make "Mac and Dennis: Manhunters" a crude but tasty episode.

Johnny Bravo (8/18/2000) "Virtual Johnny / Hold That Schmoe / Hunted!" Season 3, Episode 2. Creator: Van Partible; Director: Kirk Tingblad; Teleplay: John Crane, Gene Grillo. Cast (voices): Jeff Bennet, Brenda Vaccaro, Mae Whitman. Guest star: Jim Cummings.

Ohhhh mama! This Cartoon Network animated series details the misadventures of clueless blonde hunk Johnny Bravo (voiced by Jeff Bennet, doing a decent Elvis caricature), his mother Bunny (Brenda Vaccaro) and their neighbor Suzy (Mae Whitman).

In the 7-minute "Hunted!" segment, Bunny loses Johnny in a poker game to Colonel Fatman (Jim Cummings), who takes Johnny to his private island to "play a little game." Walking through his mansion festooned with hunting trophies, the sinister, Sydney Greenstreet-esque Fatman asks Johnny, "Are you frightened?" "Got any snacks," answers Johnny, unperturbed ... until Johnny asks, "Hey, by the way, what's that empty plaque on your wall for?" Fatman responds, "That is the one prize that has eluded me all my life. But that will change soon enough, bwa-ha-ha-ha!" Uh-oh. "Suddenly it all makes sense!" shouts Johnny.

"Well, you'll never catch me, you fiend. The stench of life is too sweet. I will survive!" Johnny plunges through the wall, followed by the hunting togs-wearing Fatman, who gloats, "And so, Johnny Bravo, our little game of hide and seek begins."

Said game, of course, is played for laughs rather than tension. As Johnny flees, he says to himself, "I don't get it; why would somebody want to hunt me for sport and put my head on the wall?" Spying his reflection in a river, he pulls up short. "Oh, that's right — I'm pretty." Johnny proves so inept, however, that Fatman ends up *helping* him. "I was hoping you'd be a more challenging prey," the Colonel laments. Johnny first tries hiding under a lampshade in the mansion, with Fatman deadpanning, "Perhaps the dense jungle forest might provide you better concealment." When Fatman finds him too easily, he suggests Johnny use camouflage. When that fails, the exasperated Colonel even points out on a map the "most ingenious hiding places on the island." Finally, Fatman has had enough, and Johnny begs the hunter not to put his head on the wall. "Heavens no," exclaims Fatman, "that space is reserved for the Best in Show prize for my cat, Mr. Pippin." It truly was just an innocent game of "hide and seek" after all.

Jonny Quest (11/20/1964) "Shadow of the Condor," Season 1, Episode 10. Directors: William Hanna, Joseph Barbera; Teleplay: William D. Hamilton. Cast (voices): Mike Road, Jon Stephenson, Tim Matthieson, Danny Bravo. Guest: Everett Sloane.

This short-lived (lasting only one season) Hanna-Barbera animated series appealed to 1960s pre-teens by pitting its protagonists (brilliant scientist Dr. Quest, his young son Jonny, Jonny's childhood friend Hadji, and their he-man helper Race Bannon) against lizard men, mummies, and spider-robots. Frequent syndicated reruns turned the sci-fi/adventure series into a cult show that eventually inspired two telefilms, a second TV series, comic books, and a set of video games in the 1990s (not to mention a funny-as-hell *Jonny Quest* parody on *The Venture Bros.*).

In "Shadow of the Condor," plane trouble forces the Quest crew to land on a private airstrip in the Andes. "Welcome to Marianberg, my humble castle in the Andes," says the strip's owner, former World War I German ace (with 84 kills) Baron Heinrich von Freulich. It seems that between hunting the local wild condors, Von Freulich uses his old World War I biplanes to hunt others in the skies and take them down in aerial dogfights. (As Dr. Quest finally remembers about him, "When the war ended he flew into a rage because he wanted to reach 100 [kills].") When the Baron secretly sabotages Dr. Quest's plane ("No one will leave here until I've played my little game," Von Freulich says to his little dachshund), Race (whom the Baron notes would "make a worthy opponent") is forced to borrow one of the Baron's biplanes to go to La Paz for a spare part. Von Freulich takes off in a second plane and attacks Race, but the timely intervention of an enraged condor sends Von Freulich crashing to his doom.

With his foreign accent; creepy, aristocratic demeanor (including an ever-present monocle); passion for hunting condors (with one of the giant birds stuffed and mounted above his dining table); and talk of his deadly "little game," the Baron becomes an obvious Zaroff figure (he even has a mute servant), though one who hunts not with a bow or rifle but with a biplane! Unfortunately, the teleplay's writing proves as simplistic as the poor animation typical of Hanna-Barbera product, while mundane meanderings and silly shenanigans involving Jonny's dog "Bandit" keep the climactic aerial "hunt" short. And none-too-sweet, either, as at one point the Baron flies directly behind Race's plane in order to literally shave off part of its tail with his propeller! Even a 10-year-old (the show's target audience) knows that this is patently ridiculous. And at the end, Von Freulich's bullets disturb a condor who flies at the Baron's plane and *sheers off the wing*(!), causing the vehicle to crash — right along with any sense of verisimilitude.

Law and Order: Special Victims Unit (2/22/2012) Season 13, Episode 15, "Hunting Ground." Creator: Dick Wolf; Director: Jonathan Kaplan; Teleplay: David Matthews, John P. Roche (story: John P. Roche, Warren Leight). Cast: Mariska Hargitay, Danny Piino, Kelli Giddish, Richard Belzer, Ice T, Dann Florek. Guest Stars: Harry Connick, Jr., Fred Arsenault.

"In the criminal justice system," begins this popular crime series' opening narration, "sexually based offenses are considered especially heinous. In New York City the detectives who investigate these vicious felonies are members of an elite squad known as the Special Victims Unit. These are their stories."

"Hunting Ground" details the search for a missing underage prostitute that leads the SVU to a serial killer who abducts these girls, transports them to an upstate nature preserve, hunts them, rapes them and kills them. Not unsurprisingly, given the show's format, the episode focuses far more on the investigation, and the SVU's attempts to identify the killer, than on the killer's actual "hunts." Apart from a few brief shots of the missing girl running through the woods, then a dart slamming into a tree next to her, there's no detailing of the human hunt at all. Referred to by the killer as "the game" (according to the one traumatized escapee the detectives finally locate), he stalks the girls in the forest with a tranquilizer rifle, bags them, then drags them, drugged, back to his shack. "He told me to run and hide," recounts the trembling girl who got away, "then he'd come after me with Orion, his dog. Then the dart would go in me." The only motivational revelations from this hunter-of-girls comes from a flip "The chase is half the fun" at the show's beginning when he "dates" a victim; and then his admission during the final confrontation with Detective Olivia Benson (Mariska Hargitay): "There's an order to everything in Nature: hunt, feed, breed. All in the now. Honest. Animals don't lie about what they want — not like you *whores!*"

Note: Series regular Ice T knows very well what it's like to be in the Most Dangerous Game crosshairs, as he played the primary prey in *Surviving the Game*.

Lost in Space (9/27/1967) "Hunter's Moon," Season 3, Episode 4. Creator/Producer: Irwin Allen; Director: Don Richardson; Teleplay: Jack Turley. Cast: Guy Williams, June Lockhart, Mark Goddard, Marta Kristen, Billy Mumy, Angela Cartwright, Jonathan Harris. Guest Star: Vincent Beck.

Silly, puerile, ridiculous, shallow, laughable. All these adjectives can be readily applied to the juvenile sci-fi show *Lost in Space*. But back in the day the series about an intergalactic "Space Family Robinson" proved a hit, particularly with the more junior set of viewers. And hey, it even featured an endearing robot (*Forbidden Planet*'s "Robbie" with a new headpiece). What it did *not* feature, however, was any sort of depth of character or story, relying instead on bright, day-glow set dressing (in this episode even the cage bars used to imprison various characters are painted a bright red, yellow and purple); a parade of cheesy monsters that make *Star Trek*'s creatures seem positively realistic; lowest-common-denominator humor (generally involving the cowardly Dr. Smith and his exasperating interactions with the literal-minded robot); and simplistic plots that resolve with a minimum of fuss. So it's no wonder the series' take on the Most Dangerous Game concept offers little excitement and even less thought.

Needing to land their spaceship "Jupiter" for repairs, the Robinsons and crew approach an unknown planet, only to be caught in a "forcefield layer" (looking like a big wad of dangling tinsel) that drags them down to the planet's surface. There, Captain John Robinson (Guy Williams) encounters a hairy creature that he shoots in self-defense. A second alien (Vincent Beck), this one sporting blue skin, an outsized unibrow, and muttonchops that go all the way around (and who speaks perfect English) arrives and takes John prisoner. "You're trespassing on a private killing preserve, Earthling," pronounces the affronted alien. "I am Megazor, future ruler of Zann. I am here undergoing certain tests to determine my suitability as ruler of our civilization." Said tests involve hunting down other sentient life forms, including the beast John killed. "I'm sorry if I interrupted your sport," John offers. So after much time-killing wandering about and pointless interactions between the various characters, Megazor ultimately determines to hunt John in order to complete his "test." (Note: Though Megazor's ostensible motivation for hunting Robinson is to prove himself worthy by passing a series of tests, said trial involves sport-hunting of sentient beings; thus this episode's inclusion.) Armed with a metal disc-shooting weapon, the alien chases John through the woods, only to be tricked in the end, leading to his defeat and demise. And leading the viewer to breathe a sigh of relief— not because of any tension built up over the course of the episode (there is none), but because the tedium is finally over.

The Middleman (July 7, 2008) "The Manicoid Teleportation Conundrum," Season 1, Episode 4. Creator: Javier Grillo-Marxuach; Director: Jeremiah Chechik; Teleplay: Tracey Stern. Cast: Matt Keeslar, Natalie Morales, Brit Morgan, Mary Pat Gleason, Jake Smollett. Guest Cast: Clint Culp, Patrick Fischler, Allison Dunbar.

Based on a run of graphic novels (by series creator Javier Grillo-Marxuach), *The Middleman* (Matt Keeslar) works for a mysterious agency dedicated to fighting evil (re: mad scientists, hostile aliens, and monsters of all sorts). Struggling artist Wendy Watson (Natalie Morales) has been recruited as a Middleman-in-training, and she must balance facing down horrible creatures with her day-to-day "ordinary" life.

"The Manicoid Teleportation Conundrum" has the Middleman and Wendy investigating the disappearance of several well-to-do plastic-surgery patients who could give Joan Rivers a run for her tightened-face money, all linked to one Dr. Newleaf (who looks like he's gone under the knife a few too many times himself). It turns out that these odd-looking socialites are actually peaceful Manicoids, aliens exiled to Earth "masquerading as humans who've had too much plastic surgery." Meanwhile, Wendy must deal with being dumped by her boyfriend, and her friends' subsequent stifling concern (with one extolling the merits of TV psychologist Dr. Gil). Realizing that the missing Manicoids are being teleported then killed, Middleman and Wendy follow the trail to a secret room at the local TV station—a room filled with hunting trophies. "They may call themselves hunters," says a disgusted Middleman, "but to me they're just serial killers of animals." But among the expected stuffed bear and boar are mounted Manicoid heads! Suddenly, in walks Dr. Gil. "Accruing wealth and power through my work as a television psychotherapist was merely a means to the end of hunting down Manicoids for sport," he admits. "So that's all this is," observes the Middleman, "'The Most Dangerous Game' with aliens." When Gil makes a break for the teleportation machine, Wendy jumps in with him, resulting in her becoming Gil's next prey at his "private hunting reserve."

Though Dr. Gil (a take-off on TV's Dr. Phil) technically hunts these human-looking (sort of) aliens for *revenge* (his father was killed by flying wreckage from the first Manicoid landing back in the day; that's where he salvaged the teleportation device), his love of hunting ("I play down my hunting nowadays; my audience don't like to think of Dr. Gil killin' Bambi"), the mounting of his victims' heads on the wall, and his eventual hunting of Wendy makes him a legitimate Zaroff surrogate. Unfortunately, actor Clint Culp's dull non-presence not only nullifies the amusing conceit of making him a sensitive relationship therapist ("It's good to cry"), he makes for a woefully uninteresting hunter-of-men as well. The hunt itself is also disappointing, consisting of Wendy running up a hill as Gil fires at her before she simply comes back down to appeal to his sensitive psychotherapist side by telling him her troubles.

This campy ABC Family TV series lasted a mere 12 episodes. No wonder, given its overly-cutesy approach, subpar scripting, and Saturday Morning–level action and effects. Filled with pop culture references (everything from *Back to the Future* to *CSI* to Lucio Fulci zombie movies), *The Middleman* comes off as little more than a cut-rate, juvenile *Men in Black* knock-off.

The Outer Limits (1/30/1998) "The Hunt," Season 4, Episode 2. Director: Mario Azzopardi; Teleplay: Sam Egan. Cast: Doug Savant, Ron White, Sarah Strange, David McNally, Don Thompson, Tobias Mehler, Bob Gunton.

In the 1990s the success of various science-fiction television series such as *The X-Files* and the Star Trek spinoffs induced MGM to produce a redux of the original 1960s cult television anthology show *The Outer Limits*. This new incarnation, broadcast primarily on the pay-cable station *Showtime*, lasted seven seasons, from 1995 to 2002, and encompassed 154 self-contained episodes (over three times as many as the original series).

The new *Outer Limits* was filmed in and around Vancouver, British Columbia (like so many productions in the 1990s and early 2000s, including *The X-Files*), with the wet Canadian woodlands serving as a perfect location for "The Hunt," a tale of human-looking androids used as prey. The episode's opening narration sets the tone: "Humankind has proven to be unique among life forms, distinguished not only by its lofty intelligence, morality and self-awareness, but also by a baser side—it is the only creature that kills for sport." A quartet of androids, no longer deemed fit for their mining work, are released into a wilderness area to be hunted by two brothers trying to recapture the "glory" days of hunting (back before animals were declared off-limits). With them is the younger brother's college-age son, who questions the morality of this "rite of passage." When two of the androids find a way to disengage their "inhibitor chip" (which keeps them from harming humans), the tables turn, leading to tragedy for both hunters and prey.

"The Hunt" not only explores the morality of hunting but the moral position of mankind in general. At one point the more human-sympathetic droid Kel opines, "They created us, they gave us life. That gives them the right to take it." Hmmm. When one droid bitterly observes, "Humans were born to love death," this prompts Kel to respond in defense, "Nothing could be further from the truth; you read Milton or Shakespeare or Thoreau, it's a celebration of beauty, of goodness, of life." At this, the third, more practical android, pipes in with, "If I had the weapons they have I'd be celebrating too." Angry about their fate, one says, "They [the hunters] want to drag this out as long as possible, savor every kill—sadistic bastards." Indeed. The androids seem all-too-human; their articulations and responses to this robotic Most Dangerous Game drives the horrors home. And "game on" it is, as once they bypass their "inhibitor" programs, these A-I prey turn and lay a trap—a spiked log that swings down to wound one of the hunters—and even manage to steal two of their pursuer's rifles.

Gradually, the elder brother takes on the primary Zaroff persona, as we learn that he had intentionally left the androids the means to overcome their inhibitor programming. "I'm trying to give you," he explains, "the thrill of the hunt. It means going after your prey on a level playing field." As he relates, "You asked me to take you on a real hunt, just like the days before they were outlawed. Well, nobody ever muzzled the big cats Dad and I tracked on the savannah, or blunted the horn of a charging rhino. That's what hunting's about — a *contest* for survival."

Unfortunately, the episode loses its way at times. For instance, cluttering up the story with a clumsy robot-love subplot proves a poor (and cliched) choice. And the circular ending provides no real resolution nor even final revelation. But overall, "The Hunt" remains an involving and thought-provoking Most Dangerous television foray.

Relic Hunter (2/12/2001) "Run Sydney, Run," Season 2, Episode 15. Director: Paulo Barzman; Teleplay: Jeff F. King. Cast: Tia Carrere, Christen Anholt, Lindy Booth. Guest Stars: Peter Stebbings, Joseph Zeigler, Kelly Grando, Kevin Rushton.

In an obvious aping of the *Indiana Jones* movies, with a nod to the *Tomb Raider* video games, this Canadian series (shot in and around Toronto) stars Tia Carrere (best known for her role in the *Wayne's World* movies) as university professor Sydney Fox whose main pursuit is to travel the world seeking out ancient artifacts for museums, often running afoul of fellow "relic hunters" and using her black-belt skills to battle her (and her assistant Nigel's) way out of danger.

In the second-season (of three) episode "Run, Sydney, Run," Sydney and Nigel are ambushed in Russia just after retrieving an ancient sword from a wilderness lake. Waking at the isolated home of a man named Tsarlov (Peter Stebbings), she soon discovers that she is to be the prey in a most dangerous game.

If imitation is indeed the sincerest form of flattery, then TV scripter Jeff F. King must be Richard Connell's number-one fan, as "Run, Sydney, Run" references/borrows from Connell's original story to a degree seldom seen in television or movies outside of the relatively faithful 1932 adaptation *The Most Dangerous Game* and 1945's *A Game of Death*. Most obvious, the hunter's name, though spelled "Tsarlov," is pronounced "Zar-loff" (and he, like Connell's Zaroff, is Russian). Tsarlov is a great hunter; his study is festooned with animal heads — but they're *old* trophies, bagged years ago. "I only hunt one game now," Tsarlov ominously intones. Catching on, Sydney responds, "The most dangerous game." This Zaroff clone even has a hulking mute servant to aid him, and a pack of vicious hunting dogs kept in a pen. Additionally, Tsarlov's "game" requires Sydney to stay alive for three days in order to win — a detail from Connell's original tale invariably discarded by every cinematic or television version. (Of course, this being a 44-minute TV episode, the hunt lasts only a few hours — and less than 10 minutes of screen time — rather than three days, but kudos to King for at least referencing this important detail of Zaroff's "game"). And unlike in so many other adaptations of Connell's concept, Tsarlov, impressed by Sydney's grit and fighting skills, initially offers to make her a partner in the hunt — just like in Connell's story. "The challenge is so much more exhilarating," enthuses Tsarlov about hunting humans. "Let me share that feeling with you, Sydney. Hunt with me." Only when Sydney refuses ("I only hunt relics," she disgustedly retorts) does Tsarlov make her his prey. During the hunt itself, Sydney, like Connell's protagonist, lays a trap for Zaroff, wounding him slightly (just like in the story). And the hunt even concludes with Sydney making it back to Tsarlov's house and finishing him off in hand-to-hand combat with a sword (like what is implied at the close of Connell's tale).

Though standing tall in its adherence to "The Most Dangerous Game," the episode comes up short in the verisimilitude department. It begins with a wetsuit-wearing Sydney retrieving a two-thousand-year-old sword from a lake, only for it to shine and gleam like it just came out of its replica box (which no doubt it did). Peter Stebbings, as Tsarlov, looks more like a California frat-boy than a hardened ex–Army Colonel who led a "hunter-seeker" unit in the Russian military before retiring to his private estate. And his calm, even bland delivery fails to capture the mania or gravitas necessary to bring a character like Tsarlov/Zaroff to life. Still, "Run, Sydney, Run" deserves credit for being one of the most Connell-conscious adaptations ever to hit the airwaves.

Note: This wasn't the first time Tia Carrere had to run for her (onscreen) life from a mad hunter-of-men (or women); she played the female half of a couple hunted for sport in the made-for-television movie *Dogboys* (see "DTV Danger").

The Simpsons (11/6/2005) "Treehouse of Horror XVI," Season 17, Episode 4. Creator: Matt Groening; Director: "Godzilla vs. Silverman" (David Silverman); Teleplay: "Marc Will Killmore" (Marc Wilmore). Cast (voices): Dan Castellaneta, Julie Kavner, Nancy Cartwright, Yeardley Smith, Hank Azaria, Harry Shearer.

The middle segment of the 16th edition of this animated show's annual Halloween episode dives right into Connell territory with "Survival of the Fattest" (the other two segments being "Bartificial Intelligence" and "I've Grown a Costume on Your Face"). It begins with Homer Simpson receiving an invitation from the wealthy Mr. Burns to a "Hunting Party." "Please don't accept this invitation, Dad," pleads his daughter Lisa. "Hunting is evil." At this, Homer solicitously reassures her, "Honey, animals don't feel death. That was proved by the scientists at Black Angus." At Burns' mansion, Homer and a score of other men from the town enjoy dinner before Burns tells them all, "You're here to participate in a hunt — for the world's most dangerous game. The game I'm hunting — is *all of you*! Any man who lives till noon tomorrow will win his freedom." With that, Burns gives his quarry a five-minuting head start and then comes after them in a jeep, a bi-plane(!) and finally on foot, picking off his prey one by one despite their best efforts to hide or flee.

An hilarious segment filled with clever sight gags and dialogue, "Survival of the Fattest" packs more Dangerous Game laughs into its scant 8 minutes than most full-length MDG episodes from other comedy series. For instance, as Burns speaks to his prospective prey in his trophy-laden dining hall, we notice on the wall behind not only the expected lions and tigers, but stuffed monkey, pig and *dog* heads. At one point during the hunt Burns says, "I smell *fear*—mixed with curry," and shoots at a bush, flushing out a Hindu.

Sometimes it just feels good to laugh at one's fear, and "Survival of the Fattest" is downright *great* at that.

Star Trek (1/12/1967) "The Squire of Gothos," Season 1, Episode 17. Creator: Gene Roddenberry; Director: Don McDougall; Teleplay: Paul Schneider. Cast: William Shatner, Leonard Nimoy, DeForest Kelley. Guest Stars: William Campbell, Richard Carlyle.

For the seventeenth "voyage of the Starship Enterprise" (the seventeenth *episode*, anyway) Captain Kirk (William Shatner) and his bridge crew are forcibly transported into the odd realm of "General Trelane," a near-omnipotent being who has made a study of Earth — to the point that he's re-created a renaissance-era castle. "I can't tell you how delighted I am to have visitors here from the very planet that I have made my hobby," he tells the bewildered Kirk. "I want to learn all about your feelings on war and killing and conquest, that sort of thing. Do you know that you're one of the few predator species that preys even on itself." When Kirk refuses to go along with Trelane's charade and demands that he and his crew be released, Trelane becomes petulant, eventually trying Kirk in a kangaroo court and sentencing him to hang. Kirk then bargains for his life and his ship — by suggesting Trelane play a most dangerous game. "Where's the *sport* in a simple hanging?" he jibes. "Sport?" queries the curious Trelane. "Yes," explains Kirk, "the terror of murder. The suspense. The *fun*." Delighted with the idea, Trelane conjures up a saber and is about to strike when Kirk interjects, "There's still not enough sport in just killing me with a sword." Trelane agrees. "That *will* be dull. We'll have to have something more fanciful. Let me see — a hunt. A royal hunt. Predator against predator." After chasing and battling Kirk through the grounds of his castle, Trelane finally has the captain cornered. Suddenly a pair of glowing green lights appear in the sky, and Trelane stops short. A disapproving voice booms forth, chastising Trelane with, "If you cannot take proper care of your pets you cannot have them at all." After whisking Trelane away, one of the voices apologizes to Kirk: "You must forgive our child. The fault is ours for indulging him too much. He will be punished." (Note: These two parental voices — male and female — were *both* provided by James Doohan, who not only played *Star Trek* regular Chief Engineer Scott, but employed his vocal and accent talents numerous times throughout the series.)

As Trelane, William Campbell (*Dementia 13* [1963], *Blood Bath* [1966]) cuts a delightfully fey figure, with his 16th-century garb, haughty courtly speech, and exaggerated manners. When he sits at his harpsichord to play, the Liberace-like image is complete. And like Zaroff, Trelane's cultured, intelligent and ostensibly civilized surface serves as a mere mask. But whereas Zaroff was a cruel, arrogant hunter-of-men, Trelane is a cruel, spoiled child who becomes angry when thwarted. And this powerful being's temper tantrum results in a certain deadly game, with the sword-wielding Trelane gleefully hunting Kirk for sport. Unfortunately, this pivotal sequence lasts a mere three minutes, and the impoverished soundstage set offers barely enough room for Kirk to scurry off into the bushes before being found by Trelane, who then engages the captain in a rather languid, poorly-choreographed fight scene (with Kirk fending off Trelane's saber with a stick). Still, the episode does provide Kirk with one particular line that, in light of the hunting-for-sport theme, offers some serious food for thought: "We're living beings, not playthings for your amusement."

Star Trek: Deep Space Nine (1/31/1993) "Captive Pursuit," Season 1, Episode 5. Creators: Rick Berman, Michael Piller; Director: Corey Allen; Teleplay: Jill Sherman Donner, Michael Piller (story: Jill Sherman Donner). Cast: Avery Brooks, Rene Auberjonois, Siddig el Fadil, Terry Farrell, Cirroc Lofton, Colm Meaney, Armin Shimerman, Nana Visitor. Guest Stars: Gerrit Graham, Scott MacDonald, Kelly Curtis.

In the 1980s and '90s, the *Star Trek* universe (like our own) was rapidly expanding — via *Star Trek: The Next Generation* (1987–1994), *Star Trek: Voyager* (1995–2001), *Star Trek: Enterprise* (2001–2005), and *Star Trek: Deep Space Nine*, which began in 1993 and lasted seven seasons. Unlike the other Trek series, which focused on ships traveling across space, *Deep Space Nine* detailed the adventures and encounters of the crew of a Federation space station guarding the opening of a stable wormhole. In the fifth episode of the fledgling series, the very first encounter with an alien life form from the galaxy quadrant on the other side of the wormhole (90,000 light years away) turns out to be one of hunters and hunted...

When a damaged ship comes through the wormhole, the space station brings it aboard for repairs and offers hospitality to its odd inhabitant, an articulate lizard-man with personal space issues named Tosk (make-up designer Michael Westmore based the alien's appearance on a picture of an alligator he saw in *Smithsonian* magazine). Nervous and wary, and more than a little naïve, Tosk (Scott MacDonald) is befriended by Chief of Operations Mr. O'Brien (Colm Meaney), who senses that the reticent Tosk has a secret — particularly after the alien attempts to break into the station's armory and ends up in the brig, refusing to explain himself. When a second ship from the same quadrant arrives through the wormhole, and a trio of aliens force their way onto Deep Space Nine in order to retrieve Tosk, it becomes apparent that "this whole thing is a hunt, and Tosk is the prey." As the lead hunter discusses the situation with the incensed station's commander, Captain Sisko (Avery Brooks), the alien asks, incredulously, "Have you nothing similar in your own society?" Sisko responds, "Centuries ago people on my world engaged in blood sports, killing lower species for pleasure. A few cultures still do. But even *they* wouldn't consider hunting a sentient being." But Tosk "has been *bred* for the hunt," answers the alien, "to make it as exciting, as interesting, as he can." Indeed, when O'Brien urges Tosk to seek asylum from the Federation, Tosk refuses, feeling that this would be the ultimate indignity. "I am Tosk, the hunted. I live to outwit the hunters for another day — to survive — until I die with honor." So O'Brien bucks protocol and helps Tosk escape back to his ship and so continue the hunt. "These guys wanted a hunt," reasons O'Brien, "I just gave them one."

Light on space-thrills but long on thought-provoking ideas and interactions, this episode focuses first on Tosk's fish-out-of-water encounters, with the burgeoning friendship and understanding between the alien and O'Brien becoming both endearing and affecting; then on such weighty notions as moral relativity, cultural differences, and the ideal of one's "purpose." The alien commander explains that the Tosk "train and condition themselves all their lives for this event; they're *proud* of their role in our culture." And Tosk himself states, "I live the greatest adventure one could ever desire." Such a thoughtful approach to such dicey moral issues offers no pat answers; but neither does it supply much in the way of action, apart from Tosk's exceedingly brief pursuit through the station at the end (the only part of the "hunt" portrayed). Short on action but long on thought, "Captive Pursuit" adds not only a space-age twist but puts a philosophical spin on the Most Dangerous Game.

Star Wars: The Clone Wars (3/19 and 3/26/2011) "Padawan Lost" and "Wookiee Hunt," Season 3, Episodes 21 and 22. Creator: George Lucas; Director: Dave Filoni; Teleplay: Bonnie Mark. Cast (voices): Ashley Eckstein, Gwendoline Yeo, Marc Lanter, James Arnold Taylor, Tom Kane.

"Without humility, courage is a dangerous game." So begins the two-part season three finale of *Star Wars: The Clone Wars*, a CGI-animated half-hour TV series created by George Lucas. Set in the *Star Wars* galaxy, the Grand Army of the Republic, led by various Jedi Knights (including Yoda and Anakin Skywalker) battles the droid army of the Separatists. In "Padawan Lost," the war-torn planet of Felucia sees Anakin leading a charge on a Separatist stronghold, aided by his protege Ahsoka. During the attack, a humanoid lizard-creature steps out of the forest and shoots an electrified net, capturing Ahsoka. "I can't believe my luck," hisses the alien, "a Jedi youngling." Ahsoka awakens in a cage, and a fellow captive informs her, "These are Transdoshans. They're going to release us and hunt us down for sport." A ship takes her and the other captives to another planet and drops them on an isolated island. When three other Jedi younglings, survivors of previous hunts, find Ahsoka, their leader explains, "We were taken by those foul lizards for their amusement, to be hunted, killed and mounted on their wall like trophies." At dawn the Transdoshans return and begin the hunt, tracking their prey from hoverpods and on foot. A frantic chase, ending in a vicious hand-to-hand battle, results in the death of both the head padawan and the reptilian hunter, son of the Transdoshan leader, who swears vengeance.

"Wookiee Hunt" picks up right where "Padawan Lost" left off, with Ahsoka galvanizing the remaining two Jedi padawans into attacking the next Transdoshan transport ship "head-on; they'll never expect it." In the fight, the ship is destroyed, but they rescue its lone captive, a Wookiee named Chewbacca(!). With Chewbacca's help, the padawans find and attack the mother ship, ending with Ahsoka taking on the reptilian leader one-on-one in his trophy room.

The impressive computer animation, inventive and startlingly imaginative alien flora and fauna, and fluid camera movement and varied angles all serve to make *Star Wars: The Clone Wars* a visually stunning series more akin to cinema than television. *The Hollywood Reporter* called it "likely the most photo-realistic animated TV series ever produced." (It proved popular with the public as well, becoming the most-watched series premier in Cartoon Network history. From season three onwards, however, viewership began to decline.) Dangerous Game–wise, the two episodes offer some thrilling hunt-and-chase scenes and savage fight sequences, as the padawans battle the brutish, powerful reptilians for their lives. Unfortunately, the episodes eschew the pivotal trap-laying of Connell's story (with the padawans generally just running and fighting), and the trophy room serves as mere background for the climactic front-and-center combat (with the horrors of the "trophies" themselves mere shadowy suggestion). Also missing is any discussion/exploration of the morality or philosophy of hunting, as well as any deeper motivation for the Transdoshans (who appear as simply a race who likes to hunt). Still, the two episodes remain a sometimes wondrous and often exciting, albeit simplistic, season finale.

Supernatural (2/14/2006) "The Benders," Season 1, Episode 15. Creator: Eric Kripke; Director: Peter Ellis; Teleplay: John Shiban. Cast: Jared Padalecki, Jensen Ackles. Guest Stars: John Dennis Johnston, Jessica Steen, Jon Cuthbert.

This popular (in its ninth season as of this writing) TV horror series follows the deadly adventures of brothers Sam (Jared Padelecki) and Dean (Jensen Ackles), two twenty-somethings who have taken on the mantle of monster hunters (inherited from their absent father) to roam small-town America investigating (and dispatching) all manner of supernatural menaces.

The season-one episode "The Benders" remains one of the few times Sam and Dean went up against a *non*-supernatural threat — a backwoods family that hunts humans for sport ("Demons I get," Dean says disgustedly, "*people* are crazy"). While the brothers investigate the mysterious disappearance of a man in a Mississippi town, Sam himself vanishes. With the help of a sympathetic female sheriff's deputy (Jessica Steen), Dean frantically searches for his brother and whatever supernatural creature has taken him. Finally, the trail leads to the surprisingly human (though *Texas Chainsaw*-esque) Bender family — father, two grown sons, and 13-year-old girl — who are keeping Sam in a cage awaiting their "hunt." "That's what this is all about," asks an incredulous Dean after being captured himself, "you yahoos hunt people?"

As far as the Dangerous Game goes, "The Benders" sorely disappoints, as the lone hunt lasts barely a minute and involves neither of the two principals — just a generic victim who runs through the rain-drenched woods only to be stabbed to death by the two spear-carrying Bender brothers. And said brothers, along with their cookie-cutter "vile redneck" pa and creepy younger sister, remain sorely underdeveloped (the two sick siblings — the only ones seen hunting — barely even speak). At least the deranged patriarch gets one opportunity to rhapsodize about his motive for hunting humans:

> I've hunted all my life. Just like my father and his before. I've hunted deer and bear. Even got a cougar once. But the best hunt is human. Ah, there's nothin' like it. Holding their life in your hands. Seeing the fear in their eyes just before they go dark. Makes you feel powerful alive.

But this sinister soliloquy, along with the sole blink-and-you'll-miss-it hunt, belongs in the too-little-too-late column. The remainder of this disappointingly weak and perfunctory episode focuses on Sam's ineffectual efforts to escape, Dean's drawn-out efforts to find and rescue his brother, and the Benders' clumsy efforts to keep those two things from happening.

The Venture Bros. (10/8/2006) "Showdown at Cremation Creek, Part 1," Season 2, Episode 12. Director: Jackson Publick; Teleplay: Doc Hammer, Jackson Publick. Cast (voices): James Urbaniak, Patrick Warburton, Michael Sinterniklaas, Chris McCulloch, Doc Hammer.

An acerbic, animated, adult-oriented parody of superheroes/supervillains (not to mention a satirical stab at *Jonny Quest*), *The Venture Bros.* follows the less-than-stellar adventures of (not so) super-scientist Dr. Venture, his two clueless teenage sons, and their deadpan he-man handler Brock Samson, who frequently face off against their arch-nemesis the Monarch (who dresses as an oversized butterfly and makes his lair in a giant flying cocoon) and his assistant Dr. Girlfriend.

In part one of the second season climax, the Monarch proposes to Dr. Girlfriend — much to the chagrin of Girlfriend's old flame, the Phantom Limb (an urbane supervillain with invisible arms and legs). While the episode's main storyline focuses on the couple's upcoming nuptials and Phantom Limb's (violent) disruption of same, a throwaway gag towards the episode's beginning has the suave Phantom Limb doing a bit of skeet shooting on his estate when the Monarch comes by to tell him of his and Girlfriend's engagement (and to "pick up her shit"). Instead of shotgunning clay pigeons, however, the Phantom Limb (decked out like the proverbial Great White Hunter) is targeting people (including several former villainous colleagues of the Monarch). "You'd be surprised at the array of wildlife here on the grounds," observes Phantom Limb. "Wonder what other game we could scare up," he adds before blasting Dr. Septopus out of a tree.

Xena: Warrior Princess (1/27/2001) "Dangerous Prey," Season 6, Episode 11. Creators: John Schulian, Rob Tapert; Director: Renee O'Connor; Teleplay: Joel Metzger. Cast: Lucy Lawless, Renee O'Connor. Guest Stars: Tsianina Joelson, Sandy Winton.

A spin-off from the popular TV series *Hercules: The Legendary Journeys*, the New Zealand–shot *Xena* became a hit in its own right, lasting six seasons, airing in 108 countries around the world, and even earning the number 9 and 10 spots on *TV Guide*'s "Top Cult Shows Ever" list in 2004 and 2007. The series' premise has former bandit warrior supreme Xena (Lucy Lawless) traveling the countryside, "in the time of the gods," seeking redemption for her past sins by aiding the downtrodden and righting wrongs.

In "Dangerous Prey," the female warrior Amazons Xena have befriended are being hunted down for sport and killed one by one by Prince Morloch (Sandy Winton), seeking new thrills for his jaded hunting palate. After Morloch kills the Amazon queen herself, Xena sets out to stop the mad hunter while simultaneously protecting the queen's hotheaded young successor, Varia (Tsianina Joelson).

Episode writer Joel Metzger originally wanted to do a *Karate Kid*–type story in which "the young Varia learned a lesson [from Xena] without realizing she learned it ... the wax-on, wax-off thing." But when series creator Rob Tapert rejected the idea, "I had two days to come up with something else," recounted Metzger. "We decided we would essentially rip off 'The Most Dangerous Game,' a short story that I think everybody had to read in high school" (a refreshingly candid and all-too-rare admission among MDG filmmakers). Hence, big-game hunter Rainsford became warrior princess Xena, General Zaroff was transformed into Prince Morloch, and Shipwreck Island became a trap-filled canyon near an Amazon village during a mythical age of sword and sorcery. Metzger fills his antagonist's mouth with some Connell-esque dialogue, paying homage to his original source by having Morloch explain, "I've hunted almost every creature that walks or crawls on this earth. Each one turned out to be an easy kill. When I set my sights a little higher I looked for something that might provide a real challenge. But even these so-called 'ultimate warriors'—the fierce, cunning Amazons—I've been disappointed. Feels like a *camping* trip." Later, Morloch tells Xena, his ultimate prey, "The gods make some men poets, some seers. They made me a hunter." When Xena protests that "a hunter hunts animals, not people," Morloch responds smugly, "In this world there *is* only the hunter and the hunted." It's all very reflective of Connell's character and dialogue (well, apart from the mention of "Amazons" and the campy "camping" comment, anyway).

Unfortunately, after the episode's brief opening stalk-and-chase scene in which the Amazon queen falls prey to various traps set by Morloch (including painfully catching her hand in a miniature bear trap), and finally to Morloch's own boomerang-type throwing weapon, the hunting-humans aspect falls by the wayside in favor of sword battles and the burgeoning mentor-student relationship between Xena and Varia. Couple this with the juvenile sensibilities of the show (reminiscent of an old Saturday Morning live-action series like *Shazam!* but with better production values and some lush New Zealand settings), the shallow characterizations, and the unlikely action set-pieces (at one point Xena catapults Varia over the forest via a bent tree, only to have her snagged in mid-air by a flying net launched by Morloch's catapult), and "Dangerous Prey" predictably limps along to its foregone conclusion.

With quotes from: "Interviews with Cast and Crew," *Xena: Warrior Princess, Season Six* DVD, Universal.

A Most Dangerous Conclusion

"When you have shot one bird flying you have shot all birds flying. They are all different and they fly in different ways but the sensation is the same and the last one is as good as the first." —Ernest Hemingway[1]

"When a man wants to murder a tiger he calls it sport; when a tiger wants to murder him he calls it ferocity." —George Bernard Shaw[2]

So what have I learned after taking this Most Dangerous Journey, watching, researching and studying all these films and videos and television shows? Most obvious, given the depth and breadth of the more than 100 adaptations, I've learned that people love to watch people hunting people for sport, and they have been doing so on a regular basis for the past 80-plus years. But in all their variations — gender (hunting humans is by no means an exclusive boys club), number (from lone individuals to large groups), weaponry (from the traditional bow to futuristic lasers and even trained tigers[!]), duration (lasting mere hours or encompassing multiple days), and location (everything from Caribbean island hunting grounds to inner city neighborhoods to outer space)—Most Dangerous Game stories feature one universal element: the mental health (or lack of same) of the antagonist(s). Upon this one point they all concur. Every would-be Zaroff is deranged. He, she, or they are portrayed as mad. Like in Connell's original tale, they may not be barking, they may not be drooling, they may even make rational-sounding arguments; but in the end they are ultimately revealed to be one biscuit shy of a full tin. The cause of this mental aberration that incites them to hunt people for sport may differ wildly (everything from sheer boredom to underlying insecurities to childhood trauma), but the characterization of madness remains constant. And so does the conclusion: No matter how rational their reasoned argument, hunters-of-humans have let their bestial impulses overcome their reasoning. As human beings they've abandoned their humanity and succumbed to their animal nature. Is this the price one pays for continually hunting the "lower" species for pleasure? Does protracted blood sport, killing over and over again merely for self-gratification, inevitably lead to the ultimate horror — insanity? As time marched on across the twentieth century, and the public zeitgeist turned away from big-game hunting to embrace a more ecological and conservation-minded viewpoint in the century's latter half, many of these films and television episodes (particularly the more modern iterations) seem to have answered in the affirmative. Yet, obviously not every big-game hunter becomes a sadistic Zaroff. So perhaps the spark of madness, already there, simply ignites into the flame of killing animals for pleasure before finally becoming the all-consuming conflagration of hunting humans. In any case, whether nature or nurture, innate bloodlust or violent experience, made them that way, almost always are the Zaroffs of the cinematic world punished for their madness. With infrequent exception, the sane overcome the *in*sane, the surrogate Rainsford ultimately defeats the alternate Zaroff, and thus restores order and balance to the world in a reassuring and cathartic victory for the viewer.

Nearly every Most Dangerous Game adaptation (even from the very first filmic incarnation in 1932) offers an anti–hunting polemic, sometimes subtle and sometimes overt, sometimes through introspective character development and sometimes via shout-it-to-the-rooftops speechifying. This seems only natural, of course, given the subtle-but-definite anti-hunting stance of Connell's original action-adventure story ("Rainsford knew now how an animal at bay feels," he dramatically concludes near the tale's end). Only the earliest adaptations cast their protagonists in the Rainsford mold by making them big-game hunters as well. And even when they do, inevitably these still-rational sport hunters learn the error of their ways by being forced into the role of the prey (walking a mile in their fur-lined shoes, as it were). Most Rainsford replacements are non-hunters, however, either ordinary people thrown into extraordinary circumstances or especially gifted individuals (military personnel, for instance) who, like Rainsford, possess the knowledge and skill (the "woodcraft") to defeat the Zaroff figure in this deadly game of "outdoor chess."

On a more general critical note, another thing I've learned is that, like with any cinematic subset, there's far more dross out there than gems (just ask my wife, who patiently put up with my bitching and moaning about the hours of my life spent watching terrible movies and television just because some crazy wants some poor soul's head as a trophy...). But there *are* some genuine Most Dangerous jewels, which sparkle with a unique intensity like no other cinema-type. And the Most Dangerous Game canon offers plenty of diamonds-in-the-rough as well for those willing to dig—films that with a little more care and polishing could have become a cinematic Star of India, but which still offer glimpses of brilliance through their celluloid surfaces. To paraphrase Connell's famous closing line: "He had never explored a more fascinating subgenre, Senn decided."

Chapter Notes

Introduction

1. Richard Connell (1893–1949) authored over 300 short stories, four novels and a number of screenplays (he became an in-demand Hollywood screenwriter in the 1930s, and subsequently devoted himself to that branch of writing, publishing no further novels or short story collections after 1937). Connell was nominated for an Academy Award for Best Original Story for 1941's *Meet John Doe*. He died of a heart attack in 1949, age 56.

2. Gregory Desilet, *Our Faith in Evil: Melodrama and the Effects of Entertainment Violence* (Jefferson, NC: McFarland, 2006).

3. Andrew Klavan, "In Praise of Fictional Violence," in *Examining Pop Culture: Violence in Film and Television*, edited by James D. Torr (San Diego, CA: Greenhaven Press, 2002).

4. Theodore Roosevelt, *African Game Trails* (New York: Cooper Square Press, 2001 [1910]).

5. In addition to film and television, Connell's story made its mark in radio as well. The radio series *Suspense* staged "The Most Dangerous Game" twice as an audio play, first on September 23, 1943, with Orson Welles as Zaroff; then on February 1, 1945, with Joseph Cotten playing Rainsford. In both productions Rainsford narrates the tale in retrospect as he waits in Zaroff's bedroom for their final confrontation, changing the story's third-person narrative to first-person (a logical adaptation to the radio medium).

6. Colin Wilson and Donald Seaman, *The Serial Killers: A Study in the Psychology of Violence* (New York: Carol Publishing Group, 1991).

7. Bernard DuClos, *Fair Game* (New York: St. Martin's Press, 1993).

8. Morc Encino, "*Hunt Me 4 Sport*," www.huntme4sport.comwww.huntme4sport.com, *6/20/2011.*

9. *Huffington Post*, "Sarah Timme, Colorado Mom, Wants School to Ban 'The Most Dangerous Game,'" www.huffingtonpost.comwww.huffingtonpost.com, *11/5/2012.*

Chapter 1

1. George E. Turner (ed.), *The Cinema of Adventure, Romance and Terror* (ASC Press, 1989).

2. Ronald Haver, *David O. Selznick's Hollywood* (New York: Alfred A. Knopf, 1980).

3. Orville Goldner and George E. Turner, *The Making of King Kong* (San Diego/New York: A. S. Barnes and Company, 1975).

4. Turner, *The Cinema of Adventure, Romance and Terror*.

5. Ibid.

Chapter 2

1. Michael G. Fitzgerald, "Ghost Ships, Body Snatchers, and Games of Death: Russell Wade," *Filmfax* 52 (September/October 1995).

2. Robert Wise, interviewed by the author, 1996.

3. "Ghost Ships, Body Snatchers, and Games of Death: Russell Wade."

Chapter 3

1. Tom Weaver, "Bri Murphy," in *Monsters, Mutants and Heavenly Creatures* (Baltimore, MD: Midnight Marquee Press, 1996).

2. Paul and Donna Parla, "Our Teenage Living Doll," *Scary Monsters Magazine* 73 (Jaunary 2010).

3. Tom Weaver, "Bri Murphy."

4. Ibid.

5. Paul and Donna Parla, "Our Teenage Living Doll."

6. Tom Weaver, "Bri Murphy."

7. Paul and Donna Parla, "Our Teenage Living Doll."

8. Tom Weaver, "Bri Murphy."

Chapter 5

1. All quotes attributed to Stu Segall are from phone interviews conducted by the author on April 19 and 26, 2013.

2. Jill C. Nelson, *Golden Goddesses* (Duncan, OK: BearManor Media, 2012).

Chapter 6

1. Tom Weaver, *Interviews with B Science Fiction and Horror Movie Makers* (Jefferson, NC: McFarland, 1988).
2. Ibid.
3. Ibid.
4. Ibid.

Chapter 7

1. Lowell Goldman, "Peter Fonda," *Psychotronic* 7 (1990).
2. Paul Gaita, "Dangerous Rhythm: An Interview with Richard Lynch," *Shock Cinema* 36 (2009).
3. Peter Fonda, *Don't Tell Dad: A Memoir* (New York: Hyperion, 1998).
4. Paul Gaita, "Dangerous Rhythm: An Interview with Richard Lynch."

Chapter 8

1. Interview with Brian Trenchard-Smith, *Escape 2000* DVD (Umbrella Entertainment, 2003).
2. "Turkey Shoot: Blood and Thunder Memories," *Escape 2000* DVD (Anchor Bay Entertainment, 2003).
3. Ibid.
4. *Not Quite Hollywood: The Wild, Untold Story of Ozploitation* DVD (Magnet Releasing/HD Net, 2008).
5. Interview with Brian Trenchard-Smith, *Escape 2000* DVD.
6. Ibid.
7. "Turkey Shoot: Blood and Thunder Memories," *Escape 2000* DVD.
8. Ibid.
9. Ibid.
10. Ibid.
11. Interview with Brian Trenchard-Smith, *Escape 2000* DVD.
12. *Not Quite Hollywood: The Wild, Untold Story of Ozploitation* DVD.
13. Ibid.
14. Ibid.
15. "Turkey Shoot: Blood and Thunder Memories," *Escape 2000* DVD.

Chapter 9

1. *Avenging Force* Presskit, Canon Films, Inc., 1986.
2. Ibid.
3. Jason Rugaard, "Interview: Sam Firstenberg," *Movie Mavericks Podcast*, http://moviemavericks.com/2010/04/interview-sam-firstenberg/, April 13, 2010.
4. *Avenging Force* Presskit.
5. Ibid.
6. Ibid.
7. Ibid.
8. Ibid.
9. *Michael Dudikoff* official website, http://michael-dudikoff.com/.
10. Marc Shapiro, "Street Fighter," *Action Heroes* 3 (1990).
11. Ian, "From Ninjas to Breakdancing: An Interview with Sam Firstenberg," *AV Manaics.com*, http://www.avmaniacs.com/features/interview_sam_firstenberg.html.
12. Jason Rugaard, "Interview: Sam Firstenberg," *Movie Mavericks Podcast*.
13. Marc Shapiro, "Street Fighter," *Action Heroes* 3 (1990).
14. Ibid.
15. Christine Pan James, "Steve James," http://www.ninjastevejames.com/media/stevejamesbio.pdf.
16. Jason Rugaard, "Interview: Sam Firstenberg," *Movie Mavericks Podcast*.

Chapter 10

1. J. R. Bookwalter, *Attack of the B-Movie Makers* (Hollywood, CA: Cinema Home Video Productions, Inc./Subtempeco Press, 1991).
2. "Slave Girls from Beyond Infinity," *Badmovies.org*, March 9, 1999.
3. Ibid.

Chapter 11

1. Phone interview with Ted V. Mikels, conducted by the author April 13, 2012.
2. Christopher Wayne Curry, *Film Alchemy: The Independent Cinema of Ted V. Mikels* (Jefferson, NC: McFarland, 2007).
3. Mikels interview, conducted by the author.
4. Curry, *Film Alchemy*.
5. Mikels interview, conducted by the author.
6. Curry, *Film Alchemy*.
7. Ibid.
8. Mikels interview, conducted by the author.
9. Ibid.
10. Ibid.
11. Ibid.
12. Ibid.
13. Curry, *Film Alchemy*.
14. Ibid.
15. Ibid.
16. Mikels interview, conducted by the author.
17. Curry, *Film Alchemy*.
18. Ibid.

Chapter 12

1. Kenneth E. Hall, *John Woo: The Films* (Jefferson, NC: McFarland, 1999).
2. Robert K. Eldger, ed., *John Woo: Interviews* (Jackson: University Press of Mississippi, 2005).
3. Ibid.
4. Barbara Scharres, "The Hard Road to *Hard Target*," *American Cinematographer*, September 1993.
5. Ibid.
6. Christopher Heard, *Ten Thousand Bullets: The Cinematic Journey of John Woo* (Los Angeles: Lone Eagle Publishing, 2000).
7. Kenneth E. Hall, *John Woo: The Films*
8. Ibid.
9. *Hard Target* Presskit, "Production Information," Universal Pictures, 1993.
10. Ibid.
11. Kenneth E. Hall, *John Woo: The Films*.
12. *Hard Target* Presskit.
13. Kenneth E. Hall, *John Woo: The Films*.
14. Robert K. Eldger, ed., *John Woo: Interviews*.
15. *Hard Target* Presskit.
16. Ibid.
17. Kenneth E. Hall, *John Woo: The Films*.
18. Christopher Heard, *Ten Thousand Bullets*.
19. *Hard Target* Presskit.
20. Ibid.
21. Christopher Heard, *Ten Thousand Bullets*.
22. Ibid.
23. Ibid.

Chapter 13

1. *Surviving the Game* Presskit, New Line Cinema, 1994.
2. Ibid.
3. Ibid.
4. Ibid.
5. Rutger Hauer, "Surviving the Game," *Rutger Hauer Official Website*.
6. Douglas Thompson, "1995 Interview with Rutger Hauer," *dougiethompson.com*.
7. "The Heart-Wrenching Tale of Prince Henry Stout," *Zimbio.com*.
8. Darlene Donlow, "Getting to Know F. Murray Abraham," *LA Stage Times*, April 12, 2011.
9. Ibid.
10. Andrew J. Rausch, *Fifty Filmmakers* (Jefferson, NC: McFarland, 2008).
11. *Surviving the Game* Presskit.
12. Rutger Hauer, "Surviving the Game," *Rutger Hauer Official Website*.
13. Ibid.
14. *Surviving the Game* Presskit.
15. Ibid.
16. Tambay A. Obenson, "Interview: Award-Winning Cinematographer, Writer and Director Ernest Dickerson, Reintroduced," Indiewire.com.
17. *The Larely Beagle*, "'Surviving the Game' Writer Still Regrets Killing Gary Busey's Character First," Larelybeagle.com.
18. Ibid.
19. Ibid.
20. "Surviving the Game," *Drinkingcinema.com*.

Chapter 14

1. "*The Pest* Production Information," *The Pest* Presskit, Tristar Pictures, 1997.
2. Ibid.
3. Ibid.
4. Ibid.
5. Ibid.
6. Ibid.
7. Ibid.
8. Nathan Rabin, "Interview: John Leguizamo" *Avclub.com*, July 25, 2001.
9. Ibid.
10. "*The Pest* Production Information."
11. Ibid.

A Most Dangerous Conclusion

1. Ernest Hemingway, *Winner Take Nothing* (New York: Scribners, 1933).
2. George Bernard Shaw, *Man and Superman* (New York: Penguin Classics, 2001 [1903]).

Bibliography

Albright, Brian. "High Concepts, Low Budgets: An Interview with Director Greydon Clark." *Shock Cinema* 29 (2005).

Avenging Force Presskit. Cannon Films, Inc., 1986.

Bene, Jason. "Late Night Classics — *Without Warning*." *Killer Film*, http://www.killerfilm.com/features/read/late-night-classics-without-warning-2-29680, April 16, 2010 (accessed February 2013).

Bookwalter, J.R. *Attack of the B-Movie Makers: A Personal and In-Depth Look at Low-Budget Filmmakers David DeCoteau and Fred Olen Ray*. Hollywood, CA: Cinema Home Video Productions, Inc., in association with Subtempeco Press, 1991.

Connell, Richard. "The Most Dangerous Game," 1924 (renewed 1952), reprinted in *The Most Dangerous Game and Other Stories of Adventure*. New York: Berkley Publishing Corp., 1957.

Curry, Christopher Wayne. *Film Alchemy: The Independent Cinema of Ted V. Mikels*. Jefferson, NC: McFarland, 2007.

Desiilet, Gregory. *Our Faith in Evil: Melodrama and the Effects of Entertainment Violence*. Jefferson, NC: McFarland, 2006.

Donlow, Darlene. "Getting to Know F. Murray Abraham." *LA Stage Times*, April 12, 2011, http://www.lastagetimes.com/2011/04/getting-to-know-f-murray-abraham/ (accessed 4/4/2013).

DuClos, Bernard. *Fair Game*. New York: St. Martin's Press, 1993.

Eisenthal, Bram. "laher$: Reality Slices." *Fangoria* 215 (August 2002).

Elder, Robert K., ed. *John Woo: Interviews*. Jackson: University Press of Mississippi, 2005.

Encino, Mork. "Hunt Me 4 Sport," http://huntme4sport.com/post/6736447139/hunt-me-for-sport, 6/20/2011 (accessed 3/15/2012).

Fitzgerald, Michael G. "Ghost Ships, Body Snatchers, and Games of Death: Russell Wade." *Filmfax* 52 (September/October 1995).

Fonda, Peter. *Don't Tell Dad: A Memoir*. New York, Hyperion, 1998.

"Formidable! The Michel Lemoine Story." *Seven Women for Satan* DVD, Mondo Macabro, 2003.

Gaita, Paul. "Dangerous Rhythm: An Interview with Richard Lynch." *Shock Cinema* 36 (2009).

Gilmour, Walter, and Leland E. Hale. *Butcher Baker: A True Account of a Serial Murderer*. New York: Penguin Books, 1991.

Goldman, Lowell. "Peter Fonda." *Psychotronic* 7 (1990).

Goldner, Orville, and George E. Turner. *The Making of King Kong*. San Diego/New York: A. S. Barnes and Company, 1975.

Hall, Kenneth E. *John Woo: The Films*. Jefferson, NC: McFarland, 1999.

Hauer, Rutger. "Surviving the Game." *Rutger Hauer Official Website*, http://www.rutgerhauer.org/plots/survi.php (accessed January 2013).

Haver, Ronald. *David O. Selznick's Hollywood*. New York: Alfred A. Knopf, 1980.

Heard, Christopher. *Ten Thousand Bullets: The Cinematic Journey of John Woo*. Los Angeles: Lone Eagle Publishing, 2000.

"The Heart-Wrenching Tale of Prince Henry Stout." *Zimbio*, http://www.zimbio.com/Rutger+Hauer/articles/10/Heart+Wrenching+Tale+Prince+Henry+Stout (accessed January 2013).

Hemingway, Ernest. *Winner Take Nothing*. New York: Scribners, 1933.

Huffington Post. "Sarah Timme, Colorado Mom, Wants School to Ban 'The Most Dangerous Game.'" 11/5/2012, http://www.huffingtonpost.com/2012/11/05/sarah-timme-colorado-mom-_n_2077063.html (accessed 3/20/2013).

Ian. "From Ninjas to Breakdancing: An Interview with Sam Firstenberg," *AV Manaics.com*, http://www.avmaniacs.com/features/interview_sam_firstenberg.html (accessed January 2013).

James, Christine Pan. "Steve James." http://www.ninjastevejames.com/media/stevejamesbio.pdf (accessed January 2013).

JimmyO. "Predators Chat with Rodriguez and Antal." *iamrogue.com*, July 5, 2010, http://www.iamrogue.com/news/interviews/item/91-predators-chat-with-rodriguez-antal.html (accessed 4/14/2013).

Johnson, Tom, and Mark A. Miller. *The Christopher Lee Filmography*. Jefferson, NC: McFarland & Co., Inc., 2004.

Klavan, Andrew. "In Praise of Fictional Violence." In *Examining Pop Culture: Violence on Film and*

Television, edited by James D. Torr. San Diego, CA: Greenhaven Press, 2002.

Kobal, John. *People Will Talk*. New York: Alfred A. Knopf, 1985.

LaMotta, Jake, Joseph Carter and Peter Savage. *Raging Bull: My Story*. New York: DaCapo Press, 1997 (reprint).

The Larely Beagle. "'Surviving the Game' Writer Still Regrets Killing Gary Busey's Character First." *Larelybeagle.com*, http://www.larelybeagle.com/2008/10/01/surviving-the-game-writer-still-regrets-killing-gary-buseys-character-first/ (accessed January 2013).

Lee, Christopher. *Lord of Misrule: The Autobiography of Christopher Lee*. London: Orion, 2003.

Lowry, Brian. "Nick Castle: 'How Do You Get Around Star Wars?'" *Starlog* 87 (October 1984).

Machete Maidens Unleashed! Directed by Mark Hartley, Dark Sky Films, 2010.

Maltin, Leonard. "Interview with Roger Corman." *Death Race 2000* DVD, Concord-New Horizons Corp., 2001.

McGee, Mark Thomas. *Roger Corman*. Jefferson, NC: McFarland & Co., Inc, 1988.

Muller, Eddie, and Daniel Faris. *Grindhouse*. New York: St. Martin's Press, 1995.

The Naked Prey: Merchandising Manual and Press Book. Paramount, 1966.

Nelson, Jill C. *Golden Goddesses: 25 Legendary Women of Classic Erotic Cinema, 1968–1985*. Duncan, OK: BearManor Media, 2012.

Not Quite Hollywood: The Wild, Untold Story of Ozploitation DVD. Magnet Releasing/HD Net, 2008.

Nutman, Philip. "Scream and Scream Again: The Uncensored History of Amicus Productions." *Little Shoppe of Horrors* 20 (June 2008).

Obenson, Tambay A. "Interview: Award-Winning Cinematographer, Writer and Director Ernest Dickerson, Reintroduced," *Indiewire.com*, http://blogs.indiewire.com/shadowandact/interview-cinematographer-director-writer-ernest-dickerson-reintroduced?page=3#blogPostHeaderPanel (accessed 4/4/2013).

Parla, Paul and Donna, et al. "Our Teenage Living Doll: An Exclusive Interview with June Kenney." *Scary Monsters Magazine* 73 (January 2010).

"*The Pest*: Production Information." *The Pest* Presskit. Tristar Pictures, 1997.

Poggiali, Chris. "Slinking Through the '70s: From *Cobra Woman* to the Cult Classic *Ganja and Hess*, Marlene Clark Lit Up Numerous Genre Films." *Fangoria* 191 (April 2000).

Pohle, Robert W. Jr., and Douglas C. Hart. *The Films of Christopher Lee*. Metuchen, NJ: The Scarecrow Press, Inc., 1983.

Rabin, Nathan. "Interview: John Leguizamo." *A.V. Club*. July 25, 2001, http://www.avclub.com/articles/john-leguizamo,13722/ (accessed 4/12/2013).

Rausch, Andrew J. *Fifty Filmmakers: Conversations with Directors from Roger Avary to Steven Zaillian*. Jefferson, NC: McFarland, 2008.

Roosevelt, Theodore. *African Game Trails: An Account of the African Wanderings of an American Hunter-Naturalist*. New York: Cooper Square Press, 2001 (1910).

Rugaard, Jason. "Interview: Sam Firstenberg." *Movie Mavericks Podcast*, http://moviemavericks.com/2010/04/interview-sam-firstenberg/, April 13, 2010 (accessed January 2013).

Scharres, Barbara. "The Hard Road to *Hard Target*." *American Cinematographer*, September 1993.

Schwarzenegger, Arnold, and Peter Petre. *Total Recall: My Unbelievably True Life Story*. New York: Simon and Schuster, 2012.

Scorsese, Martin. "*The Naked Prey* (1966) and *Apocalypto* (2006)." *DirecTV*, http://www.directv.com/DTVAPP/global/contentPage.jsp?assetId=P4480016 (accessed 4/22/2013).

Shapiro, Marc. "Predator vs. Schwarzenegger." *Fangoria* 65 (July 1987).

_____. "Street Fighter." *Action Heroes* 3 (1990).

Shaw, George Bernard. *Man and Superman*. New York: Penguin Classics, 2001 (1903).

"Slave Girls from Beyond Infinity." *Badmovies.org*, http://www.badmovies.org/forum/index.php?topic=111552.0, March 9, 1999 (accessed August 2009).

"Surviving the Game." *Drinking Cinema*, http://drinkingcinema.com/game/Surviving+the+Game (accessed 4/3/2013).

Swires, Steve. "The Real Mary Woronov," *Fangoria* 51 (1986).

Surviving the Game Presskit. New Line Cinema, 1994.

Tate, Fred. March 9, 1999, posting at www.badmovies.org, accessed August 2009.

"The Tenth Victim." *Continental Film Review* (September 1965).

Thompson, Douglas. "1995 Rutger Hauer Interview," *dougiethompson.com*, http://www.dougiethompson.com/RutgerHauer_page1.htm (accessed January 2013).

Trenchard-Smith, Brian. Interview on *Escape 2000* DVD, Anchor Bay Entertainment, 2003.

"Turkey Shoot: Blood and Thunder Memories." *Escape 2000* DVD, Anchor Bay Entertainment, 2003.

Turner, George (ed.). *The Cinema of Adventure, Romance and Terror*. ASC Press, 1989.

"Video Interview: Nimrod Antal and Robert Rodriguez." *JoBlo.com*, July 9, 2010, http://www.joblo.com/horror-movies/news/video-interview-nimrod-antal-and-robert-rodriguez (accessed 4/14/2013).

Watkins, Peter. "Director's Introduction." *Punishment Park* DVD, Asset Digital, 2004.

Weaver, Tom. *Interviews with B Science Fiction and*

Horror Movie Makers: Writers, Producers, Directors, Actors Moguls and Makeup. Jefferson, NC: McFarland, 1988.

_____. "Jan Merlin: The Thrill of the Hunt." *Chiller Theater* 20 (2004).

_____. *Monsters, Mutants and Heavenly Creatures: Confessions of 14 Classic Sci-Fi/Horrormeisters.* Baltimore, MD: Midnight Marquee Press, 1996.

Wilson, Colin, and Donald Seaman. *The Serial Killers: A Study in the Psychology of Violence.* New York: Carol Publishing Group, 1991.

Woman Hunt Pressbook. New World Pictures, 1973.

Wood, Gary. "Stephen King & Hollywood." *Cinefantastique* (February 1991).

Zuzelo, David. "An Invisible Cord: Analia Ivars on Jess Franco." *Tomb It May Concern*, 4/3/2013, http://david-z.blogspot.com/?zx=644f0a2175c85dc8 (accessed 4/4/2013).

Index

Page numbers in **_bold italics_** indicate pages with photographs.

The A-Team (series) 40, 68
Abbott, Bruce 206, 207
Abdul, Paula 223
Abraham, F. Murray 134, 137
Ackles, Jensen 267
Adams, Don 142, 254
Adamson, Al 238
Aerobicide see *Killer Workout*
African Game Trails (book) 3
Agron, Dianna 161
Airwolf (series) 242–243
Alaimo, Marc **_89_**
Alegre, Alona 66
The Alfred Hitchcock Hour (series) 40
Alice in Wonderland: An X-Rated Musical Fantasy (1976) 208
Alien (1979) 232, 236
Alien Fury: Countdown to Invasion (2000) 59
Alien vs. Predator see *AVP: Alien vs. Predator*
Alienator (1990) 243
Aliens (1986) 114, 119, 235
The All-Americans (novel) see *Open Season* (novel)
Allen, Woody 142
Altered States (1980) 155
Altweis, Jame 28
Amadeus (1984) 134, 144
American Dad! (series) 243–244
American Ninja (1985) 93, 95
American Ninja 2 (1987) 95
American Ninja 3 (1989) 95
American Ninja 4 (1990) 95
American Ninja 5 (1993) 95
Amick, Madchen 158, 160
Andress, Ursula 229
The Andromeda Strain (1971) 40
Angel (series) 245, 251
Angel of Vengeance see *War Cat*
Animal House (1978) 208
Annett, Paul 179, 181
Antal, Nimrod 236, 237
Antoyoya, Svetlana 174
Apocalypse Now (1979) 68
Apollo 13 (1995) 239
Apollo 18 (2011) 163
Archer (series) 244–245, **_244_**
Armchair Theatre (series) 76
Armed Response (1986) 110
Armendari, Pedro 193
Armstrong, Robert 15, 20, 21, 27

Arno, Alice 172, **_173_**
Aronson, John B. 161
Arribas, Fernando 75
Arrivano i titani see *My Son, the Hero*
Ashley, John 55, 66, 67–68, 210
Assante, Armand 122
Assault on Precinct 13 (2005) 144
The Astro-Zombies (1968) 109
Atkins, Tom 208
Attack of the Giant Leeches (1959) 29
Attack of the Puppet People (1958) 41
Austin, Steve 216, 217
Avenging Force (1986) 87–95, **_88_**, **_89_**, **_91_**, 120, 131
AVH: Alien vs. Hunter (2007) 231–232
AVP: Alien vs. Predator (2004) 231, 232–233, 236
AVP: Requiem see *AVPR: Aliens vs. Predator Requiem*
AVPR: Aliens vs. Predator Requiem (2007) 231, 233
The Awful Dr. Orlof (1962) 172

Bachman, Richard see King, Stephen
Back to the Future (1985) 262
Baez, Joan 199
Ballerini, Edoardo **_141_**, 143
Band, Charles 104
Banks, Leslie **_17_**, 18, **_19_**, 20, 22, 27
Barbarella (1968) 85
Barbet, Ken 220
Barrier, Edgar **_26_**, 29, 30, 31
Bartel, Paul 219
Basehart, Richard 164, 165
Bassett, Michael 213
Batman (series) 153
Bats (1999) 147
Battle Royale (2000) 215–216, 220
Battle Royale II (2003) 216
Bazelli, Bojan 131
Beach Babes from Beyond (1993) 153
Beach Blanket Bingo (1965) 68
Beal, Cindy **_97_**, 103
The Beast Must Die (1974) 179–182, **_180_**, 236
Beast of Blood (1971) 66, 185, 210
Beast of the Yellow Night (1971) 66, 68, 210
The Beastmaster (1982) 183

Beastmaster: The Eye of Braxus (1996) 59
Beck, Michael 183
Beck, Vincent 261
Becker, Tony 161
Beetlejuice (1988) 144
Benjamin, H. John **_244_**
Benmayor, Daniel 222
Bennet, Jeff 258
Bergen, Candice 186
Bernt, Eric 128, 130, 135, 136–137
Best, James 201
Bet Your Life (2004) 146–147
A Better Tomorrow (1986) 117, 122
Bicknell, Andrew 256
The Big Bird Cage (1972) 65, 67
The Big Country (1958) 211
The Big Doll House (1971) 65, 68
Big Fish (2003) 190
Big Game (1980) 147–149
Big game: la chasse aux noirs see *Big Game*
Bilingslea, Aldo 167
Billingsley, John 248
Bitter Feast (2010) 179, 182–183
Bixby, Bill 155, 257
B.J. and the Bear (series) 208
Black Jack (1981) 149
Black Sabbath (1963) 219
Black Shampoo (1976) 238
Black Werewolf see *The Beast Must Die*
Blade Runner (1982) 132
Blier, Bernard 151
Blood Bath (1966) 265
Blood Camp Thatcher see *Escape 2000*
Blood of Dracula (1957) 36
The Blood of Heroes (1990) 136
Blood Orgy of the She Devils (1972) 111
Blood Sisters see *Sisters*
Blood Trail (1997) 150
Bloodlust! (1960) 33–41, **_34_**, **_37_**
Bloodsport (1988) 122
Blow-Up (1966) 85
BMX Bandits (1983) 85
The Body Snatcher (1945) 30, 31
Bochner, Lloyd 247
Bogart, Humphrey 207
Boisset, Yves 151
Bonanza (series) 245
Bones (2001) 136

279

Index

Booth, James 90, 92
Borgnine, Ernest 242
Boswell, Glen 85
Bottoms, Sam 201
Boulois, Max 148, 149
Bower, Antoinette 204, 205
The Boy Who Could Fly (1986) 208
The Brady Bunch (series) 36, 40
The Brain That Wouldn't Die (1962) 208
Brand, Neville 239
Breaker Morant (1980) 154
Breakin' (1984) 136
Breakin' 2: Electric Boogaloo (1984) 95, 136
Brennen, Claire 165
Briant, Chris 161
Brides of Blood (1968) 68, 210
Brody, Adrien 236, 237
Bronson, Charles 243
The Bronx Executioner (1989) 157
Brook, Claudio 151
Brooke, Ralph 35, 36–38, 39–40, 41
Brooke, Walter 40
Brooks, Avery 266
Brown, Bryan 154
Brown, Jim 94
Brown, Peter 197
The Buddy Holly Story (1978) 133
Buffy the Vampire Slayer (series) 245–246, 251, 252
Bullet in the Head (1990) 122
Burr, Raymond 154
Busey, Gary *126*, 133, 136, 235, 236
Busselier, Tania 172
Byrd, Arthur *see* Segall, Stu
Byrkjeland, Havard 166

Cabot, Bruce 22
Cage, Nicholas 8, 122
Cain, Dean 154, 155
Caine, Michael 77
Calhoun, Rory 255
Campbell, William 265
Cannom, Greg 239
Capri, Ahna 197
Carlyle, Robert 230
Carnosaur 2 (1995) 147
Carpenter, Charisma 246
Carpenter, John 208
Carpenter, Russell 117–118
Carpenter, Willie 121
Carradine, David 95, 218, *218*, 219
Carradine, John 208
Carradine, Robert 206, 207, 207–208
Carrere, Tia 154, 263, 264
Carrigan, Sean 146
Caruso, David 250
Carver, Steve 65
Castle, Nick 207, 208
Castle, William 68
Cayton, Elizabeth *97*, 103
Cerdan, Marcel 48
Challenge of the Superfriends (series) 246–247

Chambers, John 205
Chambers, Marilyn 59
Chaney, Lon, Jr. 21
Chang (1927) 20
Charles-Williams, Liz 74, 75, 76
Charlie and the Chocolate Factory (2005) 190
Charlie's Angels (series) 40, 247–248
Charteris, Leslie 32
La Chasse aux noirs see *Big Game*
Chauvin, Lilyan 40
Cheyenne (series) 201
CHiPs (series) 208
Chow Yun-Fat 120
Citizen Kane (1941) 30
Clark, Carroll 18
Clark, Greydon 238, 239, 240, 241
Clark, Ken 151
Clark, Marlene 182
Clemento, Steve 21
Clockers (1995) 131
Clown Hunt (2012) 149–150
Cocktail (1988) 154
Coeur, Joelle 203
Coffy (1973) 67
Cohen, Bennett 159
Cold Case (series) 248–249
Collins, Jennifer 110
Collins, Suzanne 220
Collinson, Peter 74, 75–76, 76–77
Colter, John 194
Combat! (series) 242
The Comedy of Terrors (1963) 219
La Comtesse perverse see *The Perverse Countess*
The Condemned (2007) 216–217
Confessions of a Dangerous Mind (2002) 136
Confessions of a Psycho Cat (1968) 42–49, *43*, 55
Connell, Richard 1, 252, 273n1
Connery, Sean 191
Connors, Chuck 211, *212*
The Conqueror (1956) 68
Conquest of Space (1955) 40
Cooper, Merian C. 14, 20, 21, 22
Cooper, Stuart 160
"Cop Killer" (song) 136
Coplan paie le cerceuil (novel) 151
Coplan Saves His Skin (1968) 150–152
Coplan suave sa peau see *Coplan Saves His Skin*
Coppola, Francis Ford 68
Corman, Roger 65, 67–68, 217, 219
The Corpse Grinders (1972) 109
Corso, Marge 40
Cotten, Joseph 273n5
Cotton Comes to Harlem (1970) 179
Count Yorga, Vampire (1970) 179
Countess Perverse see *The Perverse Countess*
Crabbe, Buster 22
Craig, Michael 82, 83, 85
Creelman, James Ashmore 15, 16–17, 20, 26–27, 99

Criminal Minds (series) 249–250
Les Croqueuses see *The Perverse Countess*
Croxton, Lucius 28
CSI: Crime Scene Investigation (series) 250, 262
CSI: Miami (series) 250–251
CSI: New York (series) 250
Culp, Clint 262
Cummings, Jim 258
Cundy, Dean 239
Cunha, Richard E. 36, 41
Cunningham, Liam 230
The Curse of the Cat People (1944) 30
Curtis, Dan 201, 202
Cusack, John 8
Cushing, Peter 149, 181–182
Cyborg (1989) 122

D'Agostino, Albert 28
Dallas (series) 94
Daniels, Godfrey *see* Segall, Stu
Dark Shadows (series) 201
Dark Star (1974) 208
Darkman (1990) 123
Darwin, Charles 3
Davies, Geraint Wyn 253
The Da Vinci Treasure (2006) 231
Davis, Andrew 122, 224
Davis, B.J. 93
Dawn of the Dead (2004) 230
Dawson, Richard 224
Day, Charlie 258
The Day the Earth Stood Still (1951) 30
Dead Calm (1989) 146
Dead End Drive-In (1986) 85
Deadlier Than the Male (1967) 76
Deadly Embrace (1989) 243
Deadly Game (1991) 10, 183
Deadly Prey (1988) 108, 183–184
Deadwood (series) 144
Death Race 2000 (1975) 217–219, *218*
Death Ring (1992) 152–154, 171
Deathwatch (2002) 213
DeBell, Christine 208
La decima vittima see *The Tenth Victim*
DeCoteau, David 243
Deep Red (1975) 85
Deep Roy 190
Deep Space (1988) 103
Deliverance (1972) 130, 165, 175
The Delta Force (1986) 95
DeLuca, Daniella 168
Dementia 13 (1983) 265
Dempsey & Makepeace (series) 190
Dempsy, Sandy 54
De Nesle, Robert 174
Dennis the Menace (1993) 208
Denver, Bob 255
De Sade, Marquis 172
Desilet, Gregory 1
Destination Moon (1950) 21
Devereaux, Maurice 227
DeVilliers, Rocco 200
The Devils (1971) 155

Index

The Devil's Garden see *Coplan Saves His Skin*
DeVito, Danny 258
Dexter (series) 136
The Diabolical Dr. Z (1966) 172
Diaz, Vic **205**, 205
Dickerson, Ernest 128, 129, 130, 130–131, 132, 133, 134, 135, 136
Dietrich, Marlene 144
Diffring, Anton 181
Dillman, Bradford 257
Dirty Dancing (1987) 153
Dirty Harry (1971) 235
Disher, Catherine 254
Dixon, Ken 100–101, 101, 101–102, 102–103
Do the Right Thing (1989) 136
Dr. Jekyll and Mr. Hyde (novella) 204
Dr. Kildare (series) 40
Dogboys (1998) 154–155, 264
The Doll Squad (1973) 111
Dollhouse (series) 251–252
Donahue, Troy 184
Doohan, James 265
Double Impact (1991) 122
Doyle, David 247
Dracula (1931) 141
Dracula vs. Frankenstein (1971) 238
Dracula's Daughter (1936) 21, 28
Dragnet (series) 40
Dragstrip Girl (1957) 68
Drago, Billy 152, 153
Dressed to Kill (1980) 95
The Drew Carey Show (series) 110
Drive-In Massacre (1976) 57, 59
DuClus, Bernard 8
Dudikoff, Michael **88**, 91–92, **91**, 93, 94
Duncan, Carmen 82
Dushku, Eliza 251–252
Dutton, Charles S. 133

Earth vs. the Spider (1958) 41
The Earthling (1980) 77
Eastwood, Clint 235
Eating Raoul (1982) 219
Eberhardt, Thom 168
The Ecstasy Girls (1979) 58
Ed Wood (1994) 144
Edlund, Richard 235
Edwards, Vince 165
Eight Is Enough (series) 208
Einstein, Albert 3
The Eliminator (2004) 10, 219–220
Encino, Mork 8, 10
Endurance (series) 227
Enter the Dragon (1973) 185
Escape see *The Woman Hunt*
Escape from New York (1981) 208
Escape from Sobibor (1988) 136
Escape 2000 (1982) 78–86, **79**, **84**, 89
The Escort III (1999) 103
Esquire (periodical) 94
Eugenie (1970) 172
Evasion see *Maneater*
Everett, Edward *see* Paramore, Ted

Everybody Gets It in the End see *T.A.G.: The Assassination Game*
The Expendables 2 (2012) 122
The Exterminator (1980) 95

Face/Off (1997) 122
Fair Game (book) 8
Fantasy Island (1977 TV movie) 155–156
Fantasy Island (series) 155, 156, 252–253
Faris, Daniel 45
Fawcett, Farrah 247
The F.B.I. Files (series) 253
Feldon, Barbara 254
Ferrandini, Dean 171
Ferrier, Noel 82
Ferrigno, Lou 257
Ferris Bueller's Day Off (1986) 144
Fields, Norman 54, 58
The Final Executioner (1984) 156–157
Final Round see *Human Target*
Finder, Richard 197
Firstenberg, Sam 91, 92–93, 94, 95
Fishburne, Laurence 237
Flash Gordon (1936 serial) 22
Fleming, Ian 191
Flesh and Blood (1986) 136
Flipper (1995 series) 85
Foch, Nina 189
The Fog (1980) 208
Foley, Macka 110
Fonda, Peter 73–74, 77
Forbidden Planet (1956) 101, 260
Forever Knight (series) 253–254
Foucan, Sebastian 229
Fox, Billy 48
Franco, Jess 172, 173, 174, 176, 178, 203
Frankenfish (2004) 162
Frankenstein (1931) 208
Frankenstein (novel) 1
Frankenstein's Daughter (1958) 36, 41, 68
Freeman, K. Todd 246
Friedman, David F. 55, 57
Fright Night (1985) 235
Frontiers (2007) 157
Frozen Ground 8
The Fugitive (1993) 122
Fulci, Lucio 262
The Full Monty (1997) 230
F/X (1986) 154

Galotti, Robert "Rock" 119
Game of Death (1978) 186
A Game of Death (1945) 3, 23–32, **24**, **26**, 99–101, 102, 186, 263
The Game of Death (1974) 185–186
Games of Death see *The Game of Death* (1974)
Garcia, Eddie **64**, 66, 185, 186, 210
Garfield, J.D. 168
Gazarra, Ben 165
Geller, Sarah Michelle 245
Gemma, Giuliano 193, 194

George, Jon 80
Gerrard, Henry 18–19
Get Smart (series) 142, 254–255
Ghost (1990) 153
The Ghost Ship (1943) 31
Ghostbusters (1984) 235
The Giant Claw (1957) 31
Giant from the Unknown (1958) 36, 41
Gilligan's Island (series) 255–256
Gimme a Break! (series) 94
Ginnane, Antony 85
Glaser, Paul Michael 224
Glasser, Isabel 152
Glee (series) 161
Globus, Yoram 95
Glover, Danny 235
Godzilla 1985 (1985) 154
Golan, Menahem 95, 122
Goldfinger (1964) 255
Gothic (1986) 155
Gould, Harold 254
GQ (periodical) 94
The Graduate (1967) 40
Graff, Wilton 37, **37**, 38, 40
Grand Champion (2002) 150
Grandy, Fred 219
Granville, Alan 198
Grave Vengeance see *Hunting Season*
Graves, Peter 201
Gray, Charles 181
The Great Escape (1963) 82
Greatest American Hero (series) 231
Greenstreet, Sydney 258
Greer, Jane 200
Grier, Pam 210
Griffeth, Simone 218, **218**
Griffith, Andy 201
Griffith, Chuck 219
Grillo-Marxuach, Javier 261
Guffee, Paul 47
Gullon, Javier 163
Gunsmoke (series) 201
Guthu, Hal 55

Haase, Holger 152
Hack, Shelley 247
Hackman, Gene 186
Haig, Sid 67
Hall, Kevin Peter, 123, 235, 238, 240
Halloween (1978) 208, 239
Hamilton, Linda 206, 207
Hamlin, Harry 158, **159**, 160
Hammett, Dashell 207
Hansen, Robert 8, 168, 253
Happy Days (series) 94
Hard Boiled (1992) 122
Hard Rock Zombies (1985) 110
Hard Target (1993) 113–124, **114**, **115**, 130, 131
Hargitay, Mariska 260
Harper, Scott 231–232
Harrelson, Woody 221
Harvey (1969) 58
Harvey Swings (1970) 58
Hauer, Rutger **126**, 132–133, 135–136

The Haunting (1963) 30
Haunting Fear (1990) 243
Haven, Annette 59
Hayes, William H. 15
Head, Anthony Stewart 245
Hector, Jamie 250
Hedden, Rob 217
Hell Comes to Frogtown (1988) 154
Hell's Bloody Devils (1970) 238
Hemingway, Ernest 1, 237, 270
Hemmings, David 85
Henriksen, Lance *114*, 116, 118–119, 123, 232
Henry, Portrait of a Serial Killer (1986) 219
Hercules: The Legendary Journeys (series) 268
Hernandez, Tom 148
Hess, David 165
Hicks, Neill 80
High School Caesar (1960) 68
High Tension (2003) 157
Highlander (1986) 256
Highlander (series) 256–257
Hill Street Blues (series) 150
The Hitcher (1986) 132
The Hitcher (2007) 137
The Hitcher 2 (2003) 147
Hobo with a Shotgun (2011) 136
Hoffman, Abby 199
Hogan's Heroes (series) 138, 144
Hogue, Jeffrey C. 108, 109, 110, 111
Holden, Lansing C. 21
Holden, William 75, 77
Hollywood Chainsaw Hookers (1988) 103
The Hollywood Reporter (periodical) 267
Holmes, John 59
Hopkins, Stephen 236
Hornsby, David 258
The Horrible Dr. Hichcock (1962) 219
Hot Rod Gang (1958) 68
The Hounds of Zaroff see *The Most Dangerous Game* (1932)
The House That Dripped Blood (1971) 182
Houston, Norman 27, 99
How to Make a Monster (1958) 68
Howard, John 76
Howard, Trevor 200
Howerton, Glenn 258
Hu, Kelly 230
Human Target (1994) 10, 219, 220
The Hunchback of Notre Dame (1939) 30, 208
The Hunger Games (novel) 220
The Hunger Games (2012) 10, 215, 216, 220–221, 223
The Hunt (2012) 157–158
Hunt, J. Roy 29
The Hunted (1998) 158–160, *159*
Hunter (series) 59
The Hunters (2011) 160–161
The Hunting Party (1971) 186–187
Hunting Season (2000) 187–188
Hurt, John 153
Hussey, Olivia 82, 85

The Hustler (1961) 48
Hydra (2009) 162–163

I Am Legend (novel) 257
I Love Lucy (series) 141
I Married a Monster (1998) 59
I Spit on Your Grave (1978) 108
I Walked with a Zombie (1943) 29
I Want to Live! (1958) 30
I Was a Teenage Frankenstein (1957) 36
I Was a Teenage Werewolf (1957) 36
Ice Age (2002) 144
Ice-T *126*, 132, 134, 136, 193, 260
The Incredible Hulk (series) 257–258
The Incredible Shrinking Man (1957) 257
The Incredibly Strange Creatures Who Stopped Living and Became Mixed-Up Zombies (1964) 111
Indiana Jones (film series) 263
Insatiable (1980) 59
Inside (2007) 157
Invasion USA (1985) 94
The Invisible Ray (1936) 28
Irwin, Carl 110
The Island of Dr. Moreau (novel) 204
It Came Without Warning see *Without Warning*
The Italian Job (1969) 77
It's Always Sunny in Philadelphia (series) 258
Ivars, Analia 178
Ives, David 159

The Jackal (1997) 123
Jacks, James 114, 120, 121, 122, 123
Jackson, Kate 247
Jaktoffer see *Open Season* (film)
James, Christine 95
James, Clifton 191
James, Steve *88*, 91–92, 93, 94–95
Jameson, Joyce 219
Jaws (1975) 133
JCVD (2008) 121, 122
Jeffries, Lang 151
Jensen, Todd 198
Jobson, Richard 168–170
Joelson, Tsianina 268
Johnny Allegro (1949) 179, 188–189, *188*
Johnny Bravo (series) 258–259
Johnson, Clark 220
Johnson, Karl *89*
Johnson, Noble 21–22, *26*, 29
Johnson, Samuel 1
Johnston, Clint 194, 195
Jones, Charlene 66
Jones, Jeffrey *139*, 141–142, 143, 144
Jones, L.Q. 186
Jones, Vinnie 217
Jonny Quest (series) 259–260, 268
Jordan, Dorothy 22
Juice (1992) 136
Jumanji (book) 189
Jumanji (1995 film) 189

Jungle Fever (1991) 131, 136
Jurassic Park (1993) 239
Justine (1969) 172

Kapelos, John 254
The Karate Kid (1984) 269
Karloff, Boris 31, 133
Katt, William 231
Katz, David Bar 140, 142–143, 143–144, 144
Katzin, Lee H. 201
Kavun, Andrei 175
Keeslar, Matt 251, 261
Keith, David 149
Kenny, June 40, 41
Kenny, Paul 151
The Killer (1989) 117, 121, 122
The Killer Shrews (1959) 201
Killer Workout (1986) 184
King, Jeff F. 263
King, Stephen 224
King Kong (1933) 15, 18, 20, 21, 22, 101
King of New York (1990) 131
King of the Hill (2007) 163–164
Kinmont, Kathleen 220
Kinski, Klaus 151
Kitano, Takeshi 215
Kizer, R.J. 153–154
Klavan, Andrew 1–2
Knox, Terence 161
Kobal, John 22
Kurtzman, Nicotero and Berger EFX Group 183

Ladd, Cheryl 247
Ladyhawke (1985) 136
The Lair of the White Worm (1988) 155
Lamarr, Hedy 31
Lamas, Lorenzo 220
Lambert, Christopher 193
LaMotta, Jake 46, 48
Land of the Dead (2005) 144
Land of the Lost (series) 101
Landau, Martin 238, *238*, 239
Landon, Michael 245
Lanvin, Gerard 223
Laredo (series) 197
LaRue, Eve 250
The Last House on the Left (1972) 165
The Last Starfighter (1984) 208
Lauter, Harry 204, *205*, 205
Law, John Phillip 75–76, 77
Law and Order: Special Victims Unit (series) 136, 260
Lawless, Lucy 268
Lawrence, Jennifer 221
LeBrun, George T. 153
Lee, Bruce 185
Lee, Christopher 191, *192*, 192
Lee, Daniel 166, 167
Lee, Margaret 151
Lee, Spike 130, 136
Le Gault, Lance 242
Le Gros, James 182, 183
Leguizamo, John *139*, 142–143, 143–144

Index

Lemoine, Michel 202–203, 203–204
Leonard, Joshua 182, 183
The Leopard Man (1943) 31
Leprechaun (film franchise) 85
Leroy, Jeff 187, 188
Lethal Woman (1988) 189–190
Leung, Tony 120
Lewis, Jerry 141, 142
Libert, Jean *see* Kenny, Paul
Lifepod (1981) 208
Lime, Harold *see* Paramore, Ted
Lionheart (1990) 122
Lipton, Robert 190
Lithgow, John 236
Littler, Craig 204, 205
Live and Let Die (1973) 191
Lockhart, Calvin 179, 236
Loder, John **26**, 29, 31
Lois and Clark: The New Adventures of Superman (series) 155
Lonesome Dove (film series) 150
Long, Audrey 27, 29, 32
The Longest Yard (2005) 216
Lopez-Gallego, Gonzalo 163
Lora, Joan 39
Lord, Eileen 45, 48
The Lords of Flatbush (1974) 219
Lost in Space (series) 260–261
The Lost Weekend (1945) 32
The Love Boat (series) 219
Lucas, George 266
Lucide, Sarah 157
Luisi, James 190
Lynch, Richard **72**, 75, 76, 77

Macbeth (1948) 31
MacDonald, Scott 266
Mackenzie, Alistair 170
Macready, George **188**, 189
The Mad Doctor of Blood Island (1968) 68, 210
Mad Mex the Blackfighter see Big Game
Maggio, Joe 183
The Magnificent Ambersons (1942) 30
Majors, Lee 247
Malcolm X (1992) 136
Malony, Daniel 167
Mambo Mouth (play) 144
Mammone, Robert 216
Man Beast (1956) 41
The Man Who Changed His Mind (1936) 31
The Man Who Lived Again see The Man Who Changed His Mind
The Man with the Golden Gun (novel) 191
The Man with the Golden Gun (1974) 191–192, **192**
Maneater (1973) 164–165
Manera, Jesus Franco *see* Franco, Jess
Mang, William 156
Manhunt (2008) 165–166
Mann, Scott 230
Marnham, Christian 190

Marshek, Archie 20
Martyrs (2008) 157
M*A*S*H (series) 40
Mashkov, Vladimir 174
Mask (1985) 150
Mastroianni, Marcello 229
Matheson, Richard 257
Matheson, Richard Christian 257
Max B *see* Boulois, Max
McCarron, Bob 85
McCaulay, Charles 210
McCrae, Joel **17**, 20, 22, 27
McDowall, Roddy 183
McElhenney, Rob 258
McGinley, John C. 133–134
McLean, John 83
McQueen, Chad 152, 153
McQueen, Steve 82, 152, 153
McTiernan, John 234–235, 235
Mean Guns (1997) 136, 192–193
Meaney, Colm 266
Meatballs (1979) 208
Medford, Don 187
Medin, Harriet White 219
Meeker, Ralph 239
Meet John Doe (1941) 273n1
Mega Piranha (2010) 231
Men in Black (1997) 262
Men of Annapolis (series) 68
Mendoza, Albert **72**
Merlin, Jan 210
Metcalfe, Ken 66
Metzger, Joel 269
Meyer, Hans 151
Michael, Nanna 151
The Middleman (series) 261–262
Mighty Joe Young (1949) 29
Mikels, Ted V. 107, 108, 108–109, 110, 111, 111–112
Milland, Ray 21
Miller, George 219
Miller, Paul 143
Mills, Barbara 54, 57–58
Mironov, Yevgeny 174
Missile to the Moon (1958) 36, 41, 101
Missing in Action (1984) 122
Mitchell, Cameron 184, 239
Mitchell, Gordon 194
Michum, Robert 243
Mo' Better Blues (1990) 131
Monster from the Ocean Floor (1954) 211
Montalban, Ricardo 155, 252
Moore, Roger 191, **192**
Morales, Natalie 261
Moriarty, Lloyd 117
Morneau, Louis 147
Morris, Kathryn 248
Morris, Kirk 194
Moskow, Kenny 171
"The Most Dangerous Game" (short story) 1, 4–7, **5**, 14–15, 16–17, 18, 25, 35–36, 44–45, 52–53, 63–64, 73, 80–81, 89–90, 99–100, 107–108, 114–116, 127–130, 139–140, 143, 154, 158–159, 166, 167, 171, 175, 176, 179, 187, 190, 198, 200, 204, 232, 237, 239, 248, 255, 257, 262, 263, 269, 270, 271, 273n5
The Most Dangerous Game (1932 film) 1, **2**, **11**, 13–22, **14**, **17**, 25–26, 27, 35, 99–100, 102, 111, 114, 121, 154, 158, 166, 195, 255, 263, 271
The Most Dangerous Game (2001 short film) 166–167
The Most Dangerous Woman Alive see Lethal Woman
Motorcycle Gang (1957) 68
Mouina, Jellali 157
Muller, Eddie 45
Murawski, Bob 123
Murder by the Clock (1931) 21
Murders in the Rue Morgue (1932) 21
Murphy, Audie 28
Murphy, Bri 35, 39–40, 41
My Man Godfrey (1936) 189
My Son, the Hero (1962) 10, 193–194

Naked Fear (2007) 167–168
The Naked Prey (1966) 114, 194–197, **196**
Navy Seals (1990) 123
Near Dark (1987) 119
Nelson, Gary 255
Never Die Alone (2004) 136
New Jack City (1989) 136
New Town Killers (2009) 168–170, **169**
Newman, Amber 176
Next Action Star (series) 146
Night of the Cobra Woman (1972) 204
Night of the Demons 2 (1994) 85
The Night Stalker (series) 201
Nighthawks (1981) 136
1984 (novel) 157
Niven, Kip 165
Norris, Aaron 171
Norris, Chuck 94, 95, 122, 152, 153, 171
Norris, Mike 152, 153, 171
Not Quite Hollywood (2008) 85
Notorious (1946) 189
Nouri, Michael 171
Nurses (series) 110

Oakland, Simon 186
O'Brien, Hugh 155
O'Hara, David 110
Okhota na piranyu see Piranha (2006)
The Oklahoma Kid (1939) 58
Old Yeller (1957) 211
Olson, Kaitlin 258
"On the Blue Water" (short story) 237
Open Season (1974 film) 70–77, **71**, **72**, 89
Open Season (novel) 76
Ordung, Wyott 211
Osborn, David 74, 75, 76
The Othello Black Commando (1982) 149

Index

The Outer Limits (1960s series) 242, 262
The Outer Limits (1990s series) 262–263
Overkill (1996) 170–172

Padelecki, Jared 267
Paintball (2009) 221–222
Pal, George 21
Palance, Jack 238, 239
Panozzo, Orianna *79*
Paramore, Edward E., Jr. 58
Paramore, Ted 53, 55, 58
Parker, Eleanor 155
Pasquale, Steven 233
Pattila, Alan 75
Paturel, Dominique 151
Paul, Adrian 256
Paul, Val 21
Paulino, Justo 66
Pearson, James Anthony 170
Pena, Cindy 187, 188
Perfect Strangers (series) 110
Persson, Gene 38
The Perverse Countess (1974) 172–174, **173**, 176, 203
The Pest (1997) 138–145, **139, 141**
Peters, Don 194, 195
Petri, Elio 229
Petrovitch, Michael 82–83
Pfarrer, Chuck 114, 116, 118, 119–120, 121, 122, 123
The Phantom of the Opera (1943) 31
Pichel, Irving 16, 18, 21
Pillow of Death (1945) 40
Piranha (1972) 197–198
Piranha (1978) 197
Piranha (1995) 197
Piranha (2006) 174–175, 197
Piranha (2010) 197
Piranha, Piranha see *Piranha* (1972)
Planet of the Apes (1968) 205
Platt, Edward 254
Playboy (periodical) 208
Playgirl (periodical) 184
Pleasantville (1998) 221
Poitier, Sidney 95
Pollard, Sam 131, 134
Pollock, Tom 122
P.O.W.: The Escape 95
Poynter, Jannina **106**, 108, 110, 111
Pray for the Wildcats (1974) 201
Predator (1987) 122–123, 224, 231, 232, 234–235, **234**, 235, 236, 238, 241
Predator 2 (1990) 235–236
Predators (2010) 236–237
Prey for the Hunter (1993) 198
Principal, Victoria 155
Prior, David A. 184
Prior, Ted 184
Le Prix du danger see *The Prize of Peril*
The Prize of Peril (1983) 151, 222–223
Psycho (1960) 240
Psychon Invaders (2006) 187

Pulp Fiction (1994) 230
Pumpkinhead (1988) 119, 131
Punishment Park (1971) 198–199
Pure Race (1995) 108, 199–200

Quarry, Robert 179
Queen of Outer Space (1958) 101

Raft, George **188**, 189
Raging Bull (1980) 48
Raiders of the Lost Ark (1981) 235
Railsback, Steve 82, 83, 85
Rapid Assault (1997) 103
Rasca, Nanong 204
Rat Scratch Fever (2011) 187
Ravenous (1999) 144
Ray, Fred Olen 103–104, 243
Re-Animator (1985) 207
The Recon Game see *Open Season*
Red Planet (2000) 123
Redfield, Rochelle 256
Reed, Oliver 186
Reed, Robert 36, 38, 39–40
Reeves, Steve 194
Relic Hunter (series) 263–264
Renegade (series) 59
Rescue Me (series) 233
The Return of Count Yorga (1971) 40
Revenge of the Nerds (1984) 207
Revenge of the Ninja (1983) 95
El Rey de la Montana see *King of the Hill*
Rhames, Ving 230
Rickles, Don 142
The Rifleman (series) 211
Ringo (film series) 194
The Road Warrior (1981) 150, 219
Robinson, Edward G. 141
Robinson, Sugar Ray 48
Robot Monster (1953) 211
Robsahm, Nini Bull 166
Rock Monster (2008) 162
Rocky (1976) 219
Rodriguez, Adam 250–251
Rodriguez, Robert 236
Rodvyr see *Manhunt*
Rollerball (1975) 221
Romay, Lina 172, 173–174, 178
Romeo Must Die (2000) 137
Romero, Eddie 66, 210
Rooker, Michael 219
Roosevelt, Theodore 2–3
Rose, Lori (also Laurie) 54–55, 66
Ross, Don 211, **212**
Ross, Gary 221
Roth, Gene see Stutenroth, Gene
Rothschild, Frank (assistant district attorney) 8
Run for the Sun (1956) 10, 179, 200
The Running Man (film) 10, 220, 223, 223–226, **225**, 227
The Running Man (novella) 224
The Running Man (TV series) 224
Russell, Ken 155
Russell, Kurt 122
Rutten, Bas 219
Ryan, John P. **89**
Ryan, Mitchell 183, 186

The Saga of the Viking Women and Their Voyage to the Waters of the Great Sea Serpent (1958) 41
The Saint (character) 32
St. Elsewhere (series) 40
Sakata, Harold 255
'Salem's Lot (2004) 132
The Sand Pebbles (1966) 30
The Santa Fe Trail (1930) 58
Satan's Cheerleaders (1977) 238
Satan's Sadists (1969) 238
Saunders, John Monk 22
The Savages (1974) 201
Saw (2004) 183
Schenck, George 204, 205
Schnass, Andreas 213, 214
Schoedsack, Ernest B. 15, 16, 18, 20–21, 22, 154
Schoendorff, Mario 222
School Daze (1988) 136
Schwarzenegger, Arnold 220, 223, 224, **225**, 234, **234**, 235, 236, 238
Scorsese, Martin 48 195
Scott, Dougray 170
Scream of the Wolf (1974) 201–202
Scribner, Don 103
Seabiscuit (2003) 221
Seagrove, Jenny 183
Seale, Bobby 199
Season of the Hunted (2004) 175–176
Sebastian, Ray 58
Segall, Stu 54, 55, 56–57, 57, 58–59
Seizure (1974) 219
Sensual Encounters of Every Kind (1978) 58
Sept femmes pour un sadique see *Seven Women for Satan*
The Serial Killers: A Study in the Psychology of Violence 8
Series 7: The Contenders (2001) 226
Serpico (1973) 207
Seven Women for Satan (1974) 202–204
Seventeen (periodical) 94
Sex Revolution (album) 149
Sexy Nature see *The Perverse Countess*
Shakespeare, William 149
SharkMan (2005) 162
Sharpe, Cornelia 75
Shatner, William 264
Shaw, George Bernard 270
Shaw, Robert 133
Shazam! (series) 269
She (1935) 21
She Demons (1958) 29, 36, 41
She Freak (1967) 165
Sheinberg, Sid 142
Shelley, Mary 1
Shigeta, James 252, 253
The Siege at Firebase Gloria (1989) 85
Silent Hill: Revelation 3D (2012) 213
Silk Stalkings (series) 59, 85

Index

Silver, Joel 236
Silvera, Darrell 28
Simcox, Tom 197
The Simpsons (series) 264
Singer, Marc 183
Sisters (1973) 182
The Six Million Dollar Man (series) 247
Skerritt, Tom 245
Skull Island see *The Most Dangerous Game* (1932)
laher$ (2001) 223, 227
Slave Girls from Beyond Infinity (1987) 96–104, **97**, **98**, 131
Sleepy Hollow (1999) 144
Small, Jerome 210
Smedley, Richard 54, 55, 57
Smith, Jacqueline 247
Smith, William 197, 198
Smithsonian (periodical) 266
Snakes on a Plane (2006) 231
Snakes on a Train (2006) 231
Soldier of Orange (1977) 136
Some Girls Do (1969) 76
Somerhalder, Ian 230
The Sons of Thunder see *My Son Hero*
Soon-Teck Oh 183
The Sorcerer's Apprentice (2010) 131
The Sound of Music (1965) 30
Soylent Green (1973) 211
Spang, Laurette 165
Sparaglia, Leonardo 163
Spawn (1997) 144
Sperling, Ron 175–176
Spider Baby (1968) 67
The Spiral Staircase (1975) 77
The Spirit of Seventy Sex (1976) 59
Stallone, Sylvester 219
Stanley, Herb 47
Star Trek (series) 240, 260, 264–265
Star Trek: Deep Space Nine (series) 265–266
Star Trek: Enterprise (series) 265
Star Trek: The Next Generation (series) 265
Star Trek: Voyager (series) 265
Star Wars: The Clone Wars (series) 266–267
Stebbings, Peter 263, 264
Steckler, Ray Dennis 105, 111
Stevens, Brinke 103
Stevens, Vincent see Vincent, Steve
Stevenson, Robert Louis 1
Stoner, Lynda 84, 85
Storch, Larry 239
Storm Fear (1955) 195
The Strange Case of Dr. Jekyll and Mr. Hyde (novel) 1
Strause, Colin 233
Strause, Greg 233
Strode, Woody 156
Stults, George 162
The Stunt Man (1980) 82
Stutenroth, Gene 29
Subotsky, Milton 181
The Suckers (1972) 50–59, **51**
Summer Camp Girls (1983) 58

Summer of Sam (1999) 144
Sung, Elizabeth Fong 152, 153
Super Afro (album) 149
Superbeast (1972) 204–206, **205**
Supernatural (series) 267–268
Surviving the Game (1994) 125–137, **126**, 140, 236, 260
Suspense (radio series) 273n5
Sutherland, Donald 221
Swayze, Don 152, 153
Swayze, Patrick 152, 153
Syversen, Patrik 166
Szczepanski, Thomas 158
Szollosi, Thomas 257

T.A.G.: The Assassination Game (1982) 206–208
Tales from the Crypt (1972) 182
Tales from the Crypt: Demon Knight (1995) 136
Tales of Terror (1962) 219
Tapert, Rob 269
Targets (1968) 133
Tate, Fred 104
Teen-Age Jail Bait (1973) 58
Ten Little Indians (novel) 182
Ten Violent Women (1982) 111
Tender Flesh (1997) 176–178, **177**
The Tenth Victim (1965) 215, 223, 227–229, **228**
The Terminator (1984) 101, 224
Terminator 2: Judgment Day (1991) 236
Tessari, Duccio 194
Tetzlaff, Ted 189
Der Teufelsgarten see *Coplan Saves His Skin*
The Texas Chainsaw Massacre (1974) 77, 165, 165–166, 175, 267
The Thirsty Dead (1974) 204
30 Rock 12
Thompson, Gary 108
Thomson, H.A.R. 194
Three Godfathers (1936) 58
3 Loves of a Psycho Cat see *Confessions of a Psycho Cat*
The Three Stooges 142, 143
The Thrill Killers (1964) 111
Thriller (series) 41
Timecop (1994) 122
Timme, Sarah 10
Titanic (1997) 146
The Titans see *My Son, the Hero*
To Wong Foo: Thanks for Everything, Julie Newmar (1995) 144
Todd, Lisa **64**, 66
The Tomb (1986) 110
Tomb Raider (video game) 263
Tombstone (1993) 146
Tommy (1975) 155
Top Gun (1986) 150
Torture Ship (1939) 21
The Tournament (2009) 229–230
Tracked see *Dogboys*
Trammell, Sam 233
Transylmania (2009) 208, **209**
Trejo, Danny 237
Trenchard-Smith, Brian 81, 83, 84, 85

Trilogy of Terror (1975) 201
True Blood (series) 233
Tubb, Barry 150
Turkey Shoot see *Escape 2000*
Turkish Delight (1973) 136
TV Guide (periodical) 268
Tweed, Shannon 190
28 Weeks Later (2007) 230
The Twilight People (1972) 66, 179, 209–211
Tyler, Aisha **244**

Le ultimo guerriero see *The Final Executioner*
Under Siege (1992) 122
Universal Soldier (1992) 122
The Untouchables (1987) 153
Urban Warriors (1987) 157

Vaccaro, Brenda 258
Valley of the Zombies (1946) 40
Valverde, Maria 163
The Vampire Diaries (series) 230
Van Allsburg, Chris 189
Van Damme, Jean-Claude 114, **115**, **117**, 120–121, 122–123, 123
Van den Panhuyse, Gaston see Kenny, Paul
Van der Berg, Gert 195
Van Helsing (2004) 209
Van Kamp, Merete 190
Van Lidth, Erland 224
Vann, Lynn 54
Van Peebles, Mario 136
Van Ryck de Groot, Corinne 146
Varley's Game see *The Eliminator*
Ventura, Jesse 224, 235
The Venture Bros. (series) 259, 268
Venus in Furs (1968) 172
Verhoeven, Paul 136
Vernon, Howard 172, **173**, 174, 202
Veronica Mars (series) 59
Villechaize, Herve 155, 192, 252
Vincent, Jan-Michael 242, 243
Vincent, Steve 55–56
Violent Shit III see *Zombie Doom*
The Virginian (series) 40
Virus (comic book) 114
Virus (1999 film) 123
Vosloo, Arnold 120

Waddington, Steve 161
Wade, Russell 27, 28, 29, 31
Wagner, Robert 55
Walk the Dark Street (1956) 211–212, **212**
Walker, Clint 201–202
Walker, Texas Ranger (series) 68
The Walking Dead (series) 136
Wallace, Bill **89**
Wallace, Edgar 20
Walley, Deborah 68
War Cat (1987) 105–112, **106**
The War of the Worlds (1953) 31
Warcat see *War Cat*
Ward, Roger **79**, 85
The Warning see *Without Warning*
Warren, Jerry 41

The Warriors (1979) 95, 183
Watkins, Peter 199
Watson, Muse 176
Waycoff, Leon 21
Wayne, John 68, 243
Wayne's World (1992) 263
Weathers, Carl 234, 235
Les Week-ends maléfiques du Comte Zaroff see *Seven Women for Satan*
Welles, Orson 31, 273*n*5
Werewolf (series) 68
Werewolf by Night **9**
Werewolf in a Women's Prison (2006) 187
West Side Story (1961) 30
Westmore, Michael 266
What Ever Happened to Aunt Alice? (1969) 201
Whedon, Joss 251
Whitaker, Forest 207
Whitman, Mae 258
Whitman, Stuart 252
Whitmore, James 242
Whitmore, James, Jr. 242
Who Could Kill a Child (1976) 164
Whoever Slew Auntie Roo? (1971) 76
Widmark, Richard 200
Wild Guitar (1962) 111
The Wild Wild West (series) 40
Wilde, Cornel 194, 195, **196**, 195–197
Wilderness (2006) 212–213
Williams, Barry 40
Williams, Guy 261
Williams, Robin 189
Wings (1927) 22
Winston, Stan 123, 235
Winton, Sandy 268
Wiper, Scott 217
The Wire (series) 136
Wise, Robert 28, 29–30, 30–31
Without Warning (1980) 234, 237–241, **238**
The Woman Hunt (1973) 55, 60–69, **61**, **62**, **63**, **64**, 89, 186, 210
The Woman Who Came Back (1945) 31
Womanhunt see *The Woman Hunt*
Woo, John 116–118, **117**, 118, 120–121, 122, 123, 123–124
Wood, Lana 55
Wood, Montgomery see Gemma, Giuliano
Wood, Natalie 55
Woodell, Pat **62**, 210
Woods, Robert 172
Woronov, Mary 219
Wray, Fay 15, **17**, 20, 21, 27, 29
Wyler, Richard 151

The X-Files (series) 262
Xena: Warrior Princess (series) 268–269

Zamora, Raymond 185
Zane, Billy 146, 147
Zombie Doom (1999) 213–214